ABOUT THE AUTHOR

BEN HILLS is one of Australia's most experienced foreign correspondents. Over the past two decades he has been based in three countries, and has reported from fifty more. His latest assignment, on which this book is based, was Japan correspondent for the *Sydney Morning Herald* and the Melbourne *Age,* from 1992–95. Before that, he was in Hong Kong for two years in the early 1980s, and in London for three years in the mid-1970s, principally covering Africa and the Middle East. He spent four years on the road as a producer for the Australian '60 Minutes' television current affairs program, roaming from Belfast to Beirut and Brazil.

In 1989, Hills was 'highly commended' in the Graham Perkin Australian Journalist of the Year award, for a body of work including his previous book *Blue Murder*, a documentary on the Wittenoom asbestos tragedy in Western Australia. Two years later he won a Walkley Award, Australia's premier prize in journalism, for investigative reporting. He and photographer Mayu Kanamori live in Sydney where Ben is a journalist on the *Sydney Morning Herald.*

JAPAN •BEHIND THE LINES

BEN HILLS

PHOTOGRAPHS BY
MAYU KANAMORI

SCEPTRE

A HODDER & STOUGHTON BOOK

Published in Australia and New Zealand in 1996 by
Hodder Headline Australia Pty Limited
(A member of the Hodder Headline Group)
10–16 South Street, Rydalmere NSW 2116

National Library of Australia Cataloguing-in-Publication data

Hills, Ben.
Japan behind the lines.

Bibliography.
ISBN 0 7336 0088 3.

1. Popular culture - Japan. 2. Japan - History - 1945- .
I. Title.

952.04

Designed by Anna Soo
Printed by McPherson's Printing Group, Victoria

CONTENTS

For Mayu

PREFACE

I WAS MEANT TO GO TO CAIRO, but for reasons that were never made clear, the bureau the *Age* and the *Sydney Morning Herald* had operated there for a decade or so was suddenly closed. So they offered me the correspondent's job in Tokyo instead. Initially, I was somewhat underwhelmed. I wondered how a grown man could look at himself in the shaving mirror each morning, and then go off and write about the price of rice. Compared with the drama of the intifada, the rise of Moslem fundamentalism and the dawn of peace in the Middle East, the drudgery of Nikkei market reports, coal negotiations and the inscrutable machinations of a government that never seemed to change appeared to have little to offer. My partner Mayu took even more convincing. She had migrated to Australia in the 1980s at least partly to escape the suffocating conformity of Japanese society.

As it turned out, I fluked the most interesting three years in Japan since the 1950s. I *was* required to take a bit of an interest in rice when the Japanese opened their market, just a chink, to imports. There were, however, professional consolations: three changes of government; the worst economic slump since the Depression; an earthquake that killed 6000; a doomsday cult that flooded the subways with Nazi nerve gas and the fiftieth anniversary of the end of the world's greatest war. For light relief, there was a royal wedding, plus the discovery of Jesus Christ's real grave and a meal, literally, to die for. All this, against a backdrop of the most rapid and wrenching social changes since Japan's postwar economic miracle began.

Everyone, of course, brings his own strengths and weaknesses to the job. In my own case, economics not being a forte, I found it tedious regurgitating the lists of prices, statistics and forecasts that many correspondents, even of general interest newspapers, see as the life blood of covering Japan. Quite why this is so, I never could fathom. The United States is a much more important economy, and its bond and equity markets exercise a far greater influence on Australia than Japan's. Yet correspondents in America are not expected to cover the economy in anything like the detail devoted to Japan, if at all. Australians, as a result, know about Bill Clinton, Bill Gates, Meryl Streep and even (God save us) O. J. Simpson. The only Japanese (apart from Hirohito and Godzilla) most of us would be able to put names to are pieces of hardware: Sony, Toyota and Canon.

Perhaps in reaction to this, I made a decision early on to try and cover Japan like a 'normal country' rather than a GDP with attitude. I wanted to portray a three-dimensional society rather than a bunch of factories floating somewhere in the north-west Pacific spewing out televisions, cars and cameras. I don't mean the 'funny Jap' and 'ugly Jap' stereotypes so beloved of editors — although I must admit the story that brought the most reaction was neither the Hiroshima anniversary nor the Kobe earthquake, but the discovery of an automated Buddhist funeral parlour in Yokohama, complete with robot priest. I mean the stories that look at the changes under way in this antique, conservative society, which I have grouped together under generic headings such as health, education, the environment and minorities.

You will find a chapter on politics here — how could there not be? You will discover how the Japanese I came to know spend their leisure, raise their children and (still) grapple with their war guilt. But you will not find much on economics. The last thing the world needs is yet another book examining, debunking, resurrecting, denouncing, explaining and predicting the course of the Japanese economy. At least a dozen more were published in 1995 — and that's just in English. It is a mystery to me who buys all these weighty tomes. I suspect many finish up as unopened bookcase-dressing in the studies of other economists, businesspeople, journalists and academics.

The backbone of the book is the series of 100 or so feature articles I wrote for the *Sydney Morning Herald*, the *Age* and the *Good Weekend* magazine while I was based in Japan. I make no apology for rewriting, correcting some of the more egregious mistakes and filling in the context that, inevitably, gets swept away by the demands of daily newspaper journalism. Thanks to Mayu, I was able to see much more of the 80 per cent of Japan that is not the great gritty megalopolis of Tokyo than most other correspondents. We travelled to most of the forty-seven prefectures, from the Russian bases on the Kurile Islands to the haunted caves of Okinawa and the gilded temples of Kyoto.

We interviewed the usual grey, impassive faces of official Japan — the politicians, bureaucrats and industrialists. However, I believe we gained a greater insight into what makes the country tick from the farmers and fishermen, the doctors and teachers, the welfare workers and the homeless, the lawyers and scientists, the salarymen and journalists, the gangster boss, the foundry foreman, the unemployed salaryman, the geisha, the kamikaze pilot, the art-dealer, the chef, the Marxist historian, the Hiroshima survivor, the Catholic cardinal, the Ainu elder and all the other characters you will meet in these pages. They made the time to see us; they went to great pains to try and explain their complex society; they treated Mayu and me with unfailing courtesy and occasional kindness. This is really their story.

I have tried to be long on observation and short on generalisation, the reporter rather than the pundit. With good reason. Usually, if you see a sentence beginning 'The Japanese …' it is not worth reading on. There are some generalisations that contain a grain of truth, such as 'There are no blue-eyed, blonde-haired Japanese', but even here you risk embarrassment. A naturalised Japanese of Scandinavian descent answering exactly that description ran for election recently. The Japanese themselves are the worst offenders in this. They are continually attempting to explain every action, every attitude in terms of an ethnic stereotype. I have had people who should know better earnestly explain that Japanese drive on the left-hand side of the road because this was how samurai had to walk to avoid clashing swords with each other and provoking a fight.

On the other hand, I have not flinched from shining a little light into some of the darker corners of Japanese society. This is not because I don't like Japan or the Japanese — on the contrary. It is because I have family and many friends there that I feel the need to speak out against some of the more depressing consequences of their system of social organisation. Many Japanese secretly welcome such criticism from foreigners. They believe that *gaiatsu*, or 'outside pressure', is their only real hope of reforming the system, whether we are talking trade barriers or sexual harassment. Those whose interests are threatened will no doubt try to label this 'Japan bashing'. That is as absurd as calling a critique of Paul Keating's style of government 'Australia bashing'. Power-holders will always try to confuse what is in their own interests with what is in the interests of their country.

I pondered for some time how to deal with acknowledgments. Many, perhaps most, of the people who helped Mayu and me with our work spoke on condition of anonymity and would not thank us for naming them. We can leave, but they have to live with the consequences. They know who they are, and they know we are grateful for their information, insight, guidance and companionship. Without Mayu, of course, this book could not have been written. She was not only my eyes and ears, she made our stay in Japan a rewarding experience rather than the grim struggle with an alien culture that many foreigners endure. I have a debt of gratitude, too, to Mayu's family for making room in their lives, with warmth and hospitality, for an awkward *gaijin*-in-law.

As for written sources, since this is not intended as a work of scholarship, I have not enumerated each one. Instead, at the back of the book, I have provided a critique of all the publications which I read while in Japan and have used by way of background. However, I know of no country where second-hand sources should be treated with more suspicion. There is no substitute for going there, doing that. Where you read a description, it means that I have been there. Where you see quotation marks, what is between the inverted commas is what someone has said to me, usually via Mayu. The only exceptions are where I have been unable to contact the source, and I have made this clear by the use of some device such as 'was quoted as saying'.

Finally, a note on style. Anglicised Japanese names are given with the personal name first and the family name last. Hiroshi Sato is Mr Sato. This is the convention all the Japanese use on their business cards, and the style used in Japanese and foreign wire-services, newspapers, most books and all magazines (with the lone, odd, exception of *Asia Week*). All dollars are Australian and have been converted at the rate of A$1 = ¥75, about the average during my stay in Japan. All other Japanese measurements have been converted into their metric equivalents and dates are given according to the Western calendar, rather than the official Japanese imperial calendar.

IT IS ANOTHER ICY WINTER'S NIGHT AT A HOT springs resort on the banks of the Tokachi River, in the wilds of Hokkaido. Upstairs in the lounge, however, the lads are feeling no pain. The sake is flowing freely and the coloured spotlights are panning across the empty stage as the forty or fifty mainly middle-aged revellers, dressed in cotton *yukatas*, pink-faced and perspiring after their plunge in the communal baths, wait for the entertainment to begin.

There is one big difference between the audience at the Tokachi-gawa onsen and resorts almost anywhere else in the world. Here, there are no paid professional entertainers: the audience is the act. With a digital backup band booming from the Bose speakers and the words scrolling across a television monitor, the older men queue to take the stage to croon heart-rending *enka* (melancholy popular ballads), couples serenade each other with love duets, the odd cute teenaged 'OL' ('Office Lady', as they are called) belts out the words to the latest television soapie theme.

It's a scene that is repeated every night of the week in literally hundreds of thousands of venues the length of Japan — from grand hotels to tiny bars and purpose-built booths like freight containers. Whether it is the snowy mountain wilderness of Hokkaido or the remote tropical islands of the Ryukyus, it seems impossible to escape the din. Welcome to the world of karaoke — a mongrel contraction of the Japanese word *kara* (meaning 'empty') and the English word 'orchestra'.

Last year the term karaoke achieved the international legitimacy of being included in Webster's dictionary, along with sushi, samurai, futon and tsunami. Ever since a legendary salaryman, emboldened with drink, leapt on a

THE EMPTY ORCHESTRA

table in a Kobe bar in 1972 and burst into song, karaoke has swept Japan. It is now even a booming export.

According to Takanobu Yumoto, editor of the quarterly *Karaoke Business* magazine, about 80 per cent of the 380 000 bars in Japan have karaoke machines. Japan's Education Ministry included karaoke in its annual 'cultural white paper' after discovering in a survey that almost half the Japanese population attends a karaoke night at least once a year. Karaoke is more popular than watching television and was, in fact, second only to eating out as Japan's favourite leisure activity. In Tokyo, there are karaoke taxis where office workers can sing a duet with the cabbie while circling round on the Shuto expressway. There are McDonald's with karaoke, karaoke coffee shops and *jaraoke* places where you can sing along while eating *okonomi-yaki*, a sort of pancake. Passing tour buses throb with off-key choruses.

Purpose-built karaoke venues have been multiplying since the first one opened just ten years ago, in a converted railway carriage in the town of Okayama. Now there are 11 000 of them, together with more than 120 000 cubicles where groups of up to a dozen friends, usually schoolchildren, can party on in private, singing their favourite hits. Some of the venues are Cecil B. De Mille extravaganzas, fitted out like desert islands, Space Invaders or dinosaur parks. The chain of 400 Big Echo venues, operated by karaoke billionaire Tadahiko Hoshi's Daiichi Kosho company, claims to attract eighteen million wanna-be pop stars a year — a bigger crowd than Tokyo's Disneyland.

At the annual industry trade fair, the hottest thing in karaoke is a system called ISDN — a sort of pop-song superhighway — which links central 'libraries' holding

10 000 or more digitalised karaoke video clips with almost anywhere in Japan, via fibre-optic cables. A bar owner in the boondocks of Shikoku island can instantly dial up the latest hits for his customers, without the cost, storage space and time lag of buying individual laser discs or the new CD format.

Other stands display karaoke for the car, a dating service which can be plugged into karaoke machines, a drive-in karaoke parking station where huge speakers in the roof blast your car about, a machine called Michelangelo which can automatically paint a 640 square metre canvas to camouflage your karaoke establishment as, say, Mount Rushmore or the Colosseum. There is everything from special meal-microwaving machines to breathalysers ('Go home. Do not sing,' it says when you get into the red.). The industry is calculated to be worth $24 billion a year, and is one of the few growth areas for Japan's ailing electronics manufacturers, principally Pioneer, which is engaged in a karaoke war with Victor and Sony to defend its domination of the market.

For those who feel that even the booming echo that comes as standard with karaoke sound systems is not enough to drown out their off-key efforts, a professor at Waseda University is working on a system of sampling and feedback which can electronically alter people's voices to make them sing in tune. The ultimate Milli Vanilli.

The question no one seems able to convincingly answer is why karaoke should have taken off among Japanese, who are thought by most Westerners to be the most modest, diffident and conformist of people. More than half the world's karaoke market is in Japan, although other countries, principally in Asia, are catching on. There are tour boats plying the Yangtse Gorges in China, beach

THE
EMPTY ORCHESTRA

resorts in Bali, hotels in Taiwan and the Philippines, and the Royal Sauna in Seoul, South Korea, where patrons perform in the nude. In Sydney, a cruise boat has joined the numerous pubs and clubs which cater to the karaoke craze. Yet nowhere is it as ubiquitous as in Japan.

Mr Yumoto's explanation is hardly flattering: 'It's because Japanese have a very low degree of cultural awareness. In other countries, people are used to going to a park, a theatre or a movie, but not here. Japanese don't know what to do with their spare time, so they do karaoke.'

Certainly, the karaoke hit parade does not contain anything to cause Madonna or Michael Jackson any sleepless nights. Yes, there are specialist karaoke venues where you can go and play Placido Domingo all night, effortlessly knocking off *Carmen* and *Madame Butterfly*. However, most of the 'Top Ten' in one recent survey were either the themes of television soap operas or commercials. Robert Harris, a Japanese–American disc jockey on Tokyo's top-rating J-Wave radio station, says he 'avoids karaoke like the plague' and thinks it is dragging pop music down to its lowest common denominator. 'It's just churned out like by a machine, changing a note here and there,' he says. 'It's nothing music.'

Harris thinks the reasons for karaoke's success are social. 'Like Andy Warhol said, everyone's going to be famous for fifteen minutes. The salarymen go to a bar and have a drink and they get to take off their shy shelves and become extroverted. For a few minutes they are the centre of attention, not just a tiny cog in a wheel.'

ONE
THE LIAR ELECTION

If Voting Ever Changed Anything They'd Abolish It

— TITLE OF THE AUTOBIOGRAPHY OF 'RED' KEN LIVINGSTONE. CHAIRMAN OF THE GREATER LONDON COUNCIL UNTIL BARONESS (MARGARET) THATCHER ABOLISHED IT

ACROSS THE CARPETED FLOOR shuffled the conga line of elderly men in suits, past the rows of seats, up the steps to the dais. As his name was intoned, each member of parliament handed over his marker to an attendant who stacked it in a transparent plastic rack: a plain wooden billet for an 'aye', one painted green for 'nay'. For ten minutes or so, the voting proceeded on predictable party lines, as it had for the past four decades, and another government victory seemed the inevitable outcome. But then it was the turn of Mr Tsutomu Hata, once a senior member of the government, now a rebel with a cause. With a bow of the deepest respect to his one-time leader, Kiichi Miyazawa, he handed over a green ballot. The gallery thrilled as members of parliament cheered, shouted 'Banzai!' and clapped one another on the back. The non-Communist world's longest reigning government was over, thirty-eight years and fifteen prime ministers after the Liberal Democratic Party (LDP) first came to power. Jet airliners, colour television, antibiotics and instant noodles had all been invented since Japan last had a change of government.

At least, that was how it appeared to many of us who were there that hot July night in 1993, peering down from the balconies onto the floor of the lower house of Japan's Diet. The Meiji reformers of last century may have chosen the German word for their parliament, but the outfitting is strictly Italian baroque — red velvet, ornate carvings, bronze busts and statues. There is an elaborate stained-glass ceiling from which, should it shatter in an earthquake while parliament is in session, the 511 members of parliament will protect themselves by placing special shrapnel-proof hats like tea cosies on their heads. An appropriate setting for Act I, Scene III of the political opera which began in 1946 when the occupying Americans re-wrote Japan's constitution. Nothing much had happened since 1955, when the curtains went up on Scene II, a petrified tableau much like the still-life stage nudity which was all the Lord Chancellor once decreed decent for British audiences. The conservatives ruled, the socialists opposed, and no Japanese aged much under sixty had ever voted in an election which changed anything.

If democracy means a popularly elected government, in which parliament is 'the supreme organ of state power' (as the Japanese constitution defines it), in which parties have clearly defined alternative policies and in which power regularly changes hands, then Japan never was one. In fact, with the exceptions of one chaotic nine-month socialist-led government in the 1940s and a few years in the 1980s when the conservatives had to rely on the support of a breakaway faction, one party, the LDP and its predecessors, had had a monopoly on power. Having proudly boasted, when elections were first held in 1890, that it was the 'first democracy east of Suez', Japan had been overtaken first by the boisterous politics of the Indian subcontinent, then, with the election in 1992 of Kim Young Sam, the country's first civilian ruler, by South Korea. Taiwan, with its first popular presidential election in 1996, is likely to be the next country to demonstrate that the theories of Confucian authoritarianism with which the godfather of Singaporean independence, Lee Kuan Yew, likes to legitimise Asian dictatorships are little more than self-serving twaddle.

As in Italy, the roots of Japan's deeply entrenched conservative monopoly on power — and the chaos which followed its rout in 1993 — owe more to the Cold War than the Analects. In exchange for providing the United States with what former prime minister Yasuhiro Nakasone was proud to call 'an unsinkable aircraft carrier' in its mission to contain Asian Communism, the Americans underwrote the postwar economic miracle. They opened their markets to Japan and guaranteed its security. They also covertly and overtly supported a succession of conservative governments. In the early 1950s — after some electoral successes by the Left and militant strikes — the United States connived in a Japanese 'Red Purge' every bit as vicious as the witch hunts of Senator Joseph McCarthy on the other side of the Pacific. Recently declassified documents show conclusively that the CIA exchanged intelligence, gave policy direction and provided secret funds for the LDP and its predecessors. The authorised opposition, the Social Democratic Party, which espoused a Marxist/Leninist philosophy and still had the 'achievement of the socialist revolution' in its manifesto as recently as 1990, withered into political irrelevance.

But that is to get both behind and ahead of the story. That summer night, with cicadas screaming from the gingko trees outside the Diet windows, it really did look as if (as the *Asian Wall Street Journal* put it) a political earthquake had taken place. Miyazawa, a grinning factional don, had been swept from power for having failed to deliver on a promise for political reform.

All Japanese elections are identified by epithet, and the midsummer poll which followed his defeat at the hands of Hata and other rebels from his own party is called the 'Liar Election'. In his campaign speech, Mr Miyazawa used the word 'reform' five times, and the phrases 'truly regrettable' and 'I am deeply sorry' twice each. The voters were unimpressed and, for the first time in nearly four decades, failed to give the conservatives a majority in parliament. 'Believing their promises would have been like buying a wart-cure from a toad,' remarked an opposition MP acidly.

Three years and five prime ministers later, with the passions cooled, it is tempting to mock those who believed genuine political change was under way in Japan, rather than another familiar charade. The LDP had returned to government (albeit as part of a coalition) after less than a year in the wilderness. It seemed likely to be restored to absolute power at the next election, due by mid-1997. The electoral reorganisation of 1993–94 had yet to prove it could deliver the desired outcome — a US-style two-party democracy. The reform agenda had evaporated and the LDP was back in the *kantei*, the musty, shrubbery-surrounded prime-ministerial lodge, in the person of the sword-wielding, Elvis-haired one-time trade minister Ryutaro Hashimoto. Hashimoto, a hawkish throw-back to the 1960s, was widely seen as part of the problem rather than part of the solution.

The voters had correctly identified corruption as the major issue in that landmark election of 1993, the so-called 'black rain' which has polluted Japanese politics for more than a century. Bribery had reached such a massive scale that it perverted almost every aspect of public policy. Whether it was building a dam, buying a jet, apologising for the war or something as mundane as overhauling the *shaken* system, Japan's strict (and highly lucrative, for the service stations) vehicle inspection system, vested interests with thick cheque books and backdoor access came to dominate public life. Hence such absurdities as Japan trying to protect its ski industry by banning the import of foreign skis on the grounds that 'Japanese snow is different'. When Yuriko Koike, an opposition MP, sought to have compulsory rabies inoculations for dogs abolished, on the grounds that there had been no case of rabies in Japan since 1957, she was howled down by the veterinarians, who saw this as a threat to their nice little earner.

During the good times, when every year the system delivered rising living standards, the voters were prepared to turn a blind eye to scandals, returning the LDP to power time after time. But 1993 marked the third year of a full-scale recession that was to turn out to be the longest, and deepest, since World War II. Unemployment reached a record (if enviable by international standards) 3.2 per cent, the property market collapsed, banks went bust and shares languished at half their price at the peak of the 'bubble economy'. The voters were baying for a scapegoat and crooked LDP politicians paid the price.

Japan is not normally regarded as a country where bribery is particularly rampant. A 'Global Gauge of Greased Palms', compiled by the *New York Times* from surveys of businesspeople and journalists, ranks Indonesia, China and Pakistan the most corrupt of forty-one countries, and New Zealand, Denmark and Singapore the least. Japan comes exactly in the middle at number twenty, between South Africa and Belgium. This sort of superficial poll, however, is misleading. In Japan, no-one shakes you down for a 'gratuity' at the airport, or thinks of tucking a 10 000 yen note in their driving licence when pulled up by police. Obvious petty bribery does not exist. This tends to blind casual observers to the more serious corruption which is endemic to the system and thus neither visible nor, often, even illegal.

All countries, of course, have their share of political corruption. British politicians have been regularly accepting money to ask questions in parliament. The influence of cashed-up special influence groups over the US Congress is notorious. In Australia, who could deny the clout of the trade unions and the business interests who are the main source of finance for each side of politics? Yet the revelations in Japan of the past few years surpass even the purges of Italy's Operation Clean Hands. Bribery, influence-peddling and even ties with the notorious *yakuza* gangster gangs are well documented. Four of the past seven prime ministers have resigned over corruption issues, and perhaps a dozen Cabinet Ministers and party dons have faced charges in court.

As far as the bureaucracy is concerned, Japanese public servants see no conflict of interest in the practice of *amakudari* ('descent from heaven') in which they parachute from their government jobs in their early fifties to highly paid positions in the very industries which they are supposed to have been regulating. A vintage year for this practice was 1992, when no fewer than 314 bureaucrats 'retired' to join private companies, most notoriously in the construction, finance and telecommunications industries. One-quarter of the 1517 directors of construction companies and the heads of most of the major banks and securities houses are 'OBs' (Old Boys from the bureaucracy). One notorious 'bird of passage', the former head of the Patents' Office, of all things, managed to 'retire' three times after he left, flitting from job to job and collecting more than $6 million in fees and superannuation payments.

'They pay us nothing while we are here,' one of the Ministry of Finance's exceedingly bright young men tried to explain to me at one of the department's regular soirees for the foreign media. 'If it wasn't for the security of a job after retirement no-one would join the public service.' His arguments would have been more convincing if we hadn't been sharing a vintage bottle of Gevrey Chambertin at the time, for which you would have received little change out of $300 at a Tokyo bottle shop.

Japanese politicians, similarly, see no conflict in accepting sinecures, fat campaign donations and electoral manpower from companies which can benefit directly from their legislative activities. When an election campaign is on, even relatively clean MPs such as Kazuo Aichi in Sendai has his electoral office stacked with barrels of sake and other valuable gifts from people seeking favours; at night, he hosts glittering banquets under the chandeliers of a reception centre ballroom, where 1000 electors stuff themselves with Kirin beer and lobsters. Others are more blatant. Kishiro Nakamura, a former construction minister who is one of the few corrupt politicians to finish up behind bars, was caught pocketing $135 000 in return for trying to stop the Fair Trade Commission prosecuting a group of construction companies for bid-rigging. Not even the imperial family is above financial shenanigans. In 1995, relatives of two princes, Takamatsu and Tomohito, were forced to return $2 million they had received for illegally lending their names to sporting events such as bicycle and power-boat races.

It would be naive in the extreme to believe this mighty black current of capital does not come with strings attached. In case anyone should require proof, however, Shigeru Hayasaki, bagman to the godfather of Japanese corruption, the late prime minister Kakuei Tanaka, once spelled it out. 'The Japanese are realistic, so nobody will give big money to politicians unless they think they can get something in return,' he wrote. The enormous amounts of money needed to lubricate the wheels of Japanese politics boggle the imagination. They dwarf even the extravagance of American presidential campaigns. In 1991, nationwide, slightly more than $3 billion was donated to political parties, with $750 million of that raised by the LDP alone. By comparison, Bill Clinton expected to spend a mere $57 million on his 1996 re-election campaign.

The high-water mark of 'money politics' was 1991. Donations to political parties, according to the official figures at any rate, declined in the following three years amid nationwide revulsion. However, the introduction of public funding in 1994, one of the new government's reform measures which was supposed to reduce, if not eliminate, corruption appears merely to have driven much of it even further underground. The new law was emasculated in the Diet, and in practice proved to be neither comprehensive nor transparent, the two essentials for any serious attempt to convince voters their government is clean. Moreover, receipt of public funds was made conditional on each party continuing to raise colossal matching amounts, on a $1.25 for $1 basis. In 1994, the parties still collected around $2 billion from non-public sources.

And that is just what was declared. There are loopholes in the legislation through which you could drive a bullet train. Unlike, say, Australia, politicians' declarations of assets do not have to include their immediate families. This may explain why, to cite one of the more outrageous examples, a resort hotel in Okinawa turned out to be legally owned by the five-year-old son of a former Cabinet Minister. As an indication of the absurdity of the new law, the Japan Communist Party, which is supported by fewer than 10 per cent of voters, but which is scrupulous about declaring its income, has for many years been officially listed as the country's biggest fund-raiser, collecting more donations than even the LDP. As Kakuei Tanaka, who built the most awesomely corrupt money-machine in history once flagrantly said, 'Politics come from power. Power means numbers. Numbers depend on money.' Even the head-kickers of the right wing of the NSW Labor Party could not have come up with a more appropriate epigram.

So where does all the money go? Much of it is spent on getting re-elected: paying campaign staff, slipping to constituents in envelopes at weddings and funerals, greasing bureaucrats and journalists with gifts, travel and entertainment. There are, as well, allegations too numerous and too consistent to ignore that bundles of banknotes have been handed to opposition power brokers to buy their acquiescence in contentious legislation. According to Diet insiders, when the disgraced LDP faction boss Shin Kanemaru was in charge of the Diet program, he regularly paid off Makoto Tanabe, the former chairman of the Social Democrats, not to obstruct legislation. Parliament was once paralysed for days after an LDP maverick named Koichi Hamada yelled at socialist MPs objecting to some measure, 'You've got your money, now shut up!' Opposition politicians went on strike until he apologised.

In any event, Japan's politicians have very little to do with the way the country is governed. The Diet itself is rarely in session, and substantive debate on policy is all but unknown. In 1993, Japan's Lower House engaged in debate on legislation for just sixty-seven hours, less than any other parliament in the world. In the UK House of Commons, by comparison, debate took up 1468 hours, in the US House of Representatives 844 hours, and in Germany's Bundestag, 430. The agenda in Japan is dictated by the bureaucrats; parliamentary approval is a mere rubber stamp. Bureaucrats write the answers to parliamentary questions, and sometimes even draft the questions for the opposition. One Cabinet Minister has gone down in Diet folklore for replying to a question, 'This is such an important issue that I think the senior bureaucrat should answer the question.'

Senator Bob McMullan, Trade Minister in the Keating government, told me of a visit he paid in the early 1980s, when he was national secretary of the ALP, to his LDP counterpart in Tokyo. An election was coming up and McMullan was curious to know how the party's policies were developed. The LDP official showed him a long corridor in the party's headquarters lined with doors and said: 'Before the election, each ministry sends officials here to work in these offices. When they have drafted the policies they present them to us, and that is what we campaign on.' Knowing they cannot buck the bureaucracy, opposition parties content themselves with meaningless waffle in place of policies. At the 1993 election, arguably the most important in postwar Japanese history, the main opposition party's manifesto began: 'As history writhes on the doorstep of the twenty-first century ...' and continued for many pages without a single reference to taxation, health care, education, defence or any other identifiable issue.

The antics of Japan's powerless parliamentarians as they pose and posture around the parliament remind me of Luigi Barzini's classic description of Renaissance-era warfare in Italy:

> ... it was an elegant and practically bloodless pantomime. Highly paid *condottieri*, at the head of picturesque but small companies of armed men, staged the outward appearance of armed conflict, decorating the stage with beautiful props, flags, coloured tents, caparisoned horses, plumes. The action was accompanied by suitable martial music, rolls of drums, heartening songs, and blood-chilling cries. They convincingly manoeuvred their few men back and forth, pursued each other across vast provinces, conquered each other's fortresses. Victory was decided by secret negotiations and bribes.

And on what a scale. Japanese politicians calculate it costs around $3 million a year to run their electoral organisations, supporters' networks known as *koenkai*, and another $4 to $5 million to get elected. Much of this money also happens to stick to their fingers, even though, at about $500 000 a year (including allowances and annual bonuses), Japanese backbenchers are paid more than the British Prime Minister and the President of the United States put together. Yotaro Iida, then the vice-chairman of Keidanren (the peak body of Japanese industrial associations, which is one of the mainstays of funding for the LDP), outraged MPs, but merely confirmed the suspicions of the voters, when he declared only half-jokingly in 1993: 'Politicians are creatures who are eager for money. If we totally stop donating [to them] they may even commit robbery.'

Income and asset declarations — a novelty introduced for all MPs in 1992, over the strenuous objections of sections of the LDP — caused a sharp intake of breath all over Japan as humble politicians appealing for support were unveiled as zillionaires. The average LDP member of the Diet had assets of $1.86 million, eight times more than his typical constituent. A backbencher named Takashi Sasagawa had managed to amass $56 million while attending to his parliamentary duties. More than fifty members of parliament — including Kiichi Miyazawa and half his Cabinet — had assets of more than $10 million each, rich even by Japanese standards and scandalous in a society which pays so much lip service to an egalitarian distribution of wealth.

These declarations are merely notional numbers which ludicrously understate the real worth of politicians' ill-gotten gains. Stocks are listed at face value and land at an artificially low price calculated for tax purposes. An audit by the mass-circulation *Yomiuri* newspaper revealed that, in 1995, Foreign Minister Yohei Kono was really worth about $110 million (five times what he declared), Finance Minister Masayoshi Takemura $6.3 million (three times) and Trade Minister and future LDP leader Ryutaro Hashimoto $3.8 million (double). Even that prototypical modest man with much to be modest about, the bushy-browed left-wing prime minister Tomiichi Murayama, who was born in poverty, was discovered to have amassed nearly $5 million worth of shares and property since entering parliament. He said this was thanks to his wife, who looked after the money.

The declarations of income also caused considerable surprise. The average MP managed almost to double his official allowance with 'outside' earnings. No fewer than thirty past and present LDP MPs were on the payroll of — guess who — construction companies, which paid them up to $500 000 a year for their (unspecified) services. Little wonder cynics referred to it as the best government money could buy.

In the absence of organised independent citizens' lobbies in Japan — those that do exist are quickly 'captured' by the bureaucracy — only big business can afford political patronage on this scale. Hence the domination of the political process by vested producer interests and the futility of calls for any meaningful deregulation of the government-sponsored cartels, price-fixing and bid-rigging which force Japanese consumers to pay almost twice as much for life's essentials as people in any other rich country. Until the elections of 1993, the Japanese had long lost sight of any connection between the way they voted and the way they were governed. The yen, not the ballot, was the determinant of government policy.

Pork barrelling, influence peddling and outright bribery are, of course, not unique to Japan. However, the way in which the spoils are carved up is. Government MPs are organised in *zoku* or 'tribes', each of which has responsibility for protecting a particular cluster of vested interests, and which in return receives money and electoral support. Understanding Japanese politics is an exercise in following this money trail. The system helps explain many of the policy failures that are dealt with in later chapters: the grievous shortcomings of the health and education systems in Japan, the collapse of decision-making in times of crisis such as the Kobe earthquake and Japan's failure to acknowledge its war guilt, which still sours its international relations.

The construction 'tribe' intercedes with the bureaucrats to rig the bidding on major public works contracts. The health and welfare 'tribe' has been responsible for keeping the world's most popular and effective contraceptive, the Pill, out of Japan for thirty-five years in order to protect the lucrative abortion and condom industries. It is also, incidentally, the guardian of the nationalist myth that Japan was not to blame for World War II — the War Bereaved Families' Association, with more than a million members, is one of Japan's most powerful lobbies. The agriculture 'tribe' devised the rigged 'auction' system that ensured Japanese consumers would still pay eight times world prices for rice after the door to imports was opened a chink. It was also prepared to sink plans for an Asia–Pacific free trade zone (APEC) rather than allow any more competition for the world's most inefficient farmers. A few years earlier, Agriculture Minister (and later Prime Minister) Tsutomu Hata made himself a global laughing stock by opposing beef imports on the grounds that Japanese intestines were longer than those of Westerners, and hence they could not digest foreign beef. Japan's three million farmers — and the 300 000 bureaucrats in the *nokyo* cooperatives who control them — are said to be the 'third rail' in the subway of Japanese politics, the electrified one. Touch it and you're dead.

To quote Barzini (and the similarities with Italian politics are inescapable) again:

> … powerful groups know no other limit to their power than the power of rival groups. They play a free-for-all game, practically without rules and referee. Of course the law is allegedly supreme. The apparatus of a quasi-modern State is visibly omnipresent, with its props, cast of characters, costumes, titles and institutions. But there are important differences between such dignitaries and organisations and what they are elsewhere. Each branch of State machinery in Italy is in reality a mighty independent power which must struggle sometimes for its existence, and usually for the prosperity of its protégés and subjects against all other rival branches of the State machinery. They fight savagely at times, but more often surreptitiously, exactly like private pressure groups, for a larger place in the sun, a bigger cut of the budget, more employees, a higher rank and wider prerogatives for their leaders.

The defeat of the LDP in 1993 only temporarily disrupted the smooth functioning of this 'iron triangle' of business, bureaucrats and politicians. And it was unlikely that even the much-vaunted election-funding reforms of the Hosokawa government which followed would make a great deal of difference in the longer term. In late 1995, Keidanren resumed its funding of the LDP, which had been suspended at the height of the 'money politics' scandals. Japan Inc. agreed to ante up

$135 million over five years, apparently in exchange for massive tax breaks for big business. At the time of writing, it was also far from clear whether a new electoral system which was simultaneously introduced would have the desired result of turning Japan into a more 'normal' democracy. If the polls were right, a return to totally abnormal LDP hegemony was more likely.

The 'reformers' who came to power in 1993 believed that Japan's mongrel hybrid of an election system was not only unrepresentative, it was the root of the corruption. This system, originally introduced in 1925 (and reinstated by General Douglas MacArthur when he rewrote the constitution) was unique. Japan was divided into maxi-electorates which typically each returned four or five MPs, but each elector received only a single non-transferable vote. In 1995, for instance, in my local government precinct of Minato-ku, forty-six candidates were competing for forty seats. So, in spite of the fact that there were a third of a million voters on the roll, 4000 or 5000 votes, just 2 per cent of those cast, would be enough to get a candidate elected.

In national elections, members of the rival LDP factions — five autonomous groups, more akin to separate parties-within-a-party — found themselves fighting each other with identical policies, and nothing on which to compete but money. The reforms of 1994–95 were supposed to eliminate these factions, but in fact they merely changed their names, meeting instead as 'study groups' or 'former factions'. The faction boss who raised the most money — doling it out in wads of tens of thousands of dollars to his followers at the summer and winter gift-giving seasons — was the most successful. Every little gratuity was gratefully received. In 1995, MPs belonging to one faction received vouchers entitling them to a free pair of expensive imported shoes at a Ginza store.

Another problem is that Japan's entire democratic process is hedged around with absurd rules that seem designed to prevent the voters from finding out anything much about the people standing for election — even their names. In local elections, campaigning may be banned until just five days before the poll. Policy debates do not occur and political advertising is banned on television and radio, and in newspapers. These rules reach loony heights when even news footage of the campaign (as during the 1995 regional elections) has to be edited so that the face of the candidate is not shown, just a disembodied pair of hands in snow-white gloves to emphasise the anonymous candidate's purity. Public opinion polls ranking candidates by name are kept secret within the power elite and never published during the campaign, apparently for fear of influencing the result. Door-knocking and pamphleteering are illegal. What's left? I spent a day on the campaign trail with a Tokyo candidate in which his sole activity was walking up and down streets in the pouring 'plum blossom' rain, bowing towards people's front doors and howling out *'Yoroshiku onegaishimasu'* ('Thank you in advance for your support') over and over again in a steadily deteriorating croak. However, this was enough to get 'Mr Green' (to emphasise his environmental awareness he dressed in green, even down to his underpants) elected.

Little wonder that there is widespread disillusionment with the entire system, and even more contempt for politicians in Japan than in Australia. In 1995, non-traditional politicians (a TV 'talent' and a stand-up comedian) were elected to head Japan's two largest cities. The percentage of people even bothering to vote in the Upper House election fell below 50 per cent for the first time in history, and in the earthquake city of Kobe almost two in three voters stayed home. The popularity of Tomiichi Murayama's new coalition government dropped below 25 per cent. Even more alarmingly for advocates of an informed democracy, more than half of Japanese polled said they supported no political party at all.

Periodically, the ugly face of Japanese money politics is unmasked. These designer label scandals, to which thousands of reporters are assigned and which take on the proportions of Watergate, are named after the companies involved. The Lockheed scandal, in which Kakuei Tanaka was accused of taking millions to persuade ANA airlines to buy Lockheed Tri-Star aircraft, destroyed his prime ministership (though not his power). Recruit Cosmos ended the rule of his successor, Noboru Takeshita. Sagawa Kyubin brought down half a dozen LDP power brokers, including Shin Kanemaru, the party's elder statesman. The great banking scandals of 1995–96 are certain to require more blood sacrifices.

However, in spite of all the hue and cry, no-one ever gets seriously hurt. Japan's Dickensian justice system sees to that. When Tanaka died in 1994, he was still appealing against his conviction in a case which had begun eighteen years before. Of the sixteen people charged over the Lockheed affair, only one, Hiro Hayama, the former chairman of the Marubeni trading corporation, ever received a jail sentence. Even he was eventually let off because, by the time he exhausted his appeal process in 1995, he was eighty-five years old and the prosecutors decided that he 'could not endure the rigours of incarceration'. Shin Kanemaru was given a 'parking ticket' fine for his corruption. Few national politicians have ever had to serve a jail sentence for corruption. Most are never even charged.

As if on cue, as campaigning got under way for the 1993 election, the granddaddy of all scandals broke out, one involving the entire construction industry — the so-called *zenecon* (Japlish for 'general contractor') affair. It began with the arrest of Fujio Takeuchi, the 75-year-old former five-term governor of Ibaraki Prefecture, a sprawling province of farms and factories and dormitory suburbs 100 kilometres east of Tokyo. It would finish, more than a year later, with the arrest of half a dozen regional and national politicians (including former construction minister Nakamura) and the public disgrace of every major construction company in the country. At last count, more than thirty executives had been arrested and television news audiences were agog at footage of public prosecutors carrying truckloads of documents out of the offices of some of the biggest names in the construction industry — Hazama, Taisei, Shimizu and Kajima among them. Never before had the Japanese been presented with such a detailed picture of the sordid culture of corruption which ruled their country: of shopping bags full of banknotes handed over in the back parlours of discreet Ginza madams, of bureaucrats and businessmen cavorting at exclusive golf clubs and casinos as they carved up contracts worth billions of dollars.

It emerged that almost every important government contract — and even many in the private sector — had for years been rigged by cartels of construction companies known as *dangos*. The word literally means 'consultation group', but the phonetics are punned to mean a pair of rice dumplings sticking together. On a global scale, only drug smuggling rivals these *dangos* as a criminal enterprise. The Japanese construction industry is worth a gigantic $1.3 trillion a year, one-third of this amount being government contracts. It involves 500 000 companies, six million workers and about one-fifth of the country's entire gross national product. For all practical purposes, the price mechanism had ceased to operate in this entire sector. The Construction Ministry itself calculated that buildings in Japan cost between twice and three times as much as similar structures in London or New York. The Stalinist spires of the Tokyo city council in Shinjuku, for instance, cost $2.5 billion — double the cost of Australia's new Parliament House — much of which was syphoned off by crooked construction companies and returned as kickbacks to the politicians who fixed the contracts.

In exchange for their largesse, hundreds of the bureaucrats responsible for awarding public works contracts parachuted into lucrative sinecures in the industry after taking early retirement. Kajima, Japan's second-largest construction company, was the most blatant offender. It found jobs for no fewer than seven former Construction Ministry officials on its board of directors. The company was also revealed to have paid the salaries of seven staff members of Wataru Hiraizumi, who retired as director-general of the powerful Economic Planning Agency to go into politics. Shinichiro Shimozu, a former Welfare Minister, had a $700 000-a-year research institute specially set up for him by Kajima not long after he gave the company planning permission for a fancy golf course.

To add insult to injury, it was revealed that the ordinary Japanese taxpayer was actually subsidising this rampant bribery. Every major company is entitled to claim a tax deduction for what is called *shito fumeikin*, literally 'unaccounted-for expenditure'. This is mainly kickbacks for which, for obvious reasons, no receipts can be produced. Shimizu, Japan's largest construction company, wrote off no less than $34 million under this heading in 1992. The total for the construction industry (according to the National Tax Agency, which conveniently compiles bribe totals for each industry) was an extraordinary $540 million, much of which no doubt finished up in the coffers of the LDP. 'Paying off politicians has been seen like committing a traffic offence,' says Mr Tokunosuke Hasegawa, a former Construction Ministry insider who ought to know. 'You know it's against the law, but it is not seen as unethical.'

Unfortunately for those who were expecting radical action to uproot the corruption, this scandal — like so many before it — soon faded from the headlines. Mr Nakamura was expected to take the rap, while the rest of the industry was thrashed vigorously with a feather. Several of the more blatant offenders such as Kajima were 'suspended' from bidding for public works contracts for a couple of months; the industry cancelled its autumn advertising schedules; Construction Ministry officials were 'advised' (but not directed) not to take up quite so many post-retirement perks; and there was talk of more major contracts being opened up to 'open bidding'. Few who understand the Japanese system expected much to come of it. Too many vested interests were at stake.

Nevertheless, as politicians from all sides saddled up for the 'Liar Election', they placed their white-gloved hands on their hearts and promised reform. The introduction of tougher and more transparent election funding laws — together with state funding of political parties — would, voters were assured, at least reduce corruption. The 'rotten boroughs' of multi-member electorates would be replaced by a more representative two-tier Italian-style voting system, combining regional preferential elections with first-past-the-post single electorates. The theory was that it would be harder to bribe half an electorate in a two-horse race than one-fifth of one in the old multi-member constituencies. The system in which one country vote can be worth almost three city votes — a rural gerrymander blatant enough to make Joh Bjelke-Petersen blush — would be redressed. These reforms, albeit in a watered-down form, were passed into law in early 1994 and were due to be tested for the first time in elections for the lower house, the House of Representatives, due by mid-1997. That is, if the shaky series of coalition governments that succeeded the LDP's fall from power did not collapse altogether before then.

However, there was little confidence that, after all the anguish, the new system would produce what most Japanese say they want — an American-style democracy, free of corruption, with parties judged on their policies, power alternating regularly between two major parties and the Diet, not the bureaucracy, in charge. Psephologists who have attempted to predict the result, using huge polls and sophisticated computer models, expect either another wobbly coalition, with no single party holding a parliamentary majority, or a 'back to the future' result with the LDP returned to power. Morihiro Hosokawa, who succeeded Mr Miyazawa as prime minister after the Liar Election, predicts that it will take 'three or four' more elections before Japanese politics stabilises in a form the rest of the world can understand.

The catalyst for the reforms was the success in the 'Liar Election' of a man who managed to convince an electorate, weary of scandals and worried about the economy, that he represented change. With his saturnine good looks, stylish wife and plausible patter, Hosokawa was an unusual figure to reach the peak of Japanese politics. The first leader too young to have fought in the war (he was fifty-six when he became prime minister), Hosokawa was a millionaire aristocrat and as close to a wunderkind as Japan's strict seniority system of public advancement had seen. In a country where half the Cabinet was over sixty-five (and the Speaker nudging eighty-one), he had been progressively the youngest member of the House of Councillors (the upper house of the Diet), the youngest minister and the youngest provincial governor.

Hosokawa was the bluest of blue bloods. He traces his family back eighteen generations to the feudal lords who ruled on Japan's southernmost island, Kyushu, during the Tokugawa shogunate. If the aristocracy had not been abolished after the war, he would have inherited a title. His grandfather was Prince Fumimaro Konoye, a wartime prime minister. A law graduate from the prestigious Sophia University, Hosokawa was an award-winning journalist on the leading liberal *Asahi* newspaper. He was elected to the House of Councillors at the age of thirty-three, served as assistant finance minister and then as a popular governor. In short, there was style, but was there any substance to Morihiro Hosokawa?

Politically, Hosokawa was an improbable man to hold himself out as the Great White Hope of political reform. For twelve years he had been a member of the LDP's largest and most corrupt faction, the one founded by Kakuei Tanaka. However, in May of 1992, with the government reeling from the first revelations of what would become yet another damaging corruption scandal — the so-called Sagawa affair — Hosokawa returned to Tokyo after eight years in the balmy boondocks as Governor of Kumamoto, the castle town of his ancestors in Kyushu.

He sprang to centre stage of the debate over political reform, announcing the formation of not just a new party, the Japan New Party, but a new politics. 'It is time to change the rigid, outmoded system yoked to vested interests,' Hosokawa declared. He proclaimed policies (itself a remarkable thing for a mere politician) including challenging such sacred cows as import restrictions, Japan's non-participation in United Nations peacekeeping operations and proposed decentralisation of power from Tokyo to the provinces. It was absurd, he said, that local government should carry two-thirds of the responsibilities of government, but depend on Tokyo for two-thirds of their budget. And why should the approval of a central government bureaucrat 3000 kilometres away be necessary for even the relocation of a bus stop or the design of a pigsty in Kyushu? Most important of all, he pledged to reform the election system and to abolish corruption, which struck an instant chord with the electorate.

It is important to remember, looking back on Hosokawa's truncated term as prime minister, that although his ideas were almost universally applauded during that heady campaign, he received no popular mandate at the Liar Election. The JNP, with its motley slate of untried *tarento* ('talents') including sportsmen, media personalities, greenies and women, achieved just 7 per cent of the vote, and thirty-five of the 511 seats in Japan's lower house of parliament. Even the Communists outpolled them. When a coalition was finally cobbled together between a diverse crew of eight opposition parties, ousting the LDP, it was dominated by LDP defectors who, until a few months before, had been among the staunchest opponents of reform. Ex-LDP Ministers held most of the important jobs in the Hosokawa Cabinet, and the even shorter lived government of Tsutomu Hata which followed it. In less than a year the LDP was back in power, and the JNP had voted itself out of existence.

Just as Mr Hosokawa's rise to power did not really reflect the sort of fundamental shift of political tectonic plates that some imagined, so his fall, just eight months later, was just another variation on a familiar Japanese theme. It had not, actually, been much of a premiership. His reform legislation was gutted in parliament, his economic stimulus package was a flop and people were beginning to ridicule his midnight press conferences. At these unscheduled events, he would appear on television looking flushed and excited to make announcements (most fatuously a new 'welfare tax' dreamed up by the bureaucracy) which he would then have to retract in the morning. But, in the end, it was Hosokawa's ostensible involvement in that most traditional of Japanese political pastimes, suspect money transactions, that did him in. I say ostensibly, because there are good reasons for thinking that this was merely the *tatemae*, the public façade, rather than the *honne*, the truth of the matter.

What Hosokawa did was a mere peccadillo by the murky standards of Japanese politics. This is a country where politicians collect carry-bags containing $70 000 from supporters, and where prime ministers hobnob with organised crime figures. Hosokawa was accused of accepting a 'loan' of $1.3 million from the scandal-tainted Sagawa Kyubin trucking company, of concealing a lucrative trade in telephone company shares in the name of his late father-in-law and of accepting hundreds of thousands of dollars worth of free work on a holiday mansion he owns in the resort town of Karuizawa. Even before he became prime minister, these transgressions had been publicised. In the subsequent months, the media worked itself up into a full-scale frenzy. So, why did the media suddenly turn on Hosokawa, rather than, say, the sixty parliamentary colleagues whom Shin Kanemaru testified he paid off with bundles of bribe money — 'comrades' who were still sitting in parliament, rather than in prison where they belonged?

When one of these scandals blows up, the remarkable thing is that almost from day one a huge volume of incriminating evidence is dumped by the media. It contains (as in the case of the hapless Hosokawa) material that could only have come from the bureaucracy — tax records, lease agreements and share transactions. These documents are not ferreted out, Watergate style, by intrepid reporters determined to expose corruption. They are doled out to tame media contacts by bureaucrats, often using politicians as go-betweens. This is not a media lynching; it is the Japanese Establishment purging itself of someone who, for whatever reason, is no longer useful. In Hosokawa's case, he had antagonised several senior power centres in the bureaucracy. He had also been abandoned by his political patron, Ichiro 'Iron Arm' Ozawa, who had been scathingly critical of Hosokawa's performance as his public opinion ratings slumped after an early, heady honeymoon with the voters. It was time for him to go, and so the man whom many still consider offered Japan the best chance of real reform in a generation was unceremoniously dropped down the lift well.

Incidentally, the amount of data the Japanese bureaucracy holds on its citizens, and the total lack of legal safeguards on privacy, would give a western civil libertarian nightmares. Hundreds of databases are commercially available, lists of names and addresses categorising people according to age, income, education, occupation, bank balance and health problems. Meibo Toshokan ('Name-List Library'), in the Tokyo suburb of Shinbashi, has 150 million names on file and offers for sale lists of users of karaoke facilities, women managers of hostess bars in Ginza, participants in organised matchmaking parties and even every household which has not paid its viewer fee to the national broadcaster, NHK. When you go through a highway tollgate your car is automatically photographed. When you lose your job, your employer will telephone to warn your bank. When you register with your local council as a foreign resident (as you must), you are required to give your fingerprints, which remain on file forever. A colleague was flabbergasted to discover that to get a telephone line connected, or buy a mobile phone, he had to produce his passport.

Faced with this mountain of incriminating evidence, Hosokawa had no choice but to resign from the prime ministership, though not from the parliament where he remained as a 'supreme adviser' on his party's backbenches, an honour not refused to even the most wickedly corrupt premier hounded from office. He departed the *kantei*, feebly protesting, 'I never said I was clean' — a sorry epitaph. Yet the man who replaced him as prime minister for a fleeting fifty-nine days, a former bus conductor named Tsutomu Hata, was, if anything, even more tainted by scandal.

Hata, an avuncular man in his late fifties, campaigned as 'Mr Ordinary', the 'salaryman MP' in his nerdy short-sleeved 'energy-saving' suits. This set him apart from the majority of Japanese members of parliament who have never had a 'normal' job — one-third inherit their seats from their parents, another third are ex-bureaucrats. A quick tour around his electorate one snowy March weekend — guided by a critic who had spent several years researching Hata's background for a book — convinced me that this image being cranked out by the government PR machine was (surprise, surprise) completely unconvincing. Like Hosokawa, it was obvious Hata was to be a hostage of the bureaucracy, with the sword of scandal hanging over his head should he be rash enough to attempt to initiate any real reform.

Like Hosokawa, Hata was a disciple of Kakuei Tanaka. Even when the crooked godfather was convicted of corruption, Hata refused to renounce the 'old man in Mejiro' and told a campaign audience that Tanaka was 'a great teacher'. If you look around Hata's electorate, the Nagano No. 2 constituency in the snowy heartland of the Japanese Alps, you can see where the money comes from to maintain his electorate machine. This is where the 1998 Winter Olympics are to be held — the most expensive Olympics, summer or winter, staged on earth. By the time the torch is lit, more than $20 billion of the taxpayers' money will have been pumped into facilities and infrastructure, including a new bullet-train track and a superhighway. This is more than twenty times the cost of the 'environmentally friendly' winter games at Lillehamer in Norway. The Nagano games are nicknamed the 'zenecon Olympics' because of the gigantic contracts being carved up by crooked construction companies. It is the biggest sticky rice dumpling in history.

The big winner from all this will be Yoshiaki Tsutsumi, the ageing monarch of the Seibu group. Tsutsumi was reckoned by *Forbes Magazine* to be the world's richest man before the yen, and Japan Inc., took a dive. He is a close friend of Hata's and the biggest contributor to his campaign chest. He also assigns Seibu employees to work for Hata at election time. In addition, and this should come as no surprise by now, Tsutsumi is the biggest land-holder in Nagano. The roads and the rail link built for the Olympics will put his hotels, golf courses and resorts within a couple of hours of Tokyo, and will allow him to subdivide thousands of hectares of land for holiday homes. He will make billions more, and some of this will inevitably find its way into Hata's hands.

So why did the bureaucrats not immediately sool the media onto the 'Hata *zenecon* scandal'? Because they preferred to hold him hostage in the hope that, unlike Hosokawa, he would turn out to be someone they could do business with. As fate would have it, Hata hardly lasted long enough to find his way to the toilet in the prime minister's gloomy official residence. Within two months, the machinations of Ichiro Ozawa — the real strongman of the coalition — had broken apart the alliance, with the socialists defecting to put the LDP back in power. As for Hata, no doubt his file still sits in the back of some bureaucrat's safe. You never know when it may come in handy given the volatile state of Japanese politics.

Indeed, Taichi Sakaya, a former MITI (Ministry of International Trade and Industry) bureaucrat and historian, argues that the Japanese bureaucracy has been conducting these assassinations ever since Japan first had an elected parliament more than a century ago. He says it was the exposure, and downfall, of leading politicians in a string of scandals in the 1920s and 1930s that discredited the whole parliamentary system, opening the way for the military to seize control, plunging Asia, then the world, into war. And in all of this, of course, the media played a key role.

The function of the media in Japan is something that continually confuses Westerners who are used to a vigorous, independent press acting as a watchdog against abuse by society's other power centres. The Japanese media more closely resemble a lapdog. The proprietors, of course, regard themselves as part of the Establishment and are well aware of the arbitrary power of the politicians and bureaucrats over their businesses. They are among the largest donors to the LDP, and their boards and industry committees provide highly paid sinecures for the Posts and Telegraphs 'tribe' which controls communications and the media. NHK is Japan's equivalent of the ABC, but without even the nominal independence of the Australian national broadcaster. It can be counted on to toe the government line. Whether NHK is covering up for the authorities' disastrous bungling of the Kobe earthquake or pursuing its notorious '3T' policy of avoiding discussion of Tibet, Taiwan or the Tienanmen Square massacre to appease China, the world's second-largest news organisation is a disgrace.

Nor do editors and reporters on privately owned news organisations need reminding of the need for 'restraint', the euphemism for whitewashing stories the Establishment may not like. Tanaka once blatantly threatened reporters at a briefing: 'I am quite familiar with the inner workings of the media, and there is nothing I can't do if I want to. Even this [clutching his throat and pretending to strangle himself]. Your company presidents and editors will do exactly what I say.' When TV Asahi's head of news briefed his staff about the need to cover anti-government stories in the run-up to the 1993 election, he was sacked and hauled before a parliamentary committee to be publicly pilloried. Hiroshi Kume, the closest thing Japan has to an outspoken political critic on television, accused an LDP don of pressuring Toyota to terminate its sponsorship of his current affairs program. So it shouldn't really surprise foreign observers that most Japanese journalists interpret their role as the unquestioning distribution of the voice of authority to their audience — whether it is a police briefing, an industry association handout or a political speech — and play little part in the political reform process.

There are some honourable exceptions, particularly among Japan's weekly and monthly magazines, which were generally supportive of the Hosokawa reforms. The mainstream media, however, remained irredeemably compromised. The reporters spend their time hobnobbing behind closed doors with the people they are supposed to be keeping an eye on, swallowing, along with their food and booze, their propaganda, to be later regurgitated for public consumption. Media facilities are paid for by the organisation being covered. Even the humblest local council will spend tens of thousands of dollars wining and dining the reporters covering it — buying them presents, paying for their telephone calls and providing other fringe benefits. Hardly surprisingly, the media on the whole paid little more than lip service to the need for political reform and connived in the assassination of the only postwar government that had a brief window of opportunity to deliver it.

In return for this political docility, the Japanese media enjoy a cartel which makes them among the most profitable on earth. While newspapers are closing down across the English-speaking world, not a single title has died in Japan. The six national television networks have a virtual monopoly on the airwaves, whereas in America the networks account for less than a third of viewers. In Tokyo, only a few hundred thousand people have access to satellite channels or cable television; New Yorkers can all access more than sixty channels. So outrageous are the restrictions that the *Sydney Morning Herald* house has to have two separate satellite dishes, costing over $3000, to pick up the two permitted channels, NHK and the lone commercial channel, the oddly named WOW WOW. When I inquired about receiving the BBC's excellent Asian satellite channel, I was told I would need a third dish — this one would have to be three metres across, and would cost another $10 000.

Between Japanese information consumers and news sources stand '*kisha* clubs' of reporters attached to every important organisation — some 400 of them in Tokyo alone — which act as news cartels. The media which belong, in effect the eleven national newspapers and television networks, have exclusive access to the organisation, whether it is a government ministry, industry association, the defence forces or whatever. No power-holder would dare to defy the system by appealing directly to the public. In my time in Japan I was occasionally refused access to even the most basic official information. This led to absurdities such as, for instance, being told that I could sit and observe a meeting of the Tokyo City Government, but that I was not allowed to make any notes.

The system works both ways, of course. Not only do the reporters get exclusive access to news, the authorities get an unparalleled ability to shape what is reported, when it is reported and how. The *kisha* clubs caucus on stories, and often write an agreed group dispatch that appears, anonymously, in identical form in every paper and on every television station. Any organisation which steps out of line is likely to be expelled. Some of the most important stories, such as a cabinet minister denying Japan ever invaded Korea, are 'killed' by the *kisha* clubs for fear of embarrassing the source. This type of story only emerges if one of the reporters indiscreetly mentions it to a colleague not bound by the code of silence. On the prime minister's plane, heading to Washington for trade talks, reporters solemnly toast him in champagne and pledge to work to make his visit a success — a confusion of roles that, surely, would embarrass even the hacks of the Canberra press gallery.

This 'manufactured reality' is an essential tool of Japanese government, enabling the authorities to maintain power by keeping the citizens in a state of bewildered ignorance about what really goes on. Japan has no national freedom of information legislation, and no system requiring historical records to be released after, say, thirty or fifty years as in the West. Even material as essential to understanding how Japan is governed as the record of the Diet proceedings which approved the new constitution were kept secret until only recently. 'You can look out of the window and see the sun shining,' says a Japanese journalist friend, 'but if, for some reason, the authorities want to make out it is raining, there is nothing you can do. Look back in the records 100 years from now and you will find that it was raining.' This, I think, is what the revisionary historian Saburo Ienaga means when he rails against the 'standardisation of consciousness' that is such a feature of Japanese society.

Of equal concern to those who believe freedom of speech is an essential precondition of democracy is the way in which journalists are coopted to become part of the government process through membership of the 200-odd *shingi-kai*. These committees are the expert forums through which the Japanese bureaucracy — not the parliament — legitimises new laws and regulations. The bureaucrats control them; they set the agenda, provide the information (usually marked 'secret') and choose the staff. More than 100 of Tokyo's most influential journalists sit on these committees, and thus become captives of the system on which they are supposed to be independently reporting. It is quite bizarre, for instance, to listen to an 'agriculture expert' employed by the national broadcaster argue in apparent seriousness that it is a good thing for Japanese consumers to be paying eight times world prices for their rice. Bizarre, that is, until it emerges that he is also a paid and pampered member of a committee sponsored by the Ministry of Agriculture, Forests and Fisheries.

Nor are foreign journalists immune from such blandishments. Those who provide a 'positive' (in other words, uncritical) coverage — disparagingly referred to by their rivals as the 'chrysanthemum club' — are rewarded with lecture tours, well-paid columns in Japanese newspapers and magazines, visiting lectureships at universities, seats on government committees, free travel and preferential access to information and interviews. For my own part, I must confess to having received $100 from *Shukan Gendai*, a somewhat scandalous weekly magazine which asked me for 200 words on any subject I chose. They guaranteed it would not be censored unless I criticised the emperor or 'hea nudes' (pictures of naked women flaunting their pubic hair), a *Shukan Gendai* speciality. I have little interest in such pictures, and needed no warning about the dangers of writing about the emperor. Just a few years ago, a reporter from the *Asahi* newspaper was shot dead in his newsroom by a right-wing assassin, apparently over an article criticising Hirohito. I wrote, instead, about the *kisha* club system.

The authorities did, on one hilarious occasion, attempt to influence my writing. Curiously, it was not over my coverage of corruption and calls for political reform. I was invited to lunch at a fancy Ginza restaurant by Seiji Morimoto, who was then in charge of international media relations at the Ministry of Foreign Affairs. When we had finished eating and were enjoying a bottle of beer, he came to the point. He ticked off on his fingers, with mounting outrage, the stories he had been told to castigate me over. One was about how slow racehorses in Japan are eaten, a delicacy called *ba-sashi* or horsemeat sashimi. Another was about an enterprising doctor I had discovered who was attempting to rehabilitate *yakuza* gangsters by grafting toes onto their hands to replace amputated fingers. A third described Hokkaido hunters slaughtering protected sea lions. 'Why do you have to write such personal things?' complained Mr Morimoto. 'Why can't you write about politics and economics? This is very embarrassing for us Japanese.'

I explained, as tactfully as I could, that readers in both countries enjoy 'human interest' stories from time to time. Why, the only piece of news from Australia that had been run in Japan for weeks was a story about an airline attendant on the Gold Coast who had become the first man to enter a bikini contest. I hoped, I said, my own government would not be silly enough to call in the Japanese reporters responsible for a dressing-down. 'But, don't you want to improve relations between our countries?' he persisted. There was obviously quite a cultural gap here. 'No, that's your job. My job is to try and report what's going on, whether the Japanese government likes it or not.' Mr Morimoto looked flummoxed. I went off to write a piece about a robot priest I had discovered in Yokohama. The Japanese government never shouted me another lunch.

All this is by way of trying to explain why there was little critical media analysis of the Liar Election of 1993. The myth of an 'earthquake' was broadcast by the Japanese Establishment through the 'Mighty Wurlitzer', as the US Central Intelligence Agency once colourfully described its ability to manipulate the global media during the Cold War. It became conventional wisdom, both in Japan and overseas, that the system had changed. That suited the bureaucrats just fine, because they knew that in the most important respect of all, it had not. They, not parliament, remained in power.

It was two years before it finally dawned that the LDP had not so much been defeated as split. The twin poles of subsequent parliaments were not the forces of reform versus the forces of reaction, much as commentators struggled to characterise them as such. In fact, they were not about policies at all, but about personalities. The rise and fall of the four governments which followed the Liar Election were a gladiatorial contest for the numbers, the money, the patronage — the power — of the existing Japanese system. Behind it all was not an ideological split, but a blood feud between Japan's two most powerful politicians, both of whom lurked in the shadows and fought by proxy. An ageing don named Noboru Takeshita (once forced to resign the prime ministership for taking bribes and associating with gangsters) controlled the all-powerful Tanaka faction of the LDP. Ichiro Ozawa, one of the faction's ambitious young Turks, tried to seize it from him. When he failed, Mr Ozawa defected from the LDP, vowing vengeance. The 'new politics' was in reality the old factional politics with a new coat of arms, banner and battle cry.

Ozawa and Takeshita were merely the latest in a dark lineage of 'shadow shoguns'. It is a tradition that dates back to feudal times, and the role is often compared with the *kurogo*, the man in black who manipulates the action in *bunraku*, the colourful and highly stylised classical Japanese puppet theatre. While the audience is dazzled by the ritual clang and conflict of seventeenth-century samurai dramas, the chant of the balladeers and the twang of the *shamisen*, the puppeteer who controls the action remains invisible. In the satellite television soapie of Japan's late twentieth-century political epic, prime ministers come and go, governments rise and fall, political parties are born, divide and disappear, but the master manipulators are seen only fleetingly at the edges of public events before they disappear back into the blackness.

Mr Ozawa did not hold even the humblest post in the coalition governments that followed the downfall of the LDP. His only official title, until he was elected party leader late in 1995, was secretary-general of Shinshinto (which can be read as the 'New New Party'), which became the main opposition in the Diet. But no-one was deceived by the lack of formal titles. It was the brawny, hard-driving Mr Ozawa — a man who polished off two bottles of sake at a sitting and smoked five packets of

Parliament cigarettes a day until a heart attack slowed him down — who called the shots. He referred once to Prime Minister Hosokawa as a *mikoshi* — the portable shrine carried around on festive occasions. 'I am merely the actor; he is the playwright,' said Mr Tsutomu Hata, Mr Hosokawa's successor as Ozawa's puppet.

Mr Ozawa has been variously described (according to the political sympathies of the commentator) as the kingmaker of the coalition, the godfather of money politics and, in a *New York Times* review of his million-selling book *Japan Remodelling Plan*, as the most interesting and important politician the country has produced since World War II. It was Mr Ozawa who brought down the LDP (which his father, incidentally, helped found in 1955). It was Mr Ozawa who cobbled together the unlikely coalition — ranging from Social Democrats who wanted to cuddle up to Stalinist North Korea to hardline ex-LDP conservatives and followers of the Buddhist 'lay religion' Soka Gakkai — which took over the government. But what did it all achieve? What, if anything apart from a gluttony for power, does Mr Ozawa stand for? And where, if anywhere, does he want Japan to go in the unlikely event he becomes prime minister after the next election?

In his book, Mr Ozawa argues for Japan to become a 'normal country' playing a part in the world commensurate with its economic power — a seat on the United Nations Security Council, a role in Asian security and 'men not yen' in international peacekeeping operations. Domestically, he supports decentralisation and deregulation of Japan's highly controlled economy, and says parliament should wrestle power from the bureaucracy. But is this anything more than a few flowery lines in the overgrown garden of Japanese political verbiage?

Ozawa's puppets were in power for nearly a year. Yet, with the exception of the political reform legislation, nothing of significance was accomplished. The economy remained mired in the worst recession since the war; trade disputes festered and tax reform, urgently needed to cope with Japan's greying population, was put in the 'too hard' basket. International relations, although Mr Hosokawa did make a brave if belated apology to Korea for thirty-five years of cruel colonisation, remained poisoned by Japan's failure to acknowledge its responsibility for World War II. The power of the bureaucracy, if anything, increased in the absence of a clear political mandate for either Mr Ozawa's 'reformers' or Mr Takeshita's LDP. The media took to referring to the ruling parties (*renritsu-yoto*) and the government (*seifu*) as two distinct entities. There was little confusion about who was really in charge.

Probably the clearest and certainly the most entertaining account of just how the mandarins of Kasumigaseki, Tokyo's Whitehall, really rule the roost has been given by Masao Miyamoto, a former senior bureaucrat at the Ministry of Health and Welfare. Dr Miyamoto is a psychiatrist who spent many years in the United States, where he was assistant professor at two prestigious universities. He has an American wife, a zappy sports car, sharp designer clothes and, most damning of all from the point of view of the bureaucracy, a sense of humour. In 1994 and 1995 — until, eventually, they had to sack him — he provided, through newspaper columns and speaking engagements, a fascinating window into the world of Kasumigaseki, the 'foggy gate' down the road from the Diet where power really resides. Other insiders have written accounts of how the world's most important bureaucracy works, but few have done so with such candour and wit.

As deputy director of the ministry's mental health division, Dr Miyamoto had a bird's eye view of the way the bureaucracy dominates the legislature — making every important decision, writing the legislation, fixing the budgets and organising the parliamentary agenda. Diet 'interpellation' sessions (similar to question-time in Australian parliaments) are known to the mandarins as *okyo-yomi* or 'sutra-chanting'. Dr Miyamoto reveals that the ministries have style guides to help politicians and bureaucrats purge their words of all meaning. 'First, statements must be noncommittal and worded in such a way that any clear assignment of responsibility becomes impossible,' his superiors instructed him. 'Second, statements should support the status quo. Third, they should be as innocuous and inoffensive as possible. Fourth, answers to sharp, pointed questions should be framed in such a way as to evade the issue without really seeming to.' To this end, Dr Miyamoto provides a translation of bureaucratic double-speak that anyone doing business with Japan would be wise to study:

maemuki ni	(literally 'positively' or 'constructively') is used to give listeners the faint hope that something may happen in the distant future, though there are no immediate prospects.
eii	('assiduous' or 'energetic') is used when prospects are poor, but the politician or bureaucrat wants to impress people with his efforts.
jubun	('fully' or 'thoroughly') is used to stall for time.
tsutomeru	('to endeavour') means that the speaker is taking no responsibility.
hairyo suru	('careful consideration') means something will stay on the speaker's desk indefinitely with no likelihood of action.
kento suru	('investigate' or 'look into') means to kick something around without getting anywhere.
mimamoru	('follow closely') means you will assign the task to someone else and do nothing yourself.
okiki suru	('respectfully listen') also means the speaker plans to do nothing.
shincho ni	('cautiously') means the cause is absolutely hopeless.
muzukashii	('difficult') means impossible.

Some scholars trace the origins of this system — where the government reigns, but the bureaucrats rule — to ancient times, when Japan's emperors surrendered real power to the shogunate. Others date the tradition of the all-powerful bureaucracy to the samurai and merchants who formed the 'administration class' which modernised and industrialised

Japan after the Meiji revolution in 1868. Noribumi Tsukada, a respected economic historian, argues that the legal framework for all the main features of modern Japan — industrial cartels, rule by bureaucrats and interlocking business *keiretsu* — was set in place in the 1940s as part of Japan's mobilisation for all-out war.

Whatever its real roots, there can be no doubting the absolute authority of Japan's Sir Humphreys survived the Liar Election. Only one prime minister since the war has been brave enough to challenge them — Kakuei Tanaka, who defied convention by demanding the Ministry of Finance mandarins come to his office rather than vice versa, and is still spoken of in awe for personally initiating thirty-three pieces of legislation. And look what happened to him — driven from office in disgrace. Unlike the United States, where several hundred of the top administration jobs change with the presidency, Japan's bureaucrats are virtually unsackable and all but immune from political influence. Unlike Britain or Australia, where an increasing number of senior administrators are employed on contract with performance criteria, Japan's elite are a law unto themselves. The only system vaguely resembling it is the Grand Corps, the graduates of the Ecole Nationale d'Administration, who run France. However, it is a poor comparison. Japan has no powerful presidency to keep a check on the arrogance of its bureaucrats and its judicial process is geared to enforce the authority of the state over the individual, rather than act as a check on it.

The ministries — particularly the Ministry of Finance, which wields absolute power over Japan's $1 trillion-plus national budget, the banking system and the securities industry — control Japan in a fashion which more resembles a military dictatorship or a Communist autocracy than a modern democracy. The government's most senior tax reform adviser, for instance, has revealed how when he went to the prime minister's official residence to brief Hosokawa on a new tax proposal, he had to slither down a rockery and enter through a side door for fear his presence would be reported to the ministry. In the days when Mr Hosokawa was trying to cobble together his coalition, the mighty Ministry of Finance made it quite clear that whatever ideas for reform he might have, nothing would occur without their approval. 'So long as the [new] minister knows how to sit on a chair and read, we can use him more easily than before,' said one particularly insolent official.

Although it was Hosokawa who got the headlines, a far more important new face was appearing on the political scene during the 1993 election campaign — the new head of the Ministry of Finance. It was quite obvious that in spite of his humble title (heads of Japanese government departments are called *jimujikan,* or 'administrative vice-minister'), it was Jiro Saito who called the shots. 'Whatever the new government, and whomever the new Minister of Finance, we will continue to do what we believe in,' he admonished his *kisha* club hacks.

Much the same attitude was expressed in the hallways and famously grungy back offices of the other great ministries of state on whom Mr Hosokawa would have to depend to implement his reform agenda: the MITI (Ministry for International Trade and Industry, which is credited for the success of Japan's postwar industrial renaissance) and the Ministries of Construction, Agriculture, Posts and Telegraphs, Health and Welfare, and (a long way last because it has few retirement sinecures to offer) Foreign Affairs. Masayoshi Ohira, prime minister of the country for two years in the 1970s, spelt out who really made the decisions: 'The minister must consider himself only a temporary visitor in his government office,' wrote Ohira, '[he] must try as hard as he can not to be disliked by his officials.' Hosokawa, however, was determined to ignore this advice and take on the mandarins.

There was never any real doubt about who would win. When, in 1947, the bureaucracy was faced with Japan's first, and only, socialist government, the Ministry of Finance simply refused to fund Prime Minister Tetsu Katayama's budget. His government fell after only nine months, the victim of a bureaucratic coup. Nor is any minister allowed to occupy a portfolio long enough to assert his will; often they barely have time to find their way to the office. In the turmoil that followed the 1993 election, every government department had five ministers in thirty months, and some had six. In Japanese politics, everyone, no matter how untalented or downright daft, has to get a 'turn' at being a minister according to an arcane code of seniority and factional cronyism. Even prime ministers are rotated regularly through the revolving door of Japanese politics. There have been twenty-three in the fifty years since the postwar constitution came into force, including five in the past three years, more even than the famously unstable Italians. Cabinet meetings, in any case, are meaningless formalities which last the ten or fifteen minutes it takes to rubber-stamp the proposals of the bureaucrats.

Japan is remarkably unbureaucratised compared with other developed countries, with fewer than five public servants per 100 people. This compares with ten in the United States and fifteen in the United Kingdom, according to the author Karel van Wolferen. What they lack in numbers, however, they make up for in influence. Most are graduates of Tokyo University, the ultra-elite incubator of those who will run Japan. As well as dominating the public service, about 60 per cent of Japan's banks and trading houses and 30 per cent of manufacturing industry are headed by 'Todai' graduates. The power of these men (there has never been a female department head) is unquestioned. Much of Japanese 'law' is unwritten and subject to arbitrary interpretation and 'administrative guidance' by the bureaucrats. They have only to lift the phone to change government policy.

However, what visionaries like Ozawa's advisers (who 'ghosted' his book for him) had come to suspect was that Japan had reached the limits of what it could expect to achieve under this system. Many recent studies now indicate that undemocratic rule — whether by military dictators or autocratic bureaucrats — may be useful in the early stages as a country struggles to emerge as a developed nation. Certainly, in Japan, as bureaucrats eagerly point out at every opportunity, the system delivered an 'economic miracle' without parallel in history. It transformed a starving, war-scarred orphan into a global superpower in two short generations. But as a country reaches economic maturity, as Japan (now, by some measures, the world's wealthiest nation) undoubtedly has, the more flexible, creative and responsive strategies of functioning democracies appear to work better.

The problem in Japan, however, has always been that the bureaucracy refuses to share power, and the politicians lack the legitimacy to take it from them. Examples are not hard to find. At the Tokyo G7 summit of wealthy countries in 1993, Prime Minister Kiichi Miyazawa promised that Japan would boost its ailing economy with a supplementary budget and tax cuts. Within hours, the world witnessed the astonishing spectacle of Shusei Tanaka, administrative head of the Economic Planning Agency, calling a press conference to contradict publicly the economic strategy of his country's elected leader. An economic recovery was under way and no stimulus package was necessary, sniffed Mr Tanaka. As it turned out, like every prediction of recovery the Economic Planning Agency has made in the past five years, he was wrong. But it was Mr Miyazawa, not Mr Tanaka, who was soon out of a job.

Politicians of all political stripes campaigned with varying degrees of conviction to overturn this bureaucratic monopoly of power at the Liar Election. Kazuo Aichi, for instance, told a 'study group' of young voters I attended, one of Japan's many curious campaign forums: 'It is not up to the bureaucrats to make laws, it is up to the politicians. This iron triangle between bureaucrats, politicians and businessmen is not really democracy — information is monopolised by a small group, and the average Japanese, even many politicians, do not have access to that network. We must break the monopoly on information.'

Brave words. It is one of the supreme ironies of the four governments which followed that election that the power of the bureaucrats was, if anything, strengthened. The downfall of the Miyazawa government — in which Aichi played a leading role — killed Japan's best chance in decades of bringing the arrogant elite of its bureaucracy under political control. When parliament was prorogued, a bureaucratic reform package (which, needless to say, had to be specially drafted by a non-bureaucrat) was stillborn. The legislation would have curtailed the practice of 'administrative guidance', obliged bureaucrats to give written reasons for decisions and revised no fewer than 361 laws which give the public service almost limitless discretionary power. The two Shinshinto (non-LDP) coalitions of 1993–94 did not even attempt to put this particular reform package back on the agenda.

After the second New Frontier Party coalition fell, a new and unstable administration came to power — the so-called *ainori* or 'riding together' government in which the LDP and their archenemies for half a century, the Social Democratic Party, formed a coalition with a small LDP splinter. Few expected it to last more than a few months, but two years later it was still staggering on. Its first leader was a man with no popular mandate, who was without doubt the least qualified to lead Japan since the war — and the least able to dictate any agenda for reform. For only the second time in history, the government of the world's richest nation fell into the hands of a card-carrying socialist, a man who had spent most of his life in a party which was committed as recently as 1990 to the violent overthrow of the capitalist system in a 'socialist revolution'.

Tomiichi Murayama, aged seventy at the time, arrived at the *kantei* in the summer of 1993 with a doona over his shoulder and a daughter in attendance to cook his miso soup, his wife being a housebound invalid. A fisherman's son from the town of Oita on Japan's southern Kyushu island, he left school at the age of fourteen to help the family out by pickling sardines. He worked his way up through the local fishermen's union and prefectural government to become a member of parliament in 1972, and leader of the Social Democratic Party two decades later, having never sat on the government benches. His only policy expertise prior to becoming prime minister was in pensions. When his nomination as prime minister was announced, veteran journalists could be clearly heard on television calling out 'They must be mad.'

However, the plot soon became clear. All the major portfolios and the majority of Cabinet posts in Murayama's two Cabinets went to the LDP, who returned to power in all but name. In exchange for being installed as the nominal prime minister, Mr Murayama abandoned every policy his party had ever stood for. Where for forty-nine years they had branded Japan's armed forces unconstitutional and had campaigned to tear up the security treaty with the United States, the socialists now went along with the biggest boost in defence spending for years. Not only this, Murayama reaffirmed the security treaty when he met President Clinton. The banner across the front of the SDPJ headquarters in Tokyo which read 'Headquarters of the Campaign to Abolish the Consumption Tax' was hurriedly taken down as the government gritted its teeth and prepared to almost double the hated tax. Support for North Korea's Stalinist dictatorship was abandoned and a trip to Seoul was arranged. Opposition to nuclear power stations, the 'emperor system', the national anthem, the risen sun flag and every other sacred tenet of Japanese socialism went out of the window in Murayama's Faustian deal.

The consequences of this enormous act of betrayal were clear within a few months. Abandoned by most of their traditional allies in the trade union movement, deeply split between reformers groping for a new ideology and hardline Marxists resisting change, the party's support base collapsed. At the 1995 upper house elections it lost half its seats and polled 11 per cent of the vote, the lowest in history. The New Frontier Party, Mr Ozawa's crypto-conservative opposition grouping, was the big winner; the LDP held its ground; and the Communists won 10 per cent of the vote and three new seats. They picked up the votes of people disgusted by the antics of mainstream parties across the board, including, incidentally, Mayu's entire family: her mother, whose community activism should have put her in the socialist camp; her father, the company man who had voted LDP all his life; and Mayu herself, grateful for some help the Communists had given us with stories, and relieved that, in

1994, the party of Lenin and Marx had finally ditched its commitment to nationalise the economy.

Late in 1995, the socialists, who had once been supported by more than one-third of Japanese voters, voted their party out of existence, having been in government for just twenty-three months of their fifty-year history. This triggered yet another round of political upheaval. Japan's politics began to look even odder as the two main conservative parties, with different leaders but indistinguishable policies, squared off. While social democratic parties were reinventing themselves all over the world, Japanese voters found themselves in the unique position of having no mainstream party to the left of centre to vote for. Politics had reverted to an atavistic contest between two old-time LDP ogres — Mr Ozawa and Mr Takeshita. Conspiracy theorists nodded sagely. This had been the plan all along, they said, not to reform the system, but to destroy the socialists.

Not even a series of scandals which hit their heartland of Kasumigaseki in 1995–96 could shake the resurgent confidence of the bureaucracy. Politicians, the public and the media raged impotently as the Ministry of Finance and other elite ministries shrugged off a series of revelations which for the first time brought corruption to the front doors of the bureaucracy. This time, it was not *amakudari*, but something far more blatantly crooked at the root of the crisis which threatened to overwhelm Japan's financial system.

What brought it to a head was the collapse of a series of lending institutions, including one in Osaka which provoked a run on a bank, with people queueing in the streets to withdraw their money in scenes unparalleled since the 1930s. It was the first time the public began to grasp the extent of the debt crisis which the bureaucracy had been secretly trying to come to terms with for several years. Foreign analysts — Japanese bankers being too intimidated by the threat of retaliation from the Ministry of Finance to discuss the crisis frankly — began to talk of a disaster double the size of the United States savings and loan collapse of the 1980s, involving perhaps $800 billion. The government (that is, the Ministry of Finance) hinted that the public might be required to bail out these bankrupt bankers, who had lost billions on shonky business ventures, overpriced real estate and gambling on the stock market. The public began to ask just how these reckless investments had come to be made, and where the regulators were at the time. It emerged that the regulators, certain senior Ministry of Finance officials, had been bribed with gifts, trips, entertainment, free loans and, in one notorious case, bags of money.

As the Ministry of Finance's incompetence, greed and corruption became a political issue, headlines that would have been considered sacrilegious just a couple of years before began to appear: 'The Corrupt MOF' in the *Mainichi* newspaper; 'Monstrous Finance Ministry Should Be Disbanded' in the *Asahi*. A book called *Okurasho Kaitairon* (*Disbanding the Finance Ministry*), by an influential government backbencher, Fumihiko Igarashi, shot up the best-seller charts. For the first time, the third arm of the iron triangle was under attack — first the politicians, then big business and now the supposedly incorruptible bureaucrats.

The most blatant case was the international property empire of a company named EIE. It was once, at the height of the 'bubble economy', Australia's wealthiest landowner, with investments ranging from hotels to CBD skyscrapers and a piece of the Bond University on the Gold Coast. Its owner, Harunori Takahashi, a suave high roller, has in fact been described as an Asian Alan Bond. Although the company was hugely overgeared and technically bankrupt as far back as the early 1990s, Ministry of Finance pressure on Takahashi's bankers kept EIE afloat for years, until it finally collapsed under a mountain of debt. The senior Ministry of Finance bureaucrats responsible had been wined and dined, treated to weekends at Takahashi's exclusive golf courses and flown to casinos in Australia and Macao where they played in the high rollers' room with chips provided by EIE. This was totally unacceptable conduct, even by the opaque standards of the Japanese bureaucracy. When the Ministry of Finance devised a scheme to force the ratepayers of Tokyo to pay for the mess, their outrage was such that they threw out the LDP candidate who backed the scheme and elected a stand-up comic whose only policy was 'no public bail-out'.

Worse was to come. A series of investigations by groups of concerned citizens and lawyers began probing the money squandered by local governments on so-called *kan-kan settai* — the entertainment of central government officials, most notably those from the Ministry of Finance, at the public's expense. Lest this appear a trivial concern, let me explain how the system works. Every year, when the national budget is being framed, thousands of officials and politicians from provincial government and local councils troop into Tokyo to kowtow before the bureaucrats and beg favours. Thirty-nine of the forty-seven prefectures actually maintain full-time 'representative offices' in Tokyo for this purpose, with a staff of up to twenty-four people whose sole job is to cultivate the mandarins of Kasumigaseki.

This entertainment takes place in the most lavish *ryoteis* (exclusive restaurants), such as the now-closed Chiyoshin in Akasaka, where Prime Minister Tanaka cooked up many of his crooked deals. The cost can be astonishing — up to $1000 a head, which sometimes includes the services of a high-class prostitute, as well as food and copious quantities of drink. No-one has the faintest idea how much all this costs — 'several hundred million [dollars]' was the estimate of one investigating lawyer. Hiroshima Prefecture, by no means the most extravagant, threw one party for Ministry of Finance bureaucrats where the drinks bill alone was $13 000, and another where the cost of one plate of *fugu* (puffer fish) for eight people came to $1300. Staff of the tiny Tokushima Prefecture's Tokyo office laboured heroically to impress their guests, paying (so an audit found) for 939 meals in 245 days at an average cost of $1250.

While the Ministry of Finance was trying to explain all this away, the most damaging revelations of all came to light. They concerned Yoshio Nakajima, a former deputy head of the Ministry of Finance's National Tax Administration Agency, and a man in line to become head of the department. Nakajima, it emerged, had for years been receiving money from about a dozen people whom he was in a position to help — a public accountant and the chairman of a construction company included. All up, he had trousered over $2 million in cash and low-interest loans, which he had used to finance extensive stockmarket speculation (again, subject to Ministry of Finance supervision) and the purchase of a house. He had evaded tax on his stockmarket profits and had been involved in insider trading. The only charge he denied was that prostitutes had been procured for him.

What appalled the public was not the wrongdoing so much as the cover-up the ministries then engaged in, which left the overwhelming impression that the corruption was widespread and systemic within the bureaucracy, not just the greed of a few individuals. The Ministry of Finance's interim report attempted to dismiss Nakajima's conduct by likening the bribes to the practice of wealthy patrons 'sponsoring' sumo wrestlers. The 'penalties' imposed reflected the contempt of the bureaucrats for public opinion. Nakajima resigned, but was not charged. The Finance Minister, Masayoshi Takemura (who was later crowned by an influential international business magazine as the world's worst treasurer) and the head of the Ministry of Finance accepted a 20 per cent pay cut for two months. Another senior official received a 10 per cent pay cut and a verbal admonition, and a third got a 'serious warning in writing'. These were token punishments even by Japanese standards, demonstrating that no-one was any longer interested in, or believed attainable, the sort of structural reforms of Japan's system of government that had been on everybody's lips in the run-up to the Liar Election. Legislation was hurriedly drafted to 'break up' the Ministry of Finance, but with an old-time apparatchik like Hashimoto by now in the *kantei*, few expected anything to come of it.

So, three years down the track from that hot July night, the flame of reform, which once burned so brightly, was close to extinction. In the winter of 1995–96 Ryutaro Hashimoto, an old-style conservative with matinee idol looks, emerged as the latest torch-bearer for the Tanaka faction and was elected prime minister. Just to cover themselves in the unlikely event that Hashimoto would seek to challenge their authority, the bureaucrats quickly moved to let him know who held the power. They leaked to the media and the opposition the damaging news that Mr Hashimoto had benefited — to the tune of some $15 000 — from companies at the centre of the financial crisis when he was Finance Minister in 1990. The message was clear: hands off the bureaucracy or risk your political life.

Fresh elections were looming, but there was no sign of the new directions and leadership Japan will need to meet the challenges of the next fifty years. The democratisation of Japan is not an end in itself, it is a means of arriving at policies that best represent its people's aspirations. Where will its economy go as it reaches beyond maturity? What role will Japan have in regional security? How will trade wars be averted and global resources reallocated? How can Japan's domestic institutions be overhauled to meet challenges such as the ageing population?

These are fundamental questions that involve all the Japanese people, not just the self-appointed group of elite bureaucrats, the rabble of crooked politicians and the cartel of self-interested producers who rule the country. Their mandate, if they ever had one, has ended. However, the new era that the Liar Election was supposed to usher in has not yet begun. Until the great mass of ordinary people are included in the decision-making — in other words, until Japan discovers something that more resembles democracy — there can be little hope that she will become that 'normal nation' to which Ichiro Ozawa aspires.

THE GREY-BEARDED PRIEST KNEELS ON HIS GOLD-brocaded cushion in front of a Buddhist altar. Incense fills the air as he chants a monotonous sutra for the dead, pausing after each verse to strike a small brass gong. 'We are very proud of him,' says Isao Hirata, a hovering acolyte in a navy blue business suit. 'He's so lifelike … one of our finest creations.'

First they automated the humans out of car-making. Now, Japan's electronic whiz kids have made an even more daring breakthrough — taking the priests out of religion. On a hillside in the suburbs of Japan's second city of Yokohama, a construction magnate has spent $18 million marrying the marvels of modern robotics to the mysteries of the world's oldest religions.

In a high-tech chapel, all glass and stainless steel, computers and hydraulics do the Lord's work. Mr Hirata presses a button on his control pad and effortlessly the priest switches to another prayer routine, one of many recorded by EMI in living stereo in the most ancient temples in Japan. The priest, in his black and brown cowl, bows his head and moves his lips in sync with the chant. The perpetual electric candlelight glints off his steel-rimmed glasses. 'He's as good as anything at Disneyland,' says Mr Hirata, whose company, Elevator Systems, subcontracted the robot to the firm that built Snow White and 100 other animated figures for Tokyo's premier amusement park.

Robopriest cost nearly $500 000. He is programmed to deliver word-perfect prayers according to the rites of seven different Buddhist sects, Shinto and two Christian faiths. At the push of a button, religious statues are hydraulically pumped onto centre-stage — seven different Buddhas, a Catholic Christ on a cross and a slightly more haggard-looking one for the Protestants. There are two vacant niches to accommodate any Jewish or Hindu Yokohamans who may feel left out.

The robot is the centrepiece of a chapel built to the design of Hideo Yoshino, the gadget-mad head of a Yokohama construction company. Mr Yoshino decided in 1993 to get into ageing Japan's lucrative, and highly competitive, funeral industry. Behind the chapel, on a south-facing hill, is a cemetery where he hopes to make his real profit. There are 1300 grave sites, each 1.25 metres square, which are swept and watered every day by, of course, a robot caretaker. Purchasing a perpetual lease on one for yourself and your ancestors will set you back $44 000, plus the cost of a grey marble tombstone. The cemetery is surrounded by poles bristling with arrays of security cameras and solar-powered burglar detectors.

On top of the cost of a grave site, cremation, a cortege, lying in state in an elaborate tableau and the traditional wake for 100 or so of your closest family and friends — for which the chapel would be more than happy to rent you its facilities, which include microwave-equipped kitchens, wide-screen television and tables and benches which can be hydraulically raised and lowered — could easily cost another $100 000 or more.

Robopriest was built to promote this automated necropolis, says the chapel's curator, Tohru Sakurai. If you buy a grave, the date of your death will be programmed into his computer, and every year the priest will descend hydraulically from his attic in the ceiling and say sutras for your soul for half an hour.

'We are not trying to do human priests out of business,' says Mr Sakurai. 'However, the robot never forgets an anniversary, it never makes a mistake … and you get the service free. A real priest would charge around $600 to pray for you.'

Mr Sakurai says business has been quite brisk. Two hundred graves have been sold in a matter of months, including one for the owner's wife, Haruko. Two hundred death anniversaries have been programmed into Robopriest.

If the idea catches on, it could also provide an answer for a chronic shortage of priests in Japan. The root of this problem is a long-term loss of faith. The latest surveys, by the Cultural Affairs Agency, show that only one in three of the 125 million Japanese believe in anything spiritual; less than 10 per cent regularly practise a religion.

Buddhism, along with the often-overlapping indigenous folk faith Shinto, is the most widespread religion in Japan. It has been established for twelve centuries and there are 40 000 Buddhist temples staffed by 100 000 priests. However, most Japanese now only practise 'funeral Buddhism'; that is, attending wakes.

Most of the major Buddhist sects — with the exception of some of the dynamic 'new religions' such as Soka Gakkai — have been watching their congregations and revenues dwindle for decades. In recent years, more than 1000 poorly attended Buddhist temples have been closed permanently, and several hundred more mothballed because of lack of a chief priest. Nearly one-fifth of the 3800 temples of the mystical Tibetan Shingon sect, which has its headquarters at the sacred Mount Koya, are uninhabited because of a shortage of priests. So are fifty of the 420 Tendai-Shinsei temples.

Yoshinori Maesaka, a spokesman for the Tendai sect, blames a loss of faith and increasing materialism for the decline in both worshippers and clergy. 'We are facing a serious crisis, there is no doubt about it,' he says.

Today's Japanese are no longer prepared to accept the low pay, ascetic lifestyle and five years' training required to become a Buddhist priest. The sons of chief priests, who traditionally 'inherit' temples for generation after generation, are turning their backs on religion. Buddhist temples have had to resort to some unconventional means to survive. Famous temples such as the historic To-ji in Kyoto have begun charging admission. An increasing number of Buddhist priests in black robes, with their heads bowed under straw 'coolie hats' can be seen carrying begging bowls around the streets of Tokyo.

Some Shinto shrines and Buddhist temples have launched eyebrow-raising schemes to raise money, such as introducing betting shops and karaoke nights, and even taking the gospel into bars. There have also been lay-offs — there was a 'strike' at Kokubun-ji in Osaka, a historic temple of the Shingon sect, when two priests were fired from their $6000-a-month jobs to cut costs.

At Yokohama, Mr Sakurai thinks Robopriest may be the answer to the crisis. 'The media has been trying to get people to say that this is irreligious in some way. But most people accept it as part of progress ... we are even planning to use [the robot] to train real priests to say their sutras.'

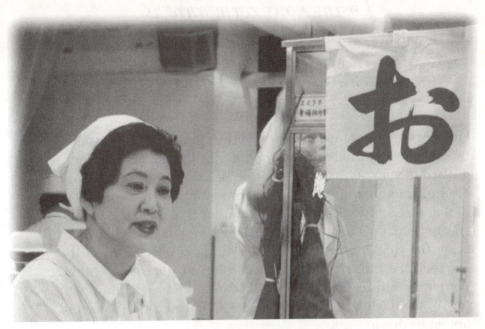

TWO
BEYOND SUSHI

'Losing your cormorant is a very basic mistake.'

— RIVER FISHERMAN IN THE TOWN OF GIFU, WHERE THE BIRDS,
ON LONG LEASHES, ARE USED TO CATCH SWEETFISH

FIRST, YOU SOAK IN THE deep, cypress pine bath downstairs, listening to the tinkle of the fountain in the courtyard. Then, dressed in your *yukata*, a light cotton dressing gown, you lounge on the tatami matting of your room, waiting for the tap on the sliding screen door signalling that dinner is about to be served. Haruji Ukai, the chef and owner of the Kinmata inn, will usually bring the first course himself. Everything is selected from the markets that morning, strictly according to what is in season. Winter, he says, is the best time of year and we took him up on this, one chilly night in the first week in February. Mr Ukai did not let us down.

Sensing the first hint of spring in the air, he had decorated our room with a bough of cherry blossom and used minuscule fernlike sprigs of *kinome*, the hothouse-raised first new shoots of *sansho* for the year, to bless the dishes with their intense, lemony fragrance. The English name for *sansho*, prickly ash, scarcely does justice to this extraordinary tree, of which only one example grows in Australia, in the Adelaide Botanical Gardens. From a simple stoneware bowl, Mr Ukai pours two measures of sake into two small medicine glasses — a silky top-of-the-line *daiginjoshu*, a term that will be explained later. We begin what the Japanese call a *kaiseki ryori*, a banquet of tiny dishes that is the crowning achievement of the country's cuisine.

Whenever Tokyo — a gritty, grey megacity aptly described as Los Angeles without the guns — began to get us down, whenever the obsession with politics and economics became too much, Mayu and I would escape to the country. Not only is there a wealth of stories Tokyo-based correspondents never come across, you are closer to what I imagine the old (that is, prewar) Japan must have been like — another country where the landscapes can be stunningly bold and beautiful, where the world walks to the beat of a different drum and the people have time for traditional values and pursuits lost in the city rat-race. It is also where the food, one of the glories of Japanese culture, can be seen at its best. What sets it apart, in this age of the microwave and the cryovac pack, is that Japanese food still manages to retain its seasonality and its regionality.

If you are at all interested in the world beyond *Maku Donarudo* (as the Japlish has it) you should, at least once, treat yourself to a *kaiseki* banquet if you visit Japan. In Australia, little is known of Japanese food beyond the second-rate sushi, sashimi, tempura and noodle shops which have proliferated in recent years. I am continually dismayed by otherwise gastronomically literate people who complain about the lack of variety, the lack of cooking techniques, the lack of sauces, the lack of spices — even, God help us, the lack of knives and forks in Japan. I remember the Sydney Rockpool's Neil Perry, one of Australia's outstanding chef/entrepreneurs blowing into Tokyo one day to show the Japanese what red curry of kangaroo and other 'nouvelle Australian cuisine' was all about. On the strength of a couple of ill-chosen ventures into hotel restaurants, he was prepared to denounce a cuisine that had been around 1300 years before Captain Cook sailed into Botany Bay to begin Australia's gastronomic ascendancy with salt beef, dog biscuits and something he called 'marmalad of yaller carrots'. Mr Perry told me he had discovered 'not much after sushi and sashimi … and the way they handle the fish, washing all the flavour out of it, is contrary to everything I believe in.'

What a pity he wasn't staying more than a couple of days or that he did not have a more intelligent guide. There is a tiny bar in the Ginza where you eat from a plain, polished wooden counter I know he would have enjoyed. It serves only sushi, only sushi topped with tuna, and only the fattest belly meat of the freshest *maguro* ('black') tuna from the Aleutian Islands. If that cut is not available at the markets, the restaurant does not open. It has no menu and, so, no prices — you pay what you think the world's finest sushi is worth. To offer $75 per piece is considered reasonable.

Tokyo's best-kept secret is that it is one of the world's great eating cities. And it is not just Japanese cooking you will find here, although the majority of the 20 000-odd registered restaurants are, naturally, of that genre. Tokyo has some superb French restaurants, many in association with the three-star royalty of France's great chefs and endorsed by the *fins becs* of Michelin. There are authentic Italian trattoria, steaming, teeming Chinatowns, Irish pubs with draft Guinness, Turkish cellars complete with belly dancers, Swedish buffets offering herring a dozen ways and even a couple of 'Australian' restaurants, though the less said about them the better. The *tsus* of Tokyo, the city's gourmets, are every bit as precious and pompous as their counterparts anywhere in the world, and just as much at home among the first growths of Burgundy as the more obscure regional sakes.

However, it is the Japanese food that I am interested in here. The first problem everyone finds trying to explore the great variety of cooking styles is that restaurants are highly specialised. Sushi restaurants do not sell steak, noodle shops do not do fish and so on. That tiny tuna bar is exceptional, but there are other 'single issue' restaurants and if you do not visit these your culinary education will be incomplete. There are restaurants which only serve eel. They are usually humble dives where the eel is marinated in sweet soy and grilled over charcoal, but, if you know where to look, you can also find quite classy 'eeleries' where snacks such as roast eel backbone and a clear soup containing eel liver are served. There are 'hormone' restaurants which serve only offal. I remember a good one in Matsuzaka, Japan's beef capital, which offered, as well as the usual things, beef cheek, three kinds of tripe (including that from the cow's third stomach) and heart, which customers grilled, *yaki-niku-*style, on tabletop barbecues. There are restaurants which are strictly vegetarian, serving Buddhist 'temple food' which eschews even such lust-inducing ingredients as ginger and onions. I have eaten in places that serve only dishes made from bean curd, oysters, beef or even mushrooms.

In fact, the restaurants specialising in mushrooms are a

delight in themselves. Probably the most exotic meal I have had in my life was in a sort of greenhouse in a forest of red pines on the slopes of Mount Suzuko in Nagano Prefecture. Here, as autumn approaches and mists shroud the mountains, men such as Shigeo Furuta, a stocky countryman of middle years who carries a sturdy stick, begin their stealthy patrols through the forest. They are not after deer or salmon, but something far more valuable — the priceless *matsutake*, Japan's truffle.

Like the French truffle, the *matsutake* has defied decades of research by the country's finest mycologists to cultivate it. The *matsutake* only grows in the wild, in dwindling numbers, on remote mountain peaks. The price reflects its rarity. The 1992 season, says Mr Furuta, was an absolute disaster. For two months, from early September to early November, he combed the mountainside and found only one kilogram of the precious fungi. On the Tokyo markets the price soared to $1150 a kilogram. A basket containing just six *matsutake*, the first of the season, sold for $1300, or more than $200 each.

Mr Furuta and his father before him have had the mushroom franchise on Mount Suzuko for more than forty years. 'In the old days the mountain was white with mushrooms and anyone from the village could come and pick them,' he says. 'Not any more.'

All the mountains where the *matsutake* grow — principally around Nagano and in the hills circling Kyoto — are reserves controlled by the national, prefectural or local governments. Mount Suzuko, for instance, is 'owned' by the little village in the valley at its foot. This year they auctioned the rights to pick mushrooms and Mr Furuta put in a bid of $30 000. This means the mountain is 'his' for the season … and woe betide any sneaky Tokyoites who are caught fossicking. Posters warn that the fine is up to $4500.

Why all the fuss? Mr Furuta offers one of the fungi — cream coloured with shreds of brown barklike skin clinging to it, the cap not yet opened. It resembles nothing so much as a largish, semi-erect penis. Botanically, it is an Asian relative of the boletus mushroom of Europe — the Italian *fungi porcini* (little pigs) beloved of Florentine cuisine, or the fleshy French *cèpe*. The *matsutake*, however, has an elusive, earthy aroma more like the white truffle of the Val D'Aosta in the Italian Alps.

So rare is it, and so expensive, that the classical way of dealing with it is *dobin mushi*: you shred it into a tiny teapot, infuse it with a delicate *dashi* (stock made of dried bonito flakes and *kombu* seaweed) and drink it from sake cups, to better savour the aroma. This is how Mr Furuta prepares it for us, sitting cross-legged in one of the most unusual restaurants to be found in Japan. Each year as August draws to a close and the *matsutake* begin pushing up through the pine needles, he erects two or three steel-framed greenhouses up on the hill among the gnarled red pines from which the fungus gets its name (*matsu* means pine and *take* means mushroom). He covers them with polythene, spreads a red carpet on the rough board floors and installs low plank tables, with a do-it-yourself gas burner in front of every place. With the sides open, you have a splendid view of the lake below, the village, the paddies of rice and the orchards of apples and grapes where a distant artillery of carbide gas guns scares off marauding birds.

The set-up may be basic, but there is nothing hick about the cooking — or the prices. The top-of-the-line menu is a $150-a-head *matsutake* banquet for which people drive from as far away as Tokyo, 150 kilometres to the south. For this you get an endless succession of dishes, all redolent of the pine fungus. A *nabe* dish is served, a delicate stew of *matsutake*, leeks, chicken and cellophane noodles; there are *dobin mushi* and *chawan mushi*, *matsutake* in an egg custard; there is *matsutake* tempura, slivers of the fungus dipped in the most delicate of batter and deep-fried; and, the grand finale, a whole *matsutake*, wrapped in foil and grilled over the gas-ring. Not much beyond sushi and sashimi?

The year we visited, Mr Furuta was hoping for a bumper harvest. Every morning he and his workers were out scouring the special places up in the mountains where *matsutake* are known to recur — often they are found in 'fairy rings', clusters of up to a dozen mushrooms. The soil must be carefully replaced or the *matsutake* will not return the following autumn. These spots are a closely guarded secret. 'Fathers promise their sons they will reveal the location before they die ... but on their deathbeds they often "forget",' the patron of a nearby sushi shop informs us. They do not use dogs or pigs to snuffle them out, as do French truffle-hunters — all you need are strong legs and good eyesight according to Mr Furuta. When we spoke in early September he had already picked five kilograms. It was too early to tell, but perhaps, for his $30 000 investment, he would harvest as much as 100 kilograms of *matsutake* for the season. Although prices would fall as the season advanced, he could still double his investment.

The falling prices in the mid-1990s, in fact, were more a reflection of cheaper imports than bumper crops. More than 90 per cent of *matsutake* in the markets are now imported from smart suppliers in Canada, North and South Korea and Morocco — and why not Australia? Connoisseurs say the imports do not have the same fragrance as the local product, but Mr Furuta is not convinced. 'I must admit that last year, when we could find no *matsutake*, we did use imports. We mixed them in with what local ones we could find, and we did not tell the customers. But this year ...' He does not finish the sentence, but looks up the hill where the warm mists of autumn are beginning to soak the rich mulch of pine needles and sniffs the air. Is it the musky aroma of the *matsutake* or a bumper harvest of ¥10 000 bills that fills his nostrils I wonder.

Then there are the restaurants that serve only noodles — and usually only one of the four main types of noodle. Never mind about whether Marco Polo pinched the idea from the Chinese, Japan has some claim to beating them both to the invention. There is *udon* (it has a fatter cousin called *kishimen*) — thick, white, rubbery strands made of wheat flour and usually served in a bowl of *dashi* broth, accompanied by things like fishcake, eggs, seaweed, chicken or onions. You can recognise an *udon* shop several blocks before you come to it by the giant sucking sound — the noodles are served scalding hot and it is de rigeur to slurp them in, along with a mouthful of cold air.

Summer is time for *soba* — these are thinner, greyish noodles made of buckwheat. *Soba* is served cold and *al dente*, on a bamboo lattice, and is dunked in a sauce containing the water in which it was boiled. *Somen* is a fine wheat noodle, about the calibre of spaghettini, which is also served cold, often Hiyashi-style, topped with shrimp, mushrooms and *mitsuba* ('Japanese parsley') and accompanied by a soy/mirin sauce and grated Japanese horseradish. We once made an expedition to the mountains north of Kyoto, where you sit with your feet in a mountain stream trying to pluck *somen* as it floats past in a bamboo pipe. Finally, there is *ramen*, originally a Chinese rice noodle served in hot, savoury broth. *Ramen* has lost a lot of face since someone worked out how to freeze-dry it and package it in polystyrene cups as 'instant *ramen*' — the bachelor salaryman's three-minute junk food.

You will hear fanatical debates between the Japanese about which are the 'best' noodles, much as Australians argue about who makes the 'best' beer. There are noodle-making clubs, noodle appreciation societies and newsletters devoted to nothing but noodles. There are all manner of subspecies and sub-subspecies. One cheerful bar in the Ginza has Kyushu-style noodles, served in a pork soup with plenty of chilli. Some people rhapsodise over *cha soba*, noodles made with powdered green tea. 'Moon-viewing' noodles have a whole egg broken on top of the bowl and 'fox noodles' contain deep-fried bean curd, said to be the fox's favourite food. Just remember, as a general guide, the buckwheat varieties come from the colder climes, say, from Tokyo north, and the soft-wheat varieties from the south. Noodles are staple budget travellers' tucker — among the few decent, reliable meals you can get for under $20 — and are thus popular not only with most Japanese, but foreign residents and travellers as well.

If that is not exotic enough for you, you could try one of the restaurants that serve only *fugu* fish, Japan's famous, and famously expensive, poisonous puffer fish. They are not hard to find — a sign or a wooden cut-out of the distinctive pudgy fish hangs outside — although, until *fugu* farming became established, they were obliged to close down during the six-month summer 'off season'. To be quite frank, I could not see what all the fuss was about. The story was a great deal more interesting than the supper, like a number of other exotic regional treats I felt obliged to sample during my travels. I swallowed live squid in a neighbourhood bar, the proprietress warning me not to bite for fear it would squirt out its ink. I horrified a visiting friend by offering her a bowl of rubbery objects which turned out to be smoked sea anenome's anuses. In a horsemeat speciality place in Kyushu, I was even persuaded to sample the house platter of raw testicle, sliced penis and stir-fried labial flaps. All these things, I suspect, are in the nature of gimmicks intended to impress the visitor, rather than delicacies to be taken seriously — although some gourmets profess to relish them, much as some Australians will tell you that the parson's nose is the best bit of the chicken.

When we finally did pluck up the courage (and the money) to sample *fugu*, it was in a *noren* (a traditional restaurant) on the outskirts of Osaka which has become a Mecca for fanciers of the fish from all over Japan. The Kitahachi restaurant is down a yellow brick road in a nondescript bayside suburb of Osaka called Kishiwada. Before we began to eat, a lugubrious waiter in a white forage cap carefully arranged the fish and vegetables in a tabletop pot, a silent, rather solemn ceremony fit for a last supper. 'If you should start to feel numb,' he confided, gesturing to his fingertips and his lips, 'then … I apologise if this is rather indelicate … it is said that eating human faeces may help save you.' If you do not fancy that particular folk remedy, you could always allow yourself to be buried in the sand on the beach as the tide comes in — the theory being that the rhythmic pounding of the waves acts as an artificial respirator when your lungs give up the ghost. Mind you, the waiter could not actually vouch for its effectiveness. Not personally. In the big ceramic bowl, the bean curd, the *enokitake* (enoki mushrooms) and Chinese cabbage began to bubble in the broth along with the creamy sacs of sperm and other bony bits of the anatomy of the centrepiece of our dinner. Mayu and I looked at each other, wondering if it was worth it.

On the menu was what is unarguably the world's most dangerous dinner — the repulsively ugly Japanese *fugu* fish, which puffs itself up into a spiky ball when angry, giving it its English name of swellfish or porcupine fish. It is, quite literally, a dish to die for. It was the storm-blowing winter month of February, when the *fugu* is at its best, and who better to entrust with our lives than the chef/proprietor, Kiichi Kitahama, who, with his late father, has been slicing and serving up *fugu* here to gourmets from far and wide since 1913. They claim it is the oldest *fugu* restaurant in Japan. And they have not had to try the faeces or the wave treatment yet, boasts Mr Kitahama — they haven't lost a single customer.

Others, however, have not been so careful — or so lucky. Since records were first kept in 1886, *fugu* fish have killed precisely 6925 Japanese. Mr Kitahama, an international authority who has a museum across the road dedicated to the *fugu*, points out an exhibit — two tiny red-capped vials, each containing perhaps a teaspoonful of white powder. One is potassium cyanide, enough to kill twenty people; the other, the *fugu*'s tetrodotoxin venom, which would kill 20 000 people.

The most famous victim was Bando Mitsugoro, one of Japan's greatest *kabuki* actors and a 'living national treasure' who sat down in a Kyoto restaurant one night in 1975, devoured four portions of *fugu* liver and declared to his wife, 'It was so delicious I feel like I am floating on air.' He died that night, and the chef was later given a suspended eight-year jail sentence for professional negligence.

It is the taste of danger that continues to lure gourmets to their deaths. To a genuine *tsu*, the deadliest parts are the most delicious — the liver and the ovaries. Even the fins, which are dried and toasted and served in a beaker of hot sake to accompany the meal, can make your lips tingle, the first sign of the nerve poison going to work. Fortunately Mayu and I did not experience this dubious pleasure. Mr Kitahama himself — although he says he will not serve it to customers — has eaten *fugu* liver many times. 'It feels as if the flavour is spearing through the top of your brains' is his verdict. I am content to take his word for it.

The Japanese authorities have been trying for centuries to get people to act sensibly about *fugu*. The shoguns, in fact, banned people from eating it altogether, on pain of death. More recently, strict rules were enforced prohibiting the eating of *fugu* liver, regulating the varieties that can be consumed (more than 100 have been identified, one of them actually named after Mr Kitahama) and prescribing a tough two-year course to perfect the surgical dissection of the poisonous parts to obtain a special licence. Even so, two or three people still die every year, victims of the belief that some things are so good they are worth risking your life for. And bankruptcy. That's the other thing about *fugu* — even in a country where a plate of sushi can set you back $75, what they charge for *fugu* is breathtaking.

Since the 'bubble economy' burst in 1991, prices at the picturesque markets at Shimonoseki on Japan's western tip — where bids for the most highly prized *fugu* are signalled to the auctioneer by hand signals inside a black cloth bag — have dropped by more than half. That still leaves the cost of a prime wild orange- and green-striped 'tiger' *fugu* at $240 a kilogram. Farmed *fugu* is a mere $70, but Mr Kitahama turns his nose up at them, claiming they taste of sardines instead of lobster or crab as they should, because of their diet. The prices at Kitahachi, in fact, make Tokyo gourmets gasp at their modesty. There are dishes as cheap as thirty or forty dollars. However, if you want the full disaster of a *kaiseki*-style set course, it will cost anything from $200 to $400 a head.

So, after all this build-up, what does it actually taste like? The typical array of dishes we consumed that night included many parts of the fish I never imagined were edible: the throat, for instance; the backbones fried crisp like crackers; an *aemono* dish of intestines set on a shiso leaf; overnight-dried sperm and several different ways with the skin. The highlight was the raw flesh, thinly sliced, crunchy and translucent. It does little for the appetite to learn that its Osaka dialect name is *tessa* — a contraction of *teppo* meaning a gun, and sashimi. *Zosui*, a rice gruel made of the remaining fragments of fish, traditionally completes the meal. The *pièce de résistance* was the presentation of a whole steamed *hakofugu*, a special kind of *fugu* served only at the Kitahachi restaurant. It sat in a bed of seaweed on a porcelain pedestal like a mottled leather purse with eyes. Everyone who orders it gets a numbered certificate. 'Us and the Tour D'Argent in Paris with its ducks — we are the only restaurants that do this,' says Japan's Claude Terrail.

The instructions are as enigmatic as the manual for a complicated Japanese domestic appliance. 'Turn your *hakofugu* upside down ... use a single chopstick, thrust its pointed end softly into the caudal area, move it forward to the direction of the head along by the vertebra, scraping off the dorsal muscles on both sides — and then eat them, which will wonderfully please your palate,' said the instruction card.

The morsels of flesh we managed to extract, and all the other skin and bone and gristle, were heavily reliant on the accessories — a sauce of red salted plums, a dip of *ponzu,* a mixture of soy sauce, the juice of a *daidai* (a sort of citron) and a heavy sprinkling of *sansho* (prickly ash). I prescribe as much sake as you can swallow. I hate to say it, so I'll let Mr Kitahama do the obituary: '*Fugu* is basically just a big lump of collagen.'

So much for gimmickry. If you are interested in the more serious side of Japanese cooking — and you do not want to go away as disappointed as Neil Perry — you must take time to seek out somewhere like Kinmata, the restaurant referred to at the start of this chapter. It is a little luxury to which Mayu and I treated ourselves when holidaying — or, occasionally, working — in beautiful old Kyoto, every foreigner's favourite Japanese city. This is the place to learn what Japan has to offer beyond sushi. Other cities, notably Osaka which fancies itself as the 'belly of Japan' and pours scorn on 'greasy' Tokyo cuisine with its 'coarse' flavours, put forward their claims to be the country's food capital. For my money, however, the elegance and style of Kyoto cuisine, which has been refined over the 1200 years since it was the imperial capital, is matchless.

Kinmata is situated down a quiet, narrow street of wooden houses black with age — firemen still patrol, rapping bamboo sticks to remind residents to extinguish fires at night. Just around the corner is the central market, one of the most interesting and colourful in Japan, where you can buy anything edible from live conger eels to a dozen varieties of rice, and the bran pickles and powdered green 'tea ceremony' tea for which Kyoto's Uji region is renowned. The handsome old inn welcomed its first customers in 1801 and maintains a tradition of service and quality that is exceptional, even by Japanese standards. Before Mr Ukai's father considered him ready to take over the kitchen, he was sent for several years to serve as an apprentice to a fishmonger. Needless to say, you cannot go wrong with his salmon, amberjack or flounder.

Kinmata is not a restaurant, nor is it a hotel: it is an establishment called a *ryokan* which combines the best features of both. You will find these places throughout Japan — not all, of course, are as refined as this — and they charge a flat amount per head for a set-course dinner, bed and usually a substantial breakfast that will include as a bare minimum fish, bean-paste soup, pickles, rice and tea. The best will feature regional specialities — one we stayed at in Toyama, for instance, specialised in 101 ways with oysters from the surrounding beds; another, in a mountain resort district north of Tokyo called Yumoto, celebrated various types of trout and char from the local lakes.

Prices range from the modest to the astronomical. One of Kyoto's most exclusive *ryokans* — a place where you will be asked for a reference from someone known to the house if you are bold enough to telephone — charges $750 per person per night. Kinmata, far less snobbish, is about $300, but it is well worth the money. If you are interested in Japanese cuisine, Mr Ukai will begin your education. He knows, of course, the classics — who hasn't heard the stories of the Japanese sushi apprentices forced to scrub pans and study the master at work for five years before they are even allowed to handle a grain of rice? But Mr Ukai is more than a master of *kata,* the technique or 'correct' way of doing things that so stultifies Japanese art and culture. His cooking has a creative flair that until quite recently would have been anathema to traditionally trained chefs. I remember, for instance, a delicious and original dish of a whole fig fried in tempura batter he presented one night. Mr Ukai represents a fusion of classical ingredients and method with modern ideas, a *nouvelle cuisine Japonais,* if that wasn't such a hackneyed phrase.

That February night, for instance, I noted in my diary a succession of eight dishes. They were brought one by one to the room in leisurely fashion, rather than being dumped all at once on the table — the usual, rather overwhelming way *kaiseki* is served in lesser establishments. First there was a *sunomono* (vinegared dish) of clams with baby asparagus and 'mountain vegetables', a mixture of things such as fiddlehead ferns, mushrooms and edible grasses supposedly gathered from the wild. After this, came an absolutely exquisite selection of crunchy-fresh raw fish: a sashimi of *akagai* (a shellfish the colour and flavour of apricots), flounder and yellowtail with a decadent dip of angler fish liver. The next course was a steamed millet dumpling containing duck meat, followed by a tempura of sweet potato and a deep-fried prawn roll dotted with 'rice hail'. Incidentally, like many Japanese who care about food, Mr Ukai regards it as a serious mistake to dunk these deep-fried morsels in a soy-based sauce thickened with grated daikon, the usual way tempura is served. At Kinmata it comes with a pinch of salt, seasoned with the ground fruit of the prickly ash tree.

My notes deteriorate somewhat about here, but I think I can make out a simmered dish of bean curd skin, the first tiny bamboo of spring and *udo,* a vegetable that looks like mutant rhubarb and has no English name. I then remember a portrait in white, a glimpse of the just-vanishing winter — 'snow salmon' marinated in white bean paste and topped with egg white. There was a perfect *dashi,* a clear broth of bonito flakes and *kombu* seaweed — the quality of the stock, the rice and (in a sushi restaurant) the omelette are the ultimate test of a Japanese chef. There was also a house speciality — luscious 'bean curd' made with ground sesame seeds instead of the usual soya beans. There must have been some rice, as always, to finish the meal, and I think after that we would probably have rolled out our mattresses on the floor and fallen soundly asleep — another great advantage of banqueting in a *ryokan*.

Without my going into any further raptures about Kinmata, you will have noticed two things about the menu — the seasonality and the regionality. In spite of modern transportation and cultivation — Japan imports something like two-thirds of its food from abroad — these two words are the hallmarks of quality Japanese cuisine. There is something tremendously sensuous about the anticipation that precedes the arrival in the shops of the first bamboo shoots of spring, the first of the new season's bonito, the first persimmon of autumn, the last *edamame* (green soya beans) of summer — something to remind you that beyond the great gritty megalopolis of Tokyo there are still fields and trees and rivers.

As for regionality, sometimes it seems as though Japan's forty-seven prefectures are really forty-seven different countries, so varied are the foods and the styles of cooking. The country sprawls from the tropical Ryukyu islands near Taiwan to Hokkaido's Shiretoko peninsula, surrounded in winter by a groaning ocean of floe ice. In Okinawa, for instance, we dined on raw goat meat, washed down with *awamori*, the fiery local hootch, with tropical berries marinated in it. At the other end of the archipelago, in a fishing town called Abashiri on the Sea of Okhotsk, there were huge, sweet Kamchatka crabs. Not only the flesh is served, but also the eggs and the muck from inside the shell which is used to make a treat whose English name scarcely does it justice: 'crab guts sushi'.

You really have to work at it to find a bad meal in Japan. Some places we discovered through guidebooks — the Japanese are as fanatical as the French about where they eat when they are away. Bookshops are stuffed with guides to every conceivable regional speciality, and it is almost impossible to turn on the television without finding some teenage *tarento* shrieking *'Oishii!'* ('Delicious!') as she scoffs down a bowl of turtle's blood. However, many of our most memorable meals came from personal recommendations or by sheer accident. Once, driving to inspect Japan's scary nuclear waste dump on the northern claw of Honshu island, we stopped for what we presumed would be a bowl of noodles at an unpromising-looking roadside shack. Inside, the television blared with the baseball finals, and there was the usual clutter of metal tables, a plastic counter, strip lighting and holiday posters.

What caught our eye, though, was a bowl of sea urchins sitting on the counter — like giant prickly brown chestnuts, so fresh their spines were still moving. After we had polished a few off, the proprietor leaned over the counter and said, 'What about I do you something special? Only 3000 yen … and if you don't like it, you don't have to pay.' We nodded. He plucked a couple of live abalone from a fish tank behind the counter, sliced them, spread them with the creamy orange roe of some more urchins and slid them under a griller for a minute. Absolutely simple and absolutely superb. We learned later that this part of the coast is famous for its urchins. Signs along the rocks warn that the 'urchin police' patrol regularly and will prosecute anyone caught collecting them without a licence.

Another time, driving through the boondocks of Shikoku island on our way to a bullfight, we stopped at a rather grander establishment to find that almost the entire restaurant was taken up by a fish tank half the size of a competition swimming pool sunk into the floor. There were benches and seats on one side and the kitchen on the other. In the tank, swimming up and down in their designated lanes like competitors in some fishy Olympics, were shoals of silver bream, *fugu,* striped bass, bonito, even giant conger eels. You pointed, and the chef whipped the designated victim out of the water in a net, weighed it, filleted it with the flash of a knife and placed it, still quivering, in front of you. Murder in the aquarium. There is, for my money, little that can beat the crunchy richness of raw bonito, served Shikoku-style with a dipping sauce of *ponzu* (soy and citrus) and a relish of grated ginger or garlic.

You only have to hop on a train to experience the regionalism of Japanese food. Trains, for some reason, are inextricably linked with food in the Japanese mind. Before the carriage even moves from the station, it will be filled with savoury odours and the sound of rustling wrappers as rice balls and bowls of soup and fried fish are laid out for a banquet. Anxious mums will have been up half the night preparing a cold collation so that little Yoshi does not die of hunger on his way to see his granny a couple of hundred kilometres away. For those who have not packed a picnic, food and drink is wheeled through the train on little trolleys that tinkle a tune as uniformed hostesses push them along. Forget your prejudices about warm beer, curly-edged sandwiches and pie with dead horse, you can have a gastronomic tour of Japan without leaving the comfort of your railway carriage.

One particular travellers' take-out we came to like was a *kamameshi* that is served to passengers heading into the Japan Alps. Mayu's parents have a log cabin in the woods near Lake Nojiri, and we rarely failed to pick some up when the train stopped at a village called Yokokawa to couple up another locomotive for the long haul up through the pine-clad mountains. The passengers begin lining up at the doors before the train arrives and, the second it stops, there is a stampede to a row of stands on the platform, piled with steaming pottery pudding basins. This is the famous *toge-no-kamameshi,* which many say makes the trip worthwhile even if you never leave the station. As the train draws slowly away five minutes later, the *kamameshi* salespeople, in their neat uniforms, line up and bow deeply to their departing customers and chorus 'Arigato' — thank you, come again. Settled in their seats, with fold-down tables (and with beer, sake or a cup of green tea from a passing trolley), the passengers quickly hoe into a rice pilaf simmered in *dashi* with chicken and chestnuts, topped with a shiitake mushroom, a quail egg, bamboo, burdock, fiddlehead ferns, daikon and green peas, with some salty eggplant pickles on the side.

Welcome to the world of *eki-ben,* the ultimate meals-on-wheels. If you thought Japan's only contributions to cuisine were sushi and sukiyaki, take a trip on a Japan Rail train some day. Fast food (literally, as the *shinkansen* bullet train tops 340 kilometres per hour) will never be the same again. There are 369 stations connected to Japan's railway network, which is as punctual as a Swiss watch and (providing you reserve your seats) as comfy as business class on a good airline. No matter how remote the station, you can count on the train arriving not only on time to the second, but with the correct door of the correct carriage aligned to the centimetre with the corresponding numbered boarding point painted on the platform. Thanks to some extraordinary bridge and tunnel feats, you can now travel the entire archipelago, from the snowy wastes of Hokkaido (where a special train with open carriages allows passengers to smell, as well as view the giant lily pads of floe ice paving the Sea of Okhotsk) to the roaring multitudes of Tokyo and the warm and steamy bamboo jungles of Kyushu.

Every tiny whistle stop has its own culinary speciality. If you want a gastronomic tour of the country, *eki-ben* is the way to go. Generically, it is type of take-out called *bento*, which has been around since the time of the shoguns. Its simplest form is the *hinomaru*, the schoolchild's lunch box, which was named after the Japanese flag because in poormouth days gone by it consisted of a single red pickled apricot on a bed of cold white rice. The Japanese have been working on perfecting it since the first railways were built a century ago. The Yokokawa crock pot, for instance, was served to Western missionaries travelling to the resort of Karuizawa in 1893. Today's *eki-ben* (literally 'station *bento*') takes the genre to its peak — the doggy bag by Louis Vuitton.

There are now more than 2900 different kinds. Think about it. You could travel around Japan by train, eating three meals a day, for nearly three years without coming across the same thing twice. Some gluttons have actually tried — the largest collection of the colourful *eki-ben* wrappers, an art form in their own right, numbers 2000. A whole foodie cult has grown up around the *eki-ben*. There are gourmet clubs which organise amazing excursions, such as travelling nearly 1000 kilometres to the seaport of Shimonoseki just to savour the raw flesh of the *fugu* fish at the peak of its season. There are books, magazines, television shows and celebrity endorsements. At Kumamoto station in Kyushu they brought out a new one called 'His Lordship' in honour of their local hero, Morihiro Hosokawa, when he became prime minister.

At Nojiri station, Mayu's mother used to pick up her favourite, a wheel of sushi rice surrounded with sliced salted trout and wrapped in bamboo leaf; in the mountains north of Kobe, travellers are offered a dish of marinated broiled boar; if you visit the famous red *torii* arches of Miyajima, do not forget to try the equally famous grilled *anago*, local sea eel; on your way to watch the cormorant fishing at Gifu, you can sample an *eki-ben* which contains nine different types of mushroom, each cooked in a different way; Osaka is worth visiting, if for nothing else than to taste its celebrated *takoyaki* or octopus fritters.

Every year, less-travelled Tokyoites have an opportunity to try 130 different *eki-ben* collected under one roof in the Keio department store, which sits on top of the world's busiest railway station in the Tokyo suburb of Shinjuku. We went along once to admire the mountains of crabs, casks of pickled mackerel, haystacks of seaweed, logs of fishcake stacked like kindling. Hundreds of workers slave from morning to night to prepare this *eki-ben* expo. Over the twelve frantic days of the celebration, more than a quarter of a million little boxes, bags, baskets, crockery pots, plastic snowmen, bamboo leaves and every other container you can possibly imagine are sold.

'This is not, strictly speaking, a gourmet product,' Mr Ryoichi Takigami, Keio's public relations man explained to us. 'To a Japanese, eating *eki-ben* is to recapture the joy of travelling when you were a child. It is like Marcel Proust's *Remembrance of Things Past*.'

Keio has a staff of dedicated foodies who continually scour Japan for as-yet-undiscovered *eki-ben*, travelling on the slowest local trains and sampling dozens of delicacies every day. The topselling *eki-ben* for most of the twenty-nine years the store has been holding this annual feast is one of the simplest and the cheapest. The insignificant little village of Mori in Hokkaido is famous throughout Japan for one thing only, its *ikameshi* — small squid stuffed with sticky rice, poached in *dashi* and seasoned with soy sauce. This *eki-ben* costs $6 (others range up to about $20), a remarkable bargain in a country where a cheap bowl of noodles can set you back $15, a platter of sushi $50 and a gourmet meal $150-plus — without wine.

Incidentally, there is no problem with the freshness of *eki-ben*. The packs do not carry a use-by *date*, they are stamped with an official use-by *hour*. Every four hours, unsold *eki-ben* are dumped and a new batch is brought in, to the great comfort of Tokyo's homeless for whom the throw-outs are a staple diet.

Another Keio favourite is *kaki meshi* from Akkeshi, also in Hokkaido, which is Japan's Tasmania when it comes to food. It is topped with oysters, marinated clams and a sort of whelk called *tsubugai*. If you should ever be in Akita, on the Sea of Japan, you must try the *eki-ben* degustation, an artist's palette of six tiny piles of rice noodles, with a dipping broth and each pile with its own topping — shredded omelette, 'vegetable caviar', *nameko* mushrooms, *kombu* seaweed, salmon flakes and spinach stalks. Other hits with the crowd, which formed queues ten and twenty metres long for the favourites, included Hokkai Hazuna, a bed of rice topped with salmon, flying fish roe and crab, garnished with shiitake mushroom and a spear of red pickled asparagus; a canvas of orange sea urchin roe decorated with grey slivers of abalone; and the thorny legs of the famous Hokkaido crab.

The list goes on ... and on ... and on. New dishes are continually evolving. If you tire of the delicate pastels of Japanese seafood, try a fat-cobwebbed Kobe steak on a bed of curried rice, with a side serve of pickled onions. If you feel in need of a boost as you pass through the town of Matsue, what about a 'joyful *eki-ben*', which contains two small bottles of local sake (one dry, one sweet), with nibblies such as simmered pond smelt, periwinkles and pickled wasabi leaf? Worthy of a detour, as Michelin would say. In fact, the detour is the whole point of the exercise — a gourmet bonus for those intrepid travellers who invest in a Japan Rail pass, which is the only way to see the country.

Much of this chapter has been taken up with fish, and for a very good reason. Japan had a long tradition of Buddhist vegetarianism and fish still makes up most of the protein in the diet. The Japanese eat six times as much fish as Australians. Red meat such as beef really only became widely eaten after World War II and (apart from the ubiquitous *Maku Donarudo*) is still regarded as something of a special occasion dish. Some people theorise that this is one reason the Japanese live longer than anyone else on earth, and I certainly regarded the opportunity to cut down on fat and cholesterol as one of the side benefits of being posted to Japan. I was in for a rude awakening. Visiting the doctor one day, I noticed a public health poster on the wall of his surgery, warning against foods with high cholesterol. There was a cross through just about all my favourites — sea urchin roe, salmon eggs, squid, chilli cod roe and prawns.

The Japanese simply cannot get enough fish and this has led to all sorts of international friction as countries try to conserve their dwindling fish stocks. In the 1970s and 1980s, Japanese fleets equipped with drift-nets — 'the walls of death' as conservationists dubbed them — scoured the earth's oceans vacuuming up anything that swam. However, with restrictions on the use of these huge nets, and with more and more countries closing off their territorial waters, the Japanese have had to turn to fish farming to satisfy their voracious appetite. In this industry, as in so many others, necessity has turned them into world-beaters.

We travelled down to Kushimoto, a small Pacific port south of Tokyo, one hot summer's day to talk to a man who can lay claim to being one of the world's great experts on the captive breeding of fish. Dr Hidemi Kumai has spent the past twenty-five years of his life on the ultimate challenge, the Everest of fish breeding — trying to raise the bluefin tuna in captivity. A sleek, stocky man in a dark blue tracksuit, he joked, 'I have been around them so long I'm starting to look like a tuna.' The official title of 'Dr Bluefin' is professor of agriculture, in charge of the fisheries department of Osaka's private Kinki University, a world leader in the artificial breeding of ocean fish. In giant concrete tanks, with computer-controlled temperature, water purity and plankton supplies, the university breeds millions of fish fry to supply the farms which ring the Japanese coast. They have mastered forty different species, including red sea bream, flounder, amberjack and the deadly poisonous *fugu* (puffer fish), but the mysteries of the tuna still elude the world's researchers. Whoever cracks the secret will win a prize worth hundreds of millions of dollars a year in the Japanese marketplace alone.

Dr Kumai thinks he is almost there. He took us out on a motor launch to a spot off Oshima Island, a speck of rock in the northwest Pacific a couple of kilometres off the coast, to show us his flock. As he slung herring by the shovelful into an enclosure the size of two Olympic swimming pools, marked out by netting suspended from orange plastic buoys, giant fish flashed to the surface, gulping down the herring whole before disappearing back into the depths. Their huge staring eyes were the size of plates; some of Dr Kumai's breeding stock weigh 50 or 60 kilograms.

The Japanese call bluefin tuna the 'diamond of the sea' because of the fabulous price they can command at Tokyo's giant Tsukiji fish market. At one new year's opening auction, a single tuna (a 200-kilogram monster), sold for $80 000. The most prized cut, the fatty meat from the belly, finished up at that exclusive restaurant in the Ginza where a single sushi can cost $75. The reason for the astronomical prices is that the oceans' stocks of bluefin tuna (one of the four species) are being fished out to satisfy Japan's greedy gourmets who consume nearly half the world's catch. Conservationists are agitating for the fish to be protected, or at least for strict limits on catches. The problem is, unlike every other fish, tuna have so far defied attempts to farm them.

'Their size and their high level of activity is one problem,' said Dr Kumai, watching his captives swirl and whirl in a feeding frenzy, their black backs breaking the waves and their great eyes staring at their captors. Bluefin tuna are the world's largest bony fish. They are believed to live up to thirty years and the largest top 330 kilograms, a third of a tonne. The North Pacific bluefin (closely related to the Australian bluefin) has an epic migratory cycle which takes it from its breeding grounds off Taiwan, up the 'black current' to Japan, across the Pacific to America and back again — a voyage of around 15 000 kilometres.

In 1979 and 1980, using as breeding stock tuna caught by long-line fishermen, Dr Kumai managed to hatch several thousand eggs. All the fish died, however, and for fourteen years he waited for his bluefin to mate again. 'I almost gave up,' he confessed. Then, in the summer of 1994, millions of fertile eggs floated to the surface of the enclosure, to be skimmed off and taken to the tank farm. More than 2000 of them survived long enough to be returned to the sea, but the last one died at 246 days of age, weighing little more than a kilogram. 'It was a great disappointment, and we still don't understand exactly why,' says Dr Kumai. 'But this is longer than anyone has ever been able to keep them alive before.'

The tuna research station on Oshima island — a new industry, incidentally, for a former whaling community — is one of four in Japan. Three are operated by private companies and the fourth, a $20 million facility owned by the fisheries department, opened in the tropical Nansei Islands near Okinawa in 1995. The idea is to breed tuna in captivity, then release them into the wild in the same way as Japan's highly successful salmon-breeding program stocks the northern waters with millions of salmon. The Japanese government was stung into getting involved in bluefin breeding when an international conference in Kyoto came close to recommending a global ban on catching the fish. In the North Atlantic, in particular, the fishery has been devastated and numbers are down as much as 80 per cent. A ban would have been a death blow to the Japanese fishing industry, which has been crippled in recent years by ever-tightening restrictions on its deep sea fleets which once roamed the earth's oceans at will — not to mention the

Japanese gourmets who are already finding it almost impossible to afford their favourite sushi.

After the banning of drift-netting and the wholesale closure of once-rich fishing grounds, the number of Japanese oceangoing boats has fallen sharply and employment in the fishing industry has halved. All over the country there are dying fishing villages where only the old men are left. From its high-water mark in 1984, the Japanese catch has fallen from thirteen million tonnes to eight million. Consumption has also dropped, although the Japanese are still the world's biggest fish-eaters, obtaining a quarter of their protein from fish, compared with 4 per cent in Australia.

The shortfall is made up by imports and fish farming. Some of the more expensive fish species in the Tokyo shops are now almost exclusively bred in facilities such as those of Kinki University. Half the flounder, 70 per cent of kingfish, more than 80 per cent of sea bream, most of the prawns and scallops are artificially raised. Some gourmets say they can detect a different taste in the farmed fish, and certainly fish that has been kept in a tank for a while develops an unpleasant 'green' taste. Dr Kumai says that when they caught one of his bluefin and ate it — 'purely for scientific purposes', he chuckles — he found the flesh softer and more fatty than wild tuna. 'But a lot of Japanese like it like that — the fat is the best part.'

However, Japan has no alternative to captive breeding if it wants to keep tuna on the menu. And time is running out. Even in the enormous expanses of the South Pacific, where Australia and New Zealand have for decades been allowing Japanese and local boats to fish for tuna at will, they are now increasingly strictly rationed. Few doubt that the Japanese will eventually find the answers. Japan without tuna sushi would be as inconceivable as England without roast beef or India without curry. First, however, Dr Kumai has to figure out how. 'In spite of all our study, there are still many mysteries,' he says.

I would hate to give the impression that this is an unmitigated rave about Japanese food. Like any other cuisine, it can pall after a while. Its repertoire of technique is limited — traditional Japanese homes do not have an oven — and flavour, even freshness, is often secondary to eye appeal. The chef is, literally, 'he who stands at the chopping board'. At home, Mayu and I used to cook as much European (primarily French and Italian) food as Japanese, and our dinner guests were always partial to a Thai or Indian curry to reawaken the taste buds. There are also some Japanese ingredients which the Western palate simply refuses to acknowledge. Even Akebono, the gigantic Hawaiian sumo wrestler, quails at the thought of *natto,* a black slime of fermented soya beans. I was particularly repulsed by 'mountain potatoes', indigenous tubers often served grated raw in a white snotty froth. Raw quail eggs also take some getting used to. On top of this, the Japanese are still having a love affair with sugar — dips, stocks and marinades are often sickly with mirin, sweetened rice wine for which, at home, we substituted sake.

Another great disappointment in Asian cuisine for Westerners is that there is no Asian wine tradition to accompany it. Japan is no exception. There are some small-scale vineyards, particularly in Yamanashi Prefecture, and I have tasted quite superb Chardonnay, made in the style of a white Burgundy by a French-trained winemaker. However, the majority of what is sold in discount stores as Japanese wine is in fact a concoction of anonymous wine imported in bulk from Europe and America, spiked with additives, and generally sweet enough to dissolve the fillings in your teeth. Tea, not wine, is the traditional drink in Japan, whatever you are eating. Most restaurants have beer: Japan makes some excellent Australian-style lagers, notably my own favourite, a malty premium brew called Yebisu. And then there is sake, usually, incorrectly, known as 'rice wine'.

Quite early on during my stay in Japan, my education in the matter of sake — in fact, the Japanese drinking culture in general — was taken in hand by a friend we will call Yoshi, a journalist on one of the country's big newspapers whom I had met some years earlier when he was a correspondent in Australia. 'Sake should never be served hot' was the first lesson, as we settled onto the tatami mats of a little bar in Asakusa. 'The alcohol evaporates.' Asakusa is a funky neighbourhood of old wooden buildings, temples, bars, betting shops and music halls where city workers come to get away from the hustle of downtown and wax nostalgic about the good old days. Yoshi used to haunt it while he was at university and knows many of the madams, the homely crones who preside over the tiny bars, often huddled 'under the girder' of railway tracks.

There is no clear demarcation in Japan between a bar and a restaurant. All restaurants serve booze and all bars serve food, an eminently sensible arrangement. You start off with your basic *nomiya,* a cheap, stand-up bar popular with workers, where the drinking is serious and usually involves *shochu,* a white spirit like vodka, which may be diluted with hot water. Then you can move up to a noodle stall — often just a cart in the street surrounded by a curtain where people stodge up at the end of a night's serious drinking. A *yakitori* bar may be next, a grill where tiny skewers of chicken, leek or liver are served with great cheer in a cloud of blue smoke that will stay in your clothes and hair for days. The little restaurant/bars identified by red paper lanterns are usually a good bet. Whenever we found ourselves hungry in a strange town we would head for the railway station, where these establishments are found. From there, it is an infinite graduation of place and price up to the refined intimacy of a screened-off room in an exclusive *ryotei* in Akasaka where the bigwigs of business and politics wheel and deal while attendant geisha refill porcelain thimbles with sake, at a price which can easily exceed $1500 a head.

Yoshi, who enjoys his food, favours establishments called *kappo.* These are usually traditional places, bars but bars that emphasise the quality of their cuisine. One of them is upstairs in a huge room like a kendo (sword) practice hall, decorated with medieval Japanese armour; another has an ornamental garden with a trickling stream and carp floating luminously in a pond. In the summer there is foamy draught beer (for some reason I never understood the brewery removes all the draught beer machines on a certain day each October, and people have to drink from bottles for the winter). Winter is time for sake, warmed to blood heat only and drunk with friendly ceremony, each drinker filling his neighbour's cup when the level dips. The food is *sakana*, literally 'things with sake'. These nibblies come in an infinite range, a definite improvement on the peanuts and barbecue chips of the Aussie pub — fresh green soya beans, strips of dried squid, grilled shiitake mushrooms, salt-grilled *ayu* (sweetfish), assorted poached eggs, vegetables and fishcake from a simmering vat called *oden*.

These are the places where Japanese males repair after work to do their bonding. Not content with working ten-hour days, they will spend another two or three hours here with their colleagues talking shop. We were occasionally invited to join such jovial groups — the long-life battery division of Sony, a group of publishers from Kodansha. If there is a problem at work, this is where it will be worked out. Freed by alcohol from hierarchical constraints, workers will sound off in the bluntest terms at their bosses. The next day, all will be forgiven, as drunks, like children and foreigners, are held not to be responsible for what they say.

There is, of course, a downside to this egalitarianism. About half the Japanese lack the enzyme needed to process alcohol, and consequently get very drunk very quickly. Occasionally, they even die. This has become a particular problem with students involved in chugging contests. Late nights at Tokyo's subway stations are a lesson for those who believe the Japanese are always prim and proper, and perfectly behaved. Station staff will be busy mopping up 'platform pizzas' as the police manhandle helpless drunks into the cells to dry out overnight. One thing I can say, however, is that I never saw a single fight, or even an aggressive piece of behaviour. The Japanese are the best-tempered drunks I ever met.

To investigate the sake culture a little further, Mayu and I went looking for Japan's equivalent of Len Evans or Hugh Johnson — a guru to explain the finer points of this unique beverage. We found him in an unlikely place, an old, red brick building modelled on a German brewery, at the end of an avenue of pink-blooming cherry trees in an obscure outer suburb of Tokyo called Takinogawa. This is the headquarters of the guardians of the Japanese sake tradition, the National Research Institute of Brewing, which, of all things, is a division of the Tax Department. Here, a staff of bureaucrats have the best job in Japan — conducting the annual sampling of sakes and awarding the prizes.

Over three mornings in April — between 10 a.m. and 1 p.m. when the palate is keenest — they taste and evaluate no fewer than 864 different sakes, from breweries scattered from Hokkaido to Okinawa. The best 300 or so are awarded gold plaques, which will hang proudly on the maker's wall and emblazon his labels for the year. The atmosphere is as intense as any Australian wine-judging — silence in the long room, lit by the pale spring sun, broken only by the slap of slippers on the linoleum or an occasional subdued gargle and splat as a mouthful of liquid hits a stainless steel spittoon. Thirty white-coated figures gather around the tables — scrutinising, sniffing, tasting, frowning and scribbling cryptic notes on pads of scorecards. The eighty or so standard terms of criticism in their vocabulary would amuse even the most effete and pretentious of Western someliers. A sake can be poised, importunate, ill-bred or even (my favourite) *kudoi,* which means garrulous.

'So, you think this is a good job?' asked Dr Shinya Kobayashi, an agricultural scientist and sake connoisseur who is in charge of proceedings. 'Well, let me tell you it is hard work. Fortunately, I don't have to drive home afterwards — I catch the train.' Just how the Tax Department got involved in the sake business is lost in the mists of Meiji history. Originally, the revenue men tested the alcohol content of each brew to assess the excise due. In more recent times, the institute expanded to become a research centre for brewing technology, a 'sake university' where young makers come from all over Japan for their training and, of course, the country's only national 'wine show'. Dr Kobayashi and his colleagues are the high priests of the cult of sake.

First mentioned in Japanese legend five centuries before

Christ (when *bijinshu*, 'beautiful woman sake', was fermented from rice chewed by virgins), it is to Japan what Scotch is to the Scottish, Calvados to the Normans and beer to the Bavarians. Sake is not just a national drink, but a way of life and an object of reverence. No important ceremony, even in modern industrial Japan, is conducted without the unction of sake. When a couple celebrate their marriage before a Shinto altar, they sip three times from a cup of sake; when a priest consecrates a building, salt and sake are sprinkled at each corner; at midnight on New Year's Eve, Japanese flock to their shrines and temples to slurp a thick, sweet porridge of rice and sake, and pray for good luck. When Japan's latest state-of-the-art jetfighter was rolled out, priests were on hand to sanctify it with salt, sake and branches of the sacred camellia tree.

Although beer has, in recent years, taken over as Japan's most popular drink — three-quarters of total consumption, according to the latest statistics — sake comes second, with an average consumption of twenty litres per head per year. This is 14 per cent of total alcohol consumption; the local moonshine, a rough white spirit called *shochu*, is around 5 per cent. There are still approximately 1600 sake brewers around the country, although — as with wine-making in the West — many of the small, local artisan makers have gone out of business. The market is dominated by three or four huge commercial conglomerates.

To call it wine is not strictly correct. The production of sake is an enormously complicated process, even at the small country breweries where lack of refrigeration means it can still only be made during the traditional 100 coldest days of the year. I visited one brewery in the mountainous province of Niigata that makes some of Japan's best sake where snow is still heaped around the huge wooden vats to slow down the fermentation process.

You start with the rice. Although many boutique brewers will tell you differently, the variety does not matter, according to Dr Kobayashi. 'It is not like wine, in this respect. You cannot taste the varietal difference. The important things are the purity of the water, the degree to which the grain is polished and the types of yeast used.' For the very finest grade of sake, the rare and extremely expensive *daiginjoshu* (Dr Kobayashi produces a series of Petri dishes containing rice grains to illustrate the point) the outer layers of rice are polished away, until less than half the volume of each grain is left. For *ginjoshu,* the rice is reduced to 60 per cent, and so on down through the grades. The outer layers contain fats and minerals which may give the sake 'off' flavours.

The fermentation itself is a double process: an enzyme called *koji* is introduced to the vats of boiled rice to convert the starch into sugar; simultaneously, a yeast is seeded into the mix to convert the sugar to alcohol. Although it is a riskier and much more complicated process than making grape wine, once the sake is filtered off, pasteurised and bottled, that's it. With rare exceptions, it does not improve with age. Indeed, most sakes are best drunk within a year of making. To illustrate the point, Dr Kobayashi dipped a scoop into a great glass container and poured out a sample of the previous season's brew. It is what they call *namasake,* draught or non-pasteurised sake. It is an extraordinary drop — a slight greenish tinge, fairly dry, but with an overpowering fruitiness, not at all unlike an old-style Australian Rhine Riesling. Dr Kobayashi warned me to be careful as *namasake* has an alcohol content of 17 or 18 per cent; sake is usually diluted down to 15 to 16 per cent, a bit stronger than grape wine, before it is bottled and sold.

In recent years there has been something of a renaissance of smaller sake brands in Japan, much like the fad for boutique wine-making in the West. Bars have sprung up — there was a particularly convivial one just around the corner in Roppongi — where you can have your pick of twenty or thirty different regional sakes, each calibrated with a number according to its sweetness. The better bottle shops, such as the one in the basement of the Seibu department store in Ginza, use the same system. The higher the number, the more residual sugar — +20 is the sweetest, –20 the driest.

There is also the vexed matter of temperature. Many Western restaurants have, for some reason, got into the habit of serving sake 'hot' — an idea which horrifies the Japanese, as it should be obvious that this drives off the delicate and volatile aromas that give sake its character. Send it back, unless you would be comfortable drinking a Margaux dunked in boiling water to bring it up to 'room temperature'. The correct temperature depends on the sake and the occasion. As a general guide, *namasake* and *tarusake* (see page 83) are drunk cool; the better quality *junmai* sakes cool or at room temperature. Only the *honzojoshu*, or *vin ordinaire* sake, should be warmed in a *bain-marie*, and then only to blood heat or slightly more. To check the temperature, some Japanese men will plunge a hand between their companion's thighs. The less adventurous should make sure the little china flask in which it is served is merely warm to the touch.

If you are drinking with the Japanese, as Yoshi demonstrated, the etiquette is to fill each other's cups when the level falls. Hold your own up when the bottle is offered, with your other hand cupped beneath it to catch any drops. Cheers is *'Kampai!'* If you want to slow down, simply stop drinking — the Japanese will understand. You can also try your luck with such cocktail novelties as red sun (a bloody Mary using sake instead of vodka), a screwdriver or even a martini made with sake, which have become faddish at bars catering for younger crowds. Some people put ice in it. Someone has actually made a sake-flavoured ice cream. There is no accounting for taste.

However, be warned before your palate embarks on its voyage of discovery. There is no *appellation d'origine contrôlée* system in Japan, and only a few self-policed rules about labelling. Sake brewers are notorious for their sharp practices. The techniques known as 'tripling the sake' were perfected in occupied Manchuria where, it is said, a chemical cocktail sold as sake was actually produced using no rice at all. Raw spirit distilled from sugar is used to spike up the cheaper brands; the powder polished off the grain is saccharised and fed back into the mix; and glucose and chemicals such as lactic acid and monosodium glutamate (MSG) are added. You often cannot even be sure who made what you are drinking — large brewers contract out with smaller sake-makers and put their own labels on it. Ill-bred, indeed.

Having said that, if the Tax Department's judgings mean anything, it is the big commercial breweries which produce the most reliable quality sake, but you have to know what you are looking for. The country's largest brewer, Gekkeikan, is the most successful, winning gold medals in all nine of the years up to 1992 — but only for two of its scores of brews, labelled Daisho. Absurdly, neither is commercially available; they are reserved for prestige corporate gift-giving. The Tokiwa brewery in Nagoya and the Kamotsuru brewery in Hiroshima came second with medals in eight of the nine years for a brand both label Daiginjo. However, instead of puzzling over the *kanji* and *katakana* on the largely decorative labels (although there are books, even in English, which can help decipher them if you really insist), the best way to get a sake education is to find a Japanese bar or bottle-shop owner who knows his stuff. Many of Japan's better sakes are now exported, and some are actually being manufactured offshore. Here are the generic varieties to look for:

Junmai The purest grade of sake, supposedly made from only rice, water, kosi and yeast. This is the bottle sake, rather than the cask. It represents about 8.5 per cent by volume of the sake made in Japan — and all the sake judged by Dr Kobayashi and his colleagues. Within this category, *ginjoshu* is made from rice with 40 per cent of its volume polished off, and *daiginjoshu* with 50 per cent or more. It may be served in the traditional tasting cup — white porcelain, with a double circle of blue, the so-called snake's eye, on the bottom.

Jisake A 'local brew', usually from one of the hundreds of smaller sake-makers. They are made to no particular standard, but may contain interesting traditional or experimental regional variations. For instance, one maker is producing a 'rosé' sake from a special yeast, which he says is popular with women.

Tarusake This is the stuff they serve in boisterous *robatayaki* restaurants where the customers sit around a bar while a chef sits cross-legged in front of a hearth, shouting orders and passing barbecued titbits around on a long-handled wooden paddle. The sake is matured for a few weeks in a cask made of cryptomeria (a type of pine) wood and is usually served in a small pine box, sometimes with a pinch of salt on the corner. It has a strong, piney aroma and is not recommended for delicate food such as sashimi.

Namasake This comes on the market in spring, two or three months after brewing, and is the 'raw' unpasteurised sake of that winter's vintage. It is high in flavour and alcohol, and must be finished once the bottle is opened otherwise it will spoil. The arrival of this 'Beaujolais Nouveau' of sakes in shops or at breweries is signalled by hanging a large ball of cryptomeria twigs under the eaves.

Koshu The exception to the rule that sake is drunk young. This sake is matured for years in the bottle. Dr Kobayashi produced one from his own cellar dated 1967. It was a tawny colour, with a slightly oxidised flavour, not unlike a sherry, and is recommended as an aperitif. Like *doburoku* (see below), it is probably impossible to obtain outside Japan. Quality department stores like the Yurakucho Seibu have some in their cellars … although at hair-raising prices.

Doburoku The 'real stuff' which farmers may invite you to sip when you visit the country, but only if they are sure you are not an excise agent. It is the 'poteen' of Japan, illegal moonshine, a sweet, milky, chewy, brew, unpasteurised and only crudely filtered. Some small country brewers make sanitised commercial versions of it and you may also find it at festivals and other special occasions.

The emphasis on fish and vegetables in Japanese cooking is no culinary accident. As I mentioned earlier, until relatively late last century, Buddhist dietary prohibitions were widely observed and little meat, particularly red meat such as beef, was eaten. There is still a strong vegetarian tradition, and any number of traditional vegetarian restaurants flourish around Tokyo. For a special, and unusual, experience many foreigners and Japanese alike seek out one of the Buddhist 'temple food' establishments, which are often set in exquisite surroundings: carp ponds, bamboo, water-splashed flagstones, ancient timbers and stone lanterns. If you can bear the schedule (pre-breakfast prayers can begin at 4 a.m.) some of the monasteries on Mount Koya, Japan's holiest mountain, take in lodgers and serve up delicacies like naturally freeze-dried bean curd. As a fringe benefit, the Japanese who attain executive rank with the larger corporations such as Mitsubishi are entitled to have their bones interred here in moss-covered corporate crypts, under the huge, gloomy cryptomeria trees.

Finally, for those whose palates are jaded with the pretty, pale watercolours of Japanese cuisine, something of a revolution has occurred in the butcher's shops over the past few years. It is now possible to sink your teeth into a hearty steak without mortgaging the family farm. Foreign beef, particularly Australian beef, is now widely available. For Mayu and me, that meant a Saturday morning stroll down to the brazenly advertised Meat Rush, on the way to our local shopping centre in Azabu Juban. A traditional German-style smallgoods manufacturer (sausage-makers by appointment to the Emperor, no less), this company decided to bypass normal distribution channels and sell the meat it imported for its hams and sausages directly to customers. When it first opened, queues of Japanese and foreigners stretched down the street and people boggled at the prices — Australian rump steak for $12 or so a kilogram, when Japanese beef sold for up to $500 a kilogram in the flash department stores up the road.

We travelled to the heartland of the Japanese beef industry to find what effect these imports were having on traditional growers of the world's most expensive — and exclusive — beef, Japan's famed *wagyu*. The most highly prized beef comes not from Kobe, as most foreigners believe, but from a historic castle town called Matsuzaka, 350 kilometres or so from Tokyo. The rolling green hills of Matsuzaka are to beef what the Champagne district is to sparkling wine, or the Caspian Sea to caviar. We arrived to find Jiro Tochigi in the middle of his morning grooming. He filled his cheeks with *shochu* spirit and spat a fine spray onto Yukimi, his favourite cow, lovingly massaging the liquor into her glossy chestnut hide with a bundle of rice-straw. Then another treat: he emptied two bottles of Kirin beer down her throat. Yukimi burped appreciatively and frothed at the mouth. This, as you might have gathered, is no ordinary cow. She is a *wagyu*, bred to produce Japan's fabulously fat-marbled beef, and worth as much as $90 000. In the gleaming showcases of posh Ginza department stores, the choicest cuts of Matsuzaka beef are displayed like jewellery and cost up to $75 per 100 gram sliver.

For the past few years, however, a shadow has been growing over the future of Mr Tochigi, a 62-year-old widower, and his fellow farmers who raise these elite cattle. With the arrival of foreign beef, particularly from Australia, on the supermarket shelves, Mr Tochigi is afraid a tradition that goes back a hundred years or more is threatened. 'We are being slowly throttled by imports,' he told us indignantly. 'Imports now have 65 per cent of the Japanese market. People are being driven out of the industry.... it is threatening our livelihoods and our lifestyles.'

Although Australian beef has been exported to Japan since the 1960s, it has been bitterly resisted by the Japanese government, who have used every trick in the book to try and prevent consumers taking advantage of the dramatically lower prices. As recently as 1987, Japan's Agriculture Minister (and, later, premier) Tsutomu Hata made his famous claim in Washington that the Japanese could not digest imported beef because their intestines were different. In Iwate Prefecture, another prestige beef-raising area, Ikko Abe, a 55-year-old beef farmer, hanged himself from a beam in his cowshed to protest the decision to open the Japanese market. Whole consignments have been impounded because of the discovery of pesticide residues that (if the Australian authorities are to be believed) would not harm a flea. There is an enormous substitution racket, with Australian beef passed off as American or even Japanese.

In spite of this, 'Aussibeef' (as housewives throughout Japan nicknamed it) has gradually carved itself out a market among the world's pickiest consumers. By 1994, it had become a $1.6 billion-a-year export, worth more to Australia than gold, iron ore or natural gas. We had overtaken the Americans in the market, and about a third of all the beef eaten in Japan now comes from the pastures and feedlots of, mainly, Queensland and New South Wales. Ironically, the dramatic opening up of the Japanese market coincided with Japanese corporations investing here. At the annual Food Expo in Tokyo, most of the stands displaying 'Aussibeef' are Japanese-owned.

Down at Matsuzaka, they take their beef seriously. The Gyugin restaurant, a 93-year-old family business in a street of ancient wooden houses below the castle ruins, is one of about thirty specialist beef-houses in Matsuzaka. On the walls are photographs of champion cows which became gourmet dinners. Here, Mayu and I had a dinner which consisted of 150 grams of fillet steak, served grilled over a charcoal brazier (it is also simmered in broth sukiyaki-style) with a bottle of beer, a bowl of rice and some slices of onion, potato and capsicum. The beef is not served with mustard, but with the soy/citrus dunking sauce called *ponzu*. The cost: $150 a head — eye-watering even by the standards of the world's most expensive country. Added to this, we were still hungry, so we went afterwards for a snack in a nearby bar and discussed the price of beef with some of the customers.

Said one woman: 'With a family to raise, I can't afford Matsuzaka beef.' The barmaid chipped in, 'Aussibeef tastes as good — and it's healthier.' Maybe they were just being polite to the foreign visitor — or maybe they were practical. At the supermarket around the corner from that exclusive restaurant you could buy three kilograms of lean Australian rump or sirloin beef for the price of that steak dinner. 'People are talking through their wallets,' acknowledged Mr Tochigi glumly.

You do not need an economics degree to work out why the cost of *wagyu* beef is so astronomical. Mr Tochigi's farm, in the picture postcard hamlet of Iinan, consists of 5400 square metres of land — a little over half a hectare on which he has a few rows of neatly manicured tea bushes, some minute rice terraces and a barn in which his entire herd of cows, all five of them, spend their blissful lives. Some of his neighbouring 'cattle farmers' own just one cow. They all have names and, to guard against substitution, which is becoming a major problem, each Matsuzaka *wagyu* comes with a birth certificate, indelibly stamped with its nose-print.

By contrast, the average Australian beef property runs 500 head of cattle, and in the Northern Territory the figure is 5000, roaming ranges of tens of thousands of hectares. 'We cannot compete with those economics. All we have is the unique taste and quality of Matsuzaka beef,' says Mr Tochigi. The *wagyu* are bought as virgin female calves from studs in the Kobe area, where centuries of selective breeding have bred the hump out of what was once a working beast used to plough the rice paddies. They are fattened on grain (and beer) for three years, then sent to the abattoir. 'After knowing them all that time, I feel lonely when they leave,' says Mr Tochigi. On the hillside above his house is a cenotaph dedicated to the souls of departed cows, where a Buddhist priest holds a memorial service every year.

There are consolations. Mr Tochigi's timber, tiled-roof house is full of coloured ribbons and silver cups. Three times he has won the Matsuzaka grand championship, once with a beast that brought the all-time record price of $450 000. A single cow worth more than his whole farm. So far, the uniqueness of genuine Matsuzaka *wagyu* — it accounts for only 1 per cent of the Japanese market — has protected the town from the cut-price imports. The number of *wagyu* cows has in fact increased, although the number of farmers has halved, from four hundred to two hundred. The imports have hurt most the farmers who fatten up the lesser grades of beef and dairy cattle, the *vin ordinaire* of the market. More than 100 000 have gone out of business in the past decade, some going bankrupt, but most retiring with no son willing to carry on the business.

Although Japanese consumption of beef has increased remarkably in recent years, from five to about eight kilograms a head (compared with thirty-five kilograms a year in Australia), imports make up most of the increase, and the Japanese beef industry is stagnant. Mr Tochigi ran his finger down Yukimi's flanks, outlining the choice cuts that would come from his pampered pet when her time was up the following autumn. 'The brisket — that's the best bit,' he said, as Yumiki slurped the beer foam from her lips. He has never eaten imported beef and has no intention of doing so. 'How could it compare?' he asks. But he, and the other farmers, worry about what will happen if it forces *wagyu* beef off the menu. 'I couldn't sell the farm — there are no buyers — and my sons say they can make more money working in office jobs,' Mr Tochigi told us.

We have travelled a long way down the food chain from that exquisite banquet at Mr Ukai's inn in Kyoto. As well as the tuna pens of the Pacific and a beef farmlet in Matsuzaka, we spent time with Japan's rice farmers, we went apple-picking in Aomori and (almost) salmon-fishing in Hokkaido — we were kept ashore by an unexpected typhoon. Food is the most fundamental part of any culture — civilisation itself begins when people change their diet from wild game to cultivated grain — and nowhere is this more under threat than in Japan.

On one front, the instant *ramen* generation is rejecting the pricey and time-consuming niceties of traditional cuisine. On the other, the efficient farming nations of the world are battering at Japan's doors, threatening not just the lifestyles of the farmers, but the landscape itself, pierced and plotted with its tiny rice paddies, its pocket handkerchiefs of orchard and ponds of carp. For the moment, it stubbornly survives. We will all, not just the Japanese, be the poorer if their great culinary culture is allowed to die.

*THE BULL WAS BIG AND BLACK AND BRAVE AND HE
pawed the ground and tossed his head and bellowed his defiance
as the men sweated and wrestled with him. But you could see that
his horns had been altered, the points had been sawn off, and he
would be no danger, and there would be no blood on the hot grey
sand of the bullring that day. There was no matador standing
there, no Cayetano, arrogant, sighting down his sword, swinging
his cape to entice the bull with a slow, beautiful faena the way the
great ones do before they go for the kill. They led the second bull
into the ring and forced down his head, until their horns locked,
and then their eyes rolled and their flanks heaved and the two
bulls began to thrust against each other, while the men shouted to
them and slapped their necks, until one dominated, and the other
ran away in defeat. This was not bullfighting, but this was how
it was that summer in Uwajima.*

The politically correct bullfights that attract the crowds to
the town of Uwajima in the boondocks of Shikoku island
will never inspire a Japanese Ernest Hemingway. In fact,
they are not even really fights, more a kinder, gentler sort
of bovine sumo wrestling. And that's how the locals like it.
'I have seen videotapes of bullfighting in Spain,' shudders
Yoshio Nakahata, the 86-year-old chairman of the Uwajima
bullfighting association. 'We would never do such a cruel
and violent thing here. We have never had a bull killed —
even when they are too old to fight they are looked after
and fed in their old age.'

This unique sport has survived at Uwajima — and in a
couple of other remote parts of Japan — for at least 500
years. The ancestors of the fighting bulls, legend has it,
were given to the islanders by grateful survivors of a Dutch
shipwreck. The fights began as scratch contests between
local farmers, who used them to pull ploughs through the
rice paddies. Twenty years ago, the civic fathers built a
special 3000-seat arena — the first covered stadium in

THE SUN ALSO RISES

Japan boasts Mr Nakahata. In its heyday, when he was a child, there were 3000 fighting bulls on the island and contests were held several times a month. However, the drift of people to the cities and the introduction of tractors for farming have cut a swathe through the herd. There are now only 200 bulls left, just enough to sustain three *corridas* a year.

Trainers prepare the bulls with a diet of eggs, rice cakes and the powdered essence of death adders. The animals are taken for four-hour hikes along steep mountain tracks to strengthen their legs. They are groomed until they gleam, as they should — a champion is worth anything up to $40 000.

The bulls are ranked like sumo wrestlers, with the bouts building up through the day until the mighty *yokozunas* (champions) are led out, wearing cloth-of-gold capes and preceded by attendants carrying purple banners and scattering salt for the ritual purification of the ring. It is quite a show. Unfortunately, the day I went the grand champion — a magnificent beast named Ichigo Shirokuch, 1100 kilograms of pure aggression — so terrified his opponent that he turned tail a bare second or two after they locked horns and ran away.

The normally docile Japanese crowd, inflamed with sake and illegal betting, erupted in a chorus of complaint. They demanded a rematch and, when it was refused, hurled cushions, sacks of garbage and abuse into the ring.

As for the cruelty, we did see one bull slammed against the rails and gored, a streak of blood running down its shoulder. It was no worse than you would see at a typical Australian rodeo.

'These bulls have a great life,' says Mr Nakahata. 'They are selected for fighting when they are calves. The ones that aren't chosen get castrated and turned into steak. Tell me what is crueller.'

都道府県　被爆者・遺族代表席

RESENTATIVES OF A-BOMB SURVIVORS
AND BEREAVED FAMILIES

THREE

DON'T MENTION
THE WAR

> 'Whoever closes his eyes to the past
> is blind to the present.
> Whoever refuses to remember the inhumanity
> is prone to the risks of new infection.'
>
> — (WEST) GERMAN PRESIDENT RICHARD VON WEIZSACKER
>
> IN A HISTORIC SPEECH TO THE BUNDESTAG, 1985

LUCKILY FOR HIM, PAPA WAS sheltered by the tunnel when they dropped the atom bomb on him. He had dug it himself, he and his young fellow officers from the Imperial Navy's accountancy unit, deep in the hillside above Kure, Hiroshima's port and one of the navy's largest bases. It wasn't to protect them from the bombing which had been going on incessantly for months — the soldiers were dispensable. It was to preserve the records, the precious leather-bound scrolls with their immaculately painted characters which recorded the names and personal details of all Admiral Yamamoto's fine young men. Like the Nazis, Emperor Hirohito's commanders were most particular about their records.

We were sitting, Satoru Tominaka and I, with our legs under a *kotatsu* — a small, heated well in the floor, covered with a tabletop and insulated with a thick blanket. There was a metre and a half of snow lying under the larch trees that surround his little wooden holiday cottage in the forest. Christmas was coming, my first in Japan, and we had cut and hung a little tree with lights. On the table were the remains of a bamboo-wrapped wheel of trout sushi and a bottle of his favourite brew — a 1.8-litre magnum of *shochu*, Downtown Napoleon, his favourite brand of moonshine.

Mayu's father was seventy-three that winter, but he still had some of his teeth, most of his hair and all of his memories. As the level in the bottle slowly fell, he began to reminisce about his war, and about that day half a century ago when the world entered the nuclear age. It was imprinted as starkly in his mind as those ghastly human silhouettes scorched into the walls of Hiroshima and Nagasaki. Eventually, I felt able to ask him the question my guilt-ridden generation clutches at as the only possible justification for the decision to drop those terrible weapons.

'Tominaka-san, if the Americans had not used those atom bombs, would the Japanese have fought on?'

'Of course,' the answer snapped back. 'We only surrendered because we did not know they only had two. We thought Kanazawa would be next.'

Of all the accounts of that fateful decision — no fewer than four hefty new historical tomes were published to mark the fiftieth anniversary of the bombing in 1995 — I still find this the most convincing. Never mind that Japanese intelligence was wrong — documents released just recently showed that the Americans were planning to build and drop another fourteen atom bombs before Christmas. Set aside for a moment the other ethical and practical objections I will deal with later. The fact remains that the ordinary soldiers and citizens of Japan such as my father-in-law were prepared to fight to the last man: 'One hundred million ready to die proudly' as the slogan went. The moral debate, which continues today, is incomplete without an understanding that President Harry Truman's fateful decision saved the lives of millions of people like my father-in-law, American and Japanese alike, who would otherwise have fought on.

In the three years I was to spend in Japan, the shadows of war would gather ever more thickly. The anniversaries followed one another as predictably as shells from a belt-fed mortar, distant explosions marking the rise and fall of the Japanese empire — Nanking, Pearl Harbour, Singapore; then, as the tide of battle turned, Leyte Gulf, Iwo Jima, Okinawa, Hiroshima. On television we watched proud old soldiers gathered on the flinty beaches of Normandy to celebrate D-Day. In Germany, withered survivors with serial numbers tattooed on their arms mourned at the Nazi death camps. In Australia, the diggers and their kin gathered at a thousand cenotaphs to commemorate what is now apparently to be called VP (for 'Victory in the Pacific') Day.

But how was the fiftieth anniversary of the end of the world's most terrible war to be remembered in Japan, the country which started it all? Would there, finally, be the acknowledgment of guilt that all Asia was waiting for? Would the ghosts of the 'comfort women', the slave labourers, the concentration camp victims finally be comforted with condolences and compensation? Most importantly of all, would new light be shed on the century's most cataclysmic event — the dropping of the atom bombs?

The year of 1995 began with an air of great optimism that Japan would at last face up to the legacy of its past, and show the world that it could once again be trusted with the future. It sputtered out in an atmosphere of mutual recrimination, a golden opportunity for reconciliation missed. Fifty years on, Japan's prime minister could not even bring himself to say 'sorry'. Instead, he chose the word *hansei*, a slippery concept usually translated as 'self-reflection'.

This much, any non-Japanese history book will tell you. Beginning with the 1932 annexation of Manchuria, with the 'last emperor' Pu Yi installed as a puppet ruler, Japan's seemingly invincible military conquered half of Asia. Millions of civilian settlers followed the sword to plunder and colonise the confiscated farmland, factories and mines. At its height, in 1942, the Greater East Asian Empire held one-seventh of the surface of the earth, and a quarter of the world's population, in its thrall.

There seemed no limit short of global conquest to the ambitions of Emperor Hirohito and his generals. Japan reached across the Pacific to explode balloon bombs over Oregon, dispatched midget submarines to torpedo shipping in Sydney Harbour and sent troops across two oceans to Sri Lanka. In the Asia–Pacific arena alone, twenty million soldiers and civilians (including three million Japanese) were killed — even more if you include the millions who died of disease and starvation. It was a decade of bloody conquest without parallel since the time of Napoleon or perhaps even Genghis Khan. That era ended with the mushroom clouds that became the symbol of the new nuclear age.

A straightforward enough account with which any Australian, Chinese or German high school student should have no difficulty. But that is not how history is seen in Japan. As I travelled around the country during that anniversary year, I must have spoken to more than 100 people about the war — old soldiers from both sides of the trenches, politicians, priests, historians and students. I visited many of the important shrines, memorials and museums dedicated to the war, and travelled to some of the battlefields in Japan, China and Russia.

The more I read and listened, the more I came to realise that, unique among all the defeated peoples of all the world's wars, the Japanese — or, more accurately, their power elite — really believe that the losers' version of history can prevail. An individual (as the historian Barbara Tuchman wrote half a century ago) can be wrong, but never a whole country:

> ... so Japan's only answer has been to tell herself that her judges are wrong, and she is right. To strengthen this contention, she has built up the belief that she acts from the purest of motives, which her fellow nations wilfully misunderstand.

In this Orwellian fantasy, the Japanese are the victims, not the villains. A brand-new history book, commissioned by the ruling Liberal Democratic Party (LDP) and published in 1995, argues that the Japanese fought a war of 'self-defence' against ruthless American aggressors, the Rape of Nanking was a 'fabrication' and the Imperial Army ventured overseas only to 'liberate' their long-suffering Asian cousins from the American and European colonial powers. This notion, incidentally, came as an especial surprise to the people of Korea who were not aware that they were anyone's colony until the Japanese army arrived in 1904, and who still refer to the forty years of brutal occupation that followed as the 'scourge of the island dwarfs'. The anniversary year should have been the time to torpedo those malign myths once and for all. Instead, the Japanese Establishment stubbornly closed its ranks.

As the anniversary approached, I watched amazed as newspapers and magazines gave space to scholars to weave fantastic fabrications 'proving' that only a communications glitch prevented an honourable warning being given before the attack on Pearl Harbour. It was 'revealed' that the Chinese leader Sun Yat-sen planned to lease Manchuria to Japan for ¥10 million, as though, by some twisted logic, that made it alright for the Imperial Army to invade and occupy the territory twenty years later. Sad old Quislings arrived on junkets from the Philippines and Sri Lanka to testify to approving audiences of veterans how their countries had welcomed their Japanese 'liberators'. Ultimately, the historians retreated behind the greatest myth of all, that no matter what Japan may have done the nation was absolved from guilt by the ultimate 'crime against humanity' of the atomic bombing.

In popular culture, as well, there was a pervasive sanitisation that rarely allowed even a pale pastiche of the truth to escape. Most notoriously, the Japanese distributors of Bernardo Bertolucci's masterwork *The Last Emperor* cut pictures — real contemporary photographs — of the Rape of Nanking from the film before allowing it to be screened. The images of war that generations of Japanese have been brought up on are those of the heroic young pilot, ready to die like a fallen cherry blossom in the service of his emperor.

As the fiftieth anniversary approached, there was a boom in such films. *Kike, Wadatsumi no Koe (Listen to the Road of the Wind)* idolised Hirohito's soldiers in a cinema tricked out with war themes. The third remake of *Himeyuri no To (Tower of the Lilies)* was packing them in with a totally fictitious account of the famous Okinawa schoolgirls drafted as nurses during the American invasion, many of them murdered by Japanese soldiers, not Americans as the movie would have it. Tear-jerking accounts of the atomic bombing of Hiroshima and Nagasaki were reworked in a dozen books and films. A new genre of 'future fact' novels appeared in which the war was re-fought with the Japanese winning. In one, Australian parliamentarians flee, wetting their pants, as Japanese bombers attack Parliament House in Canberra.

This was why, that icy winter night, I probably prodded former Lieutenant Tominaka more than was prudent or polite. I wanted to try and get a little closer to the *honne*, the truth of the situation rather than the stories peddled for public consumption by the *goyu gakusha*, the official scholars who guard the gates of Japan's authorised history. Who better to tell me than an ordinary soldier caught up in events beyond his control — and especially someone who speaks English. Mayu's stepfather has an international outlook which is unusual in people of his wartime generation, of whom it is said 'those who were there were told lies; and those who weren't were told nothing'. After the war, he worked overseas for one of Japan's giant trading companies, in Europe and the Middle East and in Iran, where he learned, among other things, to count in a dozen different languages. Also, one suspects, to express his feelings a little more freely than is usual in Japan.

Like the rest of the class of '42, Mr Tominaka hadn't wanted to sign up. He was quite content to pursue his economics and law studies at Kobe University. But a few months before he was due to graduate, the recruiting officers came calling — those who volunteered now, they said, could join the Imperial Navy as trainee officers. Those who chose to complete their studies would be drafted into the army. 'There was no choice, really,' he said, pouring another peg of Downtown Napoleon all round. 'All the intelligent people wanted to join the navy.'

In common with navy people everywhere, Mr Tominaka nurses a withering contempt for the army, whom he blames — like most Western historians — for starting the war. 'Admiral Yamamoto [the navy commander who masterminded Pearl Harbour] was an intelligent man. The navy knew about the world, and they knew they could never beat America. All the Army understood was "hurt, hurt — spirit, spirit." They thought nothing could stand up to them if they had the right spirit.' He bangs the table with some vigour as he says this. No wonder he and his college chums volunteered for the navy rather than wait to be drafted into the army.

Mayu and I went with him back to Kure on a research trip the following summer. The accounting department where he worked was long gone — firebombed one night in 1945 — but the cluster of brick buildings which are still the headquarters of Japan's second most important naval base (after Yokohama) survives. Kure is Japan's Portsmouth or Anapolis, a navy town dominated by the great shipyards which now turn out supertankers instead of warships, conquering the world with commerce where force of arms failed. It was from here that the *Akagi*, the flagship of the carrier fleet that attacked Pearl Harbour, set sail. Here, in the war's dying days, naval officers begged to be chosen to sail on the last voyage of the doomed battleship *Yamato*, which went down with 3333 men — history's greatest suicide mission.

We managed to find the filled-in entrance to the tunnel papa and his comrades had dug. He was standing here a few minutes after eight o'clock on that grey, muggy, midsummer morning in 1945. Although he couldn't see the *pikka* (the 'flash'), he heard the *don* (the 'boom') as the atom bomb went off. A huge cloud, shaped more like a jellyfish dangling from heaven than the usual mushroom simile, rose over Hiroshima. Observers were dispatched to the city, and when they returned the shock in their faces told him more than their words — the war was over. Japan had lost. Soon survivors came staggering and limping and crawling by.

A visit to the Peace Museum in Hiroshima presents an almost-too-realistic picture of what it must have been like. Nightmarish wax figures stand petrified among the ruins, faces burnt black, flesh dripping from their bones, the ghastly red glare of the burning city illuminating the apocalyptic land- scape. Nearby is a whitewashed concrete wall streaked indelibly with black radioactive rain; the shadow of a child's foot burnt onto a wooden clog; hideously deformed body parts preserved in alcohol; a greyish nest that on closer examination turns out to be a head of human hair.

Forty years and forty million visitors after they were first put on display, these exhibits in Hiroshima's Peace Museum still have an almost pornographic fascination. The relics, the dioramas, the testimonials of the victims of first atomic bombing fill the visitor, foreign and Japanese alike, with a sense of horror and revulsion that President Truman could never have imagined when he gave the order to unleash 'the force from which the sun draws its power' that August morning.

The emphasis on the macabre is understandable. When it opened in 1955, the museum presented a revisionist view of history — the Americans for years suppressed the truth about the scale of the disaster and its after-effects. The first foreign reporter into Hiroshima, Australian-born Wilfred Burchett — who made his way there from Tokyo carrying a typewriter, a black umbrella and seven days' food — was branded a liar when he reported a few days after the bombing, 'People who were uninjured in the cataclysm are still dying, mysteriously and horribly, from an unknown something which I can only describe as the atomic plague.' The only liars were the US military who, trying to conceal the enormity of the bombing, denied that radiation sickness existed.

For two generations, this museum and the monument-crowded Peace Park, which links it visually with the skeletal dome of the ruined industrial hall, have been the potent icons of the peace movement around the world. They were the images which invaded the mind whenever — from Aldermaston to Greenham Common — the cry went up to 'Ban the Bomb', to stop the nuclear arms race before the whole planet went up in flames. Anyone who was anyone in the peace movement had to be there to watch the doves released at the moment marking the fiftieth anniversary of the bomb's explosion — surely the greatest convocation of beards, batik and sandals the world has ever seen. 'Let all souls here rest in peace, for we shall not repeat the evil,' reads the enigmatic inscription on the cenotaph. But whose evil? Japan's? America's? The world's?

For two generations, this is what Japanese have thought of

whenever World War II was mentioned — not the invasion of China that started it, not the bombing of Pearl Harbour, not the battle for Okinawa, but the cataclysm that reduced one of their greatest cities to a pile of glowing cinders and redeemed their country in a nanosecond from bloody aggressor to bloodstained martyr. Japanese schoolchildren are brought here in their hundreds of thousands every year, to gawp at the blood-curdling exhibits, drape vast chains of coloured paper cranes over the monuments and pray for their dead forebears — never pausing to wonder just why it happened.

Realities collide here. Americans are taught that this was where the war *ended* — when the bomb bay of the *Enola Gay*, named after the pilot's mother, opened at 08:15:17 on the morning of August 6, 1945, and a radioactive fireball a kilometre wide incinerated the ancient castle city. 'My God, look at that son-of-a-bitch go!' cried Captain Robert Lewis, the copilot, rejoicing that the war that cost so many of his countrymen their lives must at last be over. Most Japanese people, however, sustained from their schooldays by the myths enshrined in Hiroshima, believe that instant was when it *began* — the obliteration of an innocent city; the deaths of hundreds of thousands of civilians; a crime against humanity.

That an event so seminal to this century should be so widely misunderstood — on both sides of the Pacific — is hardly surprising. If 1995 had any purpose, surely pumping the oxygen of informed debate into these musty rooms haunted by myths and legends should have been the primary one. However, no-one anticipated how bitter and painful the reassessment would become, as the former antagonists tried to lay the ghosts that still haunt what in the intervening half century has become the world's most important alliance.

Courageous historians and museum curators in the United States and in Japan came under heavy attack when they attempted to temper the prevailing national mythology with historical reality. In Washington, the Smithsonian Museum was forced to cancel its memorial exhibition after its directors were denounced for an excess of political correctness when they tried to place the victorious *Enola Gay* against a backdrop showing the holocaust it wrought. In Hiroshima, a city that has made its victimhood an international brand image (Peace Avenue, Peace Museum, Peace Pachinko Parlour, Peace Dry-Cleaners and so on), it took a nine-year battle with right-wing nationalists before the museum could open a new wing placing the bombing in its historical context.

In this wing, appropriately nicknamed 'Aggression Corner', the Japanese now for the first time have the opportunity to see what their education denied them — the reality of Japan's role in the war and the reason for the bombing. It shows a world very different from that of their bowdlerised school texts, where even the word 'defeat' has been sanitised to *shusen*, the 'ending' of the war. A single headline on a slab of text in the simple, sombre amphitheatre that houses the new display provides the epitaph: 'The Truth about the Atom Bomb: 1905–1951.' There, in one line, the most important of the myths of Hiroshima is laid to rest — that the Americans, without provocation, dropped a superweapon nicknamed 'Little Boy' (after the former US president, Franklin Delano Roosevelt) on a defenceless civilian city. The museum's acting director, Kenji Ohara, who fought for this new perspective, told me, 'Hiroshima had always been a great military base. That doesn't justify the bombing, but we thought as historians we should get the facts straight.'

Huge photographic montages show the real targets of the atom bomb: the Mitsubishi dockyards where Japan's warships were built, the munitions factories, the air strips that supported the Second General Headquarters of Emperor Hirohito's army. The new exhibition pulls few punches, either, about where responsibility for the war — and thus for Hiroshima — really lies. From the sinking of the Russian fleet in 1905 to the conquest of Korea and the occupation of Manchuria, Japan is shown as a ruthless imperial power. The 'surprise attack' on Pearl Harbour; the 'harsh working conditions' of Korean slave labourers; even Japan's greatest wartime atrocity, the Rape of Nanking, are acknowledged. Although, while the English language caption admits bluntly that 'up to 300 000 civilians' were massacred, the Japanese version concedes only that 'several tens of thousands' died.

This, since it is Japan's own painful reappraisal of its past, carries far more weight with the Japanese public than any outsider criticism or commentary, of which there has been an excess over the years. As far back as 1948, the Australian commander of the Commonwealth occupation forces, Lieutenant General Sir Horace 'Red Robbie' Robertson chose the Hiroshima memorial service to deliver this harsh verdict: 'I must remind you that you caused this disaster yourselves ... the punishment given to Hiroshima was only part of the retribution of the Japanese people as a whole for pursuing the doctrine of war.' The new exhibition does not quite go this far, but it does explicitly acknowledge for the first time that 'to save American lives' was one reason the bomb was dropped. It has been left to the next generation to decide whether to add 'and Japanese lives, too'.

As for the alleged immorality of bombing a population that included civilians, other historians have pointed out that it was Japan that pioneered this form of warfare in Asia, when it pulverised the city of Shanghai in 1937. Its own attempt at a weapon of mass destruction — the 'poor man's atom bomb' as the Japanese military called it — was germ warfare, which killed many thousands of Chinese civilians with bubonic plague and other ghastly diseases. Two wrongs, of course, do not make a right, but these facts make it difficult for Japan to claim the high moral ground.

The second great myth of Hiroshima was raised when I interviewed Takashi Hiraoka, an avuncular former journalist and tireless anti-nuclear campaigner who was mayor of Hiroshima that anniversary year. He acknowledged that 'the bomb would never have been dropped if we had not invaded China', but insisted that Hiroshima remained a unique example of the horrors of war, because of the scale of the killing, and the fact that the bomb continues to take its toll, from cancer and other radiation-caused diseases, to this day. This widespread view — that Hiroshima in some way represents a whole new magnitude of warfare, both in the quality of the killing and the quantity of the loss of life — is not supported by any impartial examination of the statistics.

It is impossible to be exact about numbers. As recently as the spring of 1994 a mass grave was discovered at Yoshidacho, thirty-five kilometres north of Hiroshima, where volunteers with picks and shovels exhumed the bones of 400 forgotten victims. Tens of thousands of Korean slave labourers who were in Hiroshima at the time were not even counted in the official records. The two official estimates usually cited are a November 1945 police report which records 78 000 dead, seriously injured or missing; and an August 1946 count by the city council, which placed the figure at 118 000 victims. The figure commonly used by Japanese historians today is 140 000, plus or minus ten thousand.

Even accepting the highest estimate, the nuclear holocaust of Hiroshima is dwarfed alongside other attacks using conventional weapons. During the apocalyptic battle for Okinawa, widely seen as a dress rehearsal for a mainland invasion, 265 000 people were killed in a matter of weeks — more than the toll for Hiroshima and Nagasaki put together. In the 1937 Japanese Rape of Nanking (according to the Allied War Crimes Tribunal), 200 000 soldiers and civilians were butchered; according to the Chinese the toll was 300 000. In a single night, March 10–11, 1945, General ('Bombs away with') Curtis LeMay's B-29 bombers burned Tokyo at the stake. He boasted that the napalm-filled fire bombs 'scorched, boiled and baked to death' 197 000 people.

One regrettable consequence of the hyperbole of Hiroshima is that it distracts from the equal awfulness of these 'acceptable' methods of warfare. I visited an exhibition at the futuristic Tokyo Edo Museum which depicted in quite gruesome detail that terrible night when one-third of Tokyo burned to the ground. The official US Army Airforce account ranks the devastation alongside Nero's torching of Rome, the Great Fire of London in 1666 and the San Francisco earthquake of 1906. The charred figures in the photographic montage are piled in the street, barely recognisable as human. All around, for mile after mile, smoke rises from the fields of ash that were once one of the world's most populous and prosperous cities. On the soundtrack, the engines of the B-29 Superfortresses, then the mightiest instrument of warfare ever built, bellow their curse of destruction over the almost-undefended Japanese capital, whose population huddled for shelter in dugouts, in temples and in the icy rivers. Just a few months earlier, the benign and courtly US Secretary of State, Henry Stimson, had explicitly ruled out the use of this sort of 'terror bombing', as he called it.

The bombs dropped on Tokyo that night totalled ten times the tonnage that the Luftwaffe unloaded over London during the entire blitz. And these were no ordinary bombs — they contained napalm, not explosives. Tokyo was the first major trial for a particularly ghastly weapon called the M-69, invented by Dr Vannevar Bush, head of the US Office for Scientific Research and Development (OSRD) at a chemical warfare centre in Dugway, Utah. Models of the weapon on display show that it was a prototype 'cluster bomb' — each 250-kilogram bomb contained thirty-eight bomblets the size of stovepipes and filled with napalm. On impact, they scattered and ignited, each squirting out a thirty-metre jet of flaming gasoline which incinerated anything in its path. According to a friend and fellow physicist, 'For years after the war, Van Bush would wake up screaming in the night because he burned Tokyo. Even the atomic bomb didn't bother him as much as jellied gasoline.'

Those who rage against the atom bombs would do well to reflect that when they were dropped, General LeMay had reached only number sixty-four on the list of 100 Japanese cities scheduled to be cremated. It is beyond rational debate that millions more Japanese civilians would have been killed in this particularly horrible, but apparently acceptable, way if the war had not been brought to an abrupt end.

Admittedly, with conventional warfare, even on this scale, most of the victims are dead within a matter of hours or days. Yet even here — the fear of the long-term effects of the blast of gene-smashing gamma rays and neutrons that accompanied the explosions — there are more myths and misunderstandings. Many of the 186 540 people whose names are inscribed on the cenotaph honour roll did not die because of the bomb — the name of a *hibakusha* (someone who was in or near the city that day) will be added to the list, even if he or she dies in a road accident. Eventually, the record will show that Hiroshima's entire population was killed by the bomb.

We called on Dr Akira Tari, a smart, Western-educated doctor who is chief of internal medicine at the Red Cross Atomic Bomb Survivors' Hospital, the main treatment centre for *hibakusha*. He had 170 beds full of ailing inpatients and said the hospital was treating more than 100 outpatients every day. 'As they get older, more and more cancers are showing up, due to damage to the carcino-suppressor gene,' he told me. Leukaemia and cancers of the lung, liver and thyroid gland, as well as heart and liver disease are prevalent.

However — and this is the point that is often overlooked — massive long-term studies in which 200 000 *hibakusha* have been monitored, have turned up no significant hereditary ill-effects. In the aftermath of the bombing, there was a widespread and hysterical fear that not a blade of grass would grow for seventy-five years. Today, Hiroshima is a thriving industrial city of 1.1 million, and its younger generations, the children and grandchildren of the bomb, are as healthy and long-lived as any other Japanese — although they may suffer irrational discrimination in matters such as marriage. It is one of the war's greater ironies that the children of Hiroshima will live longer than the descendants of the Americans who bombed them.

This is not, of course, to diminish the suffering of the survivors. I particularly remember an old woman named Yukiyo Toda, sitting on the tatami-matting floor of her little cottage on the outskirts of Hiroshima, with her arms protectively around the shoulders of her daughter Hatsumi. Hatsumi is one of the 7000 or so 'mushroom children' of Hiroshima, born with cruel handicaps after being exposed to the neutron blast of the bomb in their mothers' wombs. In Hatsumi's case, she is microcephalic (her head and brain are abnormally small) and totally dependent on her mother, who was then 75 and a widow. Mrs Toda's greatest concern was that she should not die before her daughter, because if she did there would be no-one to look after her. It is impossible not to be moved by stories like hers, but it is also important not to lose sight of the larger picture.

The third great myth of Hiroshima goes something like this: Japan was already beaten, surrender was just a matter of weeks or months away, the Russians had entered the war in Asia, the peace feelers Japan had been putting out were genuine this time and so the bomb was unnecessary — or, at any rate, it was unnecessary to drop it on a city when a 'demonstration' over Tokyo Bay would have had the same effect. Tom Uren, a minister in the Whitlam Labor government of the 1970s and a lifelong peace campaigner, saw the second bomb go off at Nagasaki from the camp where he was held as a prisoner-of-war. He goes even further: 'It was a racist act. It would never have been dropped on a Western, Christian country.'

What this conveniently ignores is the almost supernatural fighting spirit of the Japanese military. You don't have to take my father-in-law's word for it. Listen to General Sir William Slim, later to become Governor-General of Australia, after leading the 14th Army to what was then the greatest land victory of the war, killing 65 000 Japanese at the battle of Imphal-Kohima, near the India–Burma border. 'Everyone talks about fighting to the last man and the last round, but only the Japanese actually do it,' he later wrote. The samurai creed with which the Imperial Army was indoctrinated, and which the army inflicted on the civilian population, was that it is better to die than surrender. If any further proof were required, the terrifying arrival of the kamikaze squadrons at Leyte Gulf provided it — the advent of mass suicide as a battle tactic.

The deeds of the Divine Thunderbolt Corps are bound up with more than a simple accretion of half a century of adulation in Japanese popular culture — they have become a religious cult. They became gods when they died and their spirits reside at Yasukuni shrine, the Vatican of the State Shinto religion which sanctified the war. Pictures in the adjacent war museum show the young suicide pilots, some barely sixteen years old, posing before their last flights in fur-lined flying helmets with the ear muffs cocked like lopsided spaniels. Groups of schoolgirls stand by the runway waving branches of cherry blossom as they fly off to their deaths. A poem is displayed, written in blood on a piece of cloth:

I am twenty
but it is not too young to die
like the cherry-blossom
for the glory of the Emperor.

The reality, as a number of kamikaze pilots who survived explained, was rather more mundane. Sadao Seno, a historian who was training for a *kaiten* (suicide submarine) mission when the war ended, told me most of the good pilots had been killed by October 1944. The high command realised that the 'advantage of kamikazes is that it takes less time to train them; it is easier to dive onto a ship than drop a bomb on it'. Kids were taught that elementary level of flying in a week or ten days. And then, often drugged with mephamphetamines or drunk — one photograph at Yasukuni clearly shows a young pilot standing on the wing of his plane waving a huge bottle of booze — these teenage schoolboys were packed into the cabins of patched-together planes and sent to their deaths. Rather than *'Banzai!'* ('May the Emperor live 10 000 years!') as in the movies, many of them no doubt died with *'oka-san'* ('mother') on their lips.

Some of them could not even take off; they crashed on the runway. One, with a 500-pound bomb bolted onto the fuselage of his plane, strafed the control tower of the airport as he flew off to his death. Kazuo Tsunoda, a fighter ace who escorted many of these young men to their deaths, is angry at the way the kamikazes are romanticised. When we called on him, aged seventy-six and living in retirement near Tokyo, he said, 'I felt angry, watching those planes crash into the ships, watching my friends die. I was angry at the Navy commanders, and I was angry with the government. Why were they allowing the war to continue? I knew we could never win against the Americans, so why had the Emperor agreed to these useless tactics?'

The kamikazes did have a powerful psychological impact on the Allies. Admiral William 'Bull' Halsey, commander of the battle fleet which sustained the first kamikaze attack off the Philippines, wrote, 'The psychology behind it was too alien to us. Americans, who fight to live, find it hard to realise that another people will fight to die. We could not believe that the Japanese, for all their hara kiri tradition, could muster enough recruits to make such a corps really effective.' But, as for their value as a battle tactic, the statistics speak for themselves: about 4000 kamikaze planes dived to their deaths, for the loss of forty-nine Allied warships sunk, many of them small support vessels and none larger than a cruiser.

As well, in weighing up the decision whether to drop the bomb, President Truman would have been well briefed on the fanatical defence put up during the battle for Okinawa. It was a bleak warning of what an invasion of the Japanese home islands would be like. Tough field commanders were sickened by the slaughter. Japanese men, women and children fought tanks, bombers and flame-throwers with bamboo spears, scissors and sharpened farm implements. Thousands jumped off cliffs or killed themselves in the caves that honeycomb the island.

During a visit, we were taken to one of these caves near the town of Yomitan, dimly lit by candles and hung with twisted paper prayers. When the Americans came, all the women of a village were herded here by the Japanese Army and ordered to kill themselves rather than be ravished by the *akaoni*, the 'red-faced devils'. They bathed, brushed their hair and put on their best clothes before cutting their children's throats with razors, and then incinerating themselves with cooking oil. The remains of eighty-four people have been recovered from this one site. In other countries, children go collecting blackberries and mushrooms in the autumn. In Okinawa, every October 10, to commemorate the invasion, they go fossicking for pieces of human bone to give them a decent burial. Still, fifty years after the war, they discover bagsful.

Pounded by artillery, incendiaries, tanks and troops with flame-throwers, organic life ceased to exist on great swathes of the island. Those the Americans didn't kill were slaughtered by the Japanese, who still regard the Okinawans as a separate, and inferior, race. Writes George Feifer, an American authority on Okinawa's holocaust:

> Members of the [Imperial Japanese] 32nd army robbed food, refuge and life from tens of thousands of Okinawans, chiefly women and children, they had come to protect. A small but significant number bayoneted and beheaded innocents, poisoning, choking, drowning and injecting babies to silence them, tossing hand grenades into caves whose civilian occupants had decided to surrender.

Hardly surprisingly, even today, the majority of Okinawans believe the presence of Japanese military bases on the island is as great an affront as the American bases, which they lobby loudly to have removed. In early 1996, following huge public protests over the rape of a schoolgirl by three US servicemen, minor 'consolidations' in the bases were agreed, and some units were to be relocated in other parts of Japan. However, both governments insisted that Okinawa would remain the power base of US security in the region, not least (it was suspected) so the Americans could keep an eye on any resurgent militarism under the hawkish new government of Ryutaro Hashimoto.

In Okinawa, I met a man who has become a focal point for anti-Japanese, as well as anti-US sentiment. He is a supermarket-owner named Shoichi Chibana, who was once arrested for publicly burning a Hinomaru flag in a protest. He calls the wartime emperor 'Hirohitler'. The governor of the island, Masahide Ota, has compiled a gruesome album of photographs and text titled simply *Genocide,* in which he ranks the atrocities committed on Okinawa with the ovens of Belsen, the Rape of Nanking and the killing fields of Cambodia. In eighty-three days of the bloodiest fighting of the Pacific war, about a quarter of a million people, including one-third of the civilian population and 12 000 American troops, were killed.

It was with this in mind that the Allies began planning the invasion of the Japanese home islands. The date had already been set for Operation Olympic, which was due to begin on November 1, 1945, less than three months after the atom bomb was dropped. More than one million US troops were pouring across the Pacific in anything that would float, chanting 'Golden Gate in Forty-eight'. They believed it would be three years of bloody guerilla fighting before they returned to San Francisco. The troops were due to go ashore on the beaches of Kyushu, Japan's southern island, in a D-Day-style landing — and the Japanese, we now know, were waiting for them.

Although the Imperial Navy lay at the bottom of the ocean, Japan still had a formidable fighting machine, with two million men under arms, about 1000 warplanes and the entire coastline bristling with artillery. In the anniversary year of 1995, there was much hypothesising — mainly by revisionist American academics too young to know what war was like — about what the actual death toll would have been if the invasion had gone ahead. In my view, this is monumentally inconsequential. President Truman, who himself had been a combat soldier in World War I, had to rely on the best advice he had at the time. That advice, recently revealed by Chalmers Roberts, who was directly involved as a civilian analyst in assessing intercepted, decoded Japanese military intelligence, was that at least 250 000 US troops would be killed — considerably more than the toll at Hiroshima and Nagasaki. Recent revelations that the United States planned to use massive amounts of poison gas during the invasion means that Japanese casualties would have been many magnitudes larger.

Lieutenant Commander George I. Purdy, a retired navy commander who settled in Japan after the war, would have been part of that invasion. He was anchored off Okinawa when he heard the news of the atomic bombing, and later flew over Hiroshima. 'We were mighty relieved when we heard the news about this new type of bomb … I don't know how many lives the bombing saved — a million? Two million? But we were as sure as hell glad we didn't have to find out,' he told me. Other American veterans have remarked on the political impossibility of a US president going on radio and saying to the mothers and wives of those dead men, 'We had a secret weapon that might have saved them, but we didn't use it because I thought it was wrong.' Unfortunately, the ordinary fighting men who were there at the time — and whose lives were on the line — do not often get to write the histories.

Anyone who still doubts that the Japanese would not have surrendered without the devastation of the atom bombs should read the records of the Imperial Conference, the 'war cabinet' at which Emperor Hirohito presided, and reflect on whether these are the words of a beaten man:

> I believe that, if we fight through, even if it means eating grass and sleeping in the fields, we will be able to find a way out. This is the embodiment of the warrior spirit ... of doing everything to save one's country as long as one has life. I call upon all soldiers to devote themselves to defeating the enemy.

That was War Minister Korechika Anami, Japan's most powerful man (Hirohito, remember, was a god). And this was not 1942 when the Japanese empire was at its height and world conquest seemed just a few months away. He was addressing Cabinet the night Nagasaki was bombed, having already retracted his earlier assessment that 'I am convinced the Americans had only one bomb after all' — surely the most preposterous miscalculation in military history.

Japanese historians understand well that it required a cataclysm, a supernatural event such as the atom bomb, to give Hirohito a mandate to overrule his divided Cabinet. The minutes of that extraordinary midnight meeting survive and leave no doubt why the emperor made his historic decision. Briefed earlier on the bombing, and (according to one witness) with tears in his eyes, he said, 'I fear for the very survival of the

Japanese race. In order to hand down the nation called Japan to posterity, there is no alternative for me but to keep as many of its people alive [as possible] so that they may again stand on their own feet.' In his surrender speech broadcast two days later, when he famously remarked that 'the war has been progressing, not necessarily to our advantage', the emperor referred specifically to the 'new type of bomb'.

As for dropping a 'demonstration bomb' somewhere like Mount Fuji, the Manhattan Project scientists and the military argued strongly against this. The scientists were opposed to this because they could not guarantee the thing would work — serious odds were offered against it in the betting ring at Almagordo where it was tested — and a failure would certainly encourage the Japanese to fight on. The military argued against it because the Japanese high command had issued orders that every prisoner of war — they held about 100 000 Americans, Australians, British and others — be killed the moment an invasion of the mainland became imminent. Methods authorised in writing included shooting, starving to death, hanging and poisoning.

What about Tom Uren's Western Christians? The war in Europe was by then, of course, long over, but most involved believe President Truman would have been only too happy if the bomb had been built in time to be dropped on Berlin and save all those hundreds of thousands of Allied lives. As for Nagasaki — it is an ancient treaty port, and had the highest concentration of foreigners of almost any city in Japan. Many thousands of the bombing victims were ethnic Koreans, Chinese and, yes, some Europeans. This can not have been unknown to President Truman's advisers, who were so careful to spare the treasures of the historic capital of Kyoto, which had been on the original target list.

The other awful irony is that the Nagasaki bomb exploded slap bang on top of Asia's largest Catholic Cathedral, instantly uniting the priest and his congregation, who were celebrating Mass at that precise moment, with their Maker. All told, some 14 000 Christians were killed by the bomb, many of them descended from people converted by the Basque Saint Francis Xavier whose faith had survived centuries of persecution. Some of the survivors believe that this was divine retribution on Japan for having started the war. It is said that the symbol of Hiroshima is a clenched fist; the symbol of Nagasaki is two hands joined in prayer.

Finally, one might legitimately ask, if there were anything intrinsically evil about nuclear weapons, why does Japan keep its own nuclear options open while lecturing the world from the pulpit of its victimhood that they are both morally repugnant and illegal? The country is in the process of building up an enormous stockpile of plutonium to feed its out-of-control fast-breeder reactor program. No-one seriously doubts that it has the technology to turn this quite quickly into an arsenal of bombs many times the magnitude of Hiroshima, nor that Japan's HII rocket could be adapted to deliver it. Indeed, Henry Kissinger testified recently that he fully expects Japan to 'go nuclear' next century — and perhaps sooner, if America were to withdraw the 'nuclear umbrella' under which it now shelters.

There is ample evidence that Japan not only possesses the plutonium and the know-how, but actually worked on developing a bomb during World War II. I went along to the Foreign Correspondents' Club one day to listen to Japan's Robert Oppenheimer, a remarkably sprightly 83-year-old nuclear physicist named Tatsusaburo Suzuki, describe how his fifty-man team managed to separate fissionable uranium-235 — the core of the atom bomb — by 1945. Dr Suzuki was proud of his achievement, and said that if he had been given the resources, he could have built a workable bomb in twelve months. Curiously, the white-haired old scientist condemned the bombing of Hiroshima and Nagasaki, but when asked whether Japan would have dropped the bomb on America, replied, 'We had no doubts about using it if we could.'

Adding weight to Japan's nuclear ambiguity, the *Mainichi* newspaper recently unearthed what looked like conclusive evidence — a secret 1969 Foreign Ministry policy paper which declared, duplicitously, 'For the time being, we will adopt a policy of not possessing nuclear arms. But we will maintain the economic and technical potential of producing nuclear weapons ... we must protect this [potential] from foreign intervention.' When this came out, the Foreign Ministry waffled rather unconvincingly that it was ancient history, and that Japan's policy now was neither to possess, use nor allow nuclear weapons on its soil. This policy, however, has fallen into considerable disrepute since the revelation that successive Japanese governments have allowed US planes and ships carrying nuclear weapons to operate from Japanese bases.

Unfortunately — unlike Australia and the United States where 1995 was the trigger for an avalanche of analysis — little fresh thinking took place in Japan over the use of the bomb, or any of the other unresolved issues left over from the war. Yes, the Hiroshima museum finally got to open 'Aggression Corner'. Yes, the doughty Saburo Ienaga continued his forty-year-old fight to have Japan's history texts rewritten to reflect the reality of the war, although I doubt he would have called it a vintage year. The Education Ministry again red-pencilled an attempt to put the number of dead in the Nanking massacre at 200 000 ('Various experts have disagreed over the exact toll.'). And the bureaucrats demanded an entire section of one schoolbook be rewritten, omitting this outrageous sentence: 'The Japanese national flag has been taken by people of other Asian countries as a symbol of wartime aggression.' They insisted it be replaced by: 'The *hinomaru* has existed for more than a century, and should be respected regardless of Japan's wartime acts.'

Little wonder the Japanese are so vulnerable to the myths and misrepresentations of officialdom. The state of historical scholarship is lamentable, and the study of history itself, particularly modern history, including World War II, is regarded as somewhat academically disreputable. The Japanese military ordered most of their records destroyed when the war ended. Those that survived are held secretly and uncategorised in government repositories. Japan has no freedom of information law and no requirement that government documents be released after a specified time. It was not until forty-eight years after the war that a scholar unearthed proof of the 'comfort women' — slave prostitutes used by the Japanese military — whose very existence had been denied by successive governments.

One young history teacher I questioned about this said there was simply not enough time to teach the complete curriculum, so he often had to graduate entire classes without teaching them anything about 'modern history'. When I asked him what he meant by modern, he said, 'After the Meiji Restoration,' which took place in 1868. Many Japanese, as a result, are knowledgeable about ancient emperors who never existed, but know nothing about the twentieth century. A scholarly survey of the Japanese born since the war found that one in ten believed America had been Japan's ally, and two in ten did not believe the Japanese army had ever been in China.

Another black hole in Japanese history — and a vivid contrast with the way Germany dealt with its past — is the refusal even to acknowledge that its army committed war crimes. I became particularly interested in one atrocity story, that of Unit 731, Japan's infamous biological weapons research centre at Harbin in northeast China. My curiosity was first aroused when one of Japan's revisionist historians discovered, in a long-hidden wartime archive, evidence that Japan had planned to attack Australia with a diabolical weapon. Rats carrying fleas infected with bubonic plague — the dreaded 'black death' that ravaged medieval Europe — were to be transported by submarine and released in the streets of Sydney, Melbourne and Adelaide. What finally made me determined to go to Harbin, however, was when a Foreign Ministry spokesman denied point blank that Unit 731 had ever existed.

It existed alright, but the evidence only just survives. As they fled before the advancing Russian troops, the 'Imperial Water Purification Unit', as they called themselves, murdered everyone in sight, incinerated the bodies and then dynamited every building. All that's left is the gaunt skeleton of the former boiler-room, a pen where squirrels were bred and a cool room where people were frozen to death to test their resistance to cold. The rest you have to imagine, with the help of a small museum which has been established by a man named Han Xiao, a Communist Party functionary who has devoted his life to collecting relics, documents and witnesses to what happened at this 'Asian Auschwitz'.

The ruins are at a small town near Harbin called Ping Fan, which means 'one storey' in Chinese. No-one was allowed to build higher than this, for fear they would see the horrors going on behind the high walls. Under the leadership of a charismatic psychopath named Shiro Ishii — a man so gross that he once urinated through a water filter, then handed a glass of the liquid to the emperor to drink — Japan conducted a Manhattan Project of germs. Ping Fan was just one of eighteen 'death factories' located throughout Asia. It was an enormous, top-secret enterprise that consumed (in today's money) $20 million a year and employed thousands of people. It was personally approved by Emperor Hirohito, who awarded Ishii the Golden Kite (3rd order) and the Rising Sun (middle chord) he wore on his chest.

Survivors I spoke to (who included Japanese doctors who had since repented, as well as relatives of the Chinese and Korean guinea pigs) recounted some of the experiments conducted on the *maruta* or 'logs' as Ishii called them. People were infected with every imaginable disease, from plague to haemorrhagic fever, anthrax, tuberculosis, dysentery, cholera and gas gangrene. Babies were frozen to death to test their resistance to cold. The blood of horses was transfused into humans. People were injected with *fugu* fish poison, electrocuted and killed with phosgene gas. Some of the experiments were so grotesquely sadistic they can have had no conceivable scientific purpose — one man had his leg amputated and his arm sewn on in its place.

From surviving records it can be deduced that 3000 people died as a direct result of these experiments. One can only guess how many more perished in the epidemics Ishii unleashed on the countryside — 250 000 seems a reasonable estimate. When the Japanese abandoned the facility, they released hundreds of infected experimental animals, causing epidemics of plague that persist to this day. The ultimate irony was that Ishii was never able to develop a useable germ weapon. His attempts resulted only in the indiscriminate slaughter of civilian populations and the unintended deaths of some 1700 Japanese soldiers.

Apart from being a well-documented casebook study of the violation of every internationally understood principle of human rights (not to mention the 1925 Geneva Armament Convention), there are other reasons the Japanese government should drop its absurd pretence that Unit 731 never existed. What happened to Ishii and the other ring leaders sheds light on some of the sordid deals that were done after the war. To get their hands on Ishii's data for their own biological warfare experiments, the Americans guaranteed these war criminals immunity from prosecution. The only reason this story can be told is that the records are held not in Japan where they would have been hidden or destroyed, but at the US Army's chemical and biological warfare establishment at Dugway, Utah. Ishii and his lieutenants were rehabilitated and went on to become Japan's postwar medical Establishment, controlling all the important university medical schools, research establishments and the health ministry itself.

For me, this anniversary was a particular education because I also began the year with only the vaguest understanding of the Pacific war. I grew up in England. Hitler, not Hirohito, was the demon figure of my childhood, and my nightmares were the skin and bones of Auschwitz and Buchenwald, not the living dead of the Burma Railway. I had not been brought up, as Australians of my generation were, with posters depicting villainous Japanese soldiers with babies impaled on their bayonets marching down the Malayan peninsula in the general direction of Bexley. Consequently I had to spend much of 1995 burrowing through libraries and interviewing very old men.

What I found striking was the similarity between Germany and Japan at war — and the enormous contrast in the way each, after defeat, set about repairing the national psyche. Both were possessed of a sense of their racial superiority — some Japanese still imagine themselves a sort of Asian *herrenvolk* — divine mission and military invincibility. Both invaded and enslaved their neighbours, and committed terrible atrocities. Both were led by military dictators who dreamt of a global empire, and both suffered catastrophic defeats. And yet, fifty years later, Germany has long ago been absolved of its guilt, while Japan is still in a state of denial.

Here, I think, is the key. While Germany purged itself of Nazism and built new, democratic institutions on the ruins, in Japan, after a brief period of occupational penitence, the *ancien regime* quickly reasserted itself. The past cannot be exorcised, because the past is the present. Japan is the dark kingdom, where Adolf Hitler never died, but lived on to a ripe old age — opening parliament, appointing governments, hobnobbing with heads of state, stripped of his absolute powers and renouncing his divinity, but still worshipped by his people. It is the country where schoolchildren still line up each morning to salute the swastika and sing the Horst Wessel song, the anthem of the Hitler Youth; and where government ministers regularly pronounce that Auschwitz never happened and the invasion of Poland, Czechoslovakia, Holland and France was really aimed at 'liberating' those unfortunate countries.

Make a few substitutions, and this is not far from the reality of Japan fifty years after the war. For Hitler read Hirohito, for the swastika the rising sun flag and the *kimigayo* (literally 'His Majesty's Reign') for the anthem. There you have, in 1995, the imperial symbols of the Japanese Reich in whose name the war was fought. Half a century after Germany purged itself of Nazism, the 'Emperor System', as its critics call it, is alive and well in Japan. Even the much-vaunted 'peace constitution' foisted on Japan by the Americans preserves this continuity. It is, after all, merely a modification of the Meiji constitution introduced by Hirohito's grandfather.

By contrast, in Germany, the death of Hitler, the execution of his marshals and ministers, and the birth of a new republic provided a cathartic break with the past. Germany got a new flag, a new national anthem and a genuinely new constitution. Its history books face the Nazi past with unflinching honesty. In its determination never to forget the horrors of the Holocaust, German schoolchildren are taken to visit the sites of the extermination camps as a part of their education. Today, writes Ian Buruma, one of the most informed and perceptive writers on this subject, it seems the whole nation is consumed by its collective responsibility. It wallows in *trauerarbeit*, the 'labour of mourning', the essence of Germany's postwar purification and the precondition for its rehabilitation.

Compensation for Hitler's victims is no longer an issue — all outstanding claims were settled decades ago. If cash can be taken as some measure of remorse, the Germans again occupy the high moral ground — they have paid out some $92 billion over the years, with an estimated $36 billion to come in pensions and suchlike. The Japanese maintain that they settled all claims (except those of North Korea) under treaties in the 1960s, but Japan's reparations came to a paltry $3.3 billion, or one-fortieth the amount Germany came up with. Germany's rehabilitation is complete. As the century ends, it stands not just as one of the world's most successful economies, but as the mainstay of European security, with a rightful claim to a place at the global top table, the United Nations Security Council. Japan's rehabilitation has barely begun.

As the fateful fiftieth anniversary approached, defending Japan's official fiction of the war became an almost full-time occupation for successive administrations. What the rest of the world treats as history was front page news day after day after day. Ministers shot their mouths off and had to be sacked. A sorry and seemingly endless parade of victims demonstrated outside Japan's embassies around the world, appealed to the United Nations and queued in the Tokyo courts for the acknowledgment and justice denied them for half a century. Among them were Korean 'comfort women', slave prostitutes forced to work in front-line brothels; Taiwanese kidnapped to labour in the mines and munitions factories; Hong Kong people whose savings were confiscated; survivors of Arctic tribes conscripted and driven to extinction; Chinese victims of germ warfare experiments; relatives of massacred Papua New Guinean villagers; and British and Australian prisoners of war subjected to unspeakable brutality.

August is known in Japan as the 'apology season'. It is the time of Obon, the midsummer festival, when the Japanese return to their home towns to light bonfires to attract the spirits of their ancestors. It is the time when the nation's Shinto shrines resound to cries of *'Banzai!'* as old soldiers gather to remember their fallen comrades. And it is the time when Japan's erstwhile foes — particularly China and Korea — watch carefully to see if they can detect any sign of remorse in the official commemorations of the war's end; any hint that Japan is yet ready to acknowledge its past and be readmitted as a fully trusted member of the international community. This annual ritual has been going on for nearly forty years now, since prime minister Nobusuke Kishi undertook an eight-nation pilgrimage in 1957, and it is a handy barometer to the militaristic inclinations of the government of the day. Needless to say, what apologies are forthcoming are never enough.

Morihiro Hosokawa, the stylish aristocrat who overthrew thirty-eight years of conservative government in the summer of 1993, raised the hopes of Japan's neighbours that at long last there might be a change of heart. During a historic visit to Korea, he made a forthright declaration that World War II had been a 'war of aggression and a wrongful war'. This self-evident truth, which would be regarded as a bland truism anywhere else, sent his Foreign Ministry minders into fits. They even released a watered-down 'official' version of the speech to try and prevent the apology being reported back home. Later, a right-wing loony tried to shoot Hosokawa. The apology was especially poignant considering his grandfather was the weak and vacillating Prince Fumimaro Konoye who twice served as prime minister during the war, and who killed himself by swallowing cyanide just before his scheduled arrest for war crimes.

Hosokawa, however, was soon no longer prime minister, and the initiative petered out under the administrations that followed. Plans to finally draw a line under all this ancient history and get on with the next century — plans for a comprehensive apology by way of parliamentary resolution, for compensation and for correction of the historical record — were announced by the next prime minister-but-one, Tomiichi Murayama. His Social Democratic Party had had such atonement and reconciliation as an integral part of its foreign policy since it was formed in 1945. However, Murayama's allies in the coalition, the conservative Liberal Democrats who had been their arch foes for forty years, had other ideas.

For nearly a year, a bitter behind-the-scenes wrangle about the wording of the anniversary resolution threatened to bring down the government. Eventually, Mr Murayama had to threaten to resign to achieve a compromise. And what a contemptible compromise it was that emerged from that smoky backroom, a travesty of carefully crafted ambiguities that demeaned the whole process of atonement to the level of 'the dog ate my homework'. Japan admitted to 'acts of aggression' and 'colonial rule', but said that it was only one of many countries responsible for such conduct. It offered condolences for the 'unbearable suffering' caused by the war, but in the same breath extended the same sympathy to the kin of Hirohito's soldiers who caused it. Mr Murayama had to delete a promise that Japan would not repeat such aggression, and he had to delete all use of the word apology. This is the weaselish draft that was finally presented to the House of Representatives on the night of June 9, 1995:

> This Diet, in the fiftieth year after the war, offers its sincere tribute to the memory of the war dead throughout the world, and victims who suffered because of war and other deeds.
> Recalling the many instances of colonial rule and acts of aggression in the modern history of the world, we recognise those acts which our country carried out,

and the unbearable suffering inflicted on the peoples of other countries, particularly the nations of Asia, and express deep remorse.*

Transcending the differences in historical views of the past war, we must humbly learn the lessons of history, and build a peaceful international community.

This Diet links hands with the countries of the world, under the doctrine of everlasting peace enshrined in the constitution of Japan, and expresses its determination to open up a future of coexistence for humankind.

Even so, fewer than half the 510 members of the lower house could be persuaded to turn out to vote for this vacuous verbiage. The upper house refused to vote on it at all. There were swathes of empty seats in the chamber — LDP hardliners stayed away because the resolution was too tough, the Shinshinto opposition because it did not go far enough and a number of MPs simply could not be bothered and went home for the weekend. As a final irony, the sponsors of the motion raised their arms in the air and roared *'Banzai!'* as they presented the motion to the Speaker. *'Tenno heika banzai!'* ('May His Imperial Majesty live 10 000 years!') was the rallying cry of the Japanese military throughout the war.

None of the real issues was dealt with in any substantive way. There was no mention of revising the history texts. Grand plans for a $5 billion fund to compensate surviving war victims were quietly dropped. A 'private' fund was established to compensate the 'comfort women', but the government refused to contribute, claiming Japan had made full and final reparations under the San Francisco Treaty.

After all the anguish, it would really have been better for Japan to have done nothing at all. The compromise was put together for domestic political reasons — Mr Murayama was

---

* *I am being charitable here. The actual word used was* hansei, *which literally translates as 'self-reflection'. For instance, a child may 'self-reflect' over a failure to do its homework.*

facing an election the following month at which his party was to be decimated and he desperately needed a political win to make up for the policies he traded away in exchange for LDP support for his premiership. Internationally, the resolution served only to remind the world — and particularly Japan's Asian neighbours, who suffered so grievously under Japanese occupation — that Japan was still not ready to face up to its past. And so neither was it ready to be trusted with a role in regional security and diplomacy more in keeping with its economic power, let alone the seat on the United Nations Security Council after which its Foreign Ministry slavers.

In Seoul, students firebombed a Japanese cultural centre and burned effigies of the LDP don and former foreign minister Michio Watanabe in the street. He had chosen this, of all times, to remark that Japan's bloody annexation of Korea had been 'peaceful'. In Beijing, the Foreign Ministry condemned the resolution and said Japan's refusal to face up to its past placed a strain on the bilateral relationship. Curiously, the only country reported in Japan to have welcomed the resolution was Australia, but perhaps that's not so surprising, given the Australian government's long-standing policy of the pre-emptive genuflect to Japan on just about any issue. Just a few months before, they had enraged many war veterans by renaming VJ Day (Victory over Japan), as it had been commemorated for forty-nine years, 'VP Day' (Victory in the Pacific) — apparently for fear of offending 'Our Most Important Trading Partner', as the Foreign Affairs mantra has it.

So, fifty years after the war, Japan stood, an awkward, lonely figure on the fringes of Asia — admired for its economic achievements, courted for its yen, but still deeply mistrusted for its failure to atone for its past. Is Helmut Kohl, the German Chancellor, jeered and abused when he flies in for talks at the Elysées Palace, 10 Downing Street or 1600 Pennsylvania Avenue? Of course not. The most pressing international obligation of the new French President Jacques Chirac, even before his inauguration, was a hurried trip to Alsace where he and his long-ago enemy 'Helmut' (Kohl) chugged beer in a bar and did not even mention the war.

Yet, when Tomiichi Murayama, the gormless grandpa who somehow found himself prime minister of Japan, winged his way around Asia on his inaugural junket, he was met with the public hostility that still greets any Japanese leader. In Malaysia, he was heckled by 'comfort women'; in the Philippines, mass demonstrations forced the cancellation of an aid project; and in Vietnam, he was reminded that Japanese agricultural policies had resulted in two million of the Vietnamese 'liberated' from French rule dying of starvation in 1944 alone. In Singapore, he was lectured by the *Business Times* on Japan's war responsibility: 'Only when Mr Murayama can convince Asian leaders that these pretend samurai are the rump of a misguided generation, and nothing more, can Japan and other Asian countries elevate their ties to the next level.'

When Murayama paid his first visit to China the following year, 1995, he was unable to deliver on his promise of the parliamentary resolution atoning for the war that he had promised. There was no buddying in the bar with Jiang Zemin. His hosts pursed their lips and led the old man past an exhibition of Japanese atrocities at the Marco Polo Bridge outside Beijing. This is the place where, in 1937, the 'incident' took place which Japan used as a justification for launching the all-out war that China maintains killed more than twenty million of its citizens.

The 'pretend samurai' referred to in the newspaper editorial were the latest crop of government ministers who had had to be sacked for outrageous calumnies about Japan's conduct during the war — still, scarcely believably, a regular feature of Japanese public life. In six years, four ministers were forced to resign, and two or three more were lucky to survive. In a way, you had to feel sorry for them — their only real offence was to say out loud what many Japanese believe privately. One declared that the Rape of Nanking, Japan's most atrocious war crime in which upwards of 200 000 civilians died after being raped, castrated, disembowelled, beheaded, impaled and buried alive was a 'fabrication'. Another opined that Korea had actually benefited from the civilising influence of Japanese occupation, much as Africans had from European colonisation. A third repeated that tired canard — that Japan's invasion of its Asian neighbours was, in reality, to liberate them from colonial bondage.

I do not wish to belabour the point. The ministers, after all, were quite properly sacked, although after several days' dithering. However, I could not help noticing just a few months later a report from Frankfurt that more than eighty neo-Nazis had been arrested for possession of propaganda, weapons and racist music tapes while marking what would have been Hitler's 106th birthday. Among them was the unpleasant Mr Guenter Deckert, who was subsequently jailed for two years for denying that more than a million Jews died in the Auschwitz concentration camp — a crime in Germany. Japan, by contrast, has no anti-racism laws of any sort, let alone laws outlawing the sort of 'blood libel' of which its ministers are regularly guilty.

A large part of the blame for this — Germany's rehabilitation, Japan's denial — lies in the different ways in which the Allies treated their vanquished foes. In Germany, those judged war criminals were executed or jailed in their hundreds, the great wartime corporations were dismantled and public office was purged in a ruthless de-Nazification drive. In Japan, fearful of social collapse and anxious to build a bulwark against the advances of Communism on the Asian mainland, the Americans made a decision that would have been unthinkable in Europe. They restored to his throne the man in whose name the war had been fought. The pay-off, of course, was that fifty years after World War II, and five years after the Cold War ended, Japan remained America's unsinkable aircraft carrier, the cornerstone of its Asia–Pacific security strategy.

This policy was vigorously opposed at the time by the Australians, who were aware more than most of the horrors of Changi, Sandakan and the Burma Railway. It is a decision which the subsequent fifty years have failed to vindicate clearly. Many still argue that the world's war wounds would have healed more quickly and more cleanly if Hirohito had been executed, or if he had been made to accept his moral responsibility and commit *seppuku* (ritual suicide) like so many of his soldiers. At the very least, they feel he should be forced to abdicate. A dozen times during my stay in Japan people of that wartime generation, civilians as well as old soldiers, have justified anything, and everything, done during the war by saying: 'How can you say Japan did wrong? It was all done in the Emperor's name, and he was not punished. We just obeyed his orders.'

Nor were significant numbers of Hirohito's generals and ministers convicted at the Tokyo war crimes trials. Twenty-eight 'class A' war criminals (the worst sort) were placed on trial; just seven of them were eventually hanged at Sugamo Jail, including prime minister Hideki Tojo, who, it was generally agreed, took the rap for his emperor. Some 4000 Japanese guilty of the most hideous crimes imaginable under the old regime were released from jail, quietly rehabilitated and installed in positions of power in the new postwar institutions — government, industry and the bureaucracy. This, surely, is the real reason Japan cannot accept its guilt — the system that was responsible for the war is still in place. To condemn it would be to condemn today's power-holders as surely as those of yesteryear.

There can be no more poignant irony than the fact that at precisely the time, in 1960, that Adolf Eichmann was in the dock in Jerusalem for masterminding the genocide of six million Jews — the crime against humanity for which he was subsequently executed — Nobusuke Kishi was serving as prime minister of Japan. Kishi, a wartime vice-minister of munitions and gauleiter of occupied Manchuria, was responsible for the gulag in which more than a million slave labourers — most of them Korean and Chinese — were forced to work in conditions of frightful cruelty and deprivation. Tens of thousands of them died. Kishi was arrested as a class A war criminal, but was released, his reputation intact, after just a couple of years in prison and resumed his political career. The Americans could not have asked for a more obliging puppet. As prime minister in the late 1950s (so newly discovered archival records show), he even did his best to dampen public revulsion against US nuclear testing.

As the August 15 anniversary approached, the day Hirohito finally broadcast Japan's surrender, Yasukuni moved to centre stage. I went there one afternoon with Mayu and her father, who was researching a schoolmate who died on a suicide submarine mission. It is an impressive place — a great *torii* arch towering twenty metres over gravelled paths where the right-wingers in their black trucks rendezvous before demonstrations to receive a pep talk and *'Banzai!'* in the direction of the imperial palace. An avenue of cherry trees where people gather to drink and sing during the spring *hanami* festival, showered by the evanescent pink petals that symbolise the kamikaze pilots, leads to the huge bulk of the shrine itself, built of cypress logs and emblazoned with the imperial symbol of the gilded chrysanthemum.

The shrine exists 'to worship the divine spirits of those who gave their lives in defence of the empire of Japan'. In the theology of State Shinto, a young priest explained, those who lay down their lives for the emperor become immortals or 'living gods'. On the parchment scrolls kept by the priests who guard the shrine are recorded the names of 2 460 000 men who were deified in this manner in the service of the last three emperors.

A brass plaque lists the dates of those wars — an extraordinarily long list that includes three civil wars, the defeat of China and Russia, World War I and the conquest of Manchuria. Japan had hardly a dozen consecutive years of peace in the century after it ended its long isolation in the mid-1800s. Long before 1939, it had become a predatory, expansionist imperial power which gobbled up an expanse of territory four times larger than the home islands themselves — Taiwan, Korea, the Ryukyus and the Kuriles, half of Sakhalin Island and Manchuria. World War II, which is all the West is usually taught about Japanese militarism, was merely the most ambitious of those adventures — and the only one Japan lost. The Marxist writer Hayashi Fusao, jailed for his views in the 1930s, refers to this period as 'the 100 years' war'.

As well, Yasukuni has within its grounds what amounts to Japan's national war museum. Sitting in the shade of the ginkgo trees are the massive weapons Japan used to wage its wars on the world: giant field guns recovered from the bloody conquest of Manchuria (referred to in the guidebook as 'The Chinese Incident'); shells weighing a tonne or more from long-sunk battleships; the rusty hulls of *kaiten* human torpedoes, iron coffins packed with explosives which were to be Japan's last-ditch defence against the invading Allies. Inside showcases display rising sun flags signed in blood, photographs of the young kamikaze pilots, and the swords and uniforms of the generals.

If this was all there was to Yasukuni, a national war memorial, there would be little controversy and little reason for the obsessive attention the shrine draws as the annual anniversary comes around. But there is, of course, more than that. To many Japanese, attendance at the shrine symbolises a celebration, not just a commemoration, of war; a perpetuation of the worship of the emperor in whose name it was fought; and homage to State Shinto which sanctified it. Most repugnant of all was the secret inclusion (revealed only in 1979) on the honour roll of 'living gods' of hundreds of war criminals, including General Tojo, Japan's prime minister for most of the war, and the six other Class A war criminals hanged for their crimes in 1948.

Attendance by politicians at the shrine is closely watched by countries such as Korea and China, and is regarded as a litmus test of contrition for the war by the government of the day. In spite of attempts to discourage the practice (the last prime minister to visit in an official capacity had been Yasuhiro Nakasone in 1985), prominent members of both the government and the opposition continued to bow and *'Banzai!'* at the shrine throughout the three 'reform' administrations that followed the dethroning of the Liberal Democratic Party (LDP) in 1993.

Those hoping for a new beginning from the government of the erstwhile pacifist Tomiichi Murayama to mark the fiftieth anniversary of the war's end were bitterly disappointed. More than 200 of the 300 LDP MPs in his coalition paid homage at the shrine. They were led by party heavyweights including the oleaginous trade minister Ryutaro Hashimoto. Two years later, Mr Hashimoto was elected prime minister, succeeding the hapless Mr Murayama and completing the LDP's resurgence, destroying for another few years — or perhaps forever — any hope of Japan truly acknowledging its past. In 1996, ignoring international outrage, Hashimoto resumed the custom of worshipping at Yasukuni shrine.

However, many critics overlook the realpolitik of all this. The ceremonies at Yasukuni are not simply the ugly face of Japanese neo-militarism on display. Hashimoto was also president of the Association of War Bereaved Families which, with more than a million members, is one of Japan's most powerful lobby groups and the source of serious election money. The association's parliamentary *zoku*, the welfare ministry special interest 'tribe', is one of the most influential in the Diet. This is the same gang who were responsible for humiliating prime minister Murayama by gutting his war apology resolution.

The leader of this group, for those who still puzzle about Japan's lack of repentance for its war crimes, was none other than Seisuke Okuno, a prewar fossil still influential in LDP politics at the age of eighty-eight. Okuno was an officer in Japan's equivalent of the Gestapo, and is on record as saying that younger Japanese have been 'brainwashed by the erroneous education prevalent in the postwar period which characterises Japan as the aggressor'. The same Mr Okuno led the LDP committee which commissioned the notorious new history of World War II referred to earlier.

It would be unfair to pretend that all the Japanese share these views. As Mr Okuno fears, many younger Japanese, particularly those educated abroad or at private schools, have an understanding of the war quite at odds with the official version. Many more neither know nor care much about the war. Some older Japanese who were there, like my father-in-law, believe that people who deny Japan's aggression are *baka* — 'mad'. However, they are not the power-holders. It is men like Hashimoto who uphold the official mythology, and until power passes to the next generation and perhaps the generation after that, Japan will not be able to finally lay the ghosts of history to rest.

As I sat, reflecting on the war stories that dominated coverage of Japan during that anniversary year and trying to put my own thoughts in some sort of coherent order, I tuned to the Cable News Network. It was the anniversary of the liberation of Auschwitz and I saw, with some surprise, that a number of young German soldiers had been invited to lay wreaths. Some of them were openly weeping as they stood in front of the 'death wall' where so many innocent civilians, a million and a half of them, were put to death.

Suddenly, it all came together. I had no doubt, as I watched this sombre and moving display of genuine grief, that Japan would never be truly trusted again, would never be ready to be accepted back into the community of civilised nations, until some young Japanese soldiers — and politicians, bureaucrats and businessmen — lay wreaths and weep at the memorials to the dead of Nanking, Ping Fang, Sandakan and all the other killing fields of the Asian holocaust. Whether it takes fifty years or 500, one day the truth, as Richard von Weizsacker said, has to be acknowledged.

THE '100-YEAR WAR'

1853   Admiral William Perry's 'black ships' reopen Japan after
                three centuries of isolation.

1860–68   Civil wars lead to the overthrow of the shogunate, the
                'restoration' of the Meiji Emperor, and the transfer of the
                capital from Kyoto to Tokyo.

1874   'Punitive expedition' against Formosa (now Taiwan).

1879   Chinese-claimed Ryukyu Islands incorporated into Japan.

1894–95   China defeated in Sino-Japanese war; cedes Taiwan to
                Japan.

1904–05   Russian fleet sunk; Russia cedes southern Manchuria and
                half Sakhalin Island to Japan.

1910   Korean peninsula formally annexed.

1914–18   Japan enters World War I on the side of the Allies; attacks
                German possessions in the Pacific and China; wins
                territorial concessions in Treaty of Versailles.

1931   'Manchurian Incident' used as a pretext to occupy
                Manchuria. Puppet state of Manchukuo established under
                the last emperor, Pu Yi.

1937   'China Incident' signals start of full-scale invasion of China.
                Major capitals, including Nanking, Hankow and Canton
                captured.

1941   Japan attacks Pearl Harbour. United States enters Pacific
                War.

1941–43   Japan conquers about a quarter of the earth's surface,
                including most of China, eastern Russia, the Philippines,
                eastern Pacific, and Southeast Asia; attacks India, Sri Lanka,
                Australia and the United States.

1945   Atomic bombing ends World War II.

'GANBATTE,' WHISPERS THE ELDERLY GENT ON MY right as the floodlights blaze in our eyes. 'Go for it.'

I am about to be initiated in one of Japan's most arcane national rituals. Not the tea ceremony. Not kendo swordsmanship. Not the ancient masked opera of *noh*. Not even sumo wrestling, though we are in the right place for it. From the walls, huge paintings of champions past glare down on the great vaulted amphitheatre of Tokyo's Kokugikan, the Lords or Wembley of sumo.

Today, however, the pine-log shrine that normally hangs over the ring has been hoisted into the rafters, and the mound of mud on which the loin-clothed whale-men shove each other around has been levelled to provide a pink-carpeted stage. On it, under the baton of Naoto Ohtomo, two great symphony orchestras, the New Japan Philharmonic and the Tokyo Symphony Orchestra, wait for the cue, 100 bows poised over 100 violins.

A blare of brass, a thunder of drums, and the voice of the tenor soars through the uproar.

'Freude!' sings Ken Nishikiori.

'Freude!' we bellow back from the bleachers.

Another performance of *Dai ku,* as Beethoven's Ninth Symphony is known in Japan, is reaching its climax, and the world's biggest choir is in fine voice. Almost 10 000 people have packed the sumo stadium this spring afternoon, and 5000 of them are in the choir. With their bow ties, tuxedos, white blouses and long black skirts, they slightly outnumber their more casually dressed friends and relatives who make up the audience.

Beethoven would, no doubt, find it bizarre, but his last and (some would say) greatest symphony — and particularly its climactic fourth movement, with the words of Schiller's grandiloquent *Ode to Joy* — is more popular

JOY, JAPANESE—STYLE

in Japan than the Beatles *and* Jesus Christ. It is the all-time classical music hit and copies of the record (Wave, a shop in Roppongi, has more than 100 versions on its shelves) outsell many popular groups. The favourite is still Wilhelm Furtwangler conducting the Beyreuth Festival Orchestra.

First performed in Japan in 1918 by homesick German prisoners-of-war in a concentration camp on Shikoku island, *Dai ku* ('Number Nine') is the country's favourite piece of music. Compact discs are about eighty minutes long because Akio Morita, then the chairman of Sony, which invented them, gave instructions that they must be able to record the Ninth on one side.

Other countries (Rhodesia, now Zimbabwe, and more recently the European Union) have adopted it as their official anthem. But nowhere in the world is it celebrated so enthusiastically by the general public — most of whom would be hard put to name any other composer, apart, perhaps from the Roringu Stons, as the Japanese call Mick Jagger's perennial rockers.

No-one has any idea how many times it is performed, but it is a safe bet that any day of the week, any week of the year, someone, somewhere will at least be singing the chorus of *Dai ku*. It has become a particular tradition for year's end. In December 1995, no fewer than 180 performances in Tokyo alone were scheduled, six a night for a month. It is performed on occasions like high school graduation, the opening ceremonies for public buildings, company birthdays and Rotary conventions. It is the campaign anthem of Shinshinto, Japan's new opposition party. Also, Japan being Japan, it is used to sell everything from cars to coffee, whisky, Sapporo noodles, even (roll over Beethoven) Macdonald's hamburgers.

Why this extraordinary appeal? Sadamitsu Ishii, the

man who has organised the annual *Dai ku* concert in the sumo stadium for the past eleven years, says Japanese admire Beethoven's spirit — his triumph over the adversity of poverty and deafness — and respond to the universality, the *millionen*, of the Ninth.

'Also,' he adds more prosaically, 'the chorale is short. Japanese don't like performances that go on for ever and ever. They are like kamikazes — they like things in short bursts.'

Americans may dream of their fifteen minutes of fame. For the Japanese, it's eighteen minutes and eleven seconds, the time it takes to perform the chorale.

It is very much a participation event. In hired halls in every nook of the country — from the metropolis of Tokyo to the tiniest hamlet in Hokkaido — tens of thousands of Japanese struggle, not always successfully, with words like *flugelwild* and *gotterfunken*. There are 100 choirs that sing nothing but Beethoven's Ninth.

Today's performance has been sponsored by the Sumida ward council, not at all an elite borough of Tokyo. In fact, it is the smallest and poorest of the twenty-three wards, with its old wooden cottages, its brewery and its grey, greasy river. The bankers and journalists are heavily outnumbered by the pensioners, the housewives, the cooks and the carpenters. Yet Sumida has become the unofficial capital of Beethoven-worship. Busts of him decorate the council chambers and a life-size bronze statue is planned. A regular newsletter (*Freude!*, of course) is published. And then there's the annual concert.

Sumida spends about $1 million a year on it. The council recovers half of this from the audience and from the choir, who pay for weekly practice sessions, tapes, songbooks and, of course, the privilege of singing in the

JOY, JAPANESE–STYLE

world's biggest choir. Biggest to get together regularly, that is. There have been other 'one-off' choirs even larger than 5000, most notably (according to the Guinness Book of World Records) one in Breslau, Germany, in 1937 which was 60 000 voices strong. But then, *Deutschland Uber Alles* is not a patch on *Dai ku*.

From the previous summer, in groups of a few dozen in more than 100 towns and cities all over the country, the Sumida choir hopefuls have been practising their scales and their gutturals. On the first weekend of spring, with the cherry-blossoms billowing in the parks, they converge by car, train and tour bus on the Kokugikan for their eighteen minutes of fame.

It would be a lie to say we were word perfect — even buried deep among the booming basses you could hear the occasional glitch. In one corner, a crowd of intellectually handicapped people were having the time of their lives singing whatever came into their heads. But somehow it didn't matter. It was a moment of sheer musical euphoria.

I guess you have to be Japanese to appreciate Beethoven fully.

FOUR
BEING THERE

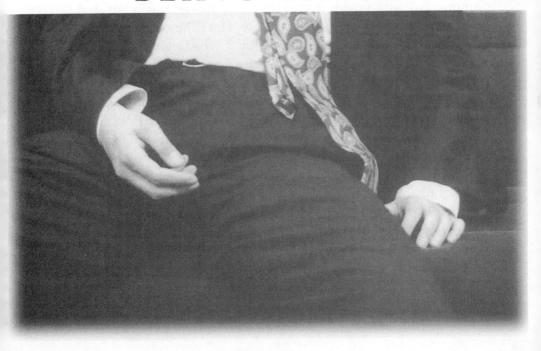

To write a poem
With seventeen syllables
is very diffic ...

In June of 1992, not long before Mayu and I arrived in Japan, the then prime minister, Kiichi Miyazawa, pledged to turn the country into a 'lifestyle superpower'. It was a fine-sounding phrase that could mean as much or as little as the listener wanted it to mean, which suits the style of Japanese politics down to the ground. He endorsed a grandiose five-year plan by the Economic Planning Agency which set specific targets for improving the quality of life in Japan — creating more city parkland, reducing working hours, cutting the cost of housing, building more nursing homes, reducing crowding on the trains and so on. The days of sacrifice were over, was the implicit message, and now was the time for Japanese to enjoy the fruits of their half a century of hard work.

It was, I think, Miyazawa's response to the growing feeling among ordinary Japanese that they were not getting a fair share of the spoils of the economic miracle. Here they were, still close to the summit of the 'bubble economy', reading every day that Japan had become 'the world's richest nation'. The site of the imperial palace in downtown Tokyo was reckoned to be worth more than the whole of Canada. Japanese corporate barons were plundering the world for trophies such as the Rockefeller Centre, Hollywood's Columbia Movies and Australia's Bond University. Flash Harry Japanese entrepreneurs with convertible Rolls-Royces were dining on sushi wrapped in gold leaf at $1000-a-head banquets.

Yet, as papa was continually complaining, Japan had become a 'rich country with poor people'. The world's highest per capita gross domestic product did not translate into money in the pocket. As a result of the inadequacies of the pension system (for all but life-long bureaucrats and salarymen in large corporations) and the breakdown of the traditional system of children looking after their ageing parents, the Japanese have to salt away an inordinate amount of money for their retirement. Even after prices deflated back to the levels of the mid-1980s, housing costs still ate up a disproportionate amount of people's incomes. It costs $750 000 for a typical ten square metre 'three LDK' (three bedrooms, living room, dining room and kitchen) apartment an hour out of Tokyo. Price-fixing cartels controlling the entire marketplace mean that Sony Walkmans are more expensive in Akihabara 'Electric City' than in New York, and food is three or four times world prices. Mayu and I found our weekly supermarket bill was usually $200 to $300.

Taxation, it's true, is relatively low for medium income-earners — the top rate of 60 per cent plus does not kick in until you earn over $200 000 a year. Also, interest rates plunged to record lows as the Bank of Japan tried with increasing desperation to reignite the economy — mortgages sank to a record 3 per cent a year and a sign in the window of 'Porsche corner' in Roppongi offered car loans at 1 per cent. In spite of this, the World Bank calculated that, in 1994, based on what money could actually buy, the Japanese were actually only the eighth best-off people in the world. They had a lower material standard of living than citizens of Luxembourg, the United States and Switzerland — but also, surprisingly, Hong Kong and Singapore.

As for living conditions, Edith Cresson, an otherwise undistinguished French prime minister, stung the Japanese when she observed that they live in 'rabbit hutches'. The criticism hurt because it happens to be true — a typical Tokyo apartment is not much more than one-third the size of a flat in Sydney or Melbourne. Many people still sleep in rolled-out futons on the dining room floor, and share a bath. Mayu's parents' place in Roppongi is typical of older style Tokyo accommodation — a walk-up flat with an outside staircase on the fifth floor of a barracks-like block originally built as company quarters for salarymen. It is a tiny, dingy place with no bath, a small stove in the dining room and a couple of minute bedrooms. Yet, at the height of the bubble, developers offered

$3 million for it. Mama, believing the boom would never end, held out for a better offer. Unfortunately, the property market then collapsed and the smiling men in suits with the chequebook stopped knocking on her door. Poor her.

Public infrastructure, even after a decade of multi-zillion dollar government spending packages, remains a disgrace: highways clogged with 120-kilometre traffic-jams on holiday weekends; people crammed into trains carrying three times their capacity and sewers (where they exist) discharging raw sewage into the ocean. In 1995, the government proudly proclaimed that half the country was now connected to a sewer; the other half, like the Tominakas' holiday house, uses a hole in the ground or a septic tank. Even in the backstreets of glittering Ginza, rats as big as cats fossick in the garbage and you can smell human faeces.

Miyazawa would also have been aware that, even in a place with such an orderly citizenry, Tokyo had become an unbearably polluted and overcrowded city. Within fifty kilometres of the old geographical centre of the city, the Nihonbashi Bridge just down the road from the *Sydney Morning Herald*'s office, live thirty million people. This is nearly double the population of Australia, and double the population of the following five largest cities in the world: New York, São Paulo, Mexico City, Shanghai and Bombay. The *average* commuting time is more than two hours a day, and some people spend four hours getting to and from work. Ask no more why on Tokyo's subways (one of the few efficient, well-run elements of this monstrous megalopolis) people slump in their seats with their eyes closed in a semi-trance. It is hard to tell which inspired more envy among visitors to Chateau Fairfax, the *Herald* house in inner-city Kamiyacho — the tiny, scrubby patch of lawn or the twenty-minute commute from the city.

Tokyo has only a fraction the public open space of any other major capital city. In fact, if it was not for the Shinto shrines and Buddhist temples all over the place, it would be one enormous lump of concrete — Los Angeles without the guns. Town planning, such as it is, seems mainly concerned with safety issues rather than public amenity. 'Pencil buildings' three metres wide and five storeys tall mark the spots where some sushi-shop owner decided to expand vertically. In Kyoto, streetscapes of historic timber tenements are bulldozed to make way for characterless concrete blockhouses which, with unconscious irony, are called *manshons*. Footpaths are either non-existent, or so narrow as to be useless. There is a famous example, running alongside the Aoyama cemetery, where in places pedestrians have to walk sideways to navigate between a wall and a light pole. It is said, with some truth, that Japan's misfortune was never to have a horse-and-buggy era — it went straight from pedestrian footpaths to the motor age. It is surprising how much you can come to miss a simple pleasure such as walking side by side with someone or sitting in a park.

It didn't have to be like this. Twice this century Tokyo had a magnificent opportunity to start from scratch and build a truly handsome and well-planned city — once on the ruins of the Great Kanto Earthquake and again after General Curtis LeMay's firebombing. Each time the government blew it. If you overlay Tokyo's modern road map on drawings of what it was like in the Edo era a century and a half ago, you will find a close correlation between today's urban layout and the rice paddies, canals and walking tracks of feudal times. This victory of individual property rights over the public interest remains one of the great contradictions of this authoritarian, consensus-driven society. It is the reason Tokyo is such an ugly, inefficient place to live and work, and why the government is continually talking about relocating it somewhere else. It is the Paris where the peasants dug in and Baron von Haussman never got to build the Champs Elysées. It is the city where half a dozen farmers have been allowed to hold tens of millions of consumers and would-be travellers hostage for more than twenty years, blocking the construction of a desperately needed second runway at the city's international airport.

Miyazawa's 'vision thing' promised action on more than thirty fronts. Working hours would be reduced and more holidays taken, hopefully ending that quintessentially Japanese affliction of *karoshi*, death from overwork. Roads and sewers would be built. Disposable income would be increased. However, with hindsight, he really missed the big picture — or perhaps he simply realised it would be impossible to talk the bureaucrats into taking the legislative measures that would strike at the root of many of Japan's social problems and make a genuine difference to the quality of life.

Ken Courtis is not the first economist to point out that Japan is not, actually, the most densely populated country in the world, as the government continually claims to justify the intolerable overcrowding — far from it. In Asia, the island nations of Hong Kong and Singapore have nearly twenty times Japan's population density, and countries as varied as the former Yugoslavia, Lebanon and even the Netherlands have more people per square kilometre, although they are not as mountainous. There is no geographical reason, says Mr Courtis, why Tokyo's trains should be more packed than those of Calcutta, nor why its capital city should not be as handsome and user-friendly as Amsterdam, which is actually more crowded. No geographical reason. The reasons are political — and this is what Miyazawa and the would-be reformers who followed him failed to address in their quest for 'lifestyle superpower' status.

Building height restrictions, barriers to land consolidation, property tax and laws upholding tenants' rights have made a joke of Tokyo's efforts to transform itself into a modern city. As a result of perverse tax incentives, the city actually still contains some registered rice paddies. The little wooden barber's shop where Mayu's ancient grandmother has lived for the past half century is a classic example of another anomaly. Twenty years or so ago, her landlord asked her to agree to a timetable to vacate so he could redevelop what is, in truth, a run-down old neighbourhood. Granny refused. For two decades they feuded, until finally granny won. 'He had a heart attack and died,' she cackled. It's hard not to admire the tough old bird, but all over Tokyo there are thousands of grannies standing in the way of the roads that should be built and the high-density housing that is needed to reduce urban sprawl and commuting times.

In the end, Miyazawa's grand theme sputtered into a modest program of capital works, and was soon forgotten. White-gloved station attendants continued cramming people into carriages on the Yamanote railway line; Tokyo and Yokohama virtually merged in a seamless megacity 100 kilometres across; Tokyo Bay filled up with garbage; and the pressures of work, if anything, increased as Japan's biggest corporations, hit by recession, began to renege on the 'jobs for life' policy which has been a cornerstone of social policy since the 1930s. However, the one legacy the 'superpower' policy did leave was a Japan which, for the first time since the war, did not feel guilty about indulging in the Western vice of leisure. Not quite so guilty, anyway.

As with every new import, the Japanese went totally over the top when they discovered the joys of recreation. More than 1000 new golf courses were planned in the decade to 1995 and, for those who could not afford the membership fees which peaked at $750 000 or more before the boom went bust, great netting enclosures of multi-storey driving ranges blossomed outside every major town and city in the country. Someone even started a 'golf religion' with driving ranges on the roofs of the churches. Gigantic 'biospheres' sprang up everywhere — fully enclosed environments where thousands of people can pay to queue on an artificial tropical beach for indoor surfing (Ocean Dome, a $2 billion extravaganza in Kyushu) or ski in midsummer on an indoor piste half a kilometre long, maintained at a constant minus two degrees (the bizarrely named La-La Port Ski-dome SSAWS which you pass on your way to Tokyo's Narita international airport). Japanese by the million took to tennis, mountain climbing, playing the piano, pet-owning, bird-watching and a hundred and one other activities. A special silent piano had to be invented so that little Kazu could practise without annoying the neighbours. Most importantly of all, the Japanese discovered travel.

Those who chronicle such things reckon that Japan came of age as a developed nation one fateful day in the early 1980s when the last shoeshine man at Narita shut up shop. Up until then, the main users of the airport had been businessmen, in their sombre suits and black leather shoes, flying off to sell the world a new Honda or a better Walkman. In fact, until as recently 1964, ordinary Japanese citizens could not get passports for holiday travel; foreign currency was reserved for business missions. In less than twenty years, the Reeboks and Nikes of leisure-seekers had taken over and the shoeshine man was out of business.

Today, Japanese domestic travel has grown into one of the country's most important industries. In 1995 it was reckoned to be worth $250 billion, around 5 per cent of the economy, and provided employment for nearly two million people. Tourism was worth twice as much as Japan's farming, forestry and fisheries sector, and was on its way to overtaking the finance and insurance industries. Internationally, countries began scrambling for a share of the additional $60 billion or so that wealthy Japanese — and even your car assembly worker from Nagoya was wealthy with the yen at 75 to the US$ — were prepared to splurge every year. Those conga lines of neatly dressed holidaymakers, following a guide with a megaphone and a banner on a pole, became a familiar sight from the Louvre to Bondi Beach. Australia, in fact, rapidly became one of Japan's favourite destinations, taking about 7 per cent of overseas tourists and ranking seventh in preference, after the United States, Korea, Hong Kong, China, Taiwan and Singapore.

Quite what they make of us is another story. Ten years and five million visitors after the Japanese began visiting Australia in large numbers, the Australian Embassy in Tokyo commissioned a poll to try and find out. The results were not at all flattering, particularly in view of the government's misconceived desire for Australia to be considered part of Asia. Seventy per cent of Japanese, the survey found, thought of Australia as a 'semi-advanced country' (compared with 16 per cent who said we were 'advanced' and 14 per cent who classified Australia as a 'developing' country). Twelve per cent thought Australia was 'part of England', 18 per cent believed we still banned nonwhite immigration, 32 per cent believed we had 'about the same population as Japan' (125 million) and 37 per cent believed Melbourne was the capital.

I would hope Australians are a bit better informed about Japan, though I know of no comparable survey. It is probably a vain hope, and the news media have to bear some of the responsibility. The only words of advice one former editor of the time had for me before I took up my post in Tokyo was 'I don't want stories full of the names of people I have never heard of.' Most Australians, in fact, would be hard pressed to name a single living Japanese — the only name recognition is for products such as Toyota, National and Toshiba, and for historical villains such as Tojo and Hirohito, and, perhaps, Godzilla. If a department store in Seoul collapses, killing 500, it will be relegated to the foreign pages. If a building is blown up in Oklahoma City, killing 150, a paper like the Melbourne *Age* will produce a special wraparound colour supplement. This is not racism, it is common sense. In spite of the aspirations of our political leaders, Australians are more interested in what goes on in Britain or America, with which we share a history and a culture, than in Japan or Korea. This is despite the fact that South Korea's economy overtook Australia's in the early 1990s, making a mockery of Winston Churchill's fatuous remark on the eve of the war that divided the peninsula: 'I can't see what's so important about it. I'd never heard of the bloody place until I was seventy.'

Japanese mass tourism is slowly redressing this information imbalance. It has another major advantage for the rest of the world — it is one of the very few industries where Japan runs a massive trade deficit. Put simply, ever increasing numbers of Japanese want to travel abroad, but very few foreigners want to visit Japan. In 1995, about 14.5 million Japanese went overseas, 80 per cent of them holidaymakers intent on sunbaking in Hawaii or getting married in Hobart. This was a sevenfold increase in a single generation. However, less than four million foreigners visited Japan. It ranked nineteenth on the list of preferred holiday destinations, behind Canada, and even tiny

Belgium where most visitors find they run out of things to do after they visit the site of the Battle of Waterloo and buy a box of chocolates. The Netherlands attracts more international conferences. Twice as many Japanese go abroad to study as foreigners who come to Japan.

Why should this be? Most surveys put the extortionate cost at the top of the list. The glory days of 360 yen to the dollar are just a fading memory to Japan's old foreign hands. Nowadays, even roughing it in a humble *minshuku*, a family-run bed-and-breakfast place, can cost $75 per person per night. A bowl of noodles, the humblest fare, might be $10 and one stop on the subway will set you back two dollars. As well, Japan Travel Bureau people dolefully point out that Japan has few cultural treasures compared with, say, Europe, China or Egypt — fire and earthquakes see to that. Medieval-looking Shuri castle in Okinawa is, for example, the sixth reincarnation of the building, which was destroyed most recently in World War II. The Japanese mind not at all that this is a replica for the tourists, completed in 1993, although foreigners may wonder why anyone would bother.

The 'Great Outdoors' does exist in Japan — Mayu and I spent many pleasant weekends fishing and bushwalking in almost virgin forest. But such spots can be remote and inaccessible; the unwary visitor is more likely to find himself swept along in a torrent of chattering, jostling, souvenir-laden humanity as he tries to enjoy a mountain waterfall, an open-air hot spring or a beach. The crowds can be intimidating — it is a serious mistake to try and travel anywhere in Japan at holiday time, especially over New Year, the spring Golden Week or midsummer *Obon* seasons. Foreigners also find it a bewildering place to find your way around; although many signs are in the Roman alphabet, most Japanese are unwilling to speak what English (or French or German) they know, and directions are notoriously confusing. Finally, as several disappointed Australian friends have remarked — apparently expecting everyone to be dressed in kimonos, riding around in rickshaws and conversing in rhyming *haiku* — 'Japan isn't foreign enough.'

However, this is a digression. The theme of this chapter is leisure and lifestyle — how the Japanese have responded to Mr Miyazawa's call for them to lighten up and enjoy life a little, and how they are handling the newish concept of 'spare' time. In actual fact, at least as far as overseas travel is concerned, they are still on a learning curve. That figure of 14.5 million looks mighty impressive, until you consider that it represents just 11 per cent of the population. By comparison, a larger proportion of Australians travel abroad (12 per cent), and even more Americans (17 per cent). The 'insular' British, who are said to believe that 'the wogs start at Calais', are proportionately five times more likely to holiday overseas (54 per cent) than the 'well-travelled' Japanese.

Some travel agents will tell you the Japanese are nervous about going abroad because they feel lost outside their normal social hierarchy, and have poor language skills. At one Queensland beach, a sign has been erected in Japanese characters advising swimmers in difficulty that it is alright to shout for help — apparently several Japanese drowned because they were embarrassed about causing a fuss. This (plus the cost) is one reason why they have clung so long to those dreadful, regimented it's-Monday-this-must-be-Surfer's Paradise package tours. Another reason is the way the media highlights the awful things that befall Japanese overseas. Whatever the real reason, Japan's xenophobia has provided a remarkable opportunity for one enterprising leisure company, which has constructed one of the world's most improbable tourist attractions. Tobu World Square is abroad without the anxiety.

The theme park is the ultimate fantasy land for nervous Japanese who would love to travel abroad, but who do not have the time, the money or the courage. Especially not the courage. On an eight-hectare site, surrounded by the pine-clad mountains of a national park ninety minutes north of Tokyo by bullet train, the Tobu travel group has spent six years and $140 million re-creating the architectural marvels of the ancient and modern world in meticulous detail, at one twenty-fifth of their real size. Looming over the mean streets of Harlem — with a bit of geographical sleight-of-hand — are the twin towers of the World Trade Centre, the Empire State Building and an anatomically perfect replica of the Statue of Liberty in an improbably clean, blue harbour.

We took a train up into the mountains to the town of Kinugawa to inspect this fascinating addition to the world of the theme park, not long after it opened. Our guide, an earnest young man named Yukio Nemoto, proudly pointed out the mayhem in progress. Two men were running from the Bank of America carrying bundles of stolen loot, pursued by police and security guards firing pistols. Just around the corner, in a dingy street daubed with graffiti, ambulances and fire engines surrounded a bloody three-car pile-up. What else would you expect in New York asked Mr Nemoto? It's a violent world out there. That's why the security-conscious Japanese were flocking to Tobu World Square in their millions rather than risk the real experience.

This, however, was just the start. There were 102 exhibits, with more on the drawing board, ranging from the Great Wall of China to the Leaning Tower of Pisa — populated with 140 000 individually modelled weatherproof plastic people six or seven centimetres tall. Place a card in a slot and a North West Airlines 747 taxies around the terminal of a miniature Narita airport, the Coldstream Guards parade outside Buckingham Palace or 2000 courtiers kowtow in Beijing's Forbidden City, in a replica of the film set for *The Last Emperor*. Big Ben chimes over the Palace of Westminster, a marble Taj Mahal glistens convincingly in the steamy summer sunshine, gondolas cruise past St Mark's in Venice, fountains play in the gardens of Versailles, workmen labour to complete Antonio Gaudí's Sagrada Famiglia cathedral in Barcelona and camels lurch past the pyramids. Long queues of tiny Japanese package tourists wait outside the attractions, watched by long queues of life-size Japanese package tourists, maintaining the illusion by peering through plastic telescopes shaped like the Leaning Tower of Pisa.

'It is, of course, much safer and much less hassle to come here rather than travel to the real thing,' agrees Mr Nemoto, whose own favourite is Dover Castle. In the three months after it opened, more than 500 000 people visited Tobu World Square, up to 30 000 a weekend — remarkable business considering the slump the rest of the Japanese leisure industry was suffering. There were queues twenty metres long at the cash registers in the souvenir shop, the restaurants were packed and the car park overflowed with more than 100 tour coaches at weekends. Cameras clicked and whirred like a deafening horde of cicadas.

Why the popularity? One reason is the widespread fear — reinforced by constant media coverage — that 'abroad' is a dangerous and unpredictable place, where harm is likely to come to an innocent Japanese traveller. Not an entirely unreasonable fear, considering that the average New Yorker is thirty-eight times more likely to be murdered, thirty-two times more likely to be raped and 446 times more likely to be robbed than the average Tokyoite. Barely a week goes by without something horrible happening to a Japanese traveller in some foreign country. In 1993, Japanese citizens were involved in 9637 'accidents and other trouble' while overseas, according to the Foreign Ministry. An extraordinary 384 died from illness, accident or homicide.

I collected newspaper cuttings for a couple of months to find out what sort of misadventures the Japanese get themselves into. These are just some of the headlines. Two Japanese students were killed in Queensland when their hire car collided with a house on the back of a truck. Japanese tourists visiting the temples of Angkor Wat had their hotel room sprayed with rifle fire by Laotian gunmen. A young Japanese woman dived into a canal in New York to save her dog and drowned (the dog lived). Five female Japanese university students in Rome were lured into an apartment on the promise of a meal of pasta and instead were all raped at the point of a sword by one man. In Austria, a man lugging a heavy suitcase through the streets of Salzburg was stopped by police. They discovered that it contained portions of his fiancée, Ms Keiko Ota, a clarinet student at the famous Mozarteum, whom he had battered to death with a table leg for suspected infidelity.

However, the incident which most shocked Japan — it was still the subject of television documentaries and magazine features nearly a year after it happened — was the shooting of a sixteen-year-old exchange student, Yoshihiro Hattori, in Baton Rouge, Louisiana. Looking for a Halloween party, he knocked on the wrong door, was told to 'freeze' and was shot dead with a .44 calibre Magnum when he failed to understand the warning. In the wake of that tragedy (the gunman was acquitted of homicide, the court ruling that his conduct was reasonable in the circumstances), travel sales to the United States slumped. Language schools cashed in by starting 'survival English' classes, teaching the meaning of 'freeze' and other useful phrases such as 'duck' and 'spread 'em'. In Osaka, a company called Gripstone introduced sheltered Japanese consumers to the first 'survival products' shop in the country, which features, along with bullet-proof jackets, tear gas pistols, electrified anti-snatching briefcases and a 'safety cable' thirty-one metres long which tourists nervous about being trapped in a blazing foreign hotel can use to escape. Provided, that is, their room is not more than thirty-one metres above the ground.

To Australians, this may appear an overreaction. Japan, however, is still surprisingly xenophobic. This fear is a major reason why theme parks in that country — particularly those such as Tobu World Square, which offer the illusion of being abroad without the risk — do such good business. The first, Tokyo's Disneyland, opened a decade ago. It is still so popular that it is advisable before planning a visit to telephone to get an estimate of the waiting time for rides. Since then, thirty-six theme parks have thrown open their gates, and another twenty or thirty are on the drawing board. Ticket sales are showing a steady 10 per cent growth per year, and in 1992 topped $6 billion. More than forty million Japanese visit a theme park each year — triple the number who travel abroad.

The 'travel experience you have when you're not travelling'

ranges from the dykes of the Netherlands to the African savanna, the Swiss Alps to the highlands of Scotland. If things get a trifle depressing while people are visiting the atomic ruins of Hiroshima, they can take a train to Obayashi and spend the day cruising in a gondola past St Mark's or casting their babies' booties in glass in Venice-on-the-Pacific. *Huis Ten Bosch* ('House in the Forest'), on 152 acres near the other atomic city of Nagasaki, offers even more excitement. Here, as well as canals, windmills and a 105-metre tall replica of Domtoren (the Netherlands' tallest church), adventurous tourists can experience the excitement of a fake flood in which '800 tonnes of water, with fog, thunder and fierce wind will appear to engulf the audience', to quote the brochure. In Saitama Prefecture, a farming area an hour by train from Tokyo, a gondola swings up into some fake Swiss Alps in an attempt to create the 'Chamonix experience', not far from an African savanna where gazelles, zebra and a dozen other tropical species shiver in the winter snow.

For reality, nothing can beat the effort of Masahiko Tsugawa, a Japanese actor, who dreamed of building a castle so that Japanese people, who mostly live in wooden houses, can 'learn about the beauty of stone'. Unlike the makers of Tobu World Square, Mr Tsugawa was not content with a replica. He wanted the real thing, and several years ago he began travelling the world looking for a castle. He set his heart on one in the Bordeaux region of France, but the local authorities banned its sale. Finally, fifty kilometres south of Edinburgh, he came across Lockhart Castle, built in 1829, but now abandoned and crumbling away.

Brick by brick — and the sandstone blocks weigh up to 60 tonnes each — Mr Tsugawa had the castle dismantled and shipped to Japan on the trans-Siberian railway. It was re-erected at a cost of some $21 million near the mountain resort village of Takayamamura. We visited it not long after it opened to the public, the Scottish experience for those who don't want to risk Scotland. It came complete with a highly accomplished Japanese bagpiper, striding in full fig along the terrace, Annie

Laurie on the Muzak and whisky-flavoured beanpaste buns for sale. As a final indignity, the Lockhart had been changed to 'Lockheart', the baronial crest had been re-forged to a sort of belt buckle with a heart rampant and an avenue of heart-shaped arches led to the chapel, where kilts were available for hire to grooms seeking the 'romantic Scottish wedding experience'. The result is 10 000 tonnes of Scottish history, transplanted around the world to form the backdrop for a sugary kitsch commercial ritual as only the Japanese can do it. The laird, we decided, would be turning in his grave.

One of the lasting legacies of the leisure boom is that there is not a town in Japan which is not trying to cash in. Outside every settlement, no matter how insignificant, you will see signs directing you to the first, the best, the biggest, the only. One municipality has constructed the world's largest wooden roller coaster. Others vie to erect colossal Kannons — the Buddhist Goddess of Mercy. At the time of writing, one at Sendai held the record at eighty metres tall. Some of the ideas are charming — a dragonfly sanctuary, for instance. Some are practical. At Nojiri, you can pay a traditional blacksmith to help you forge one of those wickedly sharp Japanese knives from an iron bar. Other ideas are so daft you wonder why the ratepayers put up with them. A dying fishing village in Tohoku, for instance, sought to revive its fortunes by building the world's first squid-racing track (complete with automatic ink-extractor). The maiden outing was judged to be a great success — after the squid completed the circuit they were sliced up for sashimi and eaten by the spectators.

One of the oddest historical claims to fame we came across was at a village in the wilds of Tohoku, where we were arrested by signs proclaiming 'the home-town of Jesus', and discovered a strange story. Christ did not die at Golgotha, you see. He escaped and made his way to Shingo Village where he married and lived to a ripe old age, leaving many descendants and a cross above a grassy mound marking his real burial place. A flourishing tourism industry has sprung up — pilgrims are offered Jesus-brand sake and candy at a nearby store, and every year Shinto priests (there are no Christians left) stage a festival here in his honour. There is a historic scroll and odd local customs to support the story, and many people appear to believe it — a variation of the 'Japanese-as-lost-tribe-of-Israel' legend.

Some towns make a virtue of their unique geography. Abashiri is a case in point — a small city way up in the north of Hokkaido on the Sea of Okhotsk that suffers from the most extreme climate of anywhere in the country. In winter, up to ten metres of snow inundate the place, howling gales blow down from the Arctic, temperatures plunge to minus thirty degrees Celsius, and may never rise above freezing point for three months. Instead of downplaying this frightful weather, Abashiri takes advantage of it. On a hill overlooking the city is a museum which is really a gigantic refrigerator containing an iceberg, complete with penguins and sea lions. People fish for *wakasagi* (tiny minnows) through holes in a frozen lake, and scuba dive under the ice floes which drift 1000 kilometres from the mouth of the Amur River. A special train with no windowpanes plies very slowly along the coast so that people can hear and smell, as well as see, the groaning, frozen ocean.

Even a place as unprepossessing as Shibukawa, a gritty little industrial city in Gunma Prefecture on the plains north of Tokyo, has its claim to fame. Its most noticeable feature is that it seems to be the power pylon capital of Japan. Shibukawa has no festivals of any note, no-one famous was born here, there are no local arts and crafts, and no national parks. In desperation, gazing at the map, one of the civic fathers noticed that Shibukawa appeared to be around the middle of Honshu, Japan's main island. He took out his ruler, and with growing excitement measured up — yes, no doubt about it, Shibukawa is the dead centre of the country. So that's what they christened the city — the 'Belly Button of Japan'.

A stone *jizo* statue has been erected, with a prominent navel of the type that used to be called an 'outie'. A souvenir shop opened which sells, among other paraphernalia, belly button boxes. I am not making this up. When Japanese babies are born, their umbilical cords are cut off, dried and placed in little boxes, usually made of fragrant cypress wood. Mayu has one, with her belly-button, like a tiny dried seahorse, nestling on a bed of cotton wool inside. We bought a new one at Shibukawa — hand-carved and painted in traditional style, like a small *matrioshka* doll. I doubt that Shibukawa is going to experience a belly button-led revival, but at least they are thinking laterally.

Probably the most unpleasant tourist draw card in Japan can be found on Shikoku, the smallest and poorest of Japan's four 'home islands'. I do not understand why, but many Japanese are very bad with animals. People like the author Taichi Sakaiya, who is always searching for some anthropological explanation, say it is because vegetarian Buddhist Japan never had a herding culture. I think it's more likely that people up until the war could not afford pets; after the war, they had no room for them, particularly if they lived in cities. They are not used to being around animals and have given no thought to what 'rights' they may have.

Whatever, possessing pets became a fashionable leisure activity during the bubble years. People spent thousands of dollars on popular breeds of cats and dogs — tens of thousands in the case of exotics like the Pyrenean mountain dog. Abandoning them when they become inconvenient is apparently acceptable — thousands are simply kicked out in the street when their owners go on holiday. My neighbourhood, like most in Tokyo, had a tribe of tough-looking feral cats. At the end of the street, there was a wooden cage provided by the council in which people could dump their unwanted pets. However, this is nothing compared with the way the people of Shikoku treat their dogs.

The first thing that hits you as you climb the stairs to the arena is the stench — a nauseating cocktail of wet dog, toilets and cheap disinfectant ... and something else you cannot quite identify. The audience, a holiday crowd of people in jeans and T-shirts, was seated around a raised arena, a three-metre circle of dirty sacking surrounded by a cage of thick iron bars. Two tough-looking types led huge scary dogs into the ring, unleashed them and leapt for metal stools out of the reach of danger as the dogs hurled themselves at each other in a riot of snarling and bared fangs. Within a few minutes, one of the dogs had been wrestled onto its back, the other dog's teeth buried in its neck, lying there as still as death. The penny then dropped — that elusive smell is blood, the dark red stain soaking the stricken dog's pelt, dripping onto the sacking.

Welcome to dog fighting Japanese-style. To its promoters, it is a sport with 200 years of honourable tradition dating back to the days of the samurai. To police and the welfare organisations which are trying to outlaw it, it is a carnival of cruelty run by criminals that is a national embarrassment. These are no ordinary dogs. The Tosa combines the smartness of the traditional Shikoku dog, which was used for boar hunting, and imported breeds — the massive bulk of the mastiff, and the aggression of the bulldog and the boxer. They have jaws that could take your leg off, and they weigh up to 105 kilograms. The favoured colour is a dark rusty brown — white is out, says the manager of this fighting ring, Takashi Tama Hirose, because 'it shows up the blood too much'.

At its peak, eighty years ago, there were thousands of these fighting dogs all over Japan. The Kochi district of Shikoku island alone, where they were first bred, had 10 000 dogs, three fighting rings and matches practically every week. Now, there are just 220 Tosa dogs left in Kochi, barely enough to support the last remaining fighting ring. Mr Hirose worries that the sport — and the breed — may become extinct within a decade. I cannot help hoping that he is right.

Elsewhere in Japan, hassled by the police and local councils, dog fights have become a clandestine, ad hoc backyard affair, controlled by *yakuza* criminals who run the illegal gambling. Tokyo banned dog fighting altogether several years ago. However, at Katsuura Beach, where the green-grey waves of the North Pacific crash against the Shikoku coastline, Mr Hirose's stadium is a shrine for dog-fight fans, a commercial extravaganza which packs in thousands of tourists who come from as far away as Tokyo. As well as the $13-a-head admission charge, the tourists spend a bundle in his souvenir shop before they leave, laden with fighting dog paraphernalia — tea towels, noodles, calendars, key rings, dried bonito and even fighting dog sake.

If appearances are any guide, many of the visitors have no idea what they are about to see. The sport is promoted as a sort of cutesy dog sumo wrestling, complete with grand champion *yokozunas* paraded around the ring dressed in traditional robes with huge gilt collars. However, the real fight which follows is not for the squeamish. The dogs, quite literally, tear each other to pieces. The audience sits there stoically, their small children stiff-faced and staring at the bloody, snarling spectacle. Several dogs are killed in the ring every year. Others are so badly mauled they have to be put down. The veterans are all ragged and covered in scar tissue. The fight goes on for up to twenty-five minutes, until one dog surrenders by yelping or running away. We saw one fight in which handlers had to thrust burning newspaper into a dog's face to stop it killing its unfortunate opponent.

Mr Hirose, the 29-year-old American-educated son of the founder of the centre, denies that this is cruel. 'These are fighting dogs. They are bred to fight and they get tense if they can't release their aggression. It is more cruel to stop them,' he says, apparently seriously. He is concerned at the shocking image attack dogs such as the Tosa have in other countries. He blames the tabloid newspapers sensationalising the killing of a child by a pit bull terrier for a ban on importing the Tosa into England, and the refusal of the US Kennel Club to recognise the breed. 'I believe they have a future as pets and watchdogs. They are not dangerous, they do not bite people …' Then, noticing my raised eyebrows, Mr Hirose adds, 'Well, if they do it's the fault of a bad owner.'

Tokyo people do not, of course, have to go as far as Shikoku to enjoy themselves. Within the loop of the Yamanote line there is probably the greatest collection of art and entertainment to be found outside New York and the old capitals of Europe.

Although government arts subsidies — such as those in Australia which subsidise the cinema, writing and music — do not exist in Japan, there is large-scale corporate patronage. Tokyo supports no fewer than eight full-scale symphony orchestras and dozens of live theatres and cinema complexes. At least 100 art galleries will be holding exhibitions at any time.

I am not commenting on the quality. Western critics are usually appalled at the lack of purpose and originality in much of modern Japanese culture. Much as Japanese of taste and refinement may shudder, comic books and karaoke are Japan's most identifiable cultural gifts to the world, the icons of its Generation X. While the rest of Asia, especially China, awakes, Japan has not made a decent movie for years. The great studios are on their last legs and cinema audiences have fallen to record lows. The umpteenth remakes of samurai dramas, sentimental war stories, and (of all things) an animated cartoon about Anne Frank dominated the releases of 1995. The pop music scene is similarly barren — bubble-gum bop squeaked out by teenage *tarento*, many of the hits are the jingles for television commercials and soapies. Japanese art commands little attention overseas — the most ridiculed exhibition in recent years featured a row of children's school bags, each lacquered a different colour, hanging from a wall. The few authors any publisher finds worth translating into English are either of little interest (Banana Yoshimoto) or completely incomprehensible (Kenzaburo Oe, Japan's 1995 Nobel Literature Prize winner, who recommends his books for those who have trouble sleeping).

However, I would prefer to talk about the quantity, rather than the quality, of entertainment available in Tokyo. Whatever your fancy, this extraordinary city has a lot of it. Leisure, for the first time, began to be taken seriously in the 1990s. Nowhere is this more obvious than in the hundreds of museums which have opened up in recent years. They are not just dusty showrooms of Jomon-era artefacts nor exhibitions of woodblock prints and celadon pottery — although you can find these if you want. The museums I found most entertaining were those devoted to some of the more obscure corners of Japanese culture and history. There are museums devoted to silk, salt, cigarettes, swords and sumo; to bags and buttons and banknotes. There are collections of kites and drums and tombstones. At Jingumae, a museum celebrates Asian shaving, including a sixth-century scalp razor. Near Meguro station is what claims to be (without much fear of challenge) the only museum devoted to parasites. The *pièce de résistance* is a three-metre tapeworm.

For sheer oddballism, Mr Kenji Sugimoto must take the cake. Mr Sugimoto is an Einstein freak, the author of three books about the great physicist and a science historian who wears his locks long like his hero. In 1994, after a fourteen-year search, he tracked down the man who souvenired Einstein's brain (it was removed for study at Princeton University after the Nobel prize-winner died in 1955) and persuaded him to part with a slice of it. Mr Sugimoto keeps it in an old Twinings tea tin. 'This is Einstein's third legacy to Japan,' he was once quoted as saying. 'The first was the Hiroshima atom bomb; and the second Nagasaki.'

Unfortunately, I never actually got to meet Mr Sugimoto, although I did read a great deal about him. However, I did once spend an entertaining couple of days in the port city of Yokohama where there are some museums which are almost as wacky. Yokohama is a city that really doesn't have a lot going for it. Its famous harbour is a rich broth of effluent, its history was bombed flat during the war and its scenery is a featureless swathe of concrete, stretching to Tokyo, an hour's train ride to the north. The premier attraction of Japan's second city is a sort of sawn-off Eiffel Tower which the Lonely Planet guide cuttingly describes thus:

> The idea is to queue for 15 minutes, fork out $8, catch a crowded lift commanded by a chirping hostess in a silly hat to the top of a 106-metre high tower, then peer through the smog at the sea on one side and an apparently infinite expanse of concrete on the other.

So what do you do to attract visitors to such a depressing dump? A few years ago, twenty-four companies with factories in the region banded together to make the best of a bad job and capitalise on the one thing grimy Kanagawa Prefecture does best — smokestack industry. The result, unintentionally, is the finest collection of truly eccentric museums to be found anywhere in the world. The sock museum, for instance, is a prime example. In an abandoned red-brick factory — once the manufacturing plant of the Naigai company, Japan's largest sock manufacturer — a museum of socks has been established. It is dedicated to Nobumasa Sakata, the company's late managing director and author of the definitive tome, *The History of Socks*.

Here, one can inspect such priceless antiques as Japan's oldest surviving sock, the Mito Komon sock, worn by the brother of the third Tokugawa Shogun (1630–1700). We were shown around by the museum's curator, Takendo Nakamura, who handled this beige, intricately embroidered garment with reverence, before confessing that, this being Japan, it wasn't the *actual* sock, but a replica carefully crafted from a photograph of the sock of the brother of the Third Tokugawa Shogun. Two to three hundred people a year find their way to this obscure haunt for connoisseurs of the absurd, to marvel at Japan's biggest sock, a red woollen windsock of a thing twenty-nine centimetres long once worn by the sumo grand champion Kitanoumi. Here are the thick, grey lambswool socks specially knitted for the writer Yasunari Kawabata when he went to collect his Nobel Prize, because he had heard that Norway was very cold. Over there are the black silk socks with special suspenders which Shigeru Yoshida, Japan's first postwar prime minister, wore on his first official visit to the United States.

There are socks of every size and shape: moth-eaten cashmere bedsocks circa 1923; silk leg socks with no feet designed for kimono-wearers; battery-operated electric socks of Shetland wool made to keep fishermen's feet warm; elbow socks for people with arthritis; and socks like gloves with a 'finger' for each toe (especially helpful, says Mr Nakamura, for people with athlete's foot). Also on display are the many trophies which

Naigai has won over the years for its stylish and innovative sock designs — the company makes thirty-five million pairs of socks a year — and examples of its bespoke sockmaking skills, including a pair of brown socks made of a blend of cashmere and vicuna wool, which you can have made for a mere $366 a pair.

If you can drag yourself away from all this, there are many other exciting museums on the Kanagawa tourist trail such as the one devoted to fishcakes. Although this is not strictly speaking a museum, you can take the train to Odawara and watch a renowned fishcake factory at work. If you like chickens, a museum at Toyoura contains a unique collection of thirty-three stuffed chickens from all over the world, including some fine examples of the so-called Yokohama chicken which has a tail up to six metres long. If this should pall, there is also a display of eggs, including the fossilised egg of the extinct elephant bird which once lived in Madagascar and a collection of 700 chicken toys.

Still wondering what to do with the kids on a rainy Saturday afternoon? What about the pen museum at the Pilot pen factory in Hiratsuka, which has a collection of more than 300 fountain pens dating back to 1918, including the largest ever made in Japan, with a nib forty-two millimetres long; the most expensive, a made-to-order pen, lacquered by hand, which takes a month to make and costs $12 195. How about the roof-tile museum at Atsugi, which also contains a fascinating collection of saws, planes and chisels, and a Japanese carpenter's lacquered ink pad, used for marking off the timber for the famous Toshougu shrine in Nikko. There is just no end to the delights of Kanagawa. Down the road there is a famous collection of light bulbs through the ages; or a fine display of micrometers and other scientific instruments may catch the eye. But be warned. These are not objects to be sniggered at by jaded *gaijin* travellers. This is serious. 'I don't want to talk to you about my collection,' snapped the curator of the roof-tile museum, when Mayu telephoned him. 'You have no understanding … it's like talking to someone who can't tell the difference between a

Picasso and a painting by a child.'

Talking about Picasso, Japan boasts one other unexpected leisure treasure. As well as the Rockefeller Centre, Pebble Beach and sundry Hollywood film studios, the tycoons of the bubble era snaffled up much of the Western world's art. In the half decade up until 1990 there was hardly an important auction anywhere in the world at which telephone bids from Tokyo — or proxies in the audience — did not provoke gasps of amazement. Driven by the mighty yen, and leveraged by reckless Japanese bankers, hundreds of the world's greatest works of art vanished into the black hole of Japan Inc., many of them never to be seen again.

Until the 1980s, the Japanese had not been serious collectors of Western art. Indeed, apart from a few sparsely endowed public museums and galleries, there were no major collections, and only a handful of serious private collectors. Takashi Seki, a Ginza art dealer we called on one evening, explained that this was because art had never been seen as a repository of wealth in Japan. In Europe, he theorised, where borders have constantly changed over the centuries, light, portable valuables such as art commanded a premium. However, because Japan had never (until 1945) been invaded or changed its borders other than to expand, land was regarded as the most secure investment. Art could be too easily destroyed by fire or earthquake.

Regardless of the explanation, Japan became caught up in arguably the most extraordinary art boom the world has ever experienced. Touring collections were mobbed — particularly the French Impressionists, who, themselves, had been influenced by Japanese art. Businessmen, discovering themselves paper billionaires almost overnight, sought respectability by becoming art patrons and purchasers, even though most could not have told a Picasso from a Pissarro. One in ten of all the Monets ever painted, 200 out of 2000, were transported to Japan, along with hundreds of Rembrandts and Renoirs, Manets, Van Goghs, Cézannes, Sisleys and Matisses.

Even outside the major cities, mad millionaires were amassing fantastic collections. Once, driving through a village called Hakuba in the foothills of the Japan Alps, I came across a sign pointing to an exhibition of paintings by Marc Chagall. A tiny, timber gallery had been built in the woods which turned out to have 150 works by the Russian/French fantasist, with another 1500 in storage. This is more than you can see at the Gallery Maeght at St Paul de Vence, owned by his greatest patron, where Chagall spent the last few years of his life. I asked the reception lady what this fabulous collection was doing here, buried in the boondocks. 'Our curator likes Chagall,' she shrugged enigmatically.

The downside, for art lovers, is that when the boom went bust in 1990, these great works of art plummeted in price. Many of them were repossessed by the banks when their highly leveraged purchasers went broke. In Osaka, for instance, a little-known lender called the Lake Finance Company has its premises in an anonymous glass-and-concrete office building. There is no hint that in its basement is stored what was just a few years ago the most expensive work of art in the world. There, protected by steel vaults and guarded by security men who are now its only audience, sits Picasso's *Wedding of Violette*, a striking painting which at the time of its sale in 1989 brought a world-record $107 million.

It would be stretching it a bit to say, as they like to in the Sotheby's catalogues, that it was once 'the property of a gentleman'. Tomonori Tsurumaki, who bought the picture with a bid over a satellite link with the auction house in Paris, was more your high-flying Japanese entrepreneur ... sort of an Alan Bond with an extra nought or two. Mr Tsurumaki, who was then in his forties, was a high-school dropout who made a paper fortune punting on real estate, shares and horse-racing during the go-go years of the 1980s. Until he made headlines with the Picasso purchase, he was best known for his plans to put Japan on the world Formula One car-racing map by building a circuit on the southern island of Kyushu.

Just three years later — like Alan Bond before him — Mr Tsurumaki and reality converged with a sickening thud. He was declared bankrupt with debts of $118 million ... and the

Picasso was repossessed by the Lake Finance Company, a large Japanese non-bank, which had lent him the money to buy it. And there it sits. 'They just don't know what to do with it,' said Mr Seki, the art dealer who is president of the Tokyo auction house Est-Ouest. 'Art prices have fallen 80 or 90 per cent since then ... if they try to sell it they will take a massive loss.'

The story of the *Wedding of Violette* is a microcosm of what happened during the boom and bust of the Japanese art market — arguably the greatest ramp since the South Sea Bubble — when prices doubled and redoubled, and redoubled again. Price was no object. In the four years to the peak of the bubble in 1990, Japan imported an astounding $19 billion worth of art. What drove the buying spree, says Mr Seki, was debt. For the first time, lenders in Japan — where land has always been the principal repository of wealth — were prepared to accept art as security. Institutions like Lake began to aggressively promote what became known as 'work-of-art mortgages'. When the bubble burst, however, the banks called in their markers and suddenly there were embarrassing pale patches on the boardroom — and bedroom — walls of Japan's richest tycoons.

Take the two paintings which are still the most expensive ever sold: two Renoirs, the *Portrait of Dr Gachet* and the equally famous *Moulin de la Galette*, which toured Australia a few years ago. These were bought, at the peak of the boom, for $321 million, a price that staggered even the boldest art speculators. The purchaser was the 77-year-old Ryoei Saito, then the billionaire chairman of the controversial Daishowa paper manufacturing company, well known to Australian woodchip protesters. Mr Saito promptly outraged the art world by declaring that when he died he would have the paintings cremated along with his body, so that his heirs would not have to pay billions of yen in death duties. As it turned out, he never got the chance. With his company teetering on the brink of bankruptcy, Mr Saito was deposed and when last seen was being driven into a police station with his head buried in his arms to be questioned about bribery and corruption. The paintings have never been seen publicly since; rumour has it they are also buried in a bank vault.

A recent survey by the Nikkei news organisation of just five of Japan's scores of non-bank financial institutions found that they were sitting on repossessed artworks that cost a staggering $1.5 billion. What they are worth today is anyone's guess — the banks certainly aren't owning up. Mr Seki estimated that since the spring of 1990 — when at one auction Est-Ouest sold a Monet and a work by the Japanese/French painter Leonardo Fujita in an auction that topped $28 million — prices have now contracted to one-eighth or one-tenth of what they were. Another $1 billion down the drain, on top of the hundreds of billions the Japanese banks lost with the collapse of the share market and the bursting of the property bubble.

Est-Ouest, incidentally, is one of the great survivors in the cut-throat Tokyo art world. Five or six auction houses have gone out of business in the past few years, along with scores of art galleries which 'sprang up like bamboo shoots in the spring' during the boom. The night we were there, their first auction of 1994, Est-Ouest offered an eclectic collection of French Art Deco glassware, oriental silk screens and some European paintings. In spite of the modest reserves (a Dufy for $73 000, a Utrillo for $107 000) and the return of some French dealers to the market, there was only a 65 per cent clearance, and the auction grossed a little over $2 million. At these prices, says Mr Seki, the banks cannot afford to put their art treasures back on the market. 'They are ashamed of what has happened, and also afraid that if they try to sell the paintings they will depress the market even further. Basically, they just don't want to have anything to do with them.'

As well as the paintings hidden in the bank vaults, a lot of the art which was vacuumed up by Japan has finished up in private collections, some of them in the oddest of places. The public museums and art galleries didn't get much of a look-in during the boom years. For instance, if you want to see one of the magnificent Van Gogh sunflower paintings — the works which really started the art madness back in 1987 — you have to catch a high-speed lift to the forty-second floor of the Yasuda Fire and Marine Insurance Company. There, high among the smog-shrouded skyscrapers of Shinjuku, flanked by two Renoirs, a Gauguin and a Cézanne — amid a highly eccentric collection that also includes several dozen works by Grandma Moses — reposes the painting which was also, in its time, the most expensive ever sold. It was the auction of *Sunflowers*, for $76 million, that inspired Alan Bond to bid a couple of million more for his Monet *Irises* canvas, since rescued for a fraction of that price and currently residing in the J. Paul Getty museum in Malibu, California. Bond is said to have measured his canvas after he bought it and to have boasted: 'Mine's bigger.'

Even further off any map the art tourist ever heard of is the Tokyo Fuji Art Museum, an hour out of town in the gritty suburb of Hachiyoji, not far from a US air base and the Tokyo fire brigade headquarters. In spite of this unprepossessing location, the museum owns the most impressive collection of European art in Japan, if not all of Asia. The fabulous paintings are the property of a Buddhist sect, Soka Gakkai. Its current guru, Daisaku Ikeda, raised several hundred million dollars from his followers to amass a collection so vast that less than a tenth of it can be put on display at any one time.

The centrepieces are two Renoir portraits, the most controversial works of art purchased in Japan during the boom. The acquisition of these paintings, for a total of $47 million, led to a year-long international police chase and still-unresolved charges of fraud. Arrayed around is a veritable history of European art — from Veronese, Bellini and Ghirlandaio, to the only Goya in Japan, works by Cézanne, Morisot and Caillebotte, and Manet's masterwork, the *Promenade*. Unfortunately, the day I visited, one of the Renoirs, a Pissarro, a Utrillo, a Sisley and God knows how many other masterpieces were stored in the cellar because there is not enough room to hang them. Like hundreds of other great paintings — a large part of the Western world's art heritage was devoured by Japanese speculators — it may be years, decades even, before they are seen again by the public.

By the beginning of 1996, there was no doubt that Japan had come at least part of the way down the track towards Miyazawa's vision of working to live, rather than living to work. In the arts and entertainment, in sport and travel, in outdoor recreation and indoor wining and dining, people in Tokyo, Osaka and Yokohama — the three vast conurbations where half the Japanese live — enjoyed access to as great a cornucopia as residents of any other great city in the world. And, battered by half a decade of slowly-rising imports, and slowly crumbling cartels, prices had finally begun to fall to the levels where people could afford to enjoy them — in spite of the long, lingering recession. Deflation might have been giving the Ministry of Finance conniptions, but it proved a godsend to Japan's long-suffering consumers.

There were, of course, some hold-outs. The latest fad, in the long, hot summer of 1995, was the introduction of 'dress down Fridays' by a number of large Tokyo corporations. The idea was to allow staff to wear casual clothes one day a week for comfort, and to encourage informality and perhaps even creativity. Unfortunately, many middle-aged salarymen, used to wearing suits and ties six days a week, and lounging on the tatami-mat floor watching television in their *yukatas* on Sundays, simply did not possess any casual clothes, apart from perhaps a musty pair of plus fours and a Polo shirt left over from the golf boom. Some borrowed from their sons' wardrobes; others walked into department stores which were quick to cash in on 'dress down' outfits, and paid $3000 for a casual 'uniform' off the back of the dummy. They complained that when they set off for work dressed like this, the neighbours whispered that they must have been sacked.

However, these were exceptions. After the great waves of staff cuts that swept through Japanese industry in the 1990s, the traditional buttoned-down, job-for-life office worker, with the company pin in his lapel and the company song on his lips, probably represented only one worker in four. The other three, or at least those who had a job, were more comfortable enjoying their leisure — although more concerned than ever about the economy, the cost of living, social security and the environment, in that order. For a progress report, I called on the Economic Planning Agency, which drafted Mr Miyazawa's 'Lifestyle Superpower' report, to see whether any measurable progress had been made on these big issues.

There was little good news, which may be of comfort to those Western critics who still believe that the bureaucrats cannot centrally plan a huge, diverse economy like Japan's. You cannot simply pull a lever and change a nation of workaholic savers into fun-loving spenders. In fact, the agency was about to quietly bury the plan — which was originally due to run for the five years from 1992 to 1997 — and come up with a new one. Economic growth forecasts were the biggest and most conspicuous blunder. The Economic Planning Agency had predicted a comfortable 3.5 per cent per year; instead, Japan had floundered in its deepest, longest recession since World War II. In the first four years of the plan, instead of 14 per cent, the economy had grown a mere 2.2 per cent. That was the bottom line. Along with stagnant growth had come stagnant salaries, falling store sales and low consumer confidence.

Working hours had declined marginally (from 1958 hours in 1992 to 1903 in 1994), but were still nowhere near the target of 1800 hours a year. Interestingly, Americans (1976) were now actually working longer hours than the Japanese, although workers in the United Kingdom (1902), France (1678) and Germany (1529) all had a far easier life. Housing affordability was the only target out of the twenty-four lifestyle goals that was likely to be achieved. The price of a seventy square metre apartment had fallen from a peak of 8.5 times annual income to a multiple of 5.1 by mid-1995 — although other statistical evidence showed that this had come at the price of ever-longer commutes. Lenders were still offering 'three generation' mortgages which could be handed down from father to son and paid off over ninety-nine years. In Sydney, Australia's most expensive city, a typical apartment is still double this size and costs considerably less.

The other statistics make equally depressing reading. Hardly a single goal was likely to be achieved, conceded one of the Economic Planning Agency's senior bureaucrats who briefed me on the plan's failures. Only 25 per cent of Japan's roads had sidewalks judged safe for the elderly and handicapped. Nursing-home beds were way short of target, a particular worry in a fast-greying society. Half the population still lived in areas that were likely to be flooded. Trains in Tokyo were still carrying 199 per cent of capacity at peak-hours. The provision of city parks and greenery had improved marginally, but there were no data on traffic flow, indicating that, if anything, congestion had got worse instead of better.

At the end of the day, you are left with the uncomfortable impression that all the diversions Japan has learned to enjoy in the past few years — the ski-domes, the Monets, the holidays in Cairns — are really just distractions from the awfulness of their daily lives. I am sure many of my Japanese friends would gladly swap them to live in a handsome, well-planned city with clean air, comfortable accommodation, reasonable working hours and a pay packet that translated into a decent lifestyle. Indeed, a few Japanese have managed to migrate to Australia in recent years. One was featured in a magazine the other day boasting that he was living like a king in a waterside house on his pension of $55 000 a year — which even enabled him to fly around in a helicopter. Unhappily for the Japanese who prefer to live in their own country, the bureaucrats' grand plans are not going to deliver them that sort of lifestyle; not in five years, not even in fifty-five.

'A nation of ants' is how former French Prime Minister Edith Cresson once described Japan. The following table, based on 1993 and 1994 data, reveals some important differences between Japanese and Australian ways of life.

SOCIAL INDICATOR	JAPAN	AUSTRALIA
Average working week	39.3 hours	35.9 hours
Annual holidays	2 weeks	4 weeks
Trade union membership as percentage of workforce	19.6	35
Strikes (days lost per 1000 employees)	1.9	76
Per capita GNP	US$34 630	US$17 980
Unemployment	3.5 per cent	8.8 per cent
People receiving government benefit (e.g. pension)	9 per cent	34 per cent
Doctors per 1000 people	1.7	2.3
Life expectancy (men)	76.1 years	75 years
Life expectancy (women)	82.2 years	80.9 years
Population	125 million	18 million
People per square kilometre	331.4	2.3
Religion	Shinto 81 per cent, Buddhist 89 per cent (many people follow both)	Christian 73 per cent
Nobel prize winners	8	3

Source: *Europa World Year Book* 1996, *The Statesman Year-book* 1995–96, *Australian Government Year Book* 1996.

'PEOPLE THINK OUR LIFE IS GLAMOROUS,' SAYS the geisha, sucking in her breath as a five-metre brocade sash is wound tightly around her middle. 'But it's hard work … imagine dancing in this!'

It has taken nearly an hour to transform Kaori Takagi, a high-school dropout from the countryside, into Hagika ('Bush Clover Blossom'), a walking, talking work of art that is — along with Mount Fuji and cherry blossoms — Japan's ultimate cultural cliche.

Her hair is stiff with camellia oil and pinned with silver combs, her face painted into a ghostly mask with black circles for eyes and a tiny scarlet rosebud of a mouth. She is trussed in ten kilograms of exquisite silk and hobbles along on wooden clogs. Tonight she will entertain a group of tourists at a local inn, pouring them sake while trading witty banter, strumming her three-string *shamisen* and performing traditional dances. She will try not to drink herself — extricating oneself from the costume to go to the toilet calls for the skills of Houdini.

For three centuries, geisha like Hagika have been entertaining the wealthy merchants and haughty samurai class of Kyoto, Japan's old imperial capital. It was here that *karyukai*, the 'world of flowers and willows' reached its peak of exquisite refinement. It is also here that the twentieth century has finally caught up with this ancient profession. Kyoto is running out of geisha.

'This is a very serious situation,' says Hiroyuki Yamasaki, planning chief of the Kyoto Tourism Committee. 'One-quarter of Kyoto's economy depends on tourism, and the geisha is the symbol of the city's culture.'

Before World War II, there were more than 1000 geisha attached to the five 'flower districts' which monopolise the business. By 1955, this was down to 674; today, there are only 199 fully trained geisha left, and seventy-eight apprentices.

THE WORLD OF

Look closely at the faces in the summer Gion *matsuri* — one of Japan's most famous festivals, when radiant geisha ride through the city on huge floats — and you can detect, beneath the pancake make-up, the lines and wrinkles of advancing age. Ninety per cent of the *jikata* (geisha who play musical instruments) are over fifty, and some are in their eighties.

Mr Yamasaki blames the vanishing geisha on the decline of traditional Japanese music (Western-style pop dominates the hit parades and karaoke machines), the collapse of Kyoto's silk industry and the corporatisation of Japanese business. 'Before, wealthy merchants owned their companies and would think nothing of paying hundreds of thousands of yen for a geisha party,' he says, 'but nowadays, shareholders might have a problem with this. Companies prefer other types of sponsorship, like boxes at J-League [Japan's new national soccer competition].'

As well, Mr Yamasaki could have added, Japan's postwar economic miracle has ended the heartbreak of poverty-stricken families forced to sell their daughters into the industry. Older geisha in Kyoto remember being traded, at the age of six or seven, for a bag of rice or 100 yen.

The cost, controlled by another ancient Japanese tradition, the price-fixing cartel, is another major problem. Book a group of four into a tea-house, turn on a few seasonal titbits of food, some sake and two geisha, and ninety minutes' of strictly non-sexual fun will set you back a minimum of $2500.

The image of geisha parties has also been tainted with sleaze following revelations of the crooked political deals and bribery conducted behind the *shoji* screens. One prefectural government has recently been exposed for squandering $12 125 of the taxpayers' money entertaining Tokyo bureaucrats at a geisha party attended by just thirteen people.

In the old days, the geisha's ambition was to snare a wealthy *danna*, a patron who would find her a place to live and support her as a mistress. In today's tough economic times, sugar daddies are hard to come by and many geisha have to make do with four or five part-time *danna* sharing the expenses.

And the costs are extortionate. Hagika's hand-crafted silken kimono is worth about $20 000, by no means the most expensive you can buy, and a popular geisha may have to maintain a wardrobe of 100 different outfits to match her age, the season of the year or the mood of the party. If she dribbles her sake, the dry cleaning costs $150.

Most important of all, the old wooden inns and tea-houses where they practise their trade are all very colourful, but conditions for the people who work there have changed little since the days of bonded serfdom.

Like many of Kyoto's geisha, Hagika came here from rural Yamaguchi at the age of fifteen hoping to earn some money to help support her widowed mother. She was taken in by the 'madam' of an *okiya* ('geisha house'), who agreed to arrange for her training, in exchange for her earnings — the only way a woman can become a geisha. That was seven years ago, and Hagika still has not graduated from the distinctive costume of a *maiko*, an apprentice. Just to qualify for the *shamisen* takes fifteen years, and there are many other skills a geisha has to acquire — singing and dancing, conversation, the tea ceremony and scent-sniffing. 'They are not just entertainers, but highly skilled performers,' says Mr Yamasaki.

In Hagika's case, she was required to work up to eighteen hours a day, and in her first year had only two days off. Geisha get no paid holidays, have no pension and, until recently, did not even have medical insurance. As for the money, Hagika calculates she was earning about $60 000 a month for her madam. All she saw of this was $500 which was tossed to her as 'pocket money'. Even her tips were confiscated.

Finally, last year, she plucked up courage to become the first geisha to walk out and sue the madam of her house. 'It's been a difficult time, but someone had to be the first to stand up for her rights,' she says. When the case was publicised, other geisha fed up with being exploited contacted her. Fujika ('Wisteria Flower'), who is performing tonight with Hagika, had been beaten and kicked, lost seven kilograms in weight and had her hair falling out with worry before she, too, quit.

Eventually, four of the women — with financial backing from a wealthy hotelier — teamed up to form Kyoto's first independent geisha agency. 'We are keeping the traditional arts, but running it like a regular business,' says Chinami Kawakita, the agency's manager. 'The girls now earn a salary and have paid holidays like any other worker.'

Traditional Kyoto closed its ranks, blackbanning Hagika and her colleagues. Their music teachers refuse to teach them, tea-houses won't take their bookings, hairdressers won't fix the special styles they need and their regular customers have been pressured into dropping them.

However, Kyoto's new-wave geisha are winning a whole new clientele of tourists, younger businessmen and even schools by cutting their prices to an unheard-of $175 an hour. 'We think that is reasonable. The "flower districts" are driving people away with their prices and their elitist attitude,' says Ms Kawakita.

Mr Yamasaki and the geisha operators have come up with a different, more traditional, solution. Instead of improving conditions and introducing a bit of competition to lure people back, they are looking for a $6 million subsidy from the local government.

'Something has to be done,' says Mr Yamasaki, who admits even he has never been able to afford to pay for a geisha party out of his own pocket. 'Kyoto without geisha — it's unthinkable.'

FIVE
NAMAZU, THE
KILLER CATFISH

> *'There will be no earthquake in Kobe. Precautions would require an enormous amount of money, and would leave a huge burden for the younger generation.'*
>
> — KOBE MAYOR KAZUTOSHI SASAYAMA, SUCCESSFULLY URGING THE CITY'S DISASTER PREVENTION COMMITTEE IN 1985 NOT TO INSTITUTE ANY MAJOR PRECAUTIONS AGAINST AN EARTHQUAKE

IN THE GLOOM OF A SHUTTERED schoolroom, the cloying smell of incense filled the air as Akihiro Harada knelt on his heels beside a still form shrouded in a fluffy floral blanket. Inside was his sister Keiko, three days dead, but as yet unburied. Mr Harada, a neatly suited man of forty-seven who works as a computer systems engineer, was naturally concerned. 'The family is very anxious that she should be buried as soon as possible,' he said. 'But what can we do?' He ticked off the problems on his fingers. 'There are no coffins left. Even if there were, we could not get her to the crematorium. And even if we could, there is no gas to cremate her. There is nothing left of Kobe.'

On the floors and tables of this makeshift morgue, in the cracked and crumbling concrete Nishinomiya school where just three days before pigtailed elementary schoolgirls recited their lessons, twenty-seven other bodies lay wrapped in blankets. Many, like Keiko, were crushed to death in bed — her house was tossed a metre in the air, and then crumpled like a discarded paper cup. It is a miracle her husband and her two children escaped, said Mr Harada, though what they are going to do now no-one knows.

Some of the dead had names in hand-painted characters on pieces of paper laid on their bosoms. Others will never be identified, crushed beyond recognition. A single yellow chrysanthemum, the Japanese funeral flower, sat in a one-cup sake jar. Someone had placed a pile of rice balls, traditional offerings to the souls of the newly dead, beside another.

Relatives knelt among the corpses sniffing back tears as they observed *otsuya*, the Buddhist equivalent of a wake, and prayed for the gas to be restored before the stench of decomposing bodies overpowered the incense.

It was three days after the most terrible natural disaster in three-quarters of a century had hit Japan, devastating the country's sixth-largest city, the great port of Kobe. Three days, and the enormity of the destruction and loss of life was still hard to comprehend. Oily pillars of smoke hung over Kobe as Mayu and I walked along the rubble-strewn streets. The injured still called in vain for help as they lay buried in the ruins. Survivors wandered in a trance, sucking water from broken pipes and scrounging handfuls of rice. 'Bury the dead. Feed the living,' was the curt command of the Marquis de Pombal when a similar calamity overwhelmed the Portuguese capital of Lisbon two centuries ago. In Kobe, 1995, after seventy-two hours they had not begun to cope with even this most basic imperative.

This was *dai jishin*, the 'Big One', that all Japanese dread. In twenty-two seconds, a monster earthquake wrought almost as much damage as General Douglas MacArthur's Superfortresses during the last weeks of the war when, for twenty-five days and nights of terror, they pounded the city with high explosives and napalm, almost obliterating it. Although the scale of the destruction from what would be called the Great Hanshin Quake would take months to tally, the toll eventually passed 6000 dead, 35 000 injured and 250 000 — one in six of Kobe's entire population — rendered homeless in the depths of a bitter midwinter. Damage estimates would range up to $125 billion, more than the annual expenditure of the Australian government.

In the days to come, the great quake would also expose to the pitiless gaze of the world's media, one of the most abiding conceits of modern Japan — that here was a country so rich, so organised, so confident in its technological prowess that it could master even the forces of nature. The world's wise men once came to Japan as humble pilgrims to the shrines of earthquake science and disaster planning. After January 17, 1995, they would come to learn only one lesson — how not to handle a great natural cataclysm.

For days, the nation sat glued in horror to the wall-to-wall television coverage. As the blundering and procrastination unfolded, one magazine compared the aftermath of the quake with the dithering between the dropping of the first atomic bomb on Hiroshima and Japan's surrender nine days and tens of thousands of lives later. 'In neither case is there a sense that the protection of the lives of the citizenry is the government's responsibility,' it editorialised. A new phrase for the quake began to dominate the media. It was no longer referred to as *tensai*, a natural disaster, but *jinsai*, a man-made calamity.

The bare statistics do not even begin to convey the real horror that was Kobe after the quake. Mayu and I flew in the following day, and walked ten kilometres through the ruins talking to survivors. All communications were paralysed. The railways and the elevated highways were wrecked, and the backroads that had survived were blocked for days by chaotic traffic jams. We were hoping that enough transmission masts had survived for our newly hired mobile phone to work, otherwise Kobe would have been the foreign correspondent's worst nightmare — sitting on the world's biggest story, with no way to get it out.

The transformation of the city was stomach-churning. The first time we came to Kobe was for a lighthearted little piece on a retired businessman and Aussiephile named Tom Morimoto who had just published the first Australian–Japanese dictionary. I remember thinking as Tom showed us around that Kobe's civic fathers had blown a splendid opportunity after the war to rebuild a city worthy of its spectacular natural setting, straddling a river delta with the forested crags of the Rokko Mountains as a backdrop, the placid blue-grey waters of the Seto Inland Sea at its feet. Now they would have another chance.

Kobe was the first port opened to foreign shipping after Commodore Mathew Perry's 'black ships' ended two centuries of isolation in 1854. Before the quake, it retained something of that 'treaty port' feel, with a rollicking nightlife and a lively international community of some 120 000 foreigners. The grand nineteenth-century mansions where the *gaijin* captains and silk traders once lived, some of them glorious Gothic Revival follies, attracted tourists to the hills. The city was famous for its fabulously fatty *wagyu* beef and the sparkling springs which feed the breweries where Japan's finest sake is made.

In the postwar decades, however, much of Kobe's character had been buried under ugly, pell-mell development. The Kansai region, of which Kobe and neighbouring Osaka are the principal cities, became Japan's second most important regional economy. If it were a country, Kansai businessmen are fond of boasting, it would be worth more than Canada. The port of Kobe, with a pre-quake population of 1.5 million, is second only to Yokohama. The city of Osaka is Japan's third most important. Only if the quake had poleaxed the capital itself could it have had a more devastating effect on Japan — on human life, on the economy and on the national psyche.

Scientists would later deduce that Awaji Island, a rural backwater of rice paddies, seaweed farms and fishing villages a few kilometres offshore in the Inland Sea, was the epicentre of the quake. Legend has it that Awajishima was the first place brought into existence by the creation gods Izanami and Izanagi. The characters that make up Kobe's name reflect this — they mean, literally, the 'Doorway of the Gods'. The two days Mayu and I spent there, it was more like the gates of Hell.

The clocks on the walls of the shops and buildings were frozen in time, their hands stopped at 5.46 — the precise moment when, in the pre-dawn darkness of that Tuesday morning, the earth's fabric ruptured, releasing the force of a hundred atom bombs ten kilometres beneath the sleeping city. If there is any consolation, it is that the quake hit when most residents were still tucked in bed. Three hours later, in the middle of the morning rush, the toll would have been even more horrific. Packed commuter trains would have plunged from collapsing bridges, killing thousands more. Down the main street of Kobe, Flower Street, supposedly quakeproof high-rise buildings had collapsed or lurched like drunks, turning the highway into a shining river of broken glass, flowing around islands of fallen concrete. If the quake had hit at 9 a.m., this would have been a street of high-rise mass graves.

The narrow backstreets, partly blocked by wooden houses which collapsed under the weight of their top-heavy blue-tiled roofs, were filled with columns of people. The world's best-dressed refugees, some in cashmere coats, dragged along their life's possessions in designer suitcases. Three days after the quake, even the most essential services had not been restored. The only way into or out of the quake-zone was on foot. The most technologically advanced society on earth had become a rabble of hunter–gatherers. The telephones did not work, so people gaffer-taped messages to the ruins of their homes — 'Sato family safe. We have gone to Auntie Hiroko's.' There was no gas, so people pulled planks from the ruins and grilled foraged balls of rice over bonfires. There was no mains water — people dropped buckets in ancient wells and greenish ponds where dead goldfish floated.

The city's life-support systems, which were supposed to withstand anything short of a nuclear attack, had been ripped apart. The *shinkansen* bullet train, for thirty years the proud symbol of Japan's technological prowess, was put out of action by the collapse of a dozen supposedly earthquake-proof bridges. The Hanshin Expressway, Kobe's great elevated highway, which its designers also boasted would survive even the most violent quake, had fallen on its side like an overturned banquet table, scattering trucks and cars like toys. The port of Kobe, Japan's largest and most modern docklands, was a wasteland.

It was spooky to realise later that, buried in the ruins we walked past, people were dying. More than 2000 were still 'missing' on this third day after the quake, and the emergency services were only now starting to dig. Friends and relatives stood outside collapsed buildings, waiting for rescuers who never came. Many of the people we stopped told harrowing stories of listening helplessly as the screams of their trapped friends and relatives got fainter and fainter and finally stopped. The police, ambulancemen and firefighters, who should have been the front line of defence against such a calamity, were paralysed.

We passed a fire station where the firemen had their engines pulled up on the sidewalk and were polishing them while Kobe burned. The water mains were busted and using sea water to put out the fires might damage their pumps, they said. The military could spare 5000 people to help carve sculptures for the upcoming Sapporo Ice Festival — we watched them on television, gobsmacked. But the law (or so it was argued) did not allow them to help out in an emergency like an earthquake unless specifically invited by the local authorities — and no-one was willing to invite them until three days later, when it was all too late.

The outside world, which rushed to offer help, was equally stunned when their offers were either ignored or rejected. Japan has no agency for handling such offers, a bureaucrat explained lamely. The reality appears to be that the Japanese bureaucracy in faraway Tokyo neither knew nor cared about the extent of the calamity. When the media coverage made it impossible to ignore Kobe's agony any longer, they were too embarrassed to admit they could not handle the disaster — and were prepared to allow people to die rather than accept assistance.

While Tokyo dithered and delayed, people trapped in the wreckage were dying needlessly from their injuries and from hunger, cold and exposure. The first forty-eight hours after any disaster are the most vital — and the government squandered these vital hours wrangling over legal niceties such as whether the Constitution allowed troops to be sent in. Some people whose bodies were finally recovered a week later were found to have chewed clothing and pieces of wood to try and stay alive. Subsequent autopsies conducted by the Hyogo Medical Examiner's Office showed that 4.1 per cent of those who eventually died were still alive at the end of Day One — around 250 people, most of whom should have been saved. This is almost certainly an underestimate. Typical of those who need not have perished was Kimie Hirakawa, a 61-year-old woman living alone, whose body was not found until an extraordinary fifty-three days after the quake. She had lain, trapped in her bed, for eight days until she finally starved to death. The body was covered in bedsores.

What emergency services were still functioning were stuck in monster traffic jams. Incredibly, no-one had yet taken responsibility for the most basic priority — clearing private traffic off the roads to let ambulances and fire appliances through. The driver of a truck with 'emergency medical supplies' hand-painted on the side told us it had taken him twelve hours to drive the twenty-five kilometres from Osaka. Flashy red fire engines sat uselessly outside fire stations. Ambulances were nowhere to be seen. Even the *omawari-san*, the usually ubiquitous local bobbies, had mysteriously disappeared. The only help the people of Kobe could count on was from the traditional neighbourhood unit that has survived since feudal times — the household on either side, and the three across the road.

Thousands of casualties were carried to the surviving hospitals and medical centres, many of them on litters improvised from planks pulled from the wreckage. The hospitals, however, had long since run out of essential supplies — they work on a 'just-in-time' delivery system, and only kept one or two days' drugs, blood and bandages on hand. We visited the casualty section of the Nishinomiya Hospital, a new and undamaged high-rise building clad in gleaming white tiles which outwardly promised the best in Japanese medicine. Inside was a scene from 'MASH', with scores of seriously injured people lying dying on the floor, tended only by their friends and families.

'I have no idea how many patients we have seen,' sighed Dr Toshiki Hongo, an internal medicine specialist with bleary eyes and brown bloodstains on his white gown. 'We have 200 inpatients — every bed is filled — and we cannot cope.'

Dr Hongo said most drugs had run out, the X-ray machine was broken and the operating theatre was out of action. 'We can offer nothing except basic care. All we can do is watch. More than 100 patients have died here already, and there will be more if we don't get help.' The hospital had ceased to function except as a warehouse for the dying — it not only could offer no medical care, there was no food, no water, not even a roll of toilet paper.

As so often happens in a disaster, it was the old and the poor and the marginalised who bore the brunt of the quake. They lived in ancient rickety houses, and in slummy barracks housing 'day labourers' which collapsed like packs of cards. Nagata ward, the suburb worst hit by the quake, was an ethnic neighbourhood housing thousands of Vietnamese boat people and Koreans, many of them descendants of people kidnapped and brought to Kobe as slave labour during World War II. Nagata-cho was a neglected ghetto of run-down tenements, narrow alleys and little iron-walled workshops where the main industry was the manufacture of plastic shoes. Overcrowded, unplanned, unserviced by parks or water reservoirs — ignored, in a word, by the Kobe authorities — fires roared through the neighbourhood unchecked, incinerating twenty blocks along with everyone in them.

Old folk, who often sleep downstairs in their children's houses, rolled in futons on the living-room floor, were especially over-represented on the casualty lists. More than half the dead were aged over sixty, and the largest single demographic group was women in their seventies. One of the great shortages in the refuges where the survivors huddled was of adult diapers.

Foreign correspondents groped for words to describe the quarter of a million survivors who crammed into every available hall, and who slept in their cars and camped out around bonfires under the stars. 'Stoic' was one favourite. 'Numb with shock' got a good workout. '*Shoganai*' from those who wanted to show off their Japanese — the universal Japanese cliche, 'It can't be helped'.

It was certainly the strangest disaster I have ever covered. No-one ran. No-one wept — not until the funeral services, at any rate. No-one cried out in anger. There was no sense of urgency. Most incomprehensible of all, in the millions of words of media coverage, there was hardly a single story of heroism. After the quake, there was a rash of divorces among survivors — often women who discovered their husbands did not love them enough not to flee the house without them when the quake hit. Families huddled passively in nests of blankets on the floors of refuges waiting for their next cold rice ball, waiting to be told what would happen to them next. They didn't seem to understand yet that the authorities — the bureaucrats — neither knew nor cared.

In the Nishinomiya primary school gymnasium — on the floor above the makeshift morgue where the twenty-eight bodies lay — 800 survivors were hunkering down among the vaulting horses on the floor of a gymnasium for the fourth night in a row. It was a refuge centre with the misery, if not the mud, of Africa — these people had lost everything but a few bags of possessions snatched from the ruins. Dogs and cats fossicked around among the encampments of cushions and blankets, each with the occupants' shoes neatly arranged outside. Must keep up appearances. Someone had rescued a tank of tropical fish, someone else a gaudy sports trophy.

'We don't know how long we will be here — two months? Three months?' said Li Young Fan, forty-nine, an ethnic Korean. He was sitting on a blanket, with his wife and four children, three days of stubble on his chin and a white towel wrapped around his neck. In fact many of the 600 public buildings requisitioned would be home for the thousands of homeless for the next seven months. 'I lived in Hokkaido and Niigata and Okinawa before I chose Kobe. I came here because they said it never snowed and it never had earthquakes. I have had a good laugh about that since last Tuesday.' Mr Li told us he wanted to take his family away from the hall. 'It's not safe.' Concrete was spalling from the school's supporting pillars, windows were shattered, walls cracked. 'But where could we go? We have nothing left, nowhere else.'

Although Mr Li had lost everything in the wreckage of his house, and had been surviving on rice-ball rations in this freezing hall, he insisted on placing a carton of milk in front of me, and a can of orange soda in front of Mayu. How could we refuse? How could we accept? As we pondered the politenesses, a massive jolt like a pile-driver pounding the floor shook the hall. There was absolute silence, apart from a dog yelping in fright — not a scream, not a word until the aftershock was over. Parents hugged their children protectively. They were used to this by now, the survivors of Kobe. There had been hundreds of aftershocks since the Big One flattened the city.

I picked myself up from the floor, dusty and embarrassed. Although I live in Tokyo, where 'minor tremblers' like this are common, I will never get used to the sudden, sickening sensation of an earthquake — something like being in a light plane which simultaneously gets slammed by a crosswind as it falls into an air pocket. Mr Li barely blinked. 'You be careful now,' he said as we left.

Each night after we walked back to our hotel in barely scathed Osaka from those scenes of utter devastation and harrowing tales of hardship, we tuned in to Tokyo television. Although it was less than 500 kilometres away, these were pictures from another planet. The prime minister, Tomiichi Murayama, waggled his white prawn-head eyebrows with concern as he expressed sympathy, then continued with his schedule of official luncheons and speeches. The National Land Agency — which is supposed to be responsible for handling disasters like this — closed down its switchboard and knocked off promptly at 5 p.m.

Three days after the quake, no-one was in charge. Thirty-two separate ministries and agencies were squabbling over the responsibility — and the juicy spoils from the reconstruction graft to come. Even the *Japan Times*, normally a staid Establishment paper, was moved to editorialise: 'It was tragically clear by the end of the week that many more victims might have been found alive if a full-scale, coordinated rescue effort had been undertaken with greater speed. Bureaucratic excuses for the tardiness and insufficiency of much of the assistance effort have been readily forthcoming, but they do not convince.'

When we trekked back to Kobe the following day, the mood

had changed. Resignation was turning to anger. We talked to Hiroshi Morimoto, who stood guard over an arcade where his damaged fruit and vegetable shop had been cordoned off. He had a black eye sustained when his wardrobe fell on him the night of the earthquake. 'What do I think of the government's relief efforts?' he spluttered. 'They sent Murayama-san down here in a helicopter — they should have left him in Tokyo and filled the helicopter with things we really need like food, water, blankets.'

The *Asahi* newspaper carried a derisive front-page banner: 'Quake Toll 3083. Response Finally On.' But, in reality, in spite of the cacophony of sirens, the army trucks finally rumbling through the streets, the mechanical pterodactyls ripping at the concrete carcasses, the government had still not begun to comprehend the scale of the disaster. In most un-Japanese style, a woman survivor denounced Mr Murayama on national television: 'We want action, not words. President Clinton has offered to help, but you can't even decide whether to accept.' On the famous Kobe baseball ground, someone inscribed in ten-metre characters 'Give us water'. Kazuo Nakagawa, the governor of Osaka Prefecture dismissed the pleas of the 250 000 cold, hungry and homeless citizens. 'There ought to be something they can do for themselves,' he sniffed — a modern-day Japanese version of Marie Antoinette's great one-liner, 'Let them eat cake.' Retribution, however, would come for him, too. A couple of weeks later Mr Nakagawa was caught up in a corruption scandal and hounded from office.

The efforts of private charities and enterprises merely highlighted the almost unimaginable neglect of the government. The 73-year-old chairman of the Daiei supermarket chain, Isao Nakauchi, helicoptered into Kobe to inspect the damage the afternoon of the quake — three days before Japan's prime minister could find the time. The company brought barges loaded with supplies into the city that same day, twenty-four hours before any government lifted a finger to help. Buddhist temples, ancient Shinto shrines, the Red Cross — even Japan's largest and most feared gang of *yakuza* Mafia, the Yamaguchi-gumi — put official relief to shame. Tom Morimoto, our friend in Kobe who lives near the gang's headquarters, sent us a fax describing how the gangsters were distributing everything from well-water to box lunches, noodles and babies' nappies to quake-affected locals. At news of this, the police magically reappeared, doorknocking the neighbourhood trying to stop people accepting the *yakuzas'* charity.

By the end of the second week, the media were running out of angles. Other events were elbowing Kobe off the international television news lists — floods in the Netherlands, trade wars with China, the saturation coverage of the O. J. Simpson 'trial of the century'. The big-name correspondents flew on to the next disaster, leaving behind the stringers to sweep up the crumbs.

For the more analytical media — particularly Japan's aggressive news magazines — the dimensions of the disaster were becoming a little clearer, and it was possible to sit back and ask some fundamental questions. Why was the quake not foreseen? Why was there no disaster plan? Why did the emergency services fail so dismally? Why did supposedly quakeproof structures collapse? And above all, who was responsible, and what should be done to prevent a repetition on an even more nightmarish scale if — God forbid — Tokyo should be hit by a quake of similar magnitude?

The Kobe quake should hardly have come as a surprise. The timing and the location, yes — but the inevitability of major quakes is something all Japanese have had to live with since the beginning of time. The Netherlands has floods; Australia has bushfires; Japan has earthquakes. Just as the Inuit people (Eskimos) are said to have a dozen words for snow, so the Japanese are connoisseurs of the quake. When one is felt, a discussion may ensue over whether it was a *keishin*, or perhaps even a *jakushin*. The gods could hardly have picked a worse place on the surface of the planet to locate what would become the richest and the most technologically advanced country of the late twentieth century.

Japan is, without question, the most geologically dangerous place on earth — ten times as likely, for instance, to experience a major quake as California, according to the eminent American geophysicist Dr Frank Press. Grinding away remorselessly beneath the shaky archipelago are four great tectonic plates — continent-sized slabs of the earth's crust. Every so often the immovable object gives way to the irresistible force, and the surface of the earth, many kilometres above, thrashes violently about. The ancient Japanese believed that a giant catfish, Namazu, lay asleep under the islands, occasionally awakening to wreak great havoc with a flick of his tail. Modern seismologists call it the 'Pacific rim of fire'.

All around as you travel through Japan is the evidence of this geological instability — a boiling underground ocean of magma, under unimaginable heat and pressure, struggling to escape. Eighty-three active volcanoes rumble continuously, threatening to vomit white-hot lava at any moment. The largest eruption in recent years, of Mount Unzen on the southern island of Kyushu, was still sweeping away small towns in an unstoppable avalanche of mud and ash four years after it first exploded in 1991, killing forty-three people. Everywhere, you can find steaming sulphurous springs — many developed as *onsen* resorts — and vast moonscapes of shattered volcanic rock, devil's playgrounds of ancient eruptions of awesome force.

Not even the most transient and insensitive visitor can fail to be aware that this is a country living on the edge. In the three years we were in Japan, there were no fewer than five earthquakes which resulted in loss of life — and dozens more which scared the daylights out of people. One of the most popular novels of recent times depicts Japan actually sinking into the Pacific after a monster quake blows a hole in it.

The first earthquake in recorded Japanese history was in the year 818. Since accurate records began to be kept after the Meiji Restoration in the middle of last century, Japan has experienced a serious earthquake every three or four years, often with the initial shock aggravated by fire and tsunami, the dreaded giant tidal waves that follow undersea tremors. By 'serious' I mean one that kills a dozen or so people and destroys several hundred buildings — about the size, say, of the 1990 Newcastle (New South Wales) earthquake. Every decade or so there is a *daijishin*, a 'Big One', that kills more than 1000. Nowhere in Japan, except possibly Okinawa, is safe — earthquakes have struck from the icy waters of the Kurile Islands to almost every prefecture of Japan's four home islands.

There is no excuse for anyone in authority not knowing these basic facts — they come from a booklet put out by the Japanese Meteorological Agency. The same publication would have informed anyone interested that the Kobe region was not an earthquake-free zone, as most people seemed later to want to believe. Within living memory, in 1925, the north of Hyogo Prefecture, in which Kobe is located, was ravaged by a major quake that killed 428 people and wrecked more than 3000 buildings.

The false sense of security that lulled the people of Kobe into foregoing precautions like insurance — only 3 per cent of residents had even a limited cover — is incomprehensible to an outsider. The complacency of the city and prefectural authorities, who declared 'it could never happen here' and failed to take more than the most rudimentary precautions, is unforgivable. The quotation at the head of this chapter is from a former bureaucrat named Kazutoshi Sasayama — the mayor of Kobe at the time of the quake — who persuaded the council that, since Kobe would never have an earthquake, it would be a waste of money to plan for anything bigger than one with a moderate strength of five on the Japanese scale. The Great Hanshin Quake which hit ten years later rated the maximum seven.

In modern Japanese history, only the famous 1923 earthquake that hit Tokyo caused more damage and loss of life. The Great Kanto Quake killed 140 000 — people crushed in the initial quake, burned to death in the fires that swept the city and drowned by the monster tsunami that came roaring up Tokyo Bay. The quake obliterated two-thirds of the city and its great port of Yokohama, causing $100 billion in damage, and wiping out half of Japan's annual gross domestic product. It took seven years for the country to recover.

This is the beast in the basement of modern Japan — the certain knowledge that in a matter of seconds the achievements of half a century of economic miracle could be crushed to dust. In his book *Sixty Seconds That Will Change the World*, the journalist Peter Hadfield has done an admirably researched job on what this would mean to Japan and the world. The headlines would read: up to 150 000 dead, more than two million homeless. The American authority Haresh Shah of Stanford University calculates the damage at $2 to $2.5 trillion, followed by a giant sucking sound as Japan becomes a global black hole into which the world's savings vanish, plunging the rest of the planet into recession. The lesson of Kobe is that, if anything, this doomsday scenario may be a gross understatement — and Japan, contrary to the reassurances of its government, is almost totally unprepared for it.

Not long after we arrived in Japan, Mayu and I went to the Meteorological Agency to find out a little about earthquake planning and prediction. I was researching a feature article at the time, but we both also thought it was a sensible idea to discover what sort of personal precautions Tokyo residents should take. The agency occupies a glass and concrete block across the moat from the Imperial Palace, just a few minutes' walk from our office in the Marunouchi district. It is the nerve centre, explained the PR man, Hiroshi Araya, for the most elaborate, and the most expensive, seismic monitoring program anywhere in the world. Since it was established in the early 1960s, it has cost more than $1.3 billion; its budget in 1995 alone was $130 million.

Buried all over Japan, more than 2000 electronic sensors keep watch on the country's geological health, much like a patient wired up in an intensive-care ward. They probe every orifice, every organ — mountaintop movements calibrated by earth-orbiting satellites; sensors dropped down kilometre-deep shafts into the earth's crust; great underwater arrays fanning out across the bottom of Suruga Bay southwest of Tokyo, supposedly one of the country's most seismically dangerous spots. Into the agency the signals pour, and onto the great banks of computers every tiny tremble is logged. Ten thousand quakes a year are recorded here, more than one an hour, and about three a day powerful enough to be felt.

The idea, however, is not just to record the seismological vital signs of the country. It is to be able to predict from the data where and when a quake may strike next — a sort of geological weather forecasting service. Indeed, Canutish as it sounds, the agency is actually required by Act of Parliament to give at least two days' warning of a *tokai*, a particular type of quake that could prove especially destructive. Some 300 scientists spend their days analysing every blip on the seismographs, searching for a meaningful pattern that may crack the earthquake code. They always find one — half a dozen scientists claim to have spotted 'precursors' to the Kobe quake — but it is always after the event. This is about as much use as picking the winner of a horse race a month after it is run.

Earthquake prediction is a dream that has been around for as long as man has been wondering, and worrying, about earthquakes. The ancient Greeks examined the entrails of chickens; the Chinese once claimed great promise in observing the behaviour of birds and fish; the Americans, Californians in particular who live under the sword of the San Andreas fault, put their faith in seismic monitoring in the 1970s. But nowhere in the world, other than in Japan, the country most at risk, is the public expected to believe that earthquake prediction is not only theoretically possible, but a scientific reality. Even after Kobe, a poll showed that 53 per cent of Japanese still believed this fantasy.

Mr Araya takes particular pride in showing visitors Room 233 at the agency. It looks like a small military command centre. In the anteroom are six grey couches, a row of metal lockers and some privacy screens. Inside is a conference room with wall maps, electronic displays, a long table with speakers and notepads in front of each chair. When a threatening pattern is detected by the monitors, this is where the six *sensei*, the wise men who form the agency's earthquake panel — six of Japan's most eminent seismologists — are supposed to gather to weigh the evidence, and decide whether to alert the prime minister that a major quake is imminent.

'And then?' I asked Mr Araya. He looked at me blankly. 'What are people supposed to do if a quake is forecast?' Mr Araya giggled in embarrassment. He didn't know. There was no plan. How could there be — think of the lives that would be lost in the panic to escape if a major quake was forecast for Tokyo. Think of the trillions of yen lost if the world's second most important economy were to shut up shop.

So, for twenty years, Room 233 has sat empty and unused. The committee has never convened. Indeed, in the thirty-odd years since Japan's world-famous earthquake prediction system has been in operation, not a single quake of any sort has ever been forecast. During that time, ten major earthquakes have occurred, culminating in the Kobe quake, killing 7000 people, and causing countless billions of dollars worth of damage. Yet the Japanese public has not been warned about a single bang for its 1.3 billion bucks. It is a safe bet that it never will be. The Japan Research Institute, one of the city's think-tanks, calculates that to bring Tokyo to a halt for a single day would wipe an eye-popping $9 billion off Japan's economy. The price is simply too high to pay, even if, by some fluke, the six wise men should see a quake coming.

In the days that followed the quake, Professor Kiyoo Mogi of Tokyo University, the chairman of the earthquake committee and Japan's best-known seismologist, became a familiar sight on television, gesturing importantly at technical charts, explaining in great scientific detail what he thought had occurred and warning of aftershocks. Professor Mogi is one of those six wise men who have been carrying special pagers in their pockets for twenty years, waiting for a call that has never come. Unfortunately, with the ruins of Kobe such an eloquent testimony to the total failure of earthquake prediction, no-one was rude enough to ask him publicly whether the hundreds of millions of dollars would not have been better spent on practical precautions against the inevitable, rather than the attempted prediction of the unpredictable. Only those outside Professor Mogi's immense, and immensely lucrative, sphere of scientific influence would be brave enough to challenge the fundamentals of Japan's failed earthquake forecasting strategy.

One of these is Associate Professor Robert Geller, an American geophysicist at the same university, a scientist of international standing and a trenchant critic of earthquake prediction. Just two months before the Great Hanshin Quake, he warned again that prediction belonged in the realm of science fiction. Without going into the algorithms of plate tectonics, he used a simple demonstration. Picking up a pencil, he began to bend it between his hands. 'Everyone knows that sooner or later it is going to break,' he explained, 'but no-one can predict exactly when, or where. There are so many variables. That is precisely the problem with earthquake prediction. Not only is it not possible to predict earthquakes reliably at all, there are good scientific reasons for thinking that in principle it's impossible.'

I visited Professor Geller, a tall gangling man in his forties, in his cramped and cluttered midden on the second floor of a postwar block on the campus — a jerry-built building he fears would probably fall to bits if a major quake hit Tokyo. He was, if anything, even more convinced after Kobe that predicting quakes was impossible, and that the 'outrageous' amounts of money being spent on the prediction program should, instead, be applied to improving building design, and to a fast and effective disaster-response plan.

He shoved a tape of the national NHK television coverage of the morning of the quake into a video cassette recorder to demonstrate. Half an hour after the quake hit, an electronic display was still showing the worst damage had occurred in the Kyoto region, 200 kilometres from Kobe — and registering a reassuring force of five on the Japanese scale. 'Look at that,' cried the professor. 'They have still not announced where the epicentre is, nor the magnitude on the Richter scale — the two most important pieces of information. If you had that, you would know that there had to be severe damage and loss of life in Kobe.' Geller laughs when I ask him how he gets on with his colleagues such as Professor Mogi. 'The whole thing is a big joke — all seismologists know prediction is impossible. Mogi says to me "Geller-sensei, do you think you could say 'very difficult' instead of 'impossible' when you are interviewed about it?"'

Geller's is not a rogue opinion. A year or so before the quake, I had listened to another international expert speak, at a luncheon organised by the Foreign Correspondents' Club. This was Dr Frank Press, one of the elder statesmen of American science, a member of the National Academy of Science, adviser to governments and a world authority on both earthquakes and disaster planning. He said more or less the same thing. 'We have made great advances in the past twenty or thirty years — with global positioning satellites, for instance, which can record the movements of the earth with an accuracy of one centimetre. But no-one as yet has the answer [to earthquake prediction]. We may have to go to chaos theory to solve the problem.'

I have read similar statements by scientists from Greece, from Russia and from South America — all places where they have been learning the hard way, for centuries, about earthquakes. Japan is the only advanced country in the world where people are still expected to believe that earthquakes can be predicted in any meaningful way. By meaningful, I mean that it is not a terribly useful piece of information to learn that somewhere in the Kanto region (an area twice the size of Tasmania which includes Tokyo as well as lots of farmland) will suffer a major earthquake between the years 1995 and 2020, as Professor Mogi seems to think.

More depressing still, this is unlikely to change — even after the shambles that was Kobe. Japanese scientists and bureaucrats defend their turf and their budgets as vigorously as their counterparts anywhere else in the world. Under the Japanese system, Professor Mogi is the *sensei*, the ultimate authority and, no matter how mistaken, his views can never be challenged. He continued to insist — even as his own minister expressed doubts that Japan had benefited from his research — that his scientists were on the right track, although it might turn out to be a '100-year project'.

This conveniently ignored his predecessors' promise — in 1962 when the program was launched amid massive hype and worldwide interest — to find an answer within ten years. Thirty-three years later, Japan was no closer to predicting earthquakes. Yet — risking the ridicule of international scientists, and the anger of their own taxpayers — the gravy-train thundered on through the darkness with no-one able to yank the brake. In fact, the Science and Technology Agency managed to gouge another $530 million out of the national treasury to expand its prediction fiasco from fiscal 1996.

So, if prediction so comprehensively failed, how did precautions fare? This is one area where — until they saw Kobe — most knowledgeable people would have bet that Japan led the world. From its building standards to its public awareness campaigns, from the automatic sensors designed to halt the bullet trains in their tracks at the first tremor to the national network of refuges for victims, it had been one of the most-admired preparedness programs in the world. To get an idea of how it was supposed to work, Mayu and I took the train one day to Tachikawa, near a US air base on the outskirts of Tokyo, where the Tokyo Fire Brigade has spent some $120 million building a sort of disaster theme park with a deadly serious purpose.

We had a ride on the earthquake machine — a mock-up of a kitchen mounted on clever hydraulics that simulate the Great Kanto Quake — crying '*Jishin da*' ('It's an earthquake'), turning off the gas, propping the door open, placing sort of tea cosies on our heads and diving under the table. This is the drill every Japanese child is taught from kindergarten. We survived this test, did well with the fire-extinguishers, learned how to resuscitate a row of wax dummies, but unfortunately choked to death trying to find our way through a smoke-filled maze. Similar exercises are held in parks all over Japan every September 1, the anniversary of the Great Kanto Quake, to raise people's quake consciousness and increase their chances of survival.

I am rather embarrassed to admit that I swallowed all this — until I saw Kobe. It just goes to show how relentless the propaganda is — and how gullible even the self-styled visiting experts. Precautions? Just 2 per cent of Kobe residents kept stocks of essentials like food and water on hand, as advised. Even after the quake, when people stripped the shops of everything from tents to little gadgets which are supposed to fix your furniture to the wall, the figure for Tokyo was only 20 per cent. After one recent earthquake in Hokkaido, people were asked the first thing they did when they felt the shock. The winner, by a handsome margin of 60 per cent, was 'Stand there waiting to see what would happen next.'

Refuges? The biggest hoax of all — it emerged after Kobe that only seven of Japan's forty-seven prefectures have done anything at all by way of stockpiling emergency supplies. The efforts of those seven are hardly reassuring. Chiyoda-ku, the heart of Tokyo's business district where my office was, has a daytime population of about one million who would be stranded if a major quake hit. The council has just twenty designated shelters, where 140 000 packets of biscuits and 35 000 tins of food are stored. Little wonder the typical Tokyoite's reaction to questions about the coming Big One is a shrug and a *'Shoganai'*.

If prediction is impossible, and precautions inadequate, prevention of catastrophic damage by clever design should be considerably easier. If you are prepared to spend the money, the technology for quakeproof buildings — well, 'quake-resistant' is the save-your-ass phrase the engineers use — certainly exists in theory. Most of Tokyo's modern skyscrapers use 'base isolation' systems in which the building floats on shock-absorbing fluid-filled cushions. Some, like the recently completed seventy-storey Landmark building in Yokohama — Japan's tallest — also incorporate massive computer-controlled weights in the roof, to automatically counterbalance the sideways force of a quake. Unfortunately, there were none of these 'smart buildings' in Kobe, so no-one yet knows whether they work in practice. What we do know is that nothing built more than about a decade ago is safe, which is probably 90 per cent of the buildings in Japan.

Seventy years before the Kobe quake, Frank Lloyd Wright boasted that his 'earthquake proof' Imperial Hotel was one of the very few high-rise buildings to come through the Great Kanto Quake virtually unscathed. The world's first government code for earthquake-proofing public roads and bridges was promulgated in Japan three years later, in 1926. The building standards have been periodically upgraded ever since, most recently in 1981, to what the government boasted were the toughest in the world. Just twelve months before Kobe, Japanese Construction Ministry bureaucrats had returned from an inspection of the Northridge quake-scene in California, shaking their heads at the destruction of high-rise buildings and highways. 'It could never happen in Japan,' they said. 'Our standards are far higher, our highways are three or four times as strong.'

It took just twenty-two seconds to destroy that hubris. Yes, many of the structures that collapsed and burnt were old wooden houses — that you would expect. The surprise, to me, was that 'traditional' Japanese housing design has not evolved in a more sensible way after centuries of experience with earthquakes. Foreign architects goggled at the massive tiled roofs supported by flimsy wooden walls which simply collapsed, crushing everyone inside. They are built like this to withstand typhoons, which were regarded as the greater menace. The post-and-rail construction methods, with large cut-outs for doors and floor-to-ceiling windows, also make for structural weakness. Canadian and American timber housing importers were falling over themselves after the quake to show how their cross-braced iron-roofed wooden houses in Kobe (which, incidentally, cost less than half the price of Japanese-style dwellings) survived unscathed.

However, many of the structures were neither old nor wooden. They were high-rise blocks of apartments, stores, hospitals, factories and offices supposedly built to the strict specifications of Japan's earthquake code. About half the commercial buildings in the city were damaged — many of them in a particularly horrible way, when one floor collapsed, turning everything inside into a ragout of crushed bodies, furniture and masonry. A thirteen-storey bank building simply fell on its face in the road — if it had happened during office hours most of the 1000 or so people who work there would have been killed. A cluster of swanky apartment buildings on reclaimed land by the harbour known as Ashiyahama Seaside Town — buildings up to twenty storeys tall and constructed as recently as 1980 — had their main support columns twisted and buckled as they sank into the mud.

Damage to government infrastructure was, if anything, even more calamitous. The supposedly indestructible *shinkansen* bullet train — for thirty years a symbol of Japan's technological pride — had its tracks collapse in a dozen places. A one-kilometre section of the elevated Hanshin Expressway, built in 1970 and supposedly subsequently reinforced, snapped and fell over, crushing scores of vehicles and killing their occupants. Eighty per cent of Kobe's vital port fell to pieces, with cranes capsizing into the sea and the concrete cracking up like peanut brittle. The docks were built on reclaimed land which suffered from a well-known phenomenon called liquefaction — earthquakes force water to the surface, turning the soil to quicksand.

Particularly chilling for Tokyo residents was footage of the subway system, with its 'quakeproof' tunnels collapsed. Two million people trapped in the dark beneath the streets of Tokyo, with a tsunami roaring towards them through the tunnels of the world's busiest subway, would have to be the ultimate urban nightmare.

Preliminary investigations found that many of the structural failures which cost so many lives were due primarily not to inadequate building codes, but to greed, incompetence and lack of supervision of the general contractors involved. Japan's *zenecon*, as they are called, are one of the principal sources of the hundreds of millions of dollars worth of bribes which keep the Japanese political system afloat. Contributions, not cost or competence, win the contracts. Directors and executives of almost all the major companies were on trial for corruption at the time of the Kobe quake.

That elevated expressway which provided the quake's most memorable image, for instance, collapsed because the contractors cut corners. They built it in eighteen months, half the usual time, to meet a March 1970 deadline for the Osaka World Exposition. To speed things up, the contractors ignored the building code and used precast concrete instead of welded steel beams to support the highway. This put almost double the load on the supporting pillars, which simply snapped under the stress of the quake. Steel reinforcing was scrimped, welding was substandard and lumps of wooden forming were left in the pillars. A magazine photograph revealed the ultimate engineering crime: a supporting column of a bridge which snapped neat as a knife-cut across the point where two concrete pours had failed to knit together.

There is also overwhelming evidence that, as well as dodgy construction practices, the government standards themselves were grossly deficient. They were supposed to resist a quake with the force of the Great Kanto Quake, 7.9 on the Richter scale. The Kobe quake, however, although closer to the city was considerably less powerful, at 7.2 — and yet nearly one-fifth of the city fell down in ruins. Quite simply, 'earthquake proofing' is a myth. Almost every building, every bridge and highway in Japan has been built to inadequate safety standards and will fall to bits if subjected — as, inevitably, one day they will be — to a quake as violent as the one that hit Kobe.

However, instead of calling a public inquiry to learn from the disaster, the bureaucrats responsible almost immediately began a cover-up of massive proportions. The companies whose negligence contributed to the disaster were lining up with their hands out for contracts to rebuild the city within hours of the quake. By ten o'clock that morning — while Kobe still burned and hundreds of people lay trapped in the ruins — Japan's

Construction Ministry agreed to allow two companies which had been banned from public works after being convicted of bribery to tender for the reconstruction work. A smirking *zenecon* executive referred to the quake as a *kamikaze* — a 'divine wind' that would save the construction companies by blowing big contracts their way.

It was left to one man to make what I thought came closest to an honest apology for the failures of construction and planning — Mr Yumio Ishii, the vice-president of a civil engineering firm called CTI Engineering Co., a major consulting firm involved in the planning and design of government public works. This is what he said:

> Tears well up in my eyes as I watch television, because facts presented on the screen show that what we have been saying for years were lies. We were arrogant. Especially the bridges which were built during the years of rapid economic growth (1965–1975) have become too scary to cross, after what happened in Kobe. Everything was booming, and we were told to build light and thin and cheap.

One other act of atonement is worth noting. Mr Takashi Nakanishi, aged thirty-seven, the council official in charge of the Kobe water supply, committed suicide by throwing himself out of a fourth-floor window. As far as I know, he was the only person — politician, bureaucrat or emergency worker — to take responsibility or to be held accountable for the man-made disaster that was Kobe.

So, if prediction proves to be a myth, precautions are largely ignored and 'quakeproof' buildings collapse, the last line of defence against the Big One should have been Japan's emergency services. We had seen them demonstrating their skills so many times — immaculately drilled firemen hosing down towering infernos, Japanese emergency medical teams flying into the chaos of refugee camps around the world, the military restoring order from Cambodia to Mozambique. So where were they when they were needed? Nowhere to be seen.

I had seen something of natural disaster before — a major earthquake in Bucharest, Romania, in 1977, in which more than 1000 people died; Darwin after Cyclone Tracy flattened the city; I was in Hobart when the Ash Wednesday bushfires swept through in 1967. But I have never seen an emergency where there was so little sense of urgency, such indifference by the authorities, such a lack of preparedness, such an unwillingness to take the initiative and such a deficit of every commodity from clean water to simple human kindness. The victims waited passively for the 'authorities' to turn up — which, of course, they never did, at least not until too late.

In Nagata ward, that densely packed district of wooden houses that was worst-hit by the quake, twenty-four firemen with four fire engines stood by helplessly without reinforcements for six hours as 3700 buildings went up in flames around them. The quake had ruptured the water mains, as might have been expected. However, there were no emergency reservoirs, no water tankers, no authorisation for pumps to take salt water from the ocean less than a kilometre away, no deployment of helicopters or planes to dump water on the flames, no dispatch of extra fire units from nearby towns and cities until far too late. All the firemen did was watch and polish their engines, as twenty city blocks turned to ashes and nearly 1000 people were incinerated in the holocaust. The fires were still burning three days later.

Many of these secondary fires erupted when ruptured gas mains were ignited, often by people stumbling around with lighted candles in their hands. It was a mystery to me for several months why the Osaka Gas Company, the private utility which supplies the region, had not immediately shut off the supply. Then I read an interview in which the company's president, 65-year-old Shinichiro Ryouki, explained how he had agonised over the decision. 'Even though we could prevent secondary disasters, would it be a good decision?' he was asking himself. 'Once we turn off the gas we have to go to every household to reconnect the supply. This will take an enormous amount of time and money — it will cost several billion yen and seriously affect our business.' So, for six hours and four minutes after the quake hit, Mr Ryouki continued to pump gas into the inferno of Kobe, valuing the lives of hundreds of his fellow citizens less than the profits of the Osaka Gas Company.

Nor did the emergency services perform any better. What units there were in the district were unable to reach the scene because no-one would take responsibility for policing access routes. While people died in the ruins, doctors, nurses, paramedics, ambulances sat jammed in the traffic for hour after hour. Hospitals and surgeries ran out of supplies in the first few hours — and many were paralysed because they had no emergency power or water. The only helicopters to be seen the first two days were those of the television news crews — there were emergency helipads, but they were too far away, too small or crowded with refugees. To complete the farce, the $80 million satellite communications system the Kobe Council had bought for just such an emergency would not work.

This total failure of disaster preparedness cannot even be blamed on a shortage of money. 'Kobe Inc.' had been notorious for years for squandering billions of dollars on showy promotions of little benefit to its citizens — the 1981 Portpia Expo, the Universiade sports extravaganza in 1985, an Urban Resort Fair in 1993. There was little interest, however, when it came to spending money on mundane but essential things such as stockpiling supplies, improving planning and facilities in the old wooden slums, and properly equipping the emergency services. Even if they had been able to find water, Kobe had less than half the number of fire engines mandated by the national government.

All this is not, incidentally, just my somewhat jaundiced opinion. By an extraordinary fluke, we have the eyewitness assessment of some of the world's most experienced disaster planners — a conference on earthquake emergencies opened in Kobe the very morning the quake struck, and quickly adjourned to allow delegates to inspect the disaster at first hand. Charles Scawthorne, a structural engineer from San Francisco, summed up the views of many of the foreign experts who came to Kobe expecting to see a slick, efficient, effective response. 'We are seeing the breakdown of the city function,' he said as Kobe burned around him. 'We did not even see that in the Northridge [Los Angeles], Loma Prieta [San Francisco] quakes, or even in Mexico City in 1985. I have seen thousands of people just wandering the streets not knowing what to do, with little assistance, and with insufficient food, water and sanitary facilities. The lifelines have broken.'

Later, there was an even blunter assessment from one of the world's most experienced disaster planners, who spent a week touring hospitals and evacuation centres. Dr Leonid Roshal, a member of the executive committee of the World Association for Emergency and Disaster Medicine, heads an emergency medical team in Russia and has seen action after disasters in Georgia, Armenia, Iran and Israel. 'Kobe is in a state of anarchy,' he said. 'I cannot understand why Japan refused to accept help. [I worry about] what would happen if there was a disaster in Tokyo.'

Elsewhere — the United States, which gave Japan its modern system of governance is the usual model — a state of emergency would be declared, the Federal Emergency Management Agency (FEMA) put in charge, and the military would be immediately called on to deal with a massive disaster such as this. The Northridge earthquake, for example, hit the Los Angeles area at 4.31 a.m. on January 17, 1994 — eerily, precisely one year before the Kobe quake. Nineteen minutes later, President Bill Clinton was woken up with the news; an hour after the quake a state of emergency was declared and FEMA took charge; and by 6.10 a.m., less than two hours later, thousands of troops had been airlifted in for search-and-rescue operations. Within five hours of the quake hitting, everyone who had been trapped was rescued, and within seven hours every fire was out.

The contrast with the chaos of Kobe could not be more stark. For a start, no-one knew how severe the earthquake had been because the Awaji Island seismic monitoring centre was broken, and the one in Kobe lost its phone-line. Even when the Japan Meteorological Agency belatedly realised something was going on, there was no procedure for an emergency alert — it sent a fax to the National Land Agency which sat there until someone arrived for work two hours later. The prime minister's office was not even on the JMA distribution list — Mr Murayama heard the news about an hour and a half later on television. Then he went to his office, where he had to wait, twiddling his thumbs, until 8 a.m. when someone on his staff turned up. The ultimate absurdity was that President Bill Clinton, aboard Air Force One en route from Denver to Los Angeles, knew about the quake hours before Japan's hapless prime minister. The shock was picked up by a spy satellite watching North Korea, and the news relayed to him within ten minutes via the National Security Agency headquarters in Maryland.

Japan does have an agency modelled on America's FEMA — the Disaster Prevention Coordination Division of the National Land Agency. It was established in the wake of another bungled disaster, the so-called Isewan typhoon of 1959, in which more than 5000 people were killed. However, in thirty-five years, Japan has never declared a state of emergency — not even after Kobe. Even if it had, it is hard to see what could have been done. The agency has a staff of thirty-six (most of them bureaucrats on loan from other agencies, and none with any special training in crisis management), no communications network and no legislative authority to do anything other than 'coordinate'. In the event, on Day One of the quake, the switchboards were unmanned after everyone went home at 5 p.m. It took five days to establish even a field headquarters in Kobe itself. Even now, more than a year after the quake, Japan still has no coherent national emergency plan.

Four hours after the quake, Cabinet met — not an emergency meeting (those are mostly reserved for 'crises' such as the yen going up on the foreign currency markets), but a regular scheduled meeting which first discussed at length the contents of a routine speech Mr Murayama planned to make. When the subject of the quake did finally come up, it was suggested that National Land Agency Minister Kiyoshi Ozawa should be sent to report on the damage. 'I don't think it is necessary for me to go that far yet. We have to watch the situation for a little longer,' he said. At that stage, television was reporting nearly 1000 people dead and showing helicopter footage of the city burning like a funeral pyre.

So where were the armed forces? Incredibly, they were not called out in any numbers until Day Three — this in spite of the fact that there are more than 50 000 troops, naval units and airforce bases in the immediate area, equipped among other things with 420 helicopters which could have been of inestimable use in the initial emergency. The troops had tents, blankets, water tankers, fully equipped field hospitals and mobile kitchens each capable of serving up 200 portions of hot rice and miso soup in forty-five minutes. None of this capacity was called on for the first two days — 250 000 people had to freeze and starve through the bitter winter nights until then. The US Navy, which had two aircraft carriers in the area, offered them as floating hotels and hospitals for the survivors — yet another offer of help which was spurned.

Politics, it later emerged, played a large part in the failure to call out the troops. Mr Murayama's Social Democratic Party had bitterly opposed Japan's so-called Self-Defence Forces for more than forty years, arguing that they were unconstitutional. Although Mr Murayama had dropped his formal opposition in the deal with the Liberal Democratic Party that delivered him the prime ministership, many in the party remained pacifist zealots at heart. The Kobe region, in particular, is a hotbed of the Left — returning, among other prominent radicals, the Parliamentary Speaker Ms Takako Doi — and had important local elections coming up. The city is so politically correct that the Japanese navy had never dared send a ship to Kobe until the quake — and when it did, there was a report (later denied) that the waterside workers refused to unload the emergency supplies. When the Daiei department store donated truckloads of water, milk, bread and rice, and delivered them to Osaka's Itami airport, the airforce was not allowed to helicopter the supplies out to the victims. 'We have never allowed the SDF [Self-Defence Forces] in to Itami airport before,' explained the airport controller.

When Mr Murayama was told the Hyogo Prefectural Governor, Toshitami Kaihara, had finally requested troops, instead of a cry of relief the prime minister exclaimed, *'Sore wa taihen na koto ja nou'* — 'That's terrible.' Mr Kaihara, who turned up for work three hours after the quake, at his usual hour of 9 a.m., snapped at reporters, 'What difference would a few hours have made, anyway?' Hundreds of lives is the answer. In any case, it later emerged that troops could have quite legally gone to help in Kobe, without the charade of a 'request' from the governor. Article 83 of the Self-Defence Forces Law states quite explicitly that the military can intervene 'if urgency is required in view of the nature of the calamity'.

In contrast with the arrogance and indifference of most in government, the commander of the Chubu district army headquarters, Lieutenant General Yusuke Matsushima seemed to have some inkling of the enormity of the bungle. He burst into tears at a press conference, apologised for the delay in despatching troops and confessed: 'I am very sorry. If we had been there we could have done many things.'

Only on Day Two was Mr Murayama persuaded to change his schedule and take a personal interest in the disaster. Even then, there was an air of total unreality about the decision-making process. Leaked minutes of a Cabinet meeting held twenty-eight hours after the quake show the following enlightening exchange, while Kobe burned and the death toll climbed past 2000:

Ms Makiko Tanaka, Science and Technology Minister: The first priority should be getting food to the survivors. Don't you think we should rush them some quick energy food supplements like bananas or cheese?
Mr Kozo Igarashi, Chief Cabinet Secretary: Isn't that just like a woman, to be thinking in those terms. What about sending them some rice?

Just as reprehensible was the failure to take advantage of the offers of help which came flooding in from more than seventy countries around the world. Surreally, it seemed as if the earthquake was regarded far more seriously in Ulan Bator (which offered gloves), Helsinki (mobile phones), Canberra (mineral water), Tunis (ten tonnes of tinned tuna) and Manila (President Fidel Ramos offered a month's pay) than it was in Tokyo. More than half the offers were rejected, and many others accepted so late, and so grudgingly, that they were of little use.

The Swiss were particularly outraged. They offered a world-renowned team of tracker dogs, a search-and-rescue outfit so conscious of the need for speed that they keep their equipment stored at Zurich airport, and boast they can be anywhere in Europe in four hours. 'The first forty-eight hours are the most vital — if we are going to find people alive it will be then,' said its leader. Japan thought otherwise. The team was held up while bureaucrats wrangled over whether or not the dogs posed a quarantine risk. They finally got to Kobe fifty-five hours after the quake and found eighteen people in the ruins — every one of them dead. A million doses of American influenza vaccine, which might have saved lives in the shelters, were rejected because the vaccine had not been approved for use in Japan.

Safe in their offices in Tokyo and Kobe, the bureaucrats went to extraordinary lengths to obstruct the rescue effort and make life even harder for the victims — there is simply no other way of interpreting it. In spite of a chronic shortage of doctors and medical supplies, the world-famous Medecins Sans Frontiers — an international team of volunteer doctors who have saved lives everywhere from Bosnia to Rwanda — was refused permission to treat people in Kobe, the first time any country in the world had rejected them. It was first claimed this was because, being foreigners, they would not understand the workings of Japanese bodies. Later, this was amended to their lack of Japanese medical qualifications. However, that still does not explain why even Japan's own international medical brigade, a fully equipped 400-strong outfit of doctors and paramedics, was barred from Kobe because (in the words of another faceless bureaucrat) 'they have no authority in domestic emergencies'.

Another search-and-rescue outfit was allowed in, but then refused permission to travel to Kobe until they had first eaten dinner, had a good night's sleep and then eaten breakfast. 'God knows how many lives we could have saved,' said an exasperated rescuer. 'These people seem to have no idea what an emergency means.' A team of Canadians arrived to erect temporary housing, bringing with them their own field rations and tents. The first question they were asked by Kobe officials was, 'Can you eat miso soup?' Chafing to get on with the job, they were then forced to sit through a welcome lunch, and a long meeting with local officials which was of little value since no-one had thought to provide interpreters. Permission was then refused for them to fly in emergency housing units by helicopter because this would violate air traffic regulations.

While hundreds of bodies rotted in school gymnasiums, out-of-town hearses were refused permission to ply in Kobe because they lacked the correct licence. The Agriculture Department sent a team to the scene — not to feed people, but to prosecute anyone charging more than the regulation $10 for a kilogram of rice. A city official refused to put emergency workers in touch with the 5000 people who had volunteered for community work unless an application was first made in writing during office hours. Even at a time of national emergency, there could be no exceptions to the bureaucratic rule book. If there wasn't a rule for it, it couldn't be done.

The sickest anecdote I heard was from a Canadian volunteer helping hand out food to refugees in a shelter. The day's meal was soup containing eggs, and vegetables and noodles. One ancient woman, who had evidently lost her false teeth in the quake, humbly asked the official ladling it out whether she could just have a bowl of soup, with no solids. He frowned and went away to ask his supervisor. The supervisor was unwilling to make a decision, and went and asked his boss. Eventually, the message came down the line that this was not allowed. The sad old lady turned away from the food line and would have gone hungry if the Canadian hadn't taken it into his own hands to give her a ladle of soup.

In other cases, there was a distinct aura of wounded pride about the whole affair — as though the quake, or at least Japan's failure to deal with it adequately, was something shameful, to be hidden from foreigners in particular. A Kobe council spokesman named Masahiro Hatanaka attempted to explain why foreign doctors had not been allowed in. He made the truly amazing claim that Kobe 'already has plenty of doctors' — obviously having never visited one of the hospitals where they were dropping with exhaustion. However, Mr Hatanaka then let slip what was really on his mind: 'I also had the impression that doctors from the West still think Japan is a developing nation.' Leaving aside the question of whether Japan is indeed part of the Third World medically (as some Japanese doctors and most patients will tell you it is), here was an official prepared to deny injured people medical attention that might save their lives rather than swallow a real or imagined slight to his nationalism.

There was one other man for whom principles counted for more than saving lives. Unfortunately, he was the man who should have been in charge of coordinating the entire emergency operation — Mr Kazutoshi Ito, the director of the National Land Agency's work-to-rule disaster prevention agency referred to earlier.

If the arrogance, the ignorance and the total contempt of the Japanese bureaucracy for the suffering of the people of Kobe has to take a human face, it should be that of Mr Ito, when he was finally cornered at a midnight press conference, some ten days after the disaster. Red-faced, chain-smoking, screeching and screaming at anyone who dared to challenge him and even ordering one reporter to leave the room for smiling, Mr Ito advanced the most preposterous excuse ever given for failing to send in troops to help a rescue operation. It deserves to be quoted in full:

Ito: In an emergency like this one, if you are referring to the central government having the power to suppress and suffocate the will of the local municipalities, it reminds me of the rebirth of Japanese militarism. In the name of the state of emergency, our country restricted the rights of the people and even trampled on the rights of the people ... I am firmly resolved that we shall never, ever return to the state of affairs that we were in fifty years ago.

Japanese reporter: Even at the price of killing thousands of people?

Ito: I cannot agree with the use of the expression 'killing' and will ignore that question. I'm very busy. I have no time to deal with critics.

He then walked out.

By year's end, the toll from the Kobe quake passed 6000 and was still mounting. Many of the additional 500 or so deaths were due to the inadequacy of the temporary shelters and the barracks-like blocks of prefabricated housing that were thrown up to house more than 50 000 families left homeless and destitute by the quake. Without heat and proper medical care, with influenza and diarrhoea reaching epidemic proportions, and often with only one hot meal a day, twenty-eight people had died in the first month at one hospital alone. Many older people succumbed to *hinanjo haien*, or 'shelter pneumonia'. Isolated an hour or more away from their old friends, family and neighbourhoods, and depressed by their losses, alcoholism and mental illness became rampant among the survivors. By November, twenty-two people who survived the quake had committed suicide by throwing themselves under trains, jumping off buildings, hanging or drug overdoses. Ritsuko Ogami, a social worker, called it Kobe's 'second agony'.

Still the bureaucrats would not end the torment. Thousands of prefabricated housing units sat on the docks in Canada, the United States and the United Kingdom while they argued for months about whether they complied with Japanese standards. As they huddled in their refuges, many of the survivors watched with envy television footage from the Netherlands showing people driven from their homes by floods. The commentators were agog. Two hundred and fifty thousand people evacuated from their homes in a matter of hours, and all were immediately housed in heated dormitories, with beds, hot food and all mod cons! The contrast with the shambles of Kobe could not have been more dramatic.

We went back to Kobe six months after the quake to see how the victims — and the reconstruction — were faring. It was a depressing picture. The air was a blizzard of asbestos fibres as wrecking balls smashed buildings to bits. In the reckless rush to rebuild, thirty-three construction workers had already been killed and 639 injured, terrible figures even for a country with Japan's dismal industrial safety record. The trains were running again and the elevated highway was being rebuilt, but there was little sign of confidence from the private sector and much of the old downtown was empty, fenced-off, rubble-strewn lots. The once-bustling entertainment district was nearly deserted, with bars, shops and restaurants boarded up and abandoned.

Those who could were packing up and leaving. The Bank of Japan estimated that since the quake 200 000 people, one in seven of Kobe's population, had already gone. Kobe's industrial base had been dealt a devastating blow — the wharves were still out of action, with many shippers switching to cheaper, more efficient facilities across the Sea of Japan in Pusan, South Korea. Some of the larger employers like Sumitomo Rubber (where the Japanese rubber industry began in 1909), Kawasaki Heavy Industry and Nippon Flour had closed. Many smaller businesses, particularly the backyard 'chemical shoe' shops in the ethnic Korean ghettos, had gone bankrupt. Unemployment was the nation's highest, and social workers were stretched to the limit.

The Kobe City Council, to be sure, was promoting a 'Phoenix Plan' for reconstruction — pretty drawings of tower blocks, parks and broad boulevards rising from the ashes. However, the plan had been drawn up in secret — with no community input — by a committee of bureaucrats, and even the planners admitted it was unlikely to happen. Prefabricated shacks were already springing up among the ruins, based on the old property boundaries which trace the outlines of the original tiny rice paddies. There was no overall reconstruction authority, and squabbling had broken out between the dozen layers of local government over basic infrastructure such as the need for wider roads. 'The reality,' said Koichi Yokoyama, a spokesman for the Kobe City Council, 'is that if people don't want to sell we won't resume their land. We don't have the money anyway.'

As for the survivors, rather than allow themselves to be exiled to the grim prefabs the government was building in the boondocks, several thousand people were still defying the police and living in tents and shacks all around the city. 'It's like living in a concentration camp,' sobbed one woman, who was being evicted from her refuge on the floor of a municipal office building. Nearly a year after people from around the world dug into their pockets so generously, most of the $2.25 billion donated for the earthquake victims had still not been distributed — a typical family which had lost its home looked like receiving around $5000, which in Kobe would not be enough to secure you a parking space for a year. On the first anniversary of the quake, 60 000 people were still living in 'temporary' accommodation.

As for learning the lessons of Kobe, there was little sign that the Japanese government would prove any more responsive than they have in the wake of similar disasters in the past. A 24-hour 'crisis management unit' was set up in the prime minister's office, but was given no legislative authority. A new 'disaster plan' was promulgated (the first in thirty-two years) — but it was dismissed as a 'useless hodgepodge' by the influential *Asahi* newspaper because it contained not even the most basic guidelines such as the force of an earthquake for which the planners should prepare. Its overriding principle, said the government, was that 'people should take care of their own safety'. As if, after Kobe, that was not obvious.

The bungling that went on at Kobe was not a one-off fluke, but just the latest and most serious in a series of failures in crisis management. Japan simply cannot handle emergencies. Just two years earlier a communications cock-up resulted in more than 200 totally unnecessary deaths. A warning that a giant tsunami tidal wave was bearing down on Okushiri Island off Hokkaido was delayed fifty minutes by bureaucratic paper-shuffling and did not arrive until after the villagers — who should have had plenty of time to reach the safety of higher ground — had been swept away and drowned. There was no inquiry, no-one was held responsible and nothing was done to improve the warning system.

In 1985, a Boeing 747 crashed into the mountains in Gunma Prefecture; within two hours a US military helicopter was overhead preparing to rappel men in to rescue survivors. According to Michael Anton, an American navigator who was there, the US command ordered the mission aborted at the last minute because 'the Japanese are on the way'. Through that long, cold night, voices of survivors, some of them children, were heard gradually fading away. Japanese rescuers did not arrive until ten hours later, when all but four of the 524 passengers were dead in what would be the world's worst single-aircraft disaster. 'Had it not been for efforts to avoid embarrassing the Japanese authorities ... many more lives would have been saved,' Anton confessed ten years later. Again, no inquiry and no-one held responsible.

Go back to the 1948 earthquake which devastated the Japan Sea city of Fukui, killing 3700 people, and you find the same pattern of indifference to human suffering and disregard of official obligation. Hitoshi Ashida was prime minister at the time, and this is what he wrote in his diary the next day:

> The morning newspapers devoted much space to reporting on the quake disaster, but they did not write much about the Cabinet crisis over the budget. This made my heart unexpectedly lighter. The feeling that I might have to resign as soon as tomorrow was dispelled.

At the end of the day, what the quake did was throw a harsh

and unforgiving light on the real nature of government in Japan. At every level, the response of the bureaucrats was what you would expect of people who will never be called to account. Buck-passing, insistence on pettifogging rules, refusal to take any initiative and inability to concede the urgency of the situation damned the relief effort. In some cases, such as the refusal of medical aid, it is impossible to avoid the conclusion that it was done from sheer bloody-mindedness.

In an attempt to quell the alarm that was felt, particularly in Tokyo, the city government produced a new assessment that in the event of a Kobe-sized earthquake, the toll in Tokyo would be only 9363 dead, 147 068 injured and 155 416 buildings destroyed. No-one took this seriously, since there was no convincing explanation of why a city eight times the size of Kobe would sustain only twice as much damage. Nor was anyone prepared to reconsider, in the light of the enormous damage caused by the liquefaction phenomenon, mega projects on reclaimed land going up around Tokyo. Indeed, the largest of these developments is sponsored by the city itself — a futuristic $130 billion plan to build a new urban centre, with a daytime population of over 150 000, on a 500-hectare artificial island in Tokyo Bay.

Some blame Japan's paralysis of leadership at such times of crisis, the inability to take fast, effective action, on the protracted consensus style of decision-making. Others say it is because no-one is in charge; there is a vacuum at the centre of power. My own view is that such unresponsive authoritarianism is inevitable in a country where people long ago lost sight of any connection between the way they vote and the way they are governed. The real government — the bureaucracy — is accountable to no-one. These appalling man-made-worse calamities will continue to occur until parliament, not the mandarins of Kasumigaseki, accepts its constitutional responsibilities and enforces its will.

Until then, the lesson of Kobe is that there is little advice one can give those who are worried about living in the planet's most dangerous place apart from 'get out, if you can'. Those who, even after Kobe, still believe the government's assurances of prediction, preparation and planning are doomed to be disappointed, or dead. The Big One is coming. The only questions remaining are when, where and what new outrage of government callousness and incompetence it will reveal.

PROFESSOR SUSUMU KATO PLUNGES HIS ARMS into a blue plastic bin and pulls out what looks like a soggy bundle of technicolour tripe. Carefully, he spreads it out on the stainless steel surface of a dissecting table in the morgue. Gradually, creepily, it becomes clear what it is — a human skin.

This skin, however, is like nothing on earth. It is luminous with orange and green and dark blue dye; it is decorated over every square centimetre with peony roses and maple leaves, with bolts of lightning, fire-breathing dragons and, in the centre, the gorgeous bare-breasted Princess Tamatori.

'This is one of the finest examples I have come across,' says Dr Kato, a professor of anatomy at Tokyo's Jikei Medical University. 'I am sure the owner, wherever he is, will be very proud that it is being preserved for posterity.'

Japan has been known for centuries as the land where tattooing has achieved, to quote the *Kodansha Encyclopaedia* 'the very highest level of artistic expression'. What has, until now, been a closely guarded secret within the inner circles of connoisseurs of this macabre art, is that techniques exist to save these living canvases from the grave.

Until a few months ago, this skin belonged to Mr Kazuhisa Takahashi, a middle-aged bank worker, who endured years of pain to have an amazingly elaborate tattoo impregnated across his back, his buttocks, his upper arms and his legs. He was obliged, as are most Japanese, to keep the masterwork a secret from all but his closest friends and family. Tattoos are associated with crime in Japan — its keenest aficionados are *yakuza* gangsters — and people who have them are banned from health clubs and swimming pools.

THE ILLUSTRATED MEN

Before his death, Mr Takahashi joined the 'white chrysanthemum society' of people who leave their bodies to science (so-called because chrysanthemums are the Japanese funeral flower) so that he could have the work, by one of Japan's greatest tattoo masters, preserved. Relatives came to Professor Kato, one of the few doctors in Japan who knows the ancient technique of flaying human skin. The method, which involves peeling off the skin and pickling it in a mixture of rice bran and salt, is not mentioned in the medical texts and was passed down by word of mouth from his old anatomy professor.

The finest collection of tattoo art is preserved in the medical museum of Tokyo University, Japan's premier university. Here, the skins of about thirty illustrated men are on display, amid an amazing collection of scientific oddities, including the bottled brains of five former Japanese prime ministers, the first man-made cancer and several Japanese human mummies.

The visitor is chillingly reminded of the penniless beggar in the Roald Dahl horror story with an Impressionist portrait tattooed on his back, who disappears one night after dinner with a wealthy art collector. Indeed, though everyone denies it, there are persistent rumours of a trade in these tattooed skins. People are said to have willed their backs for money, and the author D. M. Thomas claims that a particularly splendid specimen was sold a few years ago for US$50 000.

These tattoo art galleries are not open to the media — students and visiting doctors are their usual audience — and Mayu (with her camera) and I were among the first outsiders allowed to see the skins. This furtiveness underlines the ambivalence of the Japanese towards tattooing, which has been in and out of popularity since the time of the original inhabitants, the ancient Ainu people. Until quite recently, older Ainu women could be seen with *anchipiri*, the 'black stone mouth', which was thought to be sexually alluring.

There have always been undertones of criminality about *irezumi*, 'injecting soot', as it's called. Tattooing was used until last century to brand and ostracise criminals — in Osaka, for instance, a criminal would have a dog tattooed on his forehead. Perversely, in seventeenth-century Tokyo, it became fashionable in court circles. Courtesans would have the names of their lovers — or, more subtly, dots corresponding with their age — tattooed on their elbows.

It came back into popularity in the nineteenth century among the so-called 'naked classes' — Japanese manual labourers who traditionally wore only a loincloth. Today, holders of occupations such as carpentry, masonry, fire fighting and gambling keep the tradition alive, among the 20 000 or so Japanese who carry a tattoo. Tattooing was officially (but with little effect) banned for nearly a century on the grounds that it was 'deleterious to public morals', although in the port city of Yokohama studios were allowed to remain open with signs proclaiming 'Foreigners Only'.

Foreigners have always been fascinated by Japanese tattoos — and not only brawny Jack Tars. In the days when it was more socially acceptable, both the future King George V of England and the future Tsar Nicholas II of Russia — visiting Yokohama as midshipmen on navy goodwill visits — had dragons tattooed on their forearms.

Yokohama still has some of the world's most famous tattoo artists, men like Yoshihito Nakano. Like most

THE ILLUSTRATED

tattooists, he has adopted the nom-de-needle of the master with whom he spent an eight-year apprenticeship, and is known as Horiyoshi III. Mr Nakano comes from the classic tradition of Japanese tattoo art, many of whose themes are taken from the great fourteenth-century Chinese adventure classic, the *Suikoden* (the *Water Margin*), which became a smash hit in Japanese cultural circles when it was translated in 1805.

Nothing could be further from the crudely carved hearts, skeletons, nudes and knives that Westerners associate with tattoos. 'It is like comparing a *manga* [comic] with a Rembrandt,' says Mr Nakano.

Mr Nakano's clients' bodies are decorated with great feats of the martial arts; with fierce dragons, temple dogs and cherry blossoms; with Fudo, the fanged Buddhist guardian of Hell, brandishing a flaming sword, and Kannon, the goddess of mercy, riding a golden carp. Each carries its own symbolism of magic, health, strength, wisdom, prosperity and bravery in the pantheon of tattoo mythology.

His tattoos have been exhibited at international competitions around the world, winning prizes in places as diverse as Bologna, Italy and Amsterdam (though not, ironically, Japan which has no tattoo convention). His latest prize-winning piece of living art is Mr Genichiro Katori, aged thirty-five, the proprietor of a kimono shop. Mr Katori keeps his splendid tattoos — a dragon and a phoenix — a secret in Japan for fear of upsetting his neighbours and customers.

Kesao Shibata, a construction worker and head of the Yokohama tattoo club, is another walking work of art who has spent most of the past twenty years — and thousands of dollars — having every part of his body decorated by

Mr Nakano's fluttering needles. He even has a mouse, and a mallet, on his head.

'This is the best one,' he declares, yanking up his shirt to disclose a samurai in a battle scene, licking the blood from his opponent's severed head. 'This protects me from evil.'

A session under the needle (actually an armoury of sixty different electric, or the more traditional ivory-mounted, prongs) lasts an hour — that is as much pain as people can bear — and costs $150. To acquire a full body tattoo can take fifty sessions over a year and cost $7500.

Mr Nakano, who has two apprentices, laments the fact that the Japanese are turning away from the traditional motifs towards simplistic Western-style tattoos. Tokyo is in the middle of a tattoo boom, and new studios with names like Red Wine are springing up overnight in the entertainment districts, offering to tattoo sea horses on young women's bottoms.

'If this goes on, I am afraid it will mean the end of traditional *irezumi* culture,' says Mr Nakano. He is not, however, prepared to take the drastic step of asking any of his own clients to place their hides in Professor Kato's skilful hands.

'I would like to see my work preserved,' says Mr Nakano, 'but I think the relatives would be upset if there was no body in the coffin for them to farewell at the wake.'

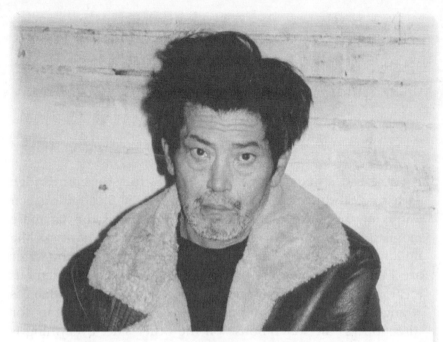

SIX

THE OUTSIDERS

It's a long time since I heard from my father
Who sold his rice paddy
to buy a German lepra drug for me

— POEM BY AN INMATE OF NAGASHIMA LEPROSARIUM

IT LOOKS LIKE A MINIATURE VERSION of the Sydney Harbour Bridge — a single, white-painted span arching over the bottle-green waters of the Seto Inland Sea. On one side is the Japanese mainland, on the other a rocky island, where low barracks-like buildings can be seen among the trees. Cobwebbing the water are hundreds of netting enclosures, leases where the famous local oysters are farmed. We drive across the bridge, which is strangely deserted of traffic and pedestrians, and stop for directions at the watch-house on the other side. Everything is unnaturally quiet in the early summer sunshine; not a soul is to be seen apart from the watchman.

Welcome to Nagashima Island, Japan's hidden shame. For sixty years crossing this strait was a one-way journey — once people were brought here they were never allowed to leave. They were neither criminals nor psychopaths, although this is how they were treated. Many were drowned trying to escape by swimming across the treacherous waters; others starved or died of exposure in tiny solitary confinement cells. The bridge itself was only built a few years ago — for decades Japanese officialdom even fought the idea of allowing the lost souls of Nagashima to be physically connected with the rest of Japan.

What unimaginable threat to Japanese society did these people pose? Nagashima is a leper colony and still, legally, none of the 1200 patients who live here (suffering from the stigma of what scientists call Hansen's disease) is allowed to cross the bridge. Under a law first passed in 1907 and never repealed, they are prisoners for life on this island of the damned.

Nagashima is the most visible symbol of Japan's almost pathological prejudice against those who are not seen to be part of society, who do not conform to its standards or respect its values. At its most fundamental, it is based on race — the belief that the Japanese are a unique people descended from the gods, and that the blood carries certain characteristics different from any other race. Not many Japanese people nowadays believe, literally, the creation myth of Izanami and Izanagi (a frightfully violent Old Testament-meets-Godzilla story, by the way). Any mother who has smacked her baby's bottom knows that Japanese are born with the 'Mongol blue spot' at the base of the spine, an anthropological marker indicating the origins of the modern Japanese on the plains of the northeast Asian mainland. However, almost all subscribe in one way or another to the theory of *nihonjinron*, literally the 'science of Japaneseness'.

Time and again, going about our business, the only explanation for some improbable event or unlikely opinion would be 'You must understand, we Japanese ...' This ethnic stereotyping is quite ruthless, and is employed to explain anything from the commission of atrocities during the war to the willingness of Japanese consumers to pay $150 for a melon. Books are written by otherwise credible scientists arguing that Japanese brains are physically different from those of non-Japanese. Five former prime ministers, in fact, donated their brains to science to help establish this point — they sit pickled in alcohol in large jars on a shelf in the medical museum of Tokyo University and look, to me at any rate, like any other brains.

More plausibly, it is argued that the socialisation — the nurture, rather than the nature — of the Japanese indoctrinates them with certain values and ways of thinking and behaving. This begins at birth and is therefore impossible to reverse, even if anyone should want to. Mayu sleeps flat on her back (and snores) because when she was a child her grandmother made her sleep in the 'correct' position for a girl, on her back with her legs together and her arms by her sides — rather than the natural foetal position.

At school, the Japanese will be taught the 'correct' way to study — engorging vast amounts of information, but not the means to process, evaluate or reason with it. At work, there will be a 'correct' way to do each job — machines are used at one department store 'bowing school' to teach new recruits the precise angle to which they should abase themselves, according to the status of the customer. Even at play there will be a 'correct' way to behave — I remember one afternoon going to a university baseball tournament, where fanatical cheerleaders were stationed throughout the audience to ensure that everyone clapped, stood, sat, sang and linked arms at the 'correct' moment. When the university anthem was played everyone had to take off their sunglasses. Little wonder that the more thoughtful Japanese bureaucrats and business leaders are alarmed at the country's lack of innovation and creativity.

This conformity is usually presented as some innate Japanese desire for consensus, but it more often struck me as what Noam Chomsky would call manufactured consent. The price for dissent is a terrible one in such a homogenous society — censure, isolation, sanctions and even, in extreme cases such as school bullying, death. 'The nail that sticks out will be hammered in' goes the Japanese saying that is such a cliche that *Tokyo Journal* magazine once devoted a whole front cover to the scores of foreign correspondents who have used it. 'Please understand', I usually feel, would be more accurately rendered as 'You have no choice but to accept'.

This chapter will look at some groups in Japan who — usually through no fault of their own — do not conform. There are many from which to choose. This outwardly harmonious society discriminates against all sorts of people who are different from the mainstream Japanese for reasons of gender, health, age and employment, but most viciously against those whose 'Japaneseness' is in question. They represent five or six million out of a population of 125 million — a small number, perhaps, in comparison with vibrant multiracial countries like Australia or the United States, but large enough to make a myth of claims that Japan is a uniquely homogenous society. Every year the numbers — particularly the number of foreigners — grow, and every year the failure of Japan to address the increasing diversity of its population becomes an uglier problem. The ways in which Japanese society marginalises and stigmatises these minorities help explain the country's frequent failures to come to terms with the rest of the world.

The list of grievances of these groups is almost endless, but because they either have no vote or are unable to exercise any influence as a lobby, they have no voice. They usually welcome any interest by foreign journalists, because — with a few worthy exceptions — their own mainstream media ignores their concerns. Japanese governments have a record of addressing long-ignored injustices only after *gaiatsu* ('outside pressure') is brought to bear. The Japanese outside the mainstream have little alternative to trying to arouse international concern.

Japan, as has already been pointed out, has no laws against discrimination and so grand and petit apartheid is conducted against its minorities at almost every level. It was one of the last countries in the world to ratify the United Nations Declaration on Human Rights, which outlaws discrimination. For more than twenty years its bureaucrats argued variations on a theme that would be familiar in Australia's Deep North or America's Deep South. Michio Watanabe, an LDP power broker (who as foreign minister outraged the Americans by criticising blacks), once explained, apparently seriously, that if Japan signed the Declaration, 'Plays such as *The Merchant of Venice* could not be performed in Japan, because it is prejudiced against Jews.'

And so laws deny government jobs to half a million ethnic Koreans, bigots are allowed to refuse to serve lepers in restaurants and bikies beat up on the homeless in the tent cities that sprang up after the Kobe earthquake. The Ainu people, Japan's original inhabitants, have a particularly tragic heritage — one which makes their leaders envious even of Australia's Aboriginal peoples. Then there are the *burakumin*, distinguishable from other Japanese only because a distant ancestor may have engaged in an 'unclean' occupation such as working in an abattoir. Racial discrimination and Japan's peculiar phobia about infectious disease combined in the frightful case of an injured Thai woman who was HIV-positive and wound up paralysed because hospitals would not admit her, and doctors refused to treat her. In 1985, Japan's top baseball team, the Yomiuri Giants, 'walked' Randy Bass, an American hitter playing for the rival Hanshin Tigers, to prevent a foreign player breaking the home run record of Sadaharu Oh.

On a personal level, I did not encounter any overt racial discrimination while I was in Japan — but then I was a temporary visitor, with no ambition to vote, work for the government or draw a welfare benefit. On the contrary, Minato-ku, the ward in which Mayu and I lived, went out of its way to be foreign-user-friendly, even publishing an English-language monthly newsletter to inform its *gaijin* residents about upcoming vaccination programs, library facilities, cooking schools and the like. Perhaps this reflects the higher regard the Japanese appear to have for pale-skinned foreigners. When Japan's half-baked neo-Nazis put up posters denouncing migrants, they are talking about the Iranians peddling dope and doctored telephone cards in Yoyogi Park, not the mums lounging poolside at the American Club. I know an Indonesian correspondent who was repeatedly refused rental apartments. Black Americans also complain of prejudice, though, thanks to the Michael Jordan factor, there was quite a fad for their fashions and music while I was in Japan, and they were popular with a certain tribe of Roppongi good-time girls.

However, these are *gaijin* — 'outside people' not of the group, not expected to understand. Children, drunks and foreigners, it is said, have the best time in Japan because they are not held responsible for their behaviour. For Japanese society at large, however, there can be no deviation from a rigidly defined 'normality'. Any transgression renders people liable to be arbitrarily expelled from the society of their peers, in the workplace, in their communities and even from their own families. The 'sending to Coventry' that British unionists used to impose on workmates who transgressed does not begin to describe the severity of this punishment. The only thing comparable I have ever heard of is the ritual 'shunning' imposed by the stricter Pennsylvania Amish. How much more tragic if this is based on a misunderstanding, a prejudice that persists beyond all rational comprehension. Such is the fate of Japan's lepers.

Masao Ishida, approaching sixty when I interviewed him, is a stocky man whose only outward signs of leprosy are a missing fingertip, pebble glasses and a certain awkwardness in moving about — the disease causes nerve damage. He is the chief executive of the All-Japan Hansen's Disease Association — although, thanks to drug therapy, he hasn't shown positive for the bacillus for forty years. Ishida has been confined on Nagashima since 1946, when he was eleven years old. He was grabbed by the police when he went for a haircut at the local barber — an early symptom of leprosy is acute sensitivity of the scalp — and packed off to the island in a freight train with no windows.

Other patients I talked to when I visited the island were carried away at night in special rickshaws reserved for the dead, drawn by those other outcasts, the *burakumin*. 'We were treated like filth, like criminals — rounded up by force and brought here. There was no treatment in those days, no medicine, not much food even,' Mr Ishida told me, more with sorrow than anger. 'My whole family was told to leave our village or commit suicide. It was nearly fifty years before I could go back and visit the family tomb. My relatives apologised, but of course by then it was too late — my whole life had been destroyed.'

Driving to Nagashima across the bridge of no return is like crossing a time warp into Biblical days. The road is deserted because the only visitors are the occasional relative — only lepers and those who care for them live here, shunned by normal Japanese society. While the rest of the world long ago abandoned legal sanctions and abolished leprosariums — the cure, a powerful drug called Promin, was discovered in 1943 — in Japan, 6000 lepers are still confined in isolated institutions such as Nagashima under legislation first passed nearly ninety years ago and never repealed.

In spite of its fearsome reputation — it has been dreaded since Old Testament times — Hansen's disease (named after the Norwegian G. Armauer Hansen who isolated the bacillus that causes it in 1873) is not particularly infectious. It attacks the skin and nerves of the 'cooler' parts of the body such as the fingers and toes, nose, throat and voice box. If untreated, it causes disfigurement, blindness and paralysis. There are 2.4 million lepers in the world, about half of them in India. It was once rife among the Aboriginal population in Australia, but the New South Wales Health Department now knows of only five cases in Australia's most populous state.

About 1200 lepers live in two institutions on the island, down from a peak of 3500 in the early 1940s. Each patient now has the luxury of a tiny flat to him or herself (twice as many men as women contract leprosy) in the long dormitory buildings. When the older patients were first transported to Nagashima, conditions were 'terrible', concedes Dr Masanao Makino, director of one of the sanatoriums. 'No staff would work here — the patients had to nurse each other — they had no medicine, no rights, no vote, they were not allowed any money ...' Some committed suicide, some drowned trying to swim ashore towing their belongings in buckets, others were caught by the guards as they tried to escape and locked for punishment in tiny prison cubicles where some died of exposure.

Among the azalea bushes is a stone monolith commemorating the 173 patients who were killed one night, when a terrible typhoon devastated the leprosarium. A Buddhist ossuary houses the bones of 2887 people who crossed the water to Nagashima never to return — even the cremated remains of lepers were deemed unfit for burial in their family tombs. Today, two large sinks at either end of his office for washing his hands are the only precaution Dr Makino thinks necessary when treating leprosy patients — washing is a simple, effective prophylactic. 'In spite of its terrible reputation, the disease is quite hard to transmit, even in intimate relationships, and no leprosarium worker has ever contracted it,' he says.

The leprosarium is a self-contained community, with its own sports fields, laundry, shop, workshops for hobbies such as pottery, and therapy rooms. In one, some elderly patients, many of them blind and with parts of their hands and feet missing, were having their fingernails and toenails cut by nurses when we visited. Old folk songs wafted in through the window from a hall where an afternoon karaoke session was in full swing. 'It is like the difference between Heaven and Hell to compare conditions now with what it was like when I came here,' says Taeko Nojima, aged seventy-seven, who putters around in an electric wheelchair. 'We were the living dead. I was told I would be allowed to leave after three months' treatment, but it was just a trick — fifty-six years later I am still here.'

The Japanese government passed the Leprosy Prevention Law in 1907 after it became alarmed at the number of young men ruled unfit to fight in the wars against China and Russia because of the disease. In 1900, it was estimated Japan had 30 000 lepers. A display in the museum of leprosy at Tama, half an hour by train west of Tokyo, gives a hint of the pitiful conditions in which they lived and died. 'They were shunned by society,' says another leprosy doctor. 'People were terrified of it — Hansen's disease was the AIDS or the Ebola virus of its day.' Lepers were driven from their jobs and homes and forced to survive by begging — a bronze statue depicts a mother and child embarking on *owari no nai tabi*, the 'journey without end' to which they were condemned.

The first to offer shelter and show any compassion to the tens of thousands of lepers roaming the countryside were foreign Franciscan missionaries who established a leprosarium near Mount Fuji in the 1890s. Old photographs show nuns in starched head-dresses bathing the feet of ragged lepers in wooden tubs, and there is one deeply moving picture of a blind leper reading Braille with his lips — Hansen's disease patients lose the feeling in their fingers and toes.

The government established a nationwide network of leprosariums — there are now thirteen of them (along with two private institutions) all originally located in remote and isolated parts of the country, six of them on islands like Nagashima. In 1931, with the military in the ascendancy, the law was made even more draconian, ordering the forcible confinement of anyone with the disease. And worse. Yasuji Hirasawa, now sixty-eight and working as a guide in the museum, has been a leprosarium inmate since he was fourteen. He says that if lepers wanted to marry, almost always to other patients, they had to consent to castration or vasectomies, a *paipu katto* ('pipe-cut') as it is called. 'It was done to me,' he confesses, shaking his head. 'I cried a lot, but eventually I chose marriage and gave up my chance of becoming a father. They thought it was hereditary in those days.'

This, incidentally, happened in the 1950s, more than a decade after Promin and other highly potent drugs against leprosy were available. In 1953, Japan's Diet reconsidered the law, against a backdrop of widespread patients' rights agitation which included hunger strikes and demonstrations. However, says Dr Makino, due to the arrogant intransigence of the association of leprosy doctors — some of whom are still alive and still refuse to accept the scientific facts about the disease — the provisions mandating the incarceration of patients for life remained on the books. 'The only glimmer of hope was that they promised to review the law "in the near future",' says Mr Ishida, the patients' association leader, with a bitter laugh. 'The "near future" turned out to be more than forty years.'

It was not until 1994 that the leprosy doctors' association passed a resolution formally apologising for half a century of injustice — the first time, incidentally, that any Japanese medical association has ever apologised for anything. 'It was a tragedy,' says Dr Minoru Narita, chairman of the association. 'We apologised to try and make amends, inadequate though they may be, to the patients who have gone through unnecessary pain and suffering most of their lives.'

However, the law remained on the books, reflecting a still-widespread public revulsion and fear of lepers in Japan. Even doctors and nurses routinely turn down jobs working with lepers because of family pressure. Patients, who for the past few years have been allowed (illegally) to visit the outside world, say they are subject to irrational stigmatisation. Restaurants won't serve them, hotels won't accept their reservations, in a couple of cases district hoop-ball (a type of croquet popular with patients) associations have refused to register leprosarium teams, fearing contamination from the handshake that precedes the game. The *Asahi* newspaper recently carried a plaintive letter from a man whose fiancée's parents had called off their wedding when they discovered there had been leprosy in his family in the Edo period, which ended in 1867.

When I left Japan, moves were finally afoot to right nearly a century of government-sanctioned wrongs against Japan's lepers. An expert committee was studying the issue, and a reform bill was expected to go before parliament in 1996. However, the ultimate irony is that for most of Japan's lepers it will be too late. Even though almost all his patients have been free from the bacillus for decades, they are too old, incapacitated and institutionalised to be able to make their way in the outside world says Dr Makino. The average age of patients at his institution is seventy-one — the oldest a remarkable 102 years old. About one third of them are blind, and many others are partly paralysed and dependent on medical care.

Tragically, some of the patients I spoke to were concerned that repeal of the law would leave them in the lurch. As well as free board and lodging and medical care, the 6000 people classified as lepers now receive a monthly allowance of $1300, which is considerably higher than other sickness or disability pensions. 'The truth of the matter,' says Dr Makino, 'is that even if the law was changed tomorrow, I doubt whether any of my patients would want to leave. This is their home — there is nothing for them outside.' Mr Ishida reluctantly agrees that, even if he was free to go, he would choose to remain on the island. However, that does not mean he and the other patients will not continue their campaign. 'We were not allowed to live our lives as human beings,' he says, 'but now they should change the law so that at least we can die with dignity.'

Like the lepers, the Ainu people, Japan's original inhabitants, have had a terrible time of it. However, unlike the lepers, and other groups such as Japan's ethnic Koreans, their campaign is not for acceptance and assimilation. The Ainu, the few that are left, want recognition as a separate people — recognition that has been denied them for centuries as their culture has been crushed, their lands taken and their language has become virtually extinct. When I spoke with some of their traditional leaders, they talked with envy about developments in white Australia's reconciliation with its Aborigines, particularly the Mabo decision on land rights. It takes a country with a truly terrible history to make Australia's record look good.

The Ainu were once the sole inhabitants of northern Japan, and their kingdom stretched from the main island of Honshu (Mount Fuji is actually an Ainu name) across Hokkaido, and up through the Kurile island chain to Sakhalin and the Kamchatka Peninsula. They are originally a hunter–gatherer people, one of the family of sub-Arctic races, whose cousins are the Inuit (Eskimos) of Canada and the Siberian aborigines. Beginning in the middle of the first millennium AD, successive invasions by the lighter skinned Yamato people, the ancestors of the modern Japanese, from the northeast Asian mainland drove the Ainu from their traditional hunting and fishing-grounds. By the sixteenth century they had been driven out of Honshu and pursued to Hokkaido, where they were almost annihilated by the Tokugawa shoguns in a series of bloody battles.

A century ago, fearing Russian territorial ambitions, Japan officially colonised Hokkaido, confiscating Ainu land-holdings and adopting a policy of assimilating them into the general community. As in Australia, this involved the forcible seizure of Ainu children as servants, brides and indentured labourers for Japanese enterprises. Their culture was suppressed; the consequent cycle of social dislocation, deprivation and sickness was ignored. The Ainu surviving today are sad actors in the tawdry theme parks of their culture, acting out plays whose words and meaning they have long lost. They carve bears with salmon in their mouths for the tourists — even though the bears, so important to Ainu ritual, face extinction, and they are banned from catching salmon, once their staple food.

Most Ainu people have simply tried to vanish into mainstream Japanese society. They are physically little different — the Ainu I met were a little sturdier, perhaps, and more hirsute (European anthropologists once called them the 'hairy Ainu'). In the cities, however, the Wajin, as the Ainu call other Japanese, soon find out their ethnic secret, and relegate them to low-paying jobs on society's margins. Those who remain in traditional communities around Hokkaido are an ageing minority who find younger Ainus uninterested in their language and traditions. Interbreeding means that there are probably no 'full-blooded' Ainu left alive, and there is a very real risk that the culture will cease to exist within as little as one generation. The story of the Ainu was one of the first Mayu and I did, and one of the saddest. It was bitterly ironic that it was 1993, the United Nations' Year of Indigenous Peoples.

We travelled north to the community of Nibutani, which is Japan's last Ainu stronghold — a hamlet of wooden houses, souvenir shops and a small museum dedicated to Ainu culture. Most of its population of 550 are of Ainu descent, and a few still remember the language. It was snowing a blizzard as we sought out Shigeru Kayano, an Ainu elder who was campaigning against the latest outrage inflicted on his people — a huge dam being built on the Saru, one of Japan's last wild rivers. It would inundate four square kilometres of traditional Ainu land where for 2000 years Kayano's ancestors farmed their rice and millet, the valley where they hunted bear and bob-tailed deer, the cemetery where they buried their dead and the secret place where they went to intercede with the fox god when he whispered that ill fortune was about to befall the village. 'The Japanese are spitting at heaven,' he growled.

Only Kayano was left to rail against the scheme — the government bought out the other owners, but he had refused to accept the $150 000 offered for his single hectare of rice paddy. 'Can't we have one river in Hokkaido where the salmon can spawn naturally, where crows and bears and foxes and owls — and Ainu — can be free and take the salmon to eat. How happy life would be,' he sighed. In his heart, however, Kayano knew that the dam could not be stopped, not with a $650 million investment at stake and the government arguing the priorities of industry — flood control and power generation. There is no such thing as land rights legislation in Japan and, indeed, the Ainu are not even officially recognised as a separate race. 'The Japanese are a mono-ethnic people' is government policy, as expressed by that notorious racist who almost became prime minister, Michio Watanabe.

Kayano was then in his early seventies and had been campaigning most of his life to preserve the last fragments of his people's culture. The Ainu have lived hereabouts for millennia. Pottery shards dug up in the excavations for the dam date to the Jomon period, more than 300 years before the birth of Christ. He proudly showed me a studio portrait of his blood ancestors which was taken in 1911. His grandfather, bearded and regal, is missing the finger he hacked off when he was a boy of thirteen to escape from serfdom to the Wajin who had kidnapped him to work on a fishing boat. His grandmother is tattooed around the mouth in the Ainu style. Both are wearing cloth made of the bark of elm trees, dyed in distinctive patterns. When he was a child, Kayano learned the *yukar* — epic oral sagas as the Ainu had no written language — of the days before the Wajin came to the Saru valley, when salmon was the basic food and the bear god prowled in the woods.

In 1876, when Kayano's grandfather was a young man, the new Meiji government in Tokyo annexed Hokkaido, forced the Ainu to adopt Japanese names and language, and took their lands. The assimilation was completed in 1899 when the Hokkaido Ainu Protection Act — the first of a series of paternalistic pieces of legislation which the Ainu have been trying to have repealed ever since — was passed. Two hectares of land per family was doled out (that is how Kayano's family acquired its rice paddy) and special schools were established for the Ainu, in which 'difficult' subjects such as science, history and geography were not taught. Salmon fishing became illegal.

From there on, it's been pretty much downhill. The Lonely Planet guide warns travellers:

Japanese tourists seem comfortable seeing the Ainu culture debased by pseudo 'Ainu villages' with

Disneyland surroundings and souvenir shops selling tacky carvings.

The old Ainu festivals and shamanic rites are acted by listless, elderly Ainu. I found these tourist circuses intensely depressing — they are often combined with caged bears in zoos ... symbolic of the freedom lost by the Ainu.

Down the road at the local council — the municipal emblem is, ironically, the lily of the valley — there was sympathy, but little else, for Shigeru Kayano's last stand against the dam. Two thousand of the 7000 ratepayers in the area are Ainu, but they have not one representative on the council. The mayor, Yoshiteru Nakamichi, said the council had been backing the dam since it was first proposed more than twenty years ago. 'This is not an Ainu versus Wajin issue,' said Mr Nakamichi. 'The government has compensated these people for their land ... sure, some Ainu culture has been lost, but the dam will stimulate the economy of the whole area.'

Kayano snorted with contempt when I told him that. 'I would like to think that [then prime minister Kiichi] Miyazawa will do something this year to return our land, but it's not going to happen,' said the last angry Ainu. 'For five years now we have been asking for new legislation dealing with Ainu affairs. Whenever Miyazawa is asked about it in the Diet he says "there is a committee thinking about it."' While they thought, the snow fell on the Saru River and the Ainu culture was another ten tonnes of concrete closer to extinction.

The dam on the Saru is a paradigm of the way Japan treats its original inhabitants. While other countries from Brazil to Australia at least paid lip service to the rights of their aborigines during the United Nations' Year of Indigenous People, in Japan the official fiction remained that the Ainu do not even exist. 'All over the world, the pale people who invaded other people's land are feeling guilty and signing treaties and giving at least something back,' said Kayano, 'but not here — there is no action, not even much talking.' Japan's biggest selling newspaper carried a massive report on the struggle for recognition and compensation by indigenous people around the world. It dealt with the land rights battle by the Yanomani Indians of the Amazon, Mapuche militants in Chile, the campaign to preserve indigenous languages in Guatemala and marches against Columbus Day in Bolivia. However, nowhere in the 5000-word article was there any mention of the Ainu, the first Japanese, who believe that for too long they have been gnawing the discarded bones from the Japanese economic feast.

Although most Japanese will deny racial discrimination exists, nearly half of all Ainu polled say they have experienced prejudice. Superficially Nibutani looks like a prosperous little village; however, the statistics paint quite a different picture of what goes on behind the stage show. It is a picture of deprivation that should bring shame to the managers of the world's richest economy. The Ainu have five times the rate of eye disease and tuberculosis as the average for Hokkaido residents. Sixty per cent of them are on some sort of government benefit — three times the average. Only 8 per cent receive tertiary education, one-third the average. The list goes on … and on. Little wonder they are trying to disappear into mainstream society, perhaps the world's first instance of autogenocide.

A government survey in 1989 found that there were fewer than 25 000 people left who claimed to be Ainu, around 0.2 per cent of the population, or proportionally only one-tenth as numerous as the Australian Aboriginal peoples. Many are believed to have been missed — turning their backs on their culture and passing themselves off as Wajin (people of Yamato ethnic origin) in the big cities. As a result of an official policy of assimilation going back more than a century — and the Ainu custom of 'marrying out' and adopting unwanted Wajin babies — none can claim to be pure-blooded. Many Ainu do not have the double eyelid fold, the luxuriant body hair and the Caucasian features of their ancestors. 'Biological assimilation of the Ainu by the Japanese, which was occurring over the centuries of trade and warfare, has become almost complete,' wrote two American anthropologists almost a generation ago.

In the three years since our visit, the dam has been completed and the Saru River has flooded Shigeru Kayano's little plot of land. In the media, the plight of another endangered species, the Japanese crested ibis, receives far more anguished attention than the Ainu. Four more prime ministers have come, made promises and gone, and Kayano was right — Japan is no closer to restoring the rights of its aboriginal minority, let alone accepting these outsiders into mainstream society. The only note of optimism is that Shigeru Kayano, by an unexpected fluke, got himself elected to parliament. There he sits, surrounded by 762 Wajin MPs, give or take a few who have died, resigned or are unavoidably detained at the prosecutors' pleasure. Speeches are made. Committees debate. You could die waiting. The Ainu probably will.

In contrast with the Ainu, Japan's ethnic Koreans are far more numerous, and far more vocal in their demands. Theirs is not a rallying cry for a dying culture, but a demand to be accepted as Japanese, to have the same rights as other citizens. They compare themselves with African Americans — their ancestors transported across the ocean, forced to work as slaves, then abandoned in their ghettos, and subject to widespread, institutionalised discrimination.

Koreans were first brought to Japan in the early seventeenth century, when the Tokugawa Ieyasu — the Japanese Napoleon — invaded the peninsula, kidnapping thousands and killing tens of thousands more in bloody battles. There is a monument on a mound in the suburbs of Kyoto known as 'ear hill' where the shogun's generals deposited thousands of ears they sliced off as proof of their battle skills. From 1910 to 1945, Japan invaded and colonised Korea, confiscating land and businesses, and attempting to obliterate the culture by forcing Koreans to undergo Japanese education, worship at Shinto shrines and even change their names to Japanese ones. This is quite ironic, since important elements of Japanese culture were originally imported from Korea. One of the reasons the Imperial Household Agency refuses to allow any more of the keyhole-shaped burial mounds of ancient 'Japanese' emperors to be opened — the equivalent of Egypt banning researchers from the pyramids — is that when archaeologists excavated one a few years ago they found it decorated in glorious, unmistakably Korean reliefs.

The legacy of Japan's brutal occupation persists. Most of the million-odd ethnic Koreans in Japan are descended from people who emigrated during the first half of this century. Some came voluntarily looking for work, some were driven into exile when their land and property was expropriated and many were simply rounded up and deported as slave labour for Japan's mines, steel mills and arms factories. A disproportionate number were killed by the atom-bombing of Hiroshima and Nagasaki — the survivors then had to fight for decades for pensions, medical care, even the right to erect monuments alongside those for the Japanese victims.

Today they are second- and third-generation residents, indistinguishable to the outsider from any other Japanese. However, they have no vote, are not allowed to work for the government, have reduced social security entitlements, have to carry ID cards and are subject to a barrage of other statutory persecution. The *ninniku-bara* ('garlic bellies') also suffer unofficial discrimination at almost every level — in housing, in marriage and in education, where Korean children are not even eligible for discounts on public transport to and from school. The big difference between ethnic Koreans and other outsider groups in Japan, however, is that the Koreans — a feisty, hot-blooded folk whose diaspora has led to them being called the Irish of Asia — are not prepared to submit meekly to discrimination. Represented by influential national organisations — one for Koreans who support the Stalinist North of the divided peninsula, the other for southerners — and funded by the powerful networks of lending institutions and *pachinko* (pinball) parlours they control, Koreans are prepared to fight for their rights. The battle for Utoro is a case in point.

This little hamlet is just a twenty-minute drive from the

Byodo-in temples, one of the great glories of Japan's Heian era, when the Fujiwara clan ruled Japan from the ancient imperial capital of Kyoto. There, floating above pools of lotus blossom, with its enormous gold-plated Buddha smiling benignly across the water, the temple is everything the well-heeled tourist imagines old Japan to be. Built at the exquisite height of the imperial court in the eleventh century, the temple is arguably the most important, and certainly the most beautiful to have survived. The name means 'hall of equality'. But drive twenty minutes from the immaculately raked gravel lawns, where visitors sip ceremonial thimbles of the famous local whisked green tea, and you come across another Japan, one the tourists never get to see.

Utoro is a cluster of huts and houses sandwiched between the grey hangers of an old Nissan car factory and the barbed wire of a military base. Cats and dogs explore piles of rusting junk, old ladies squat gossiping in the alleyways. There is no equality here, nor any roads — just laneways. Until five years ago there was no running water, just a pump; there are still no sewers, and reeking open drains carry away the waste water. Some of the tiny tumbledown shacks do not even have a bath; the nearest public facilities are three stops away by train. A Mediterranean-style three-storey mansion, whitewashed, guarded by video cameras and with both a Rolls-Royce and a latest-model Mercedes in the garage, provides a bizarre counterpoint to the general squalor. It is the headquarters of the local branch of Aizu Kotetsu, the Korean-run *yakuza* gang.

Utoro is Japan's third world — one of the hidden ghettos in the world's wealthiest country, where those ultimate outsiders, the one million people of Korean background chose, or are forced by institutionalised bigotry and discrimination, to live. For the 300-odd 'Koreans' who live here — many of them third generation, Japanese-speaking, sushi-eating youngsters indistinguishable from their 'Japanese' neighbours — there was never any hope of a fair share of the spoils of the economic miracle they helped build. We went there because Utoro had become the latest battleground between official Japan and its most outspoken minority. Like the Ainu of Nibutani, the people of Utoro were threatened with losing what little they had, in the name of progress and development.

The community was built, technically illegally, on land owned by a Nissan company when the Korean settlers were abandoned here after the war. It was secretly sold a few years ago to a development company, and now the residents — some of them in their seventies and eighties who have lived here for half a century — had been served with eviction notices. It has happened before in other parts of Japan. The bulldozers move in and the Koreans bundle up their lifetime possessions and look on in helpless rage as their homes are destroyed to make a profit for some multinational corporation in far-off Tokyo. However, this time when the wrecking crews arrived in their trucks, they were in for a surprise. The residents rallied, the police were called in and the developers beat a startled retreat. It was the beginning of a confrontation which grabbed the headlines, and galvanised Japan's Korean minority into a broader battle for its rights.

Che Chun Kyu, squatting on the porch of his little wooden cottage, cast his rheumy old eyes back more than fifty years to explain how it all began. He was twenty-six at the time, the war was three years old and the Japanese occupation army — which had ruled Korea since 1910 — had come to Taikyo city in South Korea with an ultimatum for the civic fathers: deliver up 150 fit young men for the Japanese war machine. Bidding farewell to his wife and two young children, Mr Che and 149 of his fellow citizens reported to the recruitment office in the port city of Pusan. A few weeks later they were working in brutal conditions down the coal mines of Kyushu, Japan's southernmost island. He moved to Utoro twenty-five years ago.

Mr Che is part of the great Korean diaspora in which more than six million people, mainly from the southern provinces of the peninsula, were driven from their homeland to work for the Japanese overlords in occupied Manchuria, Siberia and Japan. Millions went 'voluntarily', if you can call it that — their land expropriated for Japanese settlers, they became Asia's original boat people. Many more were press-ganged into service in the Japanese military or sent to work as slaves in the munitions factories or building roads and railways. Hundreds of thousands were forced to work as prostitutes in front-line brothels or down the mines. Many lost their lives, most tragically those executed as 'war criminals' whom the Allies mistakenly thought were enthusiastic Japanese soldiers, rather than slaves conscripted at gunpoint.

Utoro came into being in the latter years of the war. Many of the original residents worked for a corporate ancestor of Nissan which had an aircraft factory nearby — another 1300 laboured building a military airstrip. 'Times were terribly tough,' said Hang Soon Ye, who fled to Utoro with her mother and two sisters in the last months of the war from her home town of Kyoto. 'Rumour had it that Kyoto was going to be the next city to be atom-bombed.' They lived in a 'four-mat shack' — a mat is about the size of a desktop — with straw on the floor, while Mrs Hang's mother worked as a day labourer to put rice balls on the table. The remains of two of the galvanised iron and timber huts used as barracks for the single men still stand in the village.

After the war, 'the work ended and the Japanese just abandoned us here to starve,' Mrs Hang told me. Many Koreans — perhaps half the two million who had been in the country — returned to Korea. Tens of thousands made the terrible mistake of choosing North Korea, the 'paradise on earth' ruled by the bloody dictator Kim Il Sung, where they remain in what has been described as the world's biggest hostage-taking. The rest stayed, however, afraid of the civil war that was about to break out in their homeland or too poor to afford the passage.

Over the years, the Koreans stranded in Utoro began some cottage industries — bicycle-making, scrap-iron recycling, construction — and built homes for themselves and their families. Says Mrs Hang, 'This place was nothing. We collected rocks in sacks and levelled the land with our bare hands. Our blood, sweat and tears are here, and we are not going to move.'

The miracle is that this community — and the hundreds like it across Japan — survived at all in the face of the institutionalised racism that people of Korean ethnic ancestry are subject to, even if their parents and grandparents have been born in Japan. 'It is apartheid,' another resident, Om Myong Bu, told us. He invited us to share a snack of a pancake of spicy pickled cabbage in the office of his construction company in Utoro village. Mr Om is a second generation Korean-made-good, but the discrimination still rankles. He was born in 1953 in Kyushu — his father came to Japan as a labourer before the war, moved to Utoro and started a successful business building roads and other public works projects. He has kept his North Korean nationality. 'No matter how many generations we may live here, we are still Korean. But we pay our taxes like anyone else — and we believe we should have the same rights as other citizens,' says Mr Om.

Talking to him, you would never know he is not Japanese. Mr Om looks and dresses like a Japanese, he had a Japanese education, his only accent is a slight Kyoto twang. The government, however, says he is *different*. For a start, Korean Japanese cannot vote; cannot work for most levels of government, even the local council; and cannot yet draw old age pensions (although the law was recently changed) or most other welfare benefits, apart from a basic subsistence allowance. Everywhere they go, they have to carry the hated *kae p'yo* (dog tag) — the alien registration card — and until just two years ago they had to be fingerprinted annually.

Other examples of discrimination are too numerous to chronicle. Korean Japanese babies are not entitled to free vaccinations like everyone else; schoolchildren are not even allowed to compete against Japanese in interschool athletic meets. If they go to a Korean school, they will find it almost impossible to get into the elite government-run universities that are a prerequisite for entry to the civil service and the large corporations. In later life, Korean Japanese may find housing, jobs, marriage and even golf-club membership closed to them.

There is no hiding their Korean background, even if they should become 'naturalised' Japanese citizens. This is because they will be obliged to keep a *koseki*, the family household register, which records the name, address, relationship and ethnicity of everyone in the country. There is a thriving business in Japan for private detectives who specialise in ferreting out Korean, Ainu and *burakumin* 'bad blood' in prospective spouses, for employers and even for snooty golf clubs. The Korean Japanese were especially incensed when the family tree of Crown Prince Naruhito's bride-to-be was investigated — incensed because the imperial family is already of mixed race, interbred generations ago with Korean nobility. What makes all this even stranger is that there is no anthropological difference between modern-day Koreans and Japanese. Both sprang from the same northeast Asian stock.

Technically, Japanese officials assure the world, most Koreans are eligible for Japanese citizenship. In practice, however, there are formidable obstacles, which have ensured that fewer than 200 000 of the million or so Korean Japanese have become naturalised. Stories abound of bureaucratic abuse, not least an arbitrarily enforced rule that applicants for naturalisation must produce family records that may have been lost, be judged to be of 'good behaviour' and capable of 'independent living'. 'Even if I wanted to become a citizen, they don't want poor old people like me,' sighs Mr Che, who at the age of seventy-seven is still forced to go out to work for a few dollars a day as a day labourer cutting grass or any other job he can find.

Hardly surprisingly, many Korean Japanese continue to inhabit ethnic ghettos. More than 200 000, for instance, live in Osaka's bustling 'little Seoul' where they have their own FM radio station, and the streets are redolent of *kim chi* (pickled cabbage), loud with the drums and flutes of taped Korean folk music and lined with Korean-owned *pachinko* parlours, video shops and *yakiniku* barbecue restaurants. It also comes as no surprise that — like other minorities around the world — Japan's Koreans are over-represented at the bottom end of the social league ladder. Masaki Saito, a social worker in Utoro, says the village has higher than average levels of alcoholism, unemployment and disability — one-fifth of the families have no-one in regular work, compared with an unemployment rate of under 1 per cent for the rest of the region.

The immediate threat to Utoro came from a mysterious 'paper company' which six years ago bought the two hectares on which the residents' homes are built from Nissan for a mere $6 million. Its bid to have them evicted and redevelop the land was grinding its way through the Kyoto Local Court. The decision, when it comes, will be a landmark civil rights case for many other Korean communities existing 'illegally' on the riverbanks, railway embankments and other reserves at the margins of Japanese society. At least one other village near Kyoto and another in the industrial city of Kawasaki are currently under threat.

The people of Utoro, however, are not content to depend on the vagaries of Japanese justice. They have taken the imaginative step of buying a $30 000 advertisement in the *New York Times* in a slick public relations operation aimed at embarrassing Nissan, hurting the car giant's international sales and bringing a little *gaiatsu* to bear on the government. When Nissan argued that it no longer had any legal responsibility for the land, the Utoro residents hit the company with a claim for reparations, based on their exploitation of low-wage and no-wage Korean labour during World War II. In their advertisement, the residents made a pointed comparison with the Mercedes Benz company, in Germany, which paid several million dollars' compensation to its mainly Jewish slave labourers after the war.

The highly politicised struggle for land rights in Utoro has profound implications for the way Japan treats all its other unacknowledged ethnic minorities. 'This is a test case,' said Mr Om. 'It is a first step — if we win this, then we will fight for our other rights.' However, two years later, nothing had been decided — Japan's glacial legal system made sure of that. The outsiders of Utoro were standing firm and the developer had disappeared — more, one suspects, because of the collapse of the property market than out of any respect for the rights of the residents. Once again, Japan had missed an opportunity both to reconcile itself with its past and to show the world — alright, the readers of the *New York Times* — that it understood some of the elementary principles of social justice.

The largest group of outsiders in Japan has perhaps the strongest claim to injustice. The *burakumin* are not distinguishable from other Japanese by ethnicity, culture, appearance or anything else; the only way you can tell if someone belongs to this group is to check his address, and the address of his ancestors. They are shunned for no other reason than their postcodes.

One of these addresses, coincidentally, is not far from Utoro, the Sujin neighborhood of Kyoto, near the famous Higashi Hongan temple. The tourists who flock here, however, would never guess that around the corner is another world — a world of sickness, poverty, unemployment and general despair. There are streets of rickety shacks, some of them abandoned and burnt out, others with only a sheet of blue plastic for a roof. Abandoned shoe shops, hole-in-the-wall bars, budget inns and dilapidated wooden tenements jostle for space around the communal bathhouse and along laneways, some so narrow you can touch both walls with outstretched arms. Children fossick for yabbies in a rubbish-strewn creek. About 3500 people live here, although you would never know it if you had walked with Mayu and me along the nearly deserted streets one rainy afternoon. Many of the remaining residents of Sujin are old folk, bedridden or housebound with Alzheimer's and Parkinson's diseases.

What makes Sujin different from thousands of other suburbs in Japan is that it is a *buraku*, a community of people whose ancestors, hundreds of years ago, performed jobs which consigned them to the lowest levels of Japanese society. Its origins were in the Hindu/Buddhist caste system which made its way to Japan in the seventh century and the much older native Shinto folk religion. It was formalised when people in 'unclean' occupations, such as butchers, undertakers and cleaners, were classified as *eta* (literally 'filth galore') by feudal edict — the untouchable class. Even today, people insult *burakumin* by holding up four fingers, indicating the four legs of an animal.

The *burakumin* were forced to live in isolated ghettos unmarked on maps; 'marrying out' was forbidden; and they were restricted to polluting, demanding or undesirable trades such as bamboo work, leather goods, grave-sweeping and making lamp wicks. They were subject to a rigid curfew, and even their clothing was prescribed. Today *burakumin* such as Mr Masao Yamauchi, our guide, who is a health worker in the community, are indistinguishable from other Japanese people. The only way he can be identified as 'different' is from his family record of residence, the *koseki* which must be registered with his local council. His ancestors were, most likely, leather workers or executioners — this *buraku* was where Kyoto's criminals were brought to be publicly beheaded. Mr Yamauchi is still paying the price.

The remarkable thing is that, 120 years after the caste system was officially abolished, Mr Yamauchi and others who lead the Burakumin Liberation League (BLL) still complain that there is widespread discrimination against them. The majority of Japan's estimated three million *burakumin* hide their origins, and dread being 'outed' which would result in ostracism. Marriage is the most obvious example of prejudice. Many sophisticated and educated Japanese, who know there is no such thing as 'bad blood', nevertheless fear the social stigma that would attach to the whole family if anyone married on the wrong side of the tracks. Father Jesus Galeron, a Spanish missionary at Kyoto's Kawara-machi Catholic church, says weddings are often called off at the last minute because *burakumin* ancestry is discovered. On three occasions he has married such couples, but with one side of the church deserted because of a family boycott.

'Mixed' marriages, if they go ahead, often have tragic consequences. Yoshinobu Sakamoto, a Tokyo director of the BLL, recounts the story of a man living near Kyoto whose parents objected to him marrying a woman from a *burakumin* family. Two months pregnant, she threw herself to her death from the roof of a department store. Later, on the anniversary of her birthday, the man hanged himself.

The BLL, founded in the 1920s, boasts 150 000 members

and has conducted an aggressive anti-discrimination campaign in recent years. One of its most important initiatives is against discrimination in employment. Mr Sakamoto believes some companies still use a 'black book' of addresses, whose discovery caused a huge scandal twenty years ago, to avoid hiring people from *burakumin* areas. In one celebrated anti-discrimination action against the Sanwa Bank in Osaka, the BLL organised hundreds of people to paralyse the bank's business by lining up to open one yen accounts.

The BLL has forced publishers to change references in books which it believes are prejudicial, causing some to worry about freedom of expression. The most politically correct do not even use the word *burakumin*, itself a euphemism which literally means 'village people'. A volume of the *Encyclopaedia Britannica*, Edwin O. Reischauer's seminal work *The Japanese* and James Clavell's novel *Shogun* (which had historical references to Japanese names, language, geography and curses cut) were all censored to eliminate references *burakumin* found offensive.

In 1969, after at times violent protests, the Japanese government finally gave way and agreed to try and do something it consistently denied people of Korean or Ainu ancestry. The first of a series of laws and budgets designed to improve living standards of people in *buraku* like Sujin was passed by the Diet. A 1960s photograph shows the sort of problems the government wanted to fix — a flood-prone river with one bank safely clad in concrete, the other (where the *burakumin* lived) eroded mud. When the latest legislation expires in 1997, an extraordinary $50 billion will have been spent. The money has gone on public housing, on upgrading community infrastructure, on employment schemes such as re-equipping abattoirs and fisheries where the *burakumin* work, and on agricultural projects.

In Sujin, the 'barracks' — primitive sheds along the railway lines where Mr Yamauchi was born — have been pulled down and about a third of the population now lives in low-rent high-rise public housing. A gymnasium has been built, along with a library and a community centre; other projects, including preserving the district's historic buildings, are afoot. 'Materially we are better off,' says Mr Sakamoto, the son of an Osaka waste merchant whose family threatened to hang themselves when he 'came out' and joined the BLL. 'But there is still a lot of prejudice against us, even though we are Japanese like anyone else. Overcoming 300 years of discrimination is not going to happen overnight.'

Materially, their conditions have undoubtedly improved, but socially the *burakumin* are still a long way from acceptance into mainstream Japan. Just two years ago, someone who telephoned a marriage introduction agency in Kyoto was reassured that there were no *burakumin* on the books. 'We don't allow such people,' said the agency. 'Nor do we have people with harelips, epileptics, the mentally ill, people with hereditary diseases, Soka Gakkai (a Buddhist group), Communists, *boryokudan* (gangsters), people in the entertainment business, people who borrow from loan sharks, foreigners, ethnic Koreans or people who have been in prison, unless it was for a traffic offence.'

There are, officially, 1.1 million residents of 4603 official *buraku* districts in Japan — that is the people who have come forward for any of the scores of special government grants such as a $9300 wedding present, $12 500 for changing jobs, $100 to help a child's schooling or even a grant to help with driving instruction fees. However, millions of other *burakumin* have managed to escape from the ghettos and merge into the general community. The BLL says there may be three million altogether, but this is a figure they have been citing for forty years and Mr Sakamoto believes the real number could be double this.

Going by a recent survey of people residing in designated districts like Sujin, the government still has a long way to go. Thirty-nine per cent of families were receiving some sort of government benefit compared with a national average of 20 per cent. In a country that boasts universal literacy, one *burakumin* in sixty cannot read or write, and only 2.9 per cent have university degrees, one-quarter the average. In Sujin, as many as 10 per cent of people are unemployed (the national average was 3.2 per cent). During the long economic slump, they were in the jobs most likely to get the chop — day labourers on building sites, workers in tiny backyard industries. Mr Yamauchi, like many people in Sujin, left school at the age of ten to help the family income by making cardboard boxes.

As we were leaving Japan, a fierce debate was raging in the *burakumin* movement over what should happen after the March 31, 1997 deadline for an end to federal government aid. Many ordinary Japanese believe $50 billion is enough — and some *burakumin* agree with them. In the Sakuragaoka district near Osaka's Itami domestic airport, sixty families were about to declare that enough has been done to improve their standard of living. A dozen other *buraku* in prefectures (states) such as Wakayama, Hiroshima, Fukuoka and Kochi had already agreed to *kanryo sengen,* a 'completion declaration' that they should lose their subsidies and special privileges and be treated like any other community.

Akiyo Fujiwara, deputy chairperson of the All-Japan Federation of Buraku Liberation Movements, believes that discrimination itself is gradually disappearing, along with the slums. She told us that 30 to 40 per cent of the people eligible for government grants were not applying for them. She believes the law itself stigmatises people who live in *buraku* areas and should not be renewed. 'The government should be spending more money on welfare for the whole community, and targeting it better,' she says. 'The kind of special treatment we receive now just reinforces the stigma.'

However, Mr Yamauchi, who represents the mainstream *burakumin* movement, disagreed. He argued that Japan, for a start, should ratify the United Nations Declaration on Human Rights, which condemns discrimination on the grounds of race, religion or class. He also wanted more money spent on education — educating of the rest of the Japanese community that people should not be stigmatised because of an accident of their place of residence. 'Physically, conditions have improved over the past thirty years,' he says, 'but as far as people's attitudes are concerned, we still have a long way to go before the *burakumin* are treated like normal people.'

THERE IS A MOMENT WHEN THE THIN, REEDY notes of the flute pipe up, the chorus falls silent and the old woman falls to her knees clutching the scroll that you get an inkling of what it would be like to be a Martian newly arrived on earth. The action makes no sense. The words, even if you are fluent in Japanese, are barely comprehensible. The music conforms to no earthly scale. The bare pine boards of the stage and the stylised mural of pine and bamboo provide no reference.

Noh, a dramatic form that was already ancient when Shakespeare was born, more than lives up to its billing as the most arcane of all the Japanese arts — even when it deals with themes as modern as war guilt, heart transplants and Einstein's Theory of Relativity. This performance, for a near-full house at Tokyo's plush new National Noh Theatre, is the latest attempt by an eminent immunologist and connoisseur of *noh* named Tomio Tada to breathe new life into what many regard as a mummified art form that lost its relevance centuries ago.

So reactionary is the *noh* community that until Professor Tada began writing, and sponsoring, performances of his plays six years ago, most of the repertoire dated back to feudal times. Only one new play, celebrating the 1925 coronation of the Emperor Hirohito, has made it into the repertoire this century — it is as if, to use a Western analogy, no-one had written an opera since Mozart.

A form of drama incorporating chant, mime, music, masks and poetic text, *noh* bears no resemblance to any Western performing art, and little to any to be seen in Asia. Its closest cousins are the colourful Japanese *kabuki* theatre and the *kyogen* sketches which form a comic (to the initiated) interlude in a *noh* performance. Professor Tada says his critics believe the ancient repertoire is so large that there is no need for something new. 'But I believe that if a traditional art repeats the same theme over and over it is in danger of dying out. A contemporary theme, while remaining loyal to the classical form, is the way to go.'

This latest play is called *Lament for Unrequited Grief,* and it deals with an issue which is still highly controversial in Japan, even fifty years after World War II. A Buddhist priest discovers a letter written by a Korean slave labourer killed working in a coal mine in Japan, and travels to Korea to find his widow. Although the theme is contemporary, the trappings of the performance are those of classical *noh,* which have changed little in the 600 years since it was formalised from the *saru gaku* or 'monkey music' of travelling sideshows in medieval times by the father-and-son team of Kan'ami and Zeami Kiyotsugu (1333–1443).

Beneath the pine stage which juts out into the audience are ceramic urns, to enhance the stamping of stockinged feet which punctuates the performance. To one side, a narrow bridge leads to the spirit world — ghosts are popular figures in *noh.* The performance is punctuated with notes on the flute, the rapping of small drums and shrill birdlike cries. To one side, men in formal kimonos chant a commentary, much like a Greek chorus. The action by the eerily masked actors is minimalist — a fan raised in front of the face symbolises sleep, a few steps across the stage a journey of thousands of kilometres.

Like opera, *noh* has a tiny audience of connoisseurs, which has been dwindling in recent years. A senior official of the government's Cultural Agency tells me he never goes because it is 'too boring' — and, indeed, this ninety-minute performance is punctuated by snoring from the stalls. There are forty or fifty performances a month in Tokyo, in small 'art houses' like the national theatre, and all are 'one-off' events sponsored by the actors or by patrons like Professor Tada. Because *noh* plays do not have a season, it is hopelessly uncommercial.

Indeed, *noh* fans will tell you this is the whole point. 'We say it is *"ichi go, ichi go"* a one-time performance, like the tea ceremony,' says Professor Tada. 'There is no dress rehearsal — because the second performance would be predictable, not the miracle of the first.'

Professor Tada is hoping that his new plays with contemporary themes will bring the audiences back. His first, *The Well of Ignorance*, dealt with a human heart transplant — again, a controversial theme because transplants are still illegal in Japan. The only surgeon to attempt one was charged with murder.

Last year, he took this play on a tour of the United States, where it played to big houses in Cleveland, Pittsburgh and New York, receiving critical acclaim and a review in the *New York Times*. He would love to be invited to Australia. Professor Tada is hoping that once again foreign interest may revive this most Japanese of arts — *noh* very nearly died out when the courts of the shoguns, where it was the principal form of entertainment, were abolished last century. It was salvaged by the interest of such diverse Western literati as W. B. Yeats, Ezra Pound, Bertolt Brecht and the French poet Paul Claudel.

Professor Tada is a typical *noh* 'angel' — and part-time player of the *kotsuzumi*, the hand drum in the *noh* quartet — who puts up $30 000 to $40 000 of his own money to sponsor each performance. Staging *Lament* actually cost twice this amount — the premiere, the previous winter, had to be postponed for a whole year when the lead actor got stuck in a snowdrift. He wrote the play and choreographed it with Cumas Hashioka, a master of the Kanze style (one of five rival *noh* schools), who plays the lead role of the Korean widow — no women are allowed to act in *noh*. Hashioka is classified as an 'important intangible cultural property' — an eighth-generation *noh* actor who began his career at the age of three.

Although Professor Tada's works have aroused interest abroad, and from foreigners in Tokyo, the *noh* establishment in Japan is rather po-faced about his attempts to modernise the ancient art. Richard Emmert, an American who has been studying *noh* in Japan for twenty years (and who travels to Australia to workshop the theatre) says the Tada performances are not well received by traditional audiences. The troupe, and its lead actor Hashioka, are regarded as 'eccentric'.

'There is so much opportunity for creativity and reinterpretation of the traditional works … you don't say that just because Mozart lived 200 years ago his work is fossilised today,' he says.

Undeterred, Professor Tada is working on his next play — one which sounds like the greatest challenge of all. 'It's about Einstein's Theory of Relativity,' he says. '*Noh* ignores common sense. Something far away can be seen close up. Time takes on a different shape. Einstein is perfect for *noh*.'

SEVEN
MR WALKABOUT'S
MOMENT OF TRUTH

> *'This is something for crazies.*
> *Only a terrorist with a kamikaze*
> *mentality would use it.'*
>
> — SPOKESMAN FOR GERMANY'S FEDERAL CRIMINAL OFFICE (BKA)

LUCKILY, I WAS HOUSEBOUND WITH a broken leg. If it hadn't been for a skiing accident, I could have been victim number 3797 of probably the most horrifying act of urban terrorism the world is ever likely to see. As it was, I lay there watching the extraordinary scenes on television from the security of my sofa. Outside Kamiyacho station, my local stop, neatly suited salarymen and women lay on the pavement weeping, vomiting and half-blinded, while firemen rushed up the stairs with bodies on stretchers. The same scenes of chaos were flashed live from half a dozen other stations around the central city — Tsukiji, the stop for Tokyo's enormous fish markets; Hibiya, on the fringe of the glitzy Ginza shopping district; and, most ominously of all, Kasumigaseki, the sprawling subterranean warren that delivers half a million public servants every day to the great ministries of state that cluster around its exits.

For maximum destruction and ultimate terror, the target could not have been better chosen. The Tokyo subway system is the busiest in the world, carrying seven million passengers on a typical weekday. Without it Asia's largest city, and the world's second largest economy, would, literally, grind to a halt. Los Angeles has its freeways, Venice its canals and Tokyo, since the 1920s, has been the city of subways.

Kasumigaseki station, which happens to be where Mayu and I change trains every day, is typical — grey lavatory-tiled entrances lead down flights of steps and escalators 100 metres or so into the bowels of the earth. There, on pristine platforms you could eat sushi from, green-uniformed guards standing on little soapboxes orchestrate the tide of grey-suited workers to and from the government office blocks overhead. During rush-hour, a train arrives every few seconds on one of the three lines intersecting at Kasumigaseki, pulling up with its doors immaculately aligned with guidelines on the platform. People complain bitterly about the Chiyoda line, where sometimes you have to wait a whole four minutes between trains. It is not only a model of clockwork efficiency, it is a safe haven in remarkable contrast to, say, the jungle of the New York subway — children as young as five and six travel alone, and the worst a woman need fear is the wandering hand of a furtive groper. Bars and restaurants bustling with commuters line the labyrinthine pedestrian tunnels which honeycomb this cosy underworld.

Amid this nineteen-hour-a-day hustle and bustle, many of the regular Kasumigaseki commuters would have recognised the friendly, avuncular figure of Tsuneo Hishinuma, the 51-year-old stationmaster, who was always ready with a handful of change or a spot of helpful advice. At 8.20 that Monday morning, Hishinuma noticed a disturbance as a Hibiya line train pulled in. People staggered off the train choking and gagging, and pointing to a newspaper-wrapped bundle which was leaking an odd, fuming fluid.

Hishinuma, and his deputy, Kazumasa Takahashi who arrived to help a few minutes later, probably never thought that they were heroes. However, being dutiful officers of the Teito Rapid Transit Authority, their job was to maintain order and, above all, keep the trains running on schedule. They prodded the bundle, sniffed it, then picked it up and began carrying it towards their office. That was when they collapsed.

The next day, everything stopped at Kasumigaseki station for a minute's silence in remembrance of these two railwaymen, the first people to die in the subterranean nightmare that would eventually claim eleven lives, with nearly 4000 innocent commuters injured.

The subway massacre did much to destroy Japan's faith in itself as the world's safest country. Even more significantly, the extraordinary revelations of the years of ignored warnings and months of bungled investigations that preceded and followed it saw an unprecedented collapse in confidence in the country's much-vaunted security forces. Finally, the denouement, the interrogation and trial of members of the Satanic doomsday cult held responsible, shed a merciless light into the dark corners of Japan's judicial system. Seldom can a single crime, no matter how horrific, have caused such a profound reappraisal of a country's commitment to law and order.

The chemical that killed the eleven commuters was identified a few days later as isopropyl methylphosphonofluoridate, a devastatingly toxic central nervous system poison related to the organophosphate pesticides. Fortunately for the headline writers, it is popularly known as 'sarin' — an acronym of the initials of the Nazi scientists who originally developed it in 1938 as a weapon of mass destruction. However, it turned out to be so dangerous (twenty times as lethal as cyanide) and so indiscriminate that even Hitler baulked at using it. The only time sarin is known to have been used by anyone else was by Saddam Hussein in a genocidal slaughter of Kurdish villagers in 1989.

Unleashed in the claustrophobic confines of Tokyo's subway tunnels, the effect of a dozen sarin 'bombs' — planted simultaneously on different trains heading into the city vacuum-packed with rush-hour commuters — was devastating. Hospitals overflowed with victims, while frantic doctors tried to find the cause of the sinister symptoms — choking, vomiting, disorientation and partial blindness. For once the Japanese military's long and ugly experience with the use of chemical and biological weapons came in handy. Within hours, teams of soldiers in scary-looking chemical warfare 'diving suits' were lowered into the tunnels to begin a decontamination operation.

The following day, the subways were running again — albeit with an increase in the number of commuters wearing those white surgical masks the Japanese use when they have a cold. However, nearly a year later, it was clear that Tokyo would never really return to normal. The age of innocence was over. Armed police patrolled the once-peaceful tunnels, garbage bins had been removed and luggage lockers sealed, posters (and even paper lanterns) carrying mug shots of the terrorists still at large hung everywhere. In any country, such an indiscriminate act of mass murder would have been an outrage. In Japan, which prided itself on being the world's most peaceful and law-abiding place, the crime defied description. The usually sober *Japan Times'* editorial screamed: 'Someone is waging war against Japan.'

That someone, it emerged a few days later, was one of the most bizarre and extreme religious cults we have seen even in these millenarian times. Aum Shinri-kyo (the *Aum* is Japanese for the Buddhist meditational hum of 'Ommmm' and the rest means Ultimate Truth) was its name. As disaffected followers and victims came forward to tell their tales, it soon became apparent that this was a bunch of crazies in the same league as the perpetrators of the Jonestown, Branch Davidian and Solar Temple massacres. Over the weeks and months that followed, it emerged that their objective was no less than the extermination of Japan's government — not the Diet, but the bureaucrats of the all-powerful departments around Kasumigaseki — and its replacement with a theocracy headed by the cult's leader.

The gas bombs — actually plastic bags full of sarin — had been carried by followers onto five different trains, and punctured with sharpened umbrella ferrules when they converged on Kasumigaseki. Because of the meticulous mechanics of the subway, the terrorists were able to narrow the target down to one specific exit of the station — A2. This is the one used by employees of two law enforcement agencies, the Tokyo Metropolitan Police and the National Police Agency (the Japanese equivalent of the FBI), which were the prime targets. As they poured off the poisoned trains to start the day shift at 8.30 a.m., the police took the most casualties — more than seventy officers hospitalised. Other government departments and agencies also lost hundreds of key employees — the ministries of finance, trade, telecommunications and construction were all hard-hit. Only the fact that the sarin had been produced in a crude, diluted form prevented the attack from crippling Japan's government as effectively as a tactical nuclear strike.

Tokyo reacted to the news with stunned disbelief. Surely this was the stuff of lurid American airport paperbacks, not the reality of a country where the most commonly reported crime is the theft of bicycles. How could such an extremist organisation have emerged from such a grey, conformist, consensus society? How could it have been allowed to wreak its evil almost unchecked for years — a crime wave of fraud, extortion, kidnapping and murder stretching back nearly a decade? What, more fundamentally, did the subway attack tell us about law and order in a country which boasts the lowest crime rates in the world, apart from a few of the more amputationist Muslim states?

The warnings were already there that Japan was wide open for a terrorist crime of this sort. For years it had been smugly relying on its *koban* system, the network of police-boxes at almost every street corner across the country, from which the *omawari-san* ('Mr Walkabout') patrols on foot and bicycle. This had been an internationally admired model for community policing, the buzz words of the 1980s, copied with varying degrees of success by some American states and by other Asian countries, including Singapore. However, when we called on the National Police Agency two years before the subway attack, they were already worried that the *koban* system was failing to cope with an increase in the frequency and seriousness of crime — although the figures were still something about which an Australian police chief could only dream. If you live in Sydney or Melbourne, you are still three times more likely to be robbed, four times more likely to be murdered, ten times more likely to be raped and an extraordinary seventy-seven times more likely to be assaulted as you are in Tokyo.

Nevertheless, the amount of unsolved major crime was rising quite dramatically, even before Aum began its homicidal onslaught. In a little over a year, we were to see the head of the Fuji film company hacked to death on the footpath outside his home by a ritual assassin with a ceremonial sword; a campaign of bombing and extortion against the Sumitomo Bank; the shooting down of the chief of Japan's national police force; and the hijacking of a domestic 747 by a demented banker who held 200 people hostage for nearly twenty-four hours. Guns, once the preserve of a handful of professional gangsters, began flooding into the community (mainly from Russia), leading to a near doubling in shootings. In the decade to 1994, the crime clean-up rate fell from an enviable 60 per cent to an ordinary 30 to 40 per cent. For some crimes, such as theft, the rate was no better than Britain, which is continually bemoaning the breakdown of law and order.

The NPA inspector we spoke to blamed the rising tide of crime on sociological factors. Japan's homogenous, self-policing 'village society' was being gradually diluted by more than a million resident foreigners, by the increasing mobility of the workforce and the anonymity of the cities. Its famously equitable wealth distribution took a battering during the prolonged recession of the early 1990s, when hordes of dishevelled homeless people began appearing even in the subway tunnels under fashionable Ginza. The increasing violence and sophistication of crime was proving beyond traditional law enforcement, the friendly neighbourhood bobby.

We spent one afternoon on the beat with one of these 'Mr Walkabouts', an inspector named Masao Kiyota who was officer in charge of a small unit of police based in Ota-ku, a down-home residential suburb to the southwest of Tokyo. Inspector Kiyota, an affable middle-aged man with steel-rimmed glasses, headed a squad of half a dozen men based in a grey-tiled police-box — one of 15 000 or so located in every neighbourhood across the metropolis. The aim is for police, on foot or on their white bicycles with a wooden truncheon in a special holster, to be able to reach anywhere in Tokyo in ten minutes.

To visitors from the crime-ravaged cities of Europe and North America, Japan used to be a journey back in time to a vanished world where guns were for shooting ducks, not people, and drugs something you took when you were ill. Inspector Kiyota is the friendly village bobby in this urban idyll. I checked the occurrence book in his *koban* — absolutely nothing had happened since his shift came on duty. I asked the inspector and his men the most serious crime they could remember. They talked about a flasher at the local school, illegally parked bicycles and some cars which were vandalised. One young constable, eager to impress, says, 'We had a rape a few months ago,' then, when his colleagues demur, admits, 'It wasn't exactly on our patch ... but we were called in to help.'

The policing methods are based on community contact and goodwill, which some Westerners find rather Big Brotherish. Every resident is required to register with the local *koban*, and twice a year there will be a bang on the door as police come calling to check on you and ask questions about the neighbours. They regard themselves as social workers — police visit vulnerable people such as the elderly living alone, they take part in local festivals, they go drinking with community leaders to listen to their problems. If they pick up a drunk who has made a mess of himself (Inspector Kiyota swears this is true), they will put him in a cell until he sobers up, and wash his shirt and pants for him. You can borrow money from a *koban* if you lose your fare home. Often you will see a lost dog tied up outside. The inspector patted the pistol holstered on his hip. 'We do have side-arms, but nearly every Japanese policeman will retire having never fired a single shot.'

Unfortunately, as the National Police Agency rather prophetically pointed out, Japanese society is changing. The methods of policing that were appropriate for a village of rice farmers are proving increasingly inadequate to deal with the rise of professional crime, let alone a doomsday cult intent on urban terrorism. With hindsight, alarms should have been ringing in Japan's intelligence community almost from the moment a Messianic guru named Shoko Asahara began preaching death and destruction nearly a decade before the attack on the subways.

His whiskery face with its eyes half-closed in a lopsided squint and his blubbery body clad in a fuchsia-coloured robe floated above the gaping commuters on giant display screens outside railway stations all over Tokyo for days after the attack. No-one could call Shoko Asahara charismatic, the first cliche you would normally reach for to try and account for the thousands of people attracted to his cult. As he droned on, in a videotaped message from his hide-out, about how the police were trying to frame him, he merely made most people more certain of his guilt — and more furious at the police who were blundering around, day after day, for two long months on their seemingly interminable investigation.

For those who believe in the triumph-over-adversity theory of leadership, Asahara provides a case study. His real name was Chizuo Matsumoto and he came from a humble background in the backwoods of Kyushu, Japan's southern island. He was the fourth son of a poor tatami-mat maker, and was born with glaucoma, which caused the chronically poor eyesight which plagued him all his life. Asahara, however, was not completely blind. When, at the age of five, his parents managed to wangle him into a boarding school for the blind, he discovered the truth of the aphorism 'In the country of the blind, the one-eyed man is king.'

Asahara, who in his younger days was quite athletic, lorded it over his completely blind fellow students. He was something of a thug, as they remembered it, given to bullying and extortion. When they play-acted the television series 'Thunderbirds', he had to be the captain; when judo dramas became popular in Japan, Asahara marched around in iron clogs kicking people. He confiscated lollies from his classmates and used them as bribes in an unsuccessful attempt to get elected president of the school student council. He forced the other kids to fight one another, revelling in the violence. For fourteen years, Asahara ruled that closed and cowed community of children, a taste of tyranny he evidently found to his liking.

He graduated from high school with average grades, and failed dismally when he attempted to qualify for the elite Tokyo University. Married by now — he and his wife Tomoko would eventually have five children — Asahara set himself up as a traditional healer, practising massage, acupuncture and moxibustion, a Chinese remedy which involves putting a tiny pile of inflammable powder on the ailing part of the body and setting it on fire. He started a pharmacy from which he dispensed home-brewed 'cures' for various ailments. His blatant quackery soon put him on the wrong side of the law — he was fined $3000 for practising medicine without a licence for the fraudulent sale of a brew of alcohol and tangerine peel, touted as a Chinese 'Ultimate Cure-all'. That, incredibly, was the only time the authorities took any action against Asahara, until it was too late.

Asahara graduated into the cult business after a trip to India in the early 1980s, where he claimed to have studied yoga and Tibetan Buddhism under the Dalai Lama, reaching a state of *satori*, or enlightenment. Returning to Japan, he proclaimed himself His Holiness, the Master Shoko Asahara, and declared that in a previous incarnation he had been Imhotep, the vizier of the Pharaoh Zoser, responsible for designing the pyramids. Impressing the impressionable with demonstrations of ESP, levitation, breathing under water and 90 per cent winning streaks at *pachinko* (pinball), among other divine gifts, the fat swami began to attract acolytes. The cult was first called *Aum Shinsen No Kai* (the 'Group of the Legendary Hermit with Miraculous Powers').

Asahara's message was a bizarre mix of Nostradamus and Hindu and Buddhist mysticism, with strong overtones of Armageddon. He was an admirer of Adolf Hitler, Chairman Mao and Emperor Akihito, whose horoscopes he compared with his own. He preached that the world would come to an end in 1997, and that only the followers of Supreme Truth would be saved, to establish a 'thousand-year kingdom'. If this sounds a fairly unconvincing pitch, Asahara made up for it with brilliant marketing. At the top of his organisation were some extremely smart people — graduates of Tokyo University (Japan's Harvard or Oxbridge) — people with degrees in science, engineering, medicine and law. As well as salvation, Asahara offered them laboratory facilities and freedom to pursue their research. He used radio and television, books and *manga*, Japan's ubiquitous comics; he sent his disciples out into the streets, and to canvass young people in coffee shops, gyms, clubs and cramming schools. Most successfully of all, the cult used computers. It is fitting that the first guru of the information superhighway should have been Japanese. Asahara trolled the bulletin boards for the lonely, the isolated, the — well, nerdy — youngsters huddled over their screens.

Japan has always been particularly vulnerable to these cults. Some say it represents a rejection of the materialistic values which have driven Japan's postwar economic recovery. Karel van Wolferen writes, 'The main function of Japan's new religions is social. They provide havens for those who crave intensive group involvement, but are not "members" of corporations' — particularly people like housewives, students, farmers and other self-employed workers, and those in the hospitality industry. Others hold that the cults fill a vacuum left by the absence of traditional religious belief — only 26 per cent of the Japanese believe in any kind of god, compared with 68 per cent of Americans (according to an extensive study commissioned by the *Yomiuri* newspaper). This atheism is particularly pronounced among the young.

Shinto, the indigenous 'folk religion', is not really a religion at all in the sense that it involves no belief in an afterlife, worships no universal deity and has no unified body of teaching like a Bible or Koran. Buddhism, which arrived in the seventh century, is in seemingly terminal decline, mostly used nowadays to consecrate funerals. Christianity never made much headway in Japan — only about 1 per cent of the population. Religious observance, such as it is, is largely ritual. It is said, with some truth, that Japanese are born Shinto (mothers still take their newborn babies to the local shrine to be blessed), marry Christian (a church wedding is 'romantic' and cheap) and die Buddhist (their ashes interred in family tombs).

Into this spiritual void have sprung a multitude of colourful cults. Japan's Education Ministry has a mind-boggling 184 000 religious organisations registered. Ever-mindful of the religious repression which accompanied the rise of 'State Shinto' — the Emperor-worshipping cult that provided the spiritual justification for World War II — the government is extraordinarily tolerant of anything that calls itself a religion. Even organisations like The Family (a pernicious free-love cult once called the Children of God) which are banned in some overseas countries are allowed to operate in Japan. Asahara took full advantage of this constitutionally sanctioned religious tolerance.

Many of today's cults are devoted more to Mammon than God, since they pay no tax — not even, as is specifically provided by the Religious Corporations Act, if they should operate a business such as a bar, a beauty salon or even a coal mine. I once interviewed a hip Buddhist priest who conducted his mission around a tiny bar in Osaka's red light district, no doubt claiming the Four Roses bourbon he favoured as a tax deduction. In the name of religious freedom, supervision is today kept to a minimum. The Tokyo City Government, for instance, which is charged with policing 6400 registered religious groups, employs just four people to do it. Little wonder Aum escaped scrutiny for so long.

Religion in Japan is a menagerie: charismatic Christians; robot Buddhist priests; whoring Children of God; loony Moonies; Hare Krishna; Inner Peace; believers in the science-fiction author Lafayette Ron Hubbard's Dianetics; Kofuku-no Kagaku, the Institute for Research in Human Happiness; Denshin-kyo, the 'electricity religion' which worships Thomas Edison; PL Kyodan, the 'golf religion' which builds driving ranges on the roofs of its churches. All of them offer solace to the miserable multitudes — many of them demanding in return the absolute obedience and all the worldly goods of their followers. The Japanese, call them gullible if you like, flock to them in their millions.

Two years before Aum hit the headlines, I went to talk to some disaffected followers of Sun Myung Moon, the lachrymose, septuagenarian North Korean-born former arms manufacturer who runs the Unification Church, which claims five million members worldwide. The Moonies are best known for their mass weddings, in which tens of thousands of men and women who have never met are matched up and 'married' by Moon in vast outdoor spectacles. These include many naive young Japanese women, lured across the Sea of Japan, who are required to pay $13 000 a head to 'marry' farmers in poor rural districts of South Korea where brides are in short supply.

Their main complaint — leaving aside their feeling of spiritual betrayal — was that Moon had stripped them of every yen they had and turned them into door-to-door salespeople for ludicrously overpriced artefacts ($13 000 for a toy stone pagoda decorated with coloured glass) made in the cult's factories. A nurse (approached, believe it or not, in the street by a man who said she had a 'third eye' in the middle of her forehead) had donated her life savings in the hope of finding a husband. A young man had been persuaded to raise $55 million in mortgages on the family farm and hand it to the Moonies so that his father could be cured of an illness. Lawyers were pursuing more than 2000 similar cases involving nearly $600 million, and had already embarrassed the Moonies into returning much of the loot.

With Aum, however, there was no turning back once a follower had been enticed into one of the 'ashrams', grim, windowless, barracks-like buildings, surrounded by wire and guard posts, that Asahara began constructing all over the country. Classical brainwashing techniques, developed during the Korean War and adapted successfully by many cults since, were used: deprivation of sleep, food and water; isolation from friends and relatives; and endless repetition of dogma. If this was not enough, Asahara would doctor his recruits with psychotropic drugs. When his chemists succeeded in synthesising LSD, Asahara insisted on trying it first himself, and proclaimed it the highest form of enlightenment. 'I have been to the end of the universe, witnessed its origins and wet my pants,' he rejoiced. Swallowing a glass of liquid LSD became a part of the initiation ritual.

Former cult followers counselled by Dr Steven Hassan, a Boston psychologist involved in the enormous deprogramming effort that followed the collapse of Aum, spoke of being stripped, drugged and dressed in paper diapers, shut in a tiny 'meditation cell' where they were bombarded with music and slogans while they threw up, urinated, clawed their flesh until they drew blood, and experienced hallucinations. They were told this was a 'religious vision'.

When they were reduced to a sufficiently zombie-like state, the acolytes would be subjected to further grotesque rituals. Television was crowded for weeks with former followers, their faces electronically blurred to protect them from reprisals, telling of buying and drinking Asahara's sperm, blood, bath water and a tea made from his hair clippings; internal purging by swallowing huge amounts of warm water, and five metre-long bandages; being immersed in a swimming pool and ordered to hold their breath until they lost consciousness; being buried alive for weeks in wooden boxes and scalded in vats of boiling water; wearing rugby-style skullcaps wired up to batteries which delivered ten-volt shocks to their heads (three volts for children) so they could receive Asahara's 'psychic energy'; and, finally, being forced to hand over everything they owned, from apartments and bank accounts worth millions to battered pots and pans.

Once captured by the cult, they were subjected to revolting punishments for any transgressions of the rules. Couples who had sex (Aum preached abstinence, though Asahara managed to father five children and was accused of molesting some of his female followers) were stripped naked, had dog collars put around their necks and were made to crawl on all fours, eating meals of leftovers from the floor. Women who wore make-up were forced to plaster their faces with mud for a week. Followers who quarrelled were made to physically fight it out, with Asahara as the referee. Mind control was complete. 'If Asahara said black was white, then that became the reality,' said one former follower. 'That was the most terrifying part of Aum.' If anyone did escape, a squad of thugs headed by a former *yakuza* gangster Asahara recruited as his 'security chief' hunted them down, imprisoned and sometimes killed them.

Rejecting the hierarchy of Japanese society which had no place for him, Asahara built his own replica of it behind the walls and the barbed wire. His writings show that he was strongly influenced by science fiction — particularly Isaac Asimov's Foundation series, in which the prophet/hero of the book builds a new civilisation based on a harmonious blending of technology and spirituality. However, Asahara's was an inward-looking world, highly bureaucratic, authoritarian and hierarchical; there were sixteen ranks of follower, with titles such as *goshi, bocho* and *aishi*. His followers were required to slave away night and day for little personal reward for the good of the group. They were indoctrinated to believe in their own uniqueness, to reject deviants within the group and to treat the outside world as a corrupt and hostile environment. Sound familiar?

It was in 1989 that the authorities should reasonably have been expected to put a stop to Aum's increasingly antisocial activities. That was when Asahara sought the imprimatur of respectability — registration as a religion by the Tokyo Metropolitan Government. The municipal authorities were well aware of reports of kidnapping, torture and fraud that had been surfacing in the media, particularly the Sunday *Mainichi* newspaper which had long crusaded against the cult. Citizens and important politicians interceded to oppose the registration. For several months the bureaucrats hesitated — and Aum began an extraordinary campaign of harassment, dispatching up to 200 followers clad in white pyjamas to invade the Shinjuku headquarters of the city government, putting up posters denouncing individuals, telephoning and picketing their homes. Instead of citing this as further evidence of Aum's unsuitability to call itself a religion, the authorities capitulated. Ignoring a condition of registration which specifically states that followers 'must be free to enter and leave' a religion, they gave Asahara what amounted to a licence to enslave, rob and finally murder.

Apparently unsettled by this reminder that even he was subject to the laws of the land, Asahara determined to take over the country. His first attempt was by lawful means. At national by-elections for the Upper House in 1990, Asahara and twenty-four of his top lieutenants ran for election. It was a clownish campaign in which the guru was carried about sitting cross-legged on a huge cushion while his supporters, wearing giant papier-mâché caricatures of his head, capered about chanting his name. When Aum failed to get more than a handful of votes Asahara declared darkly, 'The state is bad,' and secretly began plotting its violent overthrow. He proclaimed himself 'Holy Pope' and reorganised his cult into twenty-two ministries, paralleling those of the Japanese government — most notoriously the 'science and technology agency' which was to be responsible for developing weapons of mass destruction such as sarin.

He moved his headquarters from the boondocks of Kyushu to the little farming village of Kamikuishiki, in the foothills of sacred Mount Fuji, about 100 kilometres southwest of Tokyo. Using dummy names, the cult bought up a dozen plots of land and began erecting huge barn-like structures of boilerplate sprayed with white rendering. These were the *satyams* (a Sanskrit word meaning 'place of worship') where Asahara created his evil kingdom, absolute ruler of the 1400 followers who lived there and obeyed his every command, whether it was kidnap, murder or the manufacture of weapons of mass destruction. Shoko Egawa, a cult expert we interviewed, described Aum as a 'roach motel' — gullible young people were attracted by flowery promises, but once inside found themselves glued to the floor, trapped in a nightmare.

I visited Kamikuishiki one showery day a few months after the subway attack. Spooky 'astral music' wafted out over the heads of the heavily armed *kidotai* riot police guarding the buildings and the encampments of television journalists waiting for the next act in the drama. Coaches stopped at the roadside while tourists snapped pictures. The only signs of life at the *satyams* were young blank-eyed men and women with their hair shaved to stubble, hiding inside guard boxes. We persuaded one to speak to us, although he seemed to have been programmed and long silences interspersed his monotone answers. A skinny young man, wearing a T-shirt and wire-framed glasses, he said his family name was Honma ('My other name is a secret.') and he had been a follower of Shoko Asahara for five years. At that stage, more than 200 cultists, including Asahara, had been charged with mass murder and other crimes, but Honma believed Japan's equivalent of the CIA was really responsible for the subway attack. '*Soshi* ('the founder') is not a murderer. He carries on his back the evils of the world. He is a great saviour,' he said. We asked him what would happen if the police tried to evict the remaining followers — parliament was debating whether to declare Aum a 'subversive organisation' and disband it. 'We would never use violence,' said Honma. Left hanging in the air was the possibility of mass suicide.

We had actually driven to Kamikuishiki to talk to a man who had spent six frustrating years trying to convince the authorities that they should take action against Aum. This was Seiichi Takeuchi, aged sixty-seven, a stalwart of the local Communist Party, who raises beef cattle on a property a few hundred metres from one of the *satyams*. Not long after Aum moved into the district, he became suspicious about the way the cult began harassing its neighbours — tapping telephones, taking down car registration numbers, coming and going in the middle of the night. Takeuchi actually smuggled himself into one of the buildings and took photographs of illegal construction work; but the authorities refused to take action.

Even more alarming was the testimony of followers who managed to escape from the clutches of the cult. Starving, half-naked men and women would come banging on the farmers' doors in the middle of the night seeking sanctuary. Six months or so before the subway attack, a young nurse had come to one of Takeuchi's neighbours with a chilling tale of having been kidnapped, along with her baby child, and held prisoner for three months in a freight container, handcuffed and eating her food from the floor 'like a dog'. The Kamikuishiki farmers found her a place to live and a lawyer who lodged a complaint with the police. Nothing happened. Takeuchi shook his head in disbelief. 'If only they had taken action then, all those lives would have been saved. Bureaucratic negligence and laziness caused this disaster.'

The first and most ominous warning that the cult was capable of anything came, in fact, back in November 1989, when a lawyer named Tsutsumi Sakamoto — who had been representing a number of families trying to recover their children from the cult — disappeared from his apartment in

Yokohama, along with his wife and baby son. The police were called, but even though they found an Aum badge at the scene, refused to take the investigation seriously, and claimed for years that the family disappeared of their own free will. In fact, they had been kidnapped by a squad of Aum thugs, taken to Kamikuishiki for interrogation and murdered. The dismembered bodies, buried in the countryside, were not unearthed until several months after the subway attack.

Over the following six years, at least 110 reports were made to police, linking Aum with murder, kidnapping, fraud, aggravated assault (cult followers scalded in boiling baths), manslaughter (a cult follower killed by machinery), theft, illegal detention and other crimes of the utmost seriousness. An elderly notary public trying to rescue his wealthy sister from the cult was snatched from a Tokyo street in broad daylight and never seen alive again. Another man was murdered as he walked along a busy footpath in Osaka — someone came up to him and squirted lethal VX gas in his face. Parents of more than forty young men and women appealed for help in rescuing them from the cult. Deadly poison was detected leaking from one of the Kamikuishiki compounds. In every case, the police either ignored the complaint — they told parents their missing children were a 'domestic matter' — or made a cursory and inconclusive investigation.

Shoko Egawa is a campaigning journalist who introduced Sakamoto to the parents who lost their children to Aum, and became Japan's leading authority on the cult. After publishing a series of investigative articles, she herself was attacked by noxious gas squirted through her letterbox at three-thirty in the morning. I asked her why the police time and time again refused to investigate this and other crimes quite clearly linked to Aum — what appeared to most outsiders as an incomprehensible dereliction of duty. She said that Aum was protected by its religious status, although this is quite clearly a police fabrication designed to get them off the hook. Article 86 of the Religious Corporations Law states unequivocally: 'No provision of this law should be construed as preventing the application of other rules and regulations in the event a religious organisation commits an act detrimental to the public interest.' More convincingly, she said that Sakamoto had been a member of a Yokohama Bar Association which had crossed swords with the police on human rights issues — the police refused to take the family's disappearance seriously because of personal animosity.

There are other reasons for the failure of the police to act against Aum until too late, most fundamentally the fact that they rely to an inordinate extent on the confession to obtain a conviction. It is called the 'king of evidence'. An extraordinary 99.9 per cent of people charged with crimes in Japan are convicted, and in 95 per cent of these cases police manage to extract a confession during the twenty-three days in which a suspect can legally be detained in custody. Often a suspect is held incommunicado, tied to a chair with rope, with no lawyer, no visitor, no bail and no right to silence during the long interrogation sessions. However, this reliance on confession is a double-edged sword, as the Aum investigation was to show. Faced with defiant cultists who refused to talk, the police were powerless to make a case. Their forensic techniques — which are now the front line of criminal investigation in other parts of the world — are primitive. Genetic evidence, for instance, is unknown.

The presumption of innocence, Rumpole's 'golden thread', is strained well beyond breaking point in the Japanese legal system. In 1993, both Amnesty International and the International Bar Association sent missions to Japan to investigate conditions in the *daiyo kangoku*, the police detention centres where tens of thousands of suspects are locked up until they confess. Their reports on the denial of human rights in this grim Gulag were scarifying. They uncovered a number of appalling cases of fraudulent convictions: juveniles terrorised into confessing to murder; people tied up and beaten; even one woman whose husband, a local politician accused of taking a bribe, was choked to death by police who shoved a rag down his throat with a chopstick.

I once interviewed a man named Sakae Menda who spent

thirty-four years on death row after police 'verballed' him for a murder. In 1983, he became the first convicted murderer in Japanese legal history to win an appeal. Although he was eventually released, nothing could compensate him for spending half his life waking at eight o'clock every morning in his solitary cell to the sound of the guards' heavy boots and jangling keys and wondering if it was his turn to die that day. He was the first of five convicted murderers to be released after decades on death row. No-one has any idea how many more of the eighty or so convicted murderers in Japanese jails are, in fact, innocent — nor how many innocent men have actually been hanged over the years.

The Aum investigation highlighted another weakness in the Japanese police system — the legal constraints on police powers originally designed to prevent a resurgence of anything like the dreaded *kempeitai*, the wartime secret police who terrorised Japan much as the Gestapo did Germany. Thus, police are barred basic investigation tools which law enforcement authorities elsewhere regard as essential — they are not supposed to infiltrate suspect organisations, cannot legally tap telephones, indemnify informants nor engage in plea bargaining.

As well, police organisation is weak and fragmented. The National Police Agency is actually a misnomer, since it has nothing like the authority of the US FBI with which it is often compared. It has neither the power to investigate crime nor to issue warrants or arrest criminals — its great grey fortress in the heart of Kasumigaseki serves merely as an information agency, and a severely dysfunctional one at that. Local police forces belonging to cities and prefectures do the actual work, and — as was the case with Aum — operate in an isolated, uncoordinated way. No-one sat down to make a pattern of the 110 serious complaints against the cult. No national Aum task force was set up until long after the subway attack, and many investigations were left to village 'Mr Walkabouts' with little experience of serious crime, and none at all of murder.

There is one final reason for the almost incomprehensible failure to act. During the 'bubble years' of the late 1980s when

Aum was expanding, the police had a lot more on their minds than investigating complaints against yet another loony cult. During that half decade of hectic economic growth, Japan's home-grown Mafia, the *yakuza*, had reached unprecedented heights of power and influence, and were expanding their interests overseas, including even Australia. Suddenly, a domestic problem became an international crime menace, as journalists began to write lurid accounts of these fearsome warriors with their tattoos and their amputated fingers. In 1992, Japan finally passed legislation aimed at eliminating the *yakuza*, and the police were directed to mount a full-scale campaign to disband the gangs — a campaign that, according to the *yakuza*, was conspicuously ineffective.

That came from the horse's mouth. We travelled down to Kyoto one day a little over a year after the new law came into force. An introduction had been arranged with Tokutaro Takayama, the 65-year-old boss of Aizu Kotetsu, one of Japan's larger gangs. He was not hard to find — neighbours pointed out the gang headquarters, a futuristic three-storey tiled building on the banks of a stream in a rather seedy neighbourhood of bars and bathhouses. We talked with him in a huge office dominated by a stuffed polar bear, with the gangleader's personal biographer in attendance, and the immaculately suited Takayama taking time out to practise his golf-putting. If the police campaign was having any effect, it was not noticeable — far from hiding, his 3000-odd followers, with oiled punch-perms and full body tattoos, wore a uniform of grey track suits with the gang's name emblazoned in gold on the breast pocket.

Takayama said that his gang, the third largest in Japan, had actually been increasing both its numbers and its activities. Although he declined to go into details, the National Police Agency calculated that in 1993, after a full year of the anti-gang drive, there were still 90 000 *yakuza* in 3500 gangs nationwide — around ten times the size of the Mafia in the United States. Their income, mainly from drugs, gambling, protection rackets and prostitution, was $20 billion — about the gross national product of a smallish country like Kenya. Takayama scoffed at the new law, whose constitutionality he and the other gangleaders had got together to challenge in court. Gesturing at portraits on the wall of his grim-faced predecessors dating back to the gang's foundation in 1861, he declared, 'I will not be the last boss. Aizu Kotetsu will go on for ever.'

There should have been one last line of defence against organisations like Aum, Japan's shadowy Public Safety Bureau. This is an organisation headquartered in the Justice Ministry at Kasumigaseki, which runs both domestic and foreign intelligence, and has responsibility for national security. We called on the agency one morning and had a peculiar interview with one of the young spymasters, who kept bursting into laughter at my questions. The bureau, it turned out, did not even place Aum Shinri-kyo on its surveillance list until a week after the subway attack. It was attempting to redefine its mandate in the aftermath of the Cold War, and seemed to be still spending much of its time spying on consumer groups, environmental organisations and ancient, toothless foes like the (perfectly legal and boringly respectable) Communist Party of Japan. Osamu Shimabukuro, a former officer in *koan keisatsu*, the police public security agency, has written that in some Communist Party branches government spies outnumber the actual members. Rather than identifying new and far more ferocious threats to society, such as Aum, the Public Safety Bureau was still fighting the Cold War.

With the police distracted by their ineffective war on Takamaya and his colleagues, and Japan's domestic spies chasing an imaginary Bolshevik menace, Aum was becoming a force to be reckoned with in Japan and overseas. As well as the Kamikuishiki facility, it opened centres in twenty cities across Japan, recruiting as many as 14 000 followers, of whom 1400 became full-time acolytes. It expanded into Russia, opening branches in Vladivostok — where it had a radio station — and Moscow where eventually it claimed 30 000 members. Centres were opened in New York, Bonn and near the Sri Lankan capital of Colombo. By 1995, of all the 'new religions' Japan had spawned, only Soka Gakkai (a 'lay Buddhist' organisation which claims ten million members worldwide) could claim to be larger and richer.

As his wealth and power increased, Asahara's pronouncements became increasingly apocalyptic. Hostilities would break out between the United States and Japan by 1997, he predicted, triggering World War III which only his true believers would survive. Aum was under attack from hostile governments using chemical weapons. Traitors were undermining the cult from within — Asahara began administering Sodium Pentothal, a so-called truth drug, to his followers. Any who failed the test or tried to leave were eliminated. At Asahara's command of *poa* (another Sanskrit word meaning 'ascend to heaven'), they would be dragged into a basement execution room and garrotted to death. As the murders mounted, Asahara — concerned about disposal of the bodies — experimented with a giant meat-grinder, a vat filled with nitric acid and a commercial microwave. The residue was scattered for the foxes in the foothills of Mount Fuji. Twelve months after the subway attack, forty cultists were still missing, many of them believed murdered.

While Asahara's cult spread throughout the country, it began to acquire enormous wealth from the money and property it confiscated from recruits. On joining, they were even required to write a will leaving everything to Asahara, and to sign a document indemnifying the cult against their death 'regardless of the way in which it occurs'. One of Asahara's lieutenants estimated the cult's assets at $1.5 billion — more than the annual profit of the mining multinational BHP — and this was probably no exaggeration.

In Tokyo alone (where a modest apartment will leave little change from $1 million), Aum Shinri-kyo came to own at least forty buildings, housing thriving businesses ranging from curry houses to a hospital and a computer-manufacturing company in Akihabara 'Electric City'. When police finally raided the cult compound at Kamikuishiki they discovered a safe containing

Asahara's pocket money — $18 million in cash and ten kilograms of gold bars. For a man who preached that the end of the world was nigh, Asahara relished his worldly goods. His top priority was financing the construction of weapons of mass destruction.

Confessions by former followers indicate that Asahara decided to make poison gas his ultimate weapon around April 1993. He called together members of his 'science and technology agency', who included a number of young chemistry graduates, and told them: 'The work I am about to assign you is rather dangerous, and if we go ahead with it a metropolis somewhere will be destroyed. This work is worth forty days of religious training in a solitary cell — afterwards you will all be promoted to a higher rank.' He ordered the construction of a special *satyam* — number seven — in which tonnes of the poison were to be produced in an industrial-scale plant. By August, the cult's chief chemist had succeeded in producing experimental quantities of the deadliest substance known to man.

The ease with which Asahara evaded official attention and built a massive arsenal of weapons and lethal chemicals is one of the most frightening aspects of the story. Establishing a dummy company (it was called Belle Epoch — 'Beautiful Era') fronted by one of his young scientists, he managed to lay his hands on more than 700 tonnes of chemicals needed to manufacture his deadly poison without a question being asked. Truckloads of chemicals, drums and vats and sacks of them, were carried into Satyam No. 7. This is by no means a complete inventory, just part of the stockpile later seized by the police: ninety tonnes of methanol, fifty tonnes of diethyl aniline, sixty tonnes of hexane solvent, 180 tonnes of phosphorous trichloride, half a tonne of iodine, one tonne of phosphorous pentachloride, fifty-one tonnes of isopropyl alcohol, 140 tonnes of glycerine, fifty-four tonnes of sodium fluoride, eighty tonnes of sodium chloride and sixty tonnes of sodium hydroxide.

As well, Aum was able to assemble all the equipment needed for a full-scale chemical manufacturing plant: the plumbing, electrolysis units, a reaction cauldron and air filtration plants. There were gas masks and poison gas detectors, industrial ventilation plants, centrifuges and gas chromatographs. It was a huge, highly sophisticated, computer-controlled production laboratory, a devil's kitchen that one investigator was later to describe as 'as large and as good as anything Saddam Hussein had'.

But where did the know-how come from? To the horror of the US government, it was later learned that Aum had gone to the most open marketplace in the world to get certain essential equipment and information — and even the tyres for Asahara's Rolls-Royce. Through a US-registered front company called Aum USA, Asahara's purchasing agent Yasuo Hiramatsu succeeded in buying two sophisticated air filtration systems used in making chemical and biological weapons. They almost got away with three even more alarming orders — for equipment used to measure plutonium, a military laser device and a shipment of several hundred Israeli-made gas masks. Aum downloaded much of its data from the Internet, including the formula for the poison of the highly toxic green mamba snake. They obtained invaluable information from a New Hampshire company which provided the cult with a thirty-day free trial of a computer program used for designing pharmaceuticals. The computer came back minus the hard drive that contained the information.

Seven months after the attack, a US Senate committee hearing on Aum drew attention to this failure of safeguards against the export of technology with mass destruction applications — nuclear, as well as chemical and biological. 'I believe,' said Senator Sam Nunn, 'this attack signifies that the world is entering a new era [of terrorism].' He also flagged a failure by intelligence services to identify the threat, even though Aum publications frequently referred to a war with the United States, and one article was actually headlined 'Will Clinton Be Assassinated?' over a story about the president attending an APEC summit in Osaka. 'They were not even on our radar screen,' said a spokesman for the committee —

although it did transpire that Clinton's security precautions for the summit included a gasproof car and a supply of atropine, an antidote to nerve gas that was carried by troops in the Gulf War.

As well as sarin, the cult managed to produce other almost equally horrific substances in the secret Satyam No. 7. They made two other nerve gases, Soman and VX; mustard gas; and highly toxic sodium cyanide. In vats of peptone nutrient, they cultivated biological agents — anthrax, tetanus and botulism, in particular. Even more chilling, cult followers later confessed that Aum had been toying with the idea of releasing the nightmarish Ebola virus in Tokyo. More than toying. In 1992, an outbreak of Ebola — a highly contagious virus that kills 90 per cent of its victims — in Africa received wide publicity in Japan when it was reported that a Japanese man had died of it. Under the guise of a medical mission, several Aum doctors went to Zaire, ostensibly to help in hospitals, in fact to obtain samples of the virus. Aum scientists also discussed using smallpox, yellow fever and aflatoxin as biological weapons in the apocalypse they believed was coming. Fortunately, Asahara apparently decided these agents were too unreliable after spraying them around the Imperial Palace one night in a vain attempt to murder Emperor Akihito and his family. He decided, incidentally, to try them out on people rather than using laboratory animals first 'because humans are much more vicious than animals'.

Even more alarming for Japanese security, a few months before the subway attack the cult managed to steal some of the most sensitive military secrets in the country. Aided by a sergeant in an elite paratroop regiment who had been recruited by Aum, a hit squad managed to break into Mitsubishi Heavy Industries, Japan's largest defence contractor. They tapped into the company's mainframe computer and downloaded classified data on the laser guidance system for weapons fired by Japan's main battle tank. A few weeks later, the same squad broke into Nippon Oil and Fats, which — in spite of its unprepossessing name — manufactures the solid fuel that puts Japan's H II missiles into space. Boxes of documents, including 'highly sensitive' formulae for propellants and explosives, were stolen.

The break-ins were covered up, and no-one ever linked them to Aum until too late.

Even the ultimate nightmare, nuclear weapons in the hands of terrorists, might have happened if Asahara had been more patient in his plans for Armageddon. The cult obtained plans for uranium-235 separation — the key to building an atom bomb — by infiltrating a prestigious Russian nuclear physics research establishment, the Kurchatov Institute in Moscow. Although most experts dismiss the possibility of a group like Aum actually building a bomb, it cannot be entirely ruled out given the cult's limitless wealth and easy access to other highly sensitive data. On an expedition to Australia, cultists were once seen wandering around a property they bought with Geiger counters, apparently looking for uranium deposits.

From Russia, too, using shadowy political and military connections, Aum obtained conventional military hardware. Aum's 'construction minister' Kiyohide Hayakawa visited Russia on arms purchasing expeditions more than twenty times without being detected. How they managed it, no-one has been able to satisfactorily explain, but in June of 1994 Aum bought a thirty-seat Russian MIL-17 helicopter, imported it into Japan and sent two followers to the United States to learn how to fly. Aum sent 'observers' on several occasions to Russian military manoeuvres, including simulated tank battles. One captured Aum follower was found to have a 'shopping list' on him which included prices for plutonium and for a Russian Proton rocket. They acquired AK-47 sub-machine guns — the weapon of choice of guerillas everywhere — equipped one of the *satyams* with machine tools and copied enough parts to arm an army.

Asahara did actually attempt to form a private army, though like many of his enterprises there was an element of Keystone Kops about it. Aum rented an abandoned junior high school near a remote town called Kushimoto, in Wakayama Prefecture. They rounded up about thirty day labourers — casual workers, many of them homeless — from the streets of Tokyo and Osaka, kitted them out in military fatigues and began drill practice and indoctrination about the 'coming war' in which these ragged vagrants were to be the 'Soldiers of the White Love'. Unfortunately, the neighbours — who had been told Aum was a social welfare organisation engaged in drug and alcohol rehabilitation — smelt a rat and got them evicted.

However, it was poison gas, and particularly sarin, that obsessed Asahara. He called it *maho*, 'magic'. By June of 1994, Aum's chemists had succeeded in making several litres of it, but they had not yet worked out an effective delivery system. Asahara wanted to spray it from the sky, to achieve a maximum kill. The cult spent $44 000 buying two elaborate model helicopters of the sort used in Japan to make remote observations of erupting volcanoes. Unfortunately, Yoshihiro Inoue, head of the cult's 'intelligence agency' crashed and wrecked them both on their maiden flights. An attempt to spray sarin into the street from a car equipped with a Heath Robinson-type ventilation fan also backfired — one of Aum's chemists poisoned himself and had to be injected with atropine to save his life.

In order to experiment with a substance as nightmarish as sarin, the cult's scientists needed as much space as possible — and where else in the world but Australia can you buy 190 000 hectares of land with a farmhouse attached, 800 kilometres away from the nearest city, for a mere $570 000? Their excess baggage bill added another $350 000 for two tonnes of equipment Asahara and his followers told Perth airport authorities they were importing for gold mining. In fact, undetected among the shipment, were fifty large bottles labelled 'sake' (rice wine) which actually contained sarin. Australia was where Aum did the pilot tests that would end a year later with the subway massacre 9000 kilometres away in Tokyo. The decomposed bodies of twenty sheep later discovered by police testified to its effectiveness.

Fortunately, after a few months, the cult was forced to abandon Australia when quantities of hydrochloric acid and other dangerous chemicals were discovered in their baggage at Perth airport. Two of Asahara's followers were convicted and fined for breaching airline safety regulations, and Aum finally sold the farm and departed when several other cultists were declared prohibited immigrants and turned away at the airport. By then, they had not only mastered the production of a crude, contaminated, yet still highly lethal form of sarin, but they had also decided on a delivery system. Asahara's engineers hit on the idea of mounting a fan-driven unit on the back of a small truck to vaporise the sarin and spread it through the air .

The first sarin attack in history, apart from Saddam Hussein's unspeakable slaughter of the Iraqi Kurds, occurred around midnight on a warm summer's night in June 1994. A 'stealth squad' of Aum followers drove the sarin-spraying van through the streets of the mountain resort of Matsumoto, not far from Nagano where the 1998 winter Olympics will be held. The experiment succeeded beyond Asahara's wildest expectations. The colourless, odourless vapour blew in through the open windows of bedrooms where people lay sleeping, killing them in frightful agony — investigators found fingernail claw-marks on the walls and the tatami matting floors. By the end of the night, seven people were dead and more than 200 hospitalised. The suburb looked like a necropolis — birds dropped from the sky, dead dogs and cats lay in the streets, carp and yabbies floated belly up in ornamental ponds.

Unfortunately, Mr Walkabout got the wrong man. Hassled for a quick arrest, Matsumoto police — whose only known skill is in rescuing stranded mountain climbers — picked on one of the victims of the attack, who happened to have a supply of garden chemicals in a shed. While his wife lay seriously ill in hospital, they interrogated the unfortunate man for days. Even when they failed to force a confession from him, the police remained convinced he was the real culprit, and ceased to take further investigation seriously. Asahara's followers escaped to kill again.

Evidence pointing to the cult as the real murderers did not emerge until after the subway attack, when journalists began reinvestigating the Matsumoto gassing. They discovered what the police had missed — that Aum had been involved in a bitter dispute in Matsumoto, over construction of a building on some land the cult had bought. The case had been heard in the local District Court, which had reserved its judgment — it was expected to go against the cult. The sarin gas had been aimed at a dormitory where the judges of that court lived. The assassination attempt nearly succeeded — three of the judges were hit by the gas, one seriously enough to be hospitalised.

Having missed that opportunity to stop the cult, the police proceeded over the following months to ignore a whole carillon of other alarm bells. Asahara's followers were experimenting to find the best way of producing, and disseminating, the nerve gas. Complaints of a terrible stench and corrosive fallout coming from several cult facilities were ignored. Takeuchi, the neighbouring farmer, called the police one night to complain about a stink coming from Satyam No. 7. He drew their attention to a patch of blighted land where there had apparently been a chemical spill. The police did take samples, however, and on January 1, 1995 — three months before the subway attack — the *Yomiuri* newspaper reported that laboratory tests had confirmed the presence of sarin. When Asahara read the report, he flew into a rage. Fearing a police raid, he ordered the building cleansed, equipment dismantled and a large plastic statue of the Hindu Goddess Shiva erected to disguise the poison factory as a place of worship. He need not have worried — still, incomprehensibly, the police did nothing. They swallowed a cock-and-bull story that a local fertiliser company had been responsible for the chemical spill.

Japan moved inexorably towards disaster. One frosty morning in February, a carriage full of people travelling between Tokyo and Yokohama were affected by a mysterious chemical, eleven of them requiring hospital treatment. It was a dummy run for the subway attack a month later. Mr Walkabout's 'investigation' failed to identify even the agent responsible. Convinced by now that he could get away with anything, Asahara laid his plans for war on the citizens of Tokyo.

It is now apparent that in the months leading up to the attack, Asahara was becoming increasingly, dangerously, demented. His ranting took on an ever darker doomsday tone.

He began to refer to sarin in his speeches, calling it *shoene genbaku*, literally the 'energy-saving atomic bomb'. In one apocalyptic pamphlet he warned: 'The nation's public security authorities are targeting us with the energy-saving atomic bomb. The twenty-three wards of Tokyo will shortly be annihilated.' On February 28, he called 100 of his top aides together at a Chinese restaurant and told them: 'Armageddon will certainly occur. Don't be afraid to sacrifice yourselves. You must fight to win. I think I will be captured, but I will surely return.'

The darkest secret of all, however, is not how Asahara planned his hideous crime, but what, and when, the police knew about it. Aum had deliberately targeted both the police and the military for recruitment — more than 100 followers were either serving or former officers. They provided a pipeline through which Asahara knew every move that was planned; a follower even managed to bug one of Japan's most senior military commanders. Little of this will ever appear in the Japanese media — a conspiracy of silence from the reporters attached to the cosy police '*kisha* clubs' and their editors and owners makes sure of this. However, from independent inquiries, I am certain that there was a two-way flow of information. The police knew in advance that a terrorist attack was planned, knew it would involve poison gas and knew it would be in the subways.

Exhibit A: On the Friday before the attack, police requisitioned from the military 100 gas masks and protective suits. On the Sunday morning, the day before the attack, in conditions of great secrecy, police were trained in their use at a police base in Tokyo. It was subsequently claimed that this was in preparation for the raids on Aum facilities that followed, but that does not explain why some of the masks were issued to subway police patrols. When Mayu rang the Tokyo Metropolitan Police to ask why they had done nothing to warn the public of the threat, they blustered but did not deny they had prior knowledge of the attack. Unthinkable as it would be anywhere in the real world — if only for fear of later litigation — the Japanese police kept quiet about the threat, allowing eleven people to go to their deaths, and thousands more to be injured.

Asahara's assassins struck shortly after eight o'clock on the morning of March 20, 1995, rupturing packages of sarin among rush-hour commuters before fleeing the mayhem in getaway cars. It was obvious as soon as doctors (who contacted the hospital in Matsumoto where the previous attack took place) connected the symptoms with sarin, who was responsible. Asahara's tapes and publications mentioning the chemical, as well as that *Yomiuri* report of police identifying sarin residue at Kamikuishiki, were cited as the media pointed the finger at Aum. The swami's denials, in a videotaped message from his hide-out, merely seemed to confirm his guilt. Tokyo waited for the police to raid the cult compound ... and waited ... and waited ... and waited.

For fifty-six days, Asahara remained at large. Fifty-six days in which Tokyo became a city of fear. Hundreds more people were hospitalised when at least four more poison attacks were made on trains and at railway stations, including the use of sodium cyanide and a gas identified as the World War I weapon, phosgene. The chief of the National Police Agency was gunned down outside his house, before the eyes of his four bodyguards, by a would-be assassin who escaped on a bicycle and was still at large nine months later. A parcel bomb blew off the left hand of an aide to Tokyo's mayor, Yukio Aoshima, after he announced he would move to deregister the cult. A key witness, Hideo Murai, chief of Aum's 'science and technology agency', was stabbed to death live to air on national television by a *yakuza* gangster, apparently to stop him talking.

While the police dithered, the crisis actually began to affect Japan's economy — one analyst calculated that it knocked 0.1 per cent off the gross domestic product, several billion dollars. Department store sales slumped, and travel during the Golden Week holiday was down by more than a million as people stayed home out of fear of new attacks. To add to the alarm, police were receiving fresh terrorist threats almost daily and giving secret warnings to airlines, train companies and department stores — but keeping the information from the public. Tokyo's ragged regiment of homeless people was particularly hard hit. A train travelling near Mount Fuji was halted when someone smelt something nasty, and armed police swarmed aboard to investigate. The cause of the problem turned out to be a very embarrassed tramp who was taken to a police station for a much-needed bath and change of clothes. In the 'cardboard city' in the Shinjuku railway station underpass, the homeless complained that they couldn't scavenge enough to eat because all the rubbish bins had been removed as a safety precaution.

As 'X-Day' approached, the day Aum was to be raided, Mr Walkabout had yet another blunder in store. Police ordered the Japanese media not to breathe a word about Aum being the prime suspect for the subway attack until they had completed preparations for the mother of all raids, which (because a public holiday intervened) took three days to organise. Then, hoping to gain some glory, they tipped off selected media organisations in the police *kisha* club about the cult targets they would be hitting. Asahara was thus given at least a day's notice that the police were planning to attack. His lieutenants even had time to invent a meteorological code — when the 'chance of rain' became '100 per cent', the raid was imminent.

Twelve hours before the first raids actually began, television crews began setting up lights and cameras outside the cult's headquarters in the ritzy suburb of Aoyama. Surprise, surprise, Asahara, his top lieutenants and several truckloads of incriminating evidence were spirited away into the night. By the time television viewers were admiring an impressive column of 3500 paramilitary police in full gas warfare drag — including canaries in cages, an old miner's trick to warn of gas — advancing in serried ranks through a snowstorm, the sarin had disappeared and all that was to be found of Asahara was an abandoned white Rolls-Royce. For the next few weeks he mocked the police from his hide-out, while his 'science minister', his 'foreign minister' and a bevy of smooth cult lawyers took over the afternoon television 'wide shows' to proclaim Aum's innocence. While what was advertised as the greatest dragnet in Japanese history hunted for him, Asahara unconcernedly directed fresh sarin attacks, and even dictated and published a new book.

Gradually, however, the net closed in. One by one 300 of Asahara's followers were picked up and taken into custody — not initially on charges of plotting mass destruction, but for trumped-up peccadillos such as the illegal use of a bicycle, trespass in a baseball park, registering under a false name at a hotel, possession of a paper-cutter (a breach of the Swords and Firearms Control Law), the illegal construction of a greenhouse and slander, which is a crime in Japan. One follower seen rubbing a friend's shoulders was arrested for not having a licence under the Masseurs' Act. Such is the tragicomedy of law enforcement in Japan. But of Asahara and his 'ministers' there was no trace.

Not that the police could find, at any rate. Just about everyone else in Japan seemed to know where Asahara was hiding out. NHK, the national broadcaster, had little difficulty sending the runaway guru a list of questions, and obtaining a videotaped statement from him. He was in daily telephone contact with his followers. While 220 000 police combed the country for him, he floated mockingly above the crowds at Shinjuku station on a giant screen, dressed in a fuchsia-coloured robe, blithely claiming that he had been framed — it was really the police (or the American CIA, or a rival Buddhist cult, depending on his mood) who had dumped the sarin in the subways, to discredit Aum.

Eventually, however, on the foggy morning of May 16, an army of police marched into the Aum compounds at Kamikuishiki and began to search for Asahara, who had been hiding there all along. His presence was betrayed by the rinds of the $150 musk melons, to which he was addicted, which police had found in the garbage cans. Tokyo awoke to find that, no matter what channel they turned to, all they could find on television were shots of wet, shivering reporters huddled around the Aum compound in the mist saying things like 'The police have been in there two hours now … I wonder what's going on.'

In fact, it took 3500 police four hours to find Japan's, and almost certainly the world's, most wanted man, sawing their way through steel walls and wandering in pitch darkness through a maze of secret passageways in one of the *satyams*. Finally, two officers were sitting having a smoke-oh in a locker room on the second floor, idly wondering about an odd structure like a packing-crate suspended from the ceiling. They drilled a hole in it, looked in and saw an eye looking out. Mr Walkabout's 56-day hunt was over.

It is almost impossible to describe the media frenzy that followed. After two months of terror, Tokyo could breathe again. Every TV network in the country cancelled every program for twenty hours — with the exception of one television soapie and one baseball game. Even the staid *Nikkei*, a business broadsheet, brought out a special edition. Thousands of reporters were assigned to cover the police convoy escorting him to Tokyo police headquarters — the TBS network, just one of six, had 660 reporters and technicians on the job, including cameramen on hot motorcycles relaying live coverage via helicopters hanging overhead.

Asahara cut a very different figure from the awe-inspiring guru to which his followers were accustomed. His clothes were crumpled, he hadn't bathed for days and he was clutching a cardboard box containing $120 000 in cash when police prised him from his hide-out. 'How could someone like me who cannot see have done such a thing?' he said. Then he added plaintively, 'You probably won't believe me.' As they bundled him into police headquarters, watched by crowds of thousands jamming the sidewalks, few seemed to have doubts about his guilt. Even Makoto Endo, a civil rights lawyer who appears for *yakuza* gangsters, refused to represent Asahara, claiming he was not '150 per cent' satisfied of his innocence. 'What will happen to me?' bleated the Living God.

The media's attention was by now focused on the plight of the 100-odd followers of the cult discovered imprisoned in a barracks at the Mount Fuji compound. They looked like newly released concentration camp inmates. Dehydrated, half-starved, with some of them in a drugged, zombie-like state, they told of their fears that Asahara had been planning a Solar Temple-style mass suicide. Indeed, in a broadcast the day before over the Vladivostok radio station, Asahara had told his followers to prepare to die for the cause. Parents who had travelled to the Mount Fuji compound from all over Japan clung to the wire weeping and calling out the names of their missing children. 'I have come here to kill myself if they commit suicide,' said one mother from Kobe.

Most heart-rending of all were the 100 or so little children taken into protective custody. Pale as rice-flour because they were never allowed outside for fear of 'gas attacks', and caked with filth because the compound had no bathing facilities, many of the children did not even know their real names (they were called 'boy-A' and 'girl-B'). They had been forced to chant Aum's catechisms for up to fifteen hours a day. A dozen were suffering from pneumonia and malnutrition, and had to be hospitalised while welfare officials appealed for their relatives to come forward. However, such were their feelings of shame and revulsion that many families shunned relatives who had got involved with the cult. When I visited Kamikuishiki nine months after the subway attack, there were still about 100 true believers living in the *satyams*, apparently because they had nowhere else to go.

By the end of the year, Asahara and 200 of his followers were finally behind bars, but thanks to the police bungling, at least four senior lieutenants were still at large. The charges by now included the two gas attacks, the killing of the Sakamoto family, the missing notary public and one cult follower strangled for disloyalty — a total of twenty-three murders. The National Police Agency said the whereabouts and safety of at least another forty former cult followers was still unknown. Many must be presumed murdered — former followers testified that at least two people had been boiled to death in superheated baths, and others killed by injections and electrocution. In an attempt to wipe out the memories of followers who had witnessed his crimes, Asahara connected their heads to the mains electricity and poured 110 volts through their brains until they lost consciousness. Police had little hope of finding the remains because the bodies had been variously incinerated, dissolved in acid or ground up and scattered in bushland. Aum's bloody rampage, the most diabolical string of serial killings in modern history, is matched only by the evil of the Mafia and the Colombian drug cartels.

There remained one final obstacle to the pursuit of justice and some understanding of how these terrible crimes went undetected for so long, and what Japan needs to do to prevent a repetition — the Japanese court system. If justice delayed is justice denied, then Asahara and his cohorts will never receive a fair trial. Makoto Endo, a former judge turned radical lawyer, calculates that if he pleads not guilty — as his lawyers were predicting, claiming reports of a confession were false — it will take fifteen to twenty years before the final verdict. In Japan's courts, justice is strictly rationed by the government's refusal to appoint enough judges, apparently fearing an American-style epidemic of litigation.

The country has one judge for every 44 000 people, compared with one per 16 000 in the United Kingdom and one per 8800 in the United States. Admittedly there is less litigation, but in the past forty years the number of cases before Japanese courts has trebled, while the number of judges has increased by only 30 per cent. As a result, each judge has a caseload of no fewer than 300 pending cases. Bizarrely, civil and criminal cases are typically heard for only a day, or half a day, per month. In the most extreme case I know of, that of a convicted mass murderer represented by Endo, his appeal is still going on forty-seven years after the crime, and several years after the man's death. In Asahara's case, with the prosecutors preparing no fewer than 11 983 pieces of evidence, it will be well into the next century before the judge (Japan has no juries) pronounces the final verdict, which will be death by hanging if he is found guilty.

In the meantime, Asahara had become a celebrity psychopath. Not the first in Japan — that honour goes to Issei Sagawa, the cannibal, who murdered a Dutch student in Paris in 1981 and ate portions of her body. Scores of books, several movies, and innumerable magazine articles — most notoriously one in which he was interviewed in a restaurant for the gourmet pages — have been written about him. The Asahara industry, however, became bigger than Ben Hur — Charles Manson, Jeffrey Dahmer and O. J. Simpson rolled into one fat, purple-robed package.

In Hibiya Park, 4158 people queued for the electronic raffling of fifty-six seats available at one of the preliminary trials. Aum shops sprang up across Japan selling his tapes, books, T-shirts, tunics, calendars and alms-collection boxes. A restaurant near Kamikuishiki named a takeaway rice dish 'Harumagedon', Japlish for Armageddon. A subway massacre game appeared on the Internet in which — by manipulating the time, trains and volume of poison gas — you could score ten points for a death and one for an injury. A photographer whose only claim to fame was having called an Aum spokesman a liar at a press conference was hired to do a television commercial for Suntory iced gin. Phrases like *poa suru* (to 'send to heaven' or 'kill') entered the vocabulary, as in 'my girlfriend poaed me'.

In the rush of events, and the public relief that at last Asahara was behind bars, it was easy to overlook the profound change which had come over Japanese society. Aum had shown them, just as the Kobe earthquake did two months earlier, that in the event of a disaster Japan's institutions and the people who run them are totally inadequate. A poll by the *Asahi* newspaper found that 67 per cent of Japanese no longer believed society was safe, and 45 per cent said the police were 'not doing enough'. Even the National Police Agency acknowledged this in its 1995 white paper: 'The public's assessment and assumption that Japan is a safe country have begun to fade,' said the agency.

However, what it did not address was what to do about it, how to establish the kind of system needed for preserving law and order in the post-Aum era — a modern criminal code (the current one was drawn up in 1905), a judicial system where justice is both done and seen to be done (which, surely, can't involve convicting 99.9 per cent of people charged) and, most important of all, a professional police force in which people can have confidence to prevent, detect and solve serious crime, as well as bicycle theft. This heinous crime obviously marked some sort of watershed, but it seemed as if the lessons were going to be ignored. Tomiichi Murayama's unstable coalition was tottering along, leaving the country wallowing in a policy vacuum, with no-one willing to seize the opportunity to recast Japanese law enforcement into a more effective machine to deal with such threats.

The Justice Minister did speak, softly, of the need to increase police powers to allow (for example) infiltration of terrorist organisations, phone-tapping and the establishment of an FBI-style force with power to take over investigations of national importance from local police. He was immediately howled down by the Social Democrats, who seemed to hear echoes of the pre-dawn bang on the door by the *kempeitai*. Over the protests of legitimate religions, the law was eventually changed to require religious organisations to publish their accounts — although this seemed more an attempt to harass Soka Gakkai, the Buddhist organisation which supports the opposition coalition, than a genuine attempt to supervise Japan's 185 000 registered cults. As far as the creaking, ninety-year-old Criminal Code is concerned, the only proposed change was a law to prohibit the possession of sarin, which was hurriedly rushed through the Diet as a piece of window-dressing.

Katsuya Endo, assistant professor of international law at Tokyo International University, threw up his hands in despair when I asked him what the future held. He believes that Japanese law enforcement, even in the last years of the twentieth century, still depends on the 'village system' — where everyone watches out for their neighbours and wrong-doers are sanctioned by social isolation. 'Unfortunately, the sarin gas attack has shown us that Japan is no longer a village, no longer a homogenous self-policing monoculture,' he says. 'Law enforcement simply has not developed the tools to deal with the new situation. It is a myth to talk about Japan as a "safe society". I believe it is virtually defenceless, the perfect spot for international crime or terrorism.'

IN THE GREEN GLOOM OF THE FOREST, A STARK sign stands beside the frozen trail. 'Wait!' it admonishes. 'Think again! You only have one life — value it.' It is one of a dozen warnings that have been erected by the police all through this forbidding patch of woodland on the slopes of Mount Fuji to try and stop an epidemic of suicides that has turned it into a killing field without parallel.

In the forty years since the Jukai, as it is called — the Sea of Trees — was first brought to national attention in a television drama, no fewer than 1400 people have come here from all over Japan to take their own lives. Several more have been brought here to be murdered.

Of all the world's favourite suicide sites, probably only San Francisco's Golden Gate Bridge comes close to this gruesome record. Since it opened in 1937, 985 people have jumped the forty metres to their death in the bay below.

Japan's forest of death is a much more macabre setting: 2500 hectares of an almost-impenetrable jungle of stunted, twisted pines and oak trees, their roots writhing across moss-coated boulders of black volcanic lava. Not a bird sings, this winter afternoon. Not a ray of sunlight pierces the darkness. Ice lies in black slabs on the paths. Frost rimes the pits and potholes in the frozen earth.

'Watch you don't fall in,' warns my guide, a wildlife photographer named Yuzo Nakagawa. 'If you do you will die like all the others, and your body may never be recovered.'

Many of the suicides, in fact, involve people deliberately getting lost and wandering around until they expire from exhaustion and exposure. Others, says Superintendent Sadao Jinguji, second-in-charge of the local Fujiyoshida police station, are more methodical.

TO PASS
UPON THE

Sitting in his office with his back to the snow-caped cone of the ancient volcano, the superintendent flips through photographs in looseleaf binders that contain the details of last year's suicides.

A middle-aged man in blue jeans hangs from a white rope tied to a tree branch. He has travelled here nearly 1000 kilometres to end his life. His note reads: 'I am tired of the world.' Here are the remains of a woman, aged fifty-nine, who was depressed because of a serious illness. She left her family and journeyed from faraway Kyushu Island to cut her throat in the Jukai. It took some weeks of detective work to identify her as she had faked her identity. Another picture shows only the upper half of an unidentified human skull.

'We try to warn people that this is not a pretty way to go,' says Superintendent Jinguji. 'The bodies sometimes get eaten by foxes and badgers and scattered over a wide area.'

Men outnumber women four to one among the dead, but there is no discernible pattern of age or occupation. They range from teenagers (who often kill themselves because of difficulties in their relationships) to middle-aged businessmen with financial problems, to people in their seventies worried about their health.

Every autumn, several hundred police and local fire brigade volunteers organise a day-long sweep of the Jukai, looking for bodies which they might have missed during earlier spot searches. In 1994 they found fifty-seven — the most in nearly a decade.

'The recession?' I ask the superintendent.

He purses his lips. 'The rise coincides with the publication of that book.'

'That book' is the *Complete Manual of Suicide*, a how-to manual by Tokyo journalist Wataru Tsurumi which has sold a phenomenal 800 000 copies — and plunged its author into a virulent controversy. Three of the bodies found in the Jukai that year had copies of the book by their sides, as did eight more would-be suicides the police say they saved in the nick of time. In it, Mr Tsurumi counsels:

> If you have become tired of your work and human relationships, and if you want to commit suicide without anyone ever noticing, without hesitation I recommend that you step into the Jukai.
> Your body will not be found. You will become a 'missing person' and slowly disappear from people's memory.

The Jukai was first popularised as a suicide spot 40 years ago when another book was made into a popular television drama — *Nami No To* (*Wave Tower*) by the novelist Seicho Matsumoto. It tells the story of a young woman, unhappy in love, who kills herself in the forest. The copycat suicides began increasing dramatically, however, with the publication of Mr Tsurumi's manual three years ago. As well as advice on how to kill yourself (he says hanging is best) it gives directions to the forest from the nearest railway station, recommends several hotels for one's last night on earth and advises on bushwalking tracks from which it is easy to get lost.

The book includes a map showing would-be suicides how to avoid areas searched by the police, and warns: 'Beware of the locals. Some long-time residents say they can spot suicides just by looking at them. If you are spotted, don't hang about — go quickly into the forest.'

Telephoned, Mr Tsurumi said he did not feel responsible for the epidemic of deaths. 'All my book may have done is encourage them to change the venue. I don't think suicide is a bad thing, anyway. People who want to take their own lives should be free to do so.'

Superintendent Jinguji is not convinced. 'It is not a very nice thing to be known as the suicide capital of Japan. This is an important tourist area, and local businessmen think it is bad for business. Also, my men have more important things to do than search for bodies all the time.'

Even more alarming than the suicides, the Jukai is now becoming a trendy spot to commit murder — in the past few years at least four people have been lured there and killed. They include a young mother who strangled her three-year-old daughter, a man who killed his lover and a *yakuza* gangster driven there to be garrotted.

Police are still searching for the body of one of the five victims of one of Japan's most notorious serial killers in recent years, which is said to lie buried in the forest. The so-called 'Osaka dog trainer murderer' killed his victims with poison injections and dismembered them.

To try and cut down on the toll, a police/citizens' committee has been formed to detect and deter would-be suicides. Hotel staff, taxi and bus drivers, and people running souvenir shops have been asked to look out for warning signs such as people looking depressed, travelling on their own or without baggage. Backed up by a telephone lifeline — and the posters — the committee claims to have stopped sixty-six people from killing themselves in the Jukai last year. For hundreds of other world-weary Japanese, however, it remains the favourite place for life's last exit.

For the record, the Japanese are not — as is popularly imagined because of kamikaze pilots and hara kiri — a particularly suicidal people. Some comparative figures (annual deaths per 100 000 population) follow:

Hungary	40 (60 for men)
Sri Lanka	33
Finland	29
Denmark, Austria	24
Switzerland, former Soviet Union	22
France	21
China	17
Japan	16
Canada	13
Australia, United States	12
Portugal	9
United Kingdom	8
Israel, Argentina	7
Greece	4

(*Source:* World Health Organisation)

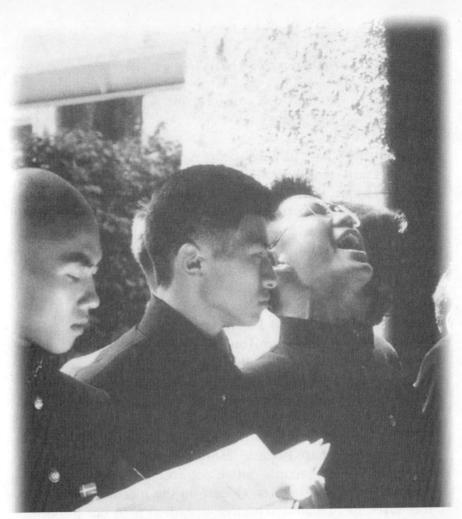

EIGHT
SUFFER THE CHILDREN

'Older brother, sorry for the inconvenience.'

— SUICIDE NOTE OF KIYOTERU OKOCHI, AGED THIRTEEN, WHO WAS BULLIED TO DEATH

HIS MOTHER FOUND THE BODY HANGING from a persimmon tree in the backyard of his home one Sunday afternoon. Kiyoteru Okochi was just thirteen years old, a quiet and studious lad who had been a pupil at the junior high school in Nishio, a small town not far from Japan's auto-making capital Nagoya. His suicide was to turn out to be not just a private tragedy for the Okochi family, but the trigger for an extraordinary outpouring of public grief and national soul-searching that was to convulse Japan for weeks. Newspaper columns were filled with commentary. The Japan Bar Association established a special hotline. Prime minister Tomiichi Murayama — himself a doting grandfather — called a special Cabinet meeting. Lugubrious television newscasters began signing off their evening bulletins appealing to children: 'Don't do it. Don't kill yourself. What you are facing now won't last for ever.'

Why should one child's death have caused such a commotion? Perhaps because it shone a pale light on one of the dirty secrets of Japan's much-admired education system. Topping most world tables, at least on the mechanical skills of the 'three Rs', Japanese children are often held out to be the best educated in the world. What is often not realised is the price they pay, the way in which they are robbed of their childhood to meet the priorities of the national education policy — the regimentation, the indoctrination, the denial of individuality the suppression of creativity and the brutality with which the system is enforced.

What tens of thousands of young Japanese are facing in the schoolyard — what eventually drove young Kiyoteru to take his own life — is called *ijime*, a word usually translated as 'bullying', but which carries much darker linguistic echoes. Used in conjunction with different Japanese qualifying characters, the Chinese kanji can mean 'tyranny' or even 'genocide'. Bullying, of course, is a feature of school society everywhere in the world. What makes it much more sinister in Japan is the extreme forms it can take, and the silent connivance of those responsible in the toll it takes on the innocent youth of the country — suicide, but also murder by fellow students, and even by the teachers who are supposed to be their protectors.

Japanese parents are smugly proud of what they suppose to be their crime-free playgrounds. They shudder theatrically when television footage is shown of youngsters passing through gun detectors on their way into classrooms in the Bronx. Indeed, superficially the children are neat, polite and well disciplined. You rarely see any rowdyism or hear of theft. Drug-taking usually means sniffing glue or thinners — that's not to diminish the ghastly consequences this can have, merely to observe that it isn't in the same self-destructive league as crack cocaine. Lulled by this into a false sense of security, people rarely want to rock the boat by taking a closer look at the statistics. If they had, Kiyoteru Okochi's death would have come as less of a sensation.

In the ten years to 1992 (the official body count, unfortunately, lags more than somewhat behind the times), no fewer than 5724 young people took their own lives in Japan — 'young' here means under twenty, the legal age of voting, drinking, smoking and going to grown-up court. This might not appear so monstrous in a country with a school population of 15 million, but it is a considerably higher youth suicide rate than in most other countries with comparable statistics. Twice as many kids take their own lives in Japan as in the United Kingdom, for example. Even more alarmingly, after falling steadily for more than a decade, the suicide rate seems to have begun to climb again, perhaps partly because of the hard times that followed the collapse of the bubble economy in 1990.

Of those who committed suicide in that decade, 101 were primary school students (five, incredibly, aged nine or younger); 850 were junior high school students, typically aged thirteen to fifteen; and 1722, high school seniors — the rest had left school. An average of 267 schoolchildren, or one every working day of the week, takes his or her life in Japan each year. Hanging is the favoured method with nearly half the children. Wataru Tsurumi, author of the *Complete Manual of Suicide*, recommends it as 'by far the best method — it's painless, easy and almost always fatal'. Jumping off buildings was the next most popular way for kids to do away with themselves, followed by leaping in front of trains, gas, poison, drowning, self-immolation and knifing.

However, what really brought this story to life, what catapulted a personal tragedy into a national crisis, were the heart-rending suicide notes, painstakingly written in pencil on four pages of an exercise book, which Kiyoteru had apparently spent several days composing. The boy's father, Yoshiharu, released them to the media as a warning to other parents, and as a spur to the school authorities to investigate what he said had been nearly a year of systematic abuse of his son by upwards of a dozen of his fellow students. It's worth quoting a few extracts here to try and explain why Kiyoteru and hundreds of other teenagers like him every year feel there is no other way out of their torment than death:

> ... four people (sorry I can't name them) frequently extorted money from me. I can't find the money to take to them today ...
>
> ... I first became a target of bullying from around the time I was a sixth grader, and in the first year of junior high school ... it became even harder in my second year ...
>
> ... they demanded as much as $900 before holidays [and at other times] $400 to $500 ... they visited our home. They searched a number of places, found money and took it. Later, when they had no money for playing, they ordered me to get some ...
>
> ... I was taken to a river and they forced my head under water. They did this many times, and I was scared, because I could not touch the river bottom with my feet. Since then, I had to do as my friends told me.

Don't blame the people who took money from me. I gave them the money obediently [although] it was wrong. I went early and brought tea to school for them. I hated all that.

I should have refused to comply with their demands, then things would not have become like this. I'm sorry. I wanted to live longer. I was most happy when I was at home. I was taken on a number of trips. I had no complaints.

Thank you very much for the last fourteen years. I am leaving on a trip. We will surely meet again some day. I am truly sorry about the money. I thought that I would be able to repay it by working, but that dream has ended.

Grandmother, I want you to live for a long time. Father, thank you for the trip to Australia. Mother, thank you for making tasty food. Older brother, sorry for being an inconvenience.

Why did I not die earlier? Because my family was gentle to me. It was easy to forget what happened at school. However, these days they bully me so hard and demand large sums of money, although I have none. I can't stand it any more ...

Kiyoteru's death was neither isolated nor unique in the degree of torment to which the boy had been subjected — it was one frame of a twelve-reel tragedy that has been going on for decades. A glance through the file of cuttings I made over the past three years puts it into context. A thirteen-year-old girl hangs herself from a utility pole when her classmates scrawl 'Liar. Fool. You ought to die.' in her schoolbook after she breaks a date to go ice-skating. In her suicide letter she says, 'Please place my comic books in my coffin. Give my belongings to my sister.' Another girl of thirteen, derided because of her plumpness, leaps in front of a train. Two fourteen-year-olds are charged with manslaughter for beating to death a classmate who refused to take the blame for them being caught smoking.

Seven boys aged twelve to fourteen are sent to detention centres for beating a class-mate, rolling him up in a gymnasium mat and stuffing him in a cupboard to die. A fifteen-year-old bully, about to be exposed and apparently overcome with remorse, kills himself by jumping in front of a train. Five girls leap from the top of an apartment block after a session sniffing thinners, killing three of them and seriously injuring the other two. In an especially tragic copycat consequence of the publicity following Kiyoteru's death, no fewer than eleven children commit suicide in less than a month. One is a fourteen-year-old boy who hangs himself from a beam at school, leaving a note saying it was an experiment. 'I just want to find out if people go to heaven or hell,' he wrote.

As for the number who are killed — or forced to commit suicide — by their teachers, the evidence is equally damning. Although corporal punishment has been illegal in Japanese schools for years, it still occurs, and is occasionally violent enough to kill. Officially (and this may be a gross underestimate) 1000 cases of assaults by teachers on students occurred in 1993, with 344 teachers disciplined or sacked. Physical education teachers were the most frequent culprits, accounting for about a third of all assaults. Of the victims, fifty-seven students were injured sufficiently seriously to need hospital treatment for wounds or broken bones — the injuries included one child with both eardrums shattered by blows and another whose spleen was ruptured after his teacher gave him a kicking.

In another quite bizarre case, the principal of a special school for 'problem children' managed to murder two of his young charges. Yukio Sakai, then aged sixty-six, was the headmaster of the poetically named Kazenoko Gakuen (Academy for Children of the Winds) located on a small island near Hiroshima, which was supposed to be a sanctuary for kids with 'school phobia'. This is a condition that (according to the Education Ministry) keeps more than 75 000 children out of school for more than thirty days a year through fear of being bullied or of failure in their studies or sporting activities. In the summer of 1991, Sakai had caught a boy aged fourteen and a girl of sixteen smoking, and by way of punishment handcuffed them and threw them into a freight container which was sitting in the hot sun in the school grounds. When they were eventually released, the two children had collapsed and later died of heatstroke. At his trial, Sakai said he had used the container on a number of other occasions and regarded it as a legitimate way to 'educate' his wards. The court disagreed, but not without misgivings, and eventually sentenced him to a relatively lenient six years in prison.

The case which received the most publicity during my time in Japan was that of a teacher who slammed a quarter-tonne iron gate on a fifteen-year-old girl who was running late for school, crushing her head and killing her. On this occasion, the teacher was dismissed and sentenced to a suspended jail term; but there have been other equally tragic and inexcusable cases where the teacher escaped punishment. A fifteen-year-old boy doing badly at baseball practice collapses and dies after he is forced to bat 100 times in scorching summer heat. A girl of seventeen hangs herself in shame after her teacher keeps her in detention for four hours, shouts at her and hits her with a wooden kendo sword. Her parents sue the school and are awarded $40 000 damages.

Exactly how many others died because of bullying can never be known, because of the secrecy and the shame which shroud child suicide, particularly in Japan. Even the raw numbers may grossly understate the extent of the crisis. Schools lie to protect their reputations, teachers to conceal their lack of concern, parents lest their child be tainted by association. In at least one recent case, a school tried to conceal a suicide by reporting it as a 'sudden death'. The circumstantial evidence, however, is strong. According to National Police Agency statistics, in those cases where the cause of death is known — three-quarters of kids leave suicide notes — 'problems at school' is the leading reason for a child taking its own life, around one suicide in four. This is followed by mental illness, family problems, unhappy love and illness. There is no category for extortion, which appears to have been the immediate cause of Kiyoteru's death — as well as an increasing number of the 22 000 other bullying cases which were reported to the education authorities in 1994.

'Wasn't there anyone at the school to whom the boy could speak frankly and pour out his woes?' asked the principal, Mamoru Miyama, at the memorial service which was held a few days later. Good question, and one which could equally have been put to his parents who had apparently sat back as Kiyoteru stole an extraordinary $15 000 from them in a matter of months to pay off his tormentors — surely a sign of trouble if ever there was one. I put it to a rather earnest young schoolteacher I met on assignment in Nara just a few weeks later. 'Perhaps the teachers just didn't want to know. As long as the class is giving them no trouble, why should they worry?' he said. This young man was unusual in that he had experience in a foreign education system — in his case a posh public school in Sydney. He believed you have to look deeper to find the real roots of the cult of violence and intimidation at Japanese schools — to the authoritarian nature of the system itself.

The finger-pointing pundits who rushed forward to try and explain Japan's uniquely horrible tradition of *ijime* focused on three main themes. First, they condemned the outlandish pressures to which Japanese children are subjected in the first eighteen years of their lives as they struggle for a place in the educational hierarchy which will determine their place in society for life — not just their job prospects, but where they will live, who they will marry and what opportunities will be open to their children. Secondly, they lamented the social isolation of the younger generation from their parents — particularly absentee salaryman fathers who play little or no part in the upbringing of their children — and from the teachers, who deliver lectures at classes of up to fifty students with no opportunity for feedback or personal contact. Finally, perhaps most convincingly, they took issue with the crushing pressure for conformity in Japanese schools, for belonging to a group which allows not even the most minor deviation from the norm. That most hackneyed of all cliches about the Japanese applies to the umpteenth degree to school society. 'The nail that sticks out will be hammered in.'

The fourth theme, the one I came to believe was the most important of all, was mentioned only obliquely. Nearly all my Japanese friends — Mayu is an exception because she went to an American school — say that teachers rely on the students to enforce discipline because they themselves often have no statutory punishments available, such as detention or 'lines'. In the elaborate hierarchy of a typical school, students are attached to a variety of groups, each headed by monitors, like the Australian public school prefect system — a group for cleaning the classroom, a group for planning excursions, a group for organising sport. When a child is seen to be straying from the norm for whatever reason, the teachers encourage his fellow students to discipline him. If excessive zeal results in the child's death, the teacher can avoid responsibility.

To look a little more closely at the education system, Mayu and I spent an afternoon talking to teachers and students at a junior high school in Hachioji, a gritty dormitory suburb southwest of Tokyo. The school seemed odd by Australian standards; the students, aged twelve to fourteen, were all from the same cookie-cutter mould. They all wear uniforms (the day we visited it was a uniform of yellow and blue tracksuits) and have a rigid code of dress and behaviour, including a ban on dyed hair and perms. At some schools, even the colour of umbrellas and satchels, the width of belts and the length of skirts are mandatory. 'We try to encourage individuality,' said the headmaster, a well-meaning, middle-aged man named Hiroo Yamazaki, 'but it is difficult.' The students themselves do not help — the girls have an unofficial regulation of their own, mandating that their white socks must be worn at identical half-mast height. An enterprising Japanese company has made a fortune selling schoolgirls an adhesive product called *sokkutachi* to hold them in place.

School at Hachioji is from eight o'clock in the morning until four o'clock in the afternoon, and very recently the government gave the kids the luxury of two Saturdays off a month. Class sizes here average thirty-five, although other schools can have forty, and some as many as fifty students in a class. After lessons — which mainly consist of rote recitation and reading, with little student/teacher interaction — the kids sweep the floor with twig brooms and then get down on their hands and knees to polish them with wax and dusters. Japan's schools do not employ cleaners, even for the toilets. The school hours go nowhere near accurately reflecting the time students really spend on their studies. Almost all the kids we spoke to were loaded down with homework, and attended Japan's dreaded *juku* (cramming schools) after hours.

The Hachioji school had been chosen for us by the teachers' association because it was said to be leading the way in bullying prevention strategies. Bullying had been rife. A questionnaire sent to 101 junior high schools and primary schools in the area found that about a quarter of all students had experienced *ijime*, ranging from teasing to verbal abuse and physical violence. Typically those picked on are the less socially skilled — *guzu* ('slow'), *debu* ('fat') and *kitanai* ('dirty') are the most common terms of abuse. 'It's an extremely serious problem and we are determined to eradicate it,' says the headmaster, Mr Yamazaki. The school and the district have set up free '110' telephone hotlines, organise seminars and encourage children to report bullying.

However, the school's counsellor, Kozo Watanabe, said the campaign had had little effect, and thought that society tolerated *ijime* because it was regarded as a 'training for life' which would never be eradicated. 'Parents and teachers are reluctant to stop bullying because they see it as an essential part of education,' he said.

Kiyoteru was part of this system. Look at the picture released to the media by his grieving parents. It's your standard Japanese schoolboy from central casting — you would be hard pressed to tell him from the thousands of other kids who strap-hang to and from school on Tokyo's crowded subways. Black woollen jacket, buttoned to the neck, with brass buttons and a stand-up collar — this is the standard uniform of 80 per cent of Japanese middle and high school boys, copied originally from the Bremen Naval Academy in nineteenth-century Germany. The girls wear blue and white uniforms with a similar military theme — except these were adopted after World War I and copied, instead, from the victorious British Navy. Kiyoteru's hair is short, although not the notorious *marugari*, a sort of convict-cut with the hair shaved to a billiard-table nap no more than one centimetre long, which many kids are forced to endure. Regulations strictly control everything from the width of his belt to his school badge (left breast) and winter muffler (banned). So extreme is the discipline in many Japanese schools that children with naturally brownish or wavy hair are required to produce a 'certificate of authenticity' for their abnormality. There have been cases of Japanese girls being forced to dye their hair black before being allowed into school.

To some Japanese, this look is a disturbing reminder of the country's militaristic past. The schools were the incubators for the Japanese war machine. Dragooned into the cadet corps, drilled by their masters in the martial virtues, Japan's teenagers were sent off to die in their thousands in the latter years of World War II — every boy dreamed of becoming a kamikaze pilot, every girl of becoming a heroic little helper, like the tragic Himeyuri girls of Okinawa. This is why, even today, there is violent controversy over the flying of the Hinomaru, the rising sun flag, and the singing of the Kimigayo ('The Emperor's Reign') anthem at school assemblies. The haircut, the uniform, the discipline, the absolute obedience demanded of Japan's children are still supported by many as an idealised *suparuta kyoiku* — a concept of 'spartan education' that has overtones of the cold water, rough towels, fagging, flogging and gruelling cross-country runs of the more unpleasant British public schools.

One person who took particular exception to the system was Ryoko Akamatsu, one of the brighter people to serve as education minister in Japan — the first woman, and the first non-politician, in the job, she was coopted from a top position in the Labour Ministry into the Cabinet of Morihiro Hosokawa in 1993, promising to blow a warm breeze of reform into the rigid system. 'I feel a chill whenever I see the *marugari*. It is because I remember the soldiers with this haircut during the war,' said Ms Akamatsu, outraging her more conservative Cabinet colleagues. Unfortunately, she lasted only a few months in the job, not long enough even to repeal the haircut rules, let alone tackle the more serious issue of bullying.

Anyone who deviates even slightly from the norm is liable to be singled out for persecution — or even worse, being sent to Coventry, isolation from the group. The intellectually handicapped are frequent targets, as are kids of *burakumin* background, the descendants of Japan's under-caste. Students who have studied abroad are soon hammered back into the mould; some who have learned to speak fluent English are forced to fake the funny pronunciations of their classmates so as not to stand out. Kids newly arriving from other parts of the country, kids who are a bit fatter, or thinner, or smarter or dumber are subjected to an escalating regime of *ijime*. It may begin with teasing and rough-housing, putting glass in the lunch box and letting bike tyres down, and escalate (to quote a couple of the nastier cases that have come to light) to putting laxatives in a child's lunch and hiding all the toilet paper, or forcing a boy to eat a used sanitary napkin.

Nobuto Hosaka, an education expert who was in much demand for his advice after Kiyoteru's suicide, was especially scathing. 'Many Japanese incorrectly believe that our education has been a success because there aren't as many dropouts or drug-abuse cases as in the United States,' he said, 'but, in fact, Japanese schools are akin to prisons ruled by fear, where kids must constantly be looking around to make sure they're behaving like everyone else.'

Masao Miyamoto recounts the case of a primary school child who was subjected to a mock funeral by his classmates with the connivance of their teacher — they even passed around a large card on which they wrote condolences. Dr Miyamoto is the psychiatrist who became an overnight celebrity in Japan when he returned from ten years in America to become the unlikeliest senior bureaucrat in the Health Ministry. In his exposé on the bureaucracy, the *Straightjacket Society*, he develops the theme that *ijime* is used as a tool of social control at all levels of Japanese society, not just in school:

> Japan has its own distinctive brand of bullying not found in other countries. In Japan, bullying is condoned by society, even by adults ... it uses the threat of ostracism to attack people's deep psychology and arouse anxiety. In the West, a bully is thought of as someone who enjoys watching others suffer, and bullying is diagnosed as an abnormal state of mind — [they] are looked on with contempt as cases of arrested development or people with immature personalities. When stories about bullying no longer fill the pages of our newspapers, then — and only then — can we say that Japanese society has become truly international.

Small wonder foreigners in Tokyo with high-school-age children approach the education system with apprehension, generally opting for one of the foreign schools. The son of a friend, Shun, had a particularly tough time fitting back into Japanese society after several happy years at Blackheath in the Blue Mountains west of Sydney. After attending a typical Australian high school, he found himself abruptly plunged back into the regimentation of the Japanese education system. 'They took him away on a camp the other day,' complained his father. 'Everything was organised down to the last detail — what they would be doing every fifteen minutes, night and day — even what time they were expected to go to the lavatory. Can you imagine that? And this is supposed to be their time off. He can't wait to get back to Australia, and nor can I.'

Some people blame the pressure. A child like Kiyoteru will spend about 240 days of the year at school, more than a student in any other education system in the world. In the United States, for instance, the school year is only 180 days long. Moves to reduce this are afoot (eventually students may even get every

Saturday off), but they are being fought by parents, who argue that this is an unnecessary indulgence. And the formal hours at school are nowhere near the end of it.

In order to keep your footing on the ferociously competitive escalator of the Japanese education system, regular attendance at a *juku* or cramming school is almost compulsory. Some 8 per cent of preschool children — preschool children, for goodness sake — are sent to these crammers. In the run-up to the crucial exams that mark the transition from junior high to high school, two-thirds of students will be spending three or four hours a day, five days a week, memorising mind-numbing reams of answers to anticipated questions. Then there's homework — an hour or two every night. 'Four and pass — five and fail' is the motto of Japan's students, referring to the number of hours of sleep you should allow yourself if you are serious about your exams.

And if this is not enough to consume every waking minute, most students — regardless of ability or inclination — will be sent to a neighbourhood workshop to study calligraphy, keyboard, abacus or kendo, Japanese swordsmanship. For Japan's notorious 'education mamas', the achievements of their sons (daughters still, in 1996, tend to finish up in second-class colleges and tea-lady jobs) is everything. It is spooky to find yourself on an underground train late at night, filled with uniformed schoolchildren silently snatching a few moments' sleep on their way to or from some assignment. When, as a foreigner, you try to talk to the Japanese about what are supposed to be the happiest days of their lives, you usually get some noncommital comments and a shrug — much as if you tried to discuss the Vietnam War with a veteran. If you weren't there, you wouldn't understand. Little wonder suicide is often an attractive option.

In the West it has become fashionable — among those who care more about academic results than about what education actually achieves in realising human potential — to praise the Japanese system. It certainly delivers a workforce which is as close to 100 per cent literate as is possible, and which outperforms most other countries in mechanical disciplines like mathematics and science. Walk into any classroom in Tokyo, however, and you will soon realise that is as far as it goes. Teaching is a one-way street — nothing could be further from the Western concept of *educare*, or drawing out a child's abilities. Education in Japan consists almost exclusively of the ingestion of thousands of facts, to be regurgitated on cue in multiple-option exam papers. Creative essays and *viva voce* examinations in languages are gradually creeping into the system, but are still regarded as radical experiments which disadvantage traditionally educated students.

The process is not helped, of course, by the amount of time it takes to master the written Japanese language. As well as thousands of Chinese-origin kanji characters which have to be learned by heart (you are not considered literate unless you have about 3000 of them at your command) there are two 48-character Japanese syllabaries to master. *Kokugo*, the study of the national language, will occupy 250 hours a year of a student's life for the twelve years he or she is at school. Go beyond this formidable rote learning, however, and look at the ability of Japanese students to reason and draw conclusions from the material they have absorbed, to express themselves, form opinions or engage in any original or creative activity, and you draw a blank. Japan's universities are full of so-called 'black hole professors' with a prodigious capacity to suck in every shred of information about their subject, but a total inability to shed any light on it.

Foreigners are continually amazed, for example, that after learning English for a minimum of six years, as the national syllabus requires, the Japanese are usually unable to speak a word of it — or of any other language they may study. This is usually put down to the fact that it is taught, like Latin, as a 'dead language' rather than a means of communication. A friend of Mayu's, in her final year of English language studies, had little interest in practising her conversation, but was obsessed with whether or not 'diamond' was a collective noun, as in 'There is a lot of diamond in South Africa.' I told her it sounded funny to me, but then I only make a living writing in

English for English-speakers. She insisted hers was the 'correct' usage, as well it might be — it's just that no-one ever says it. On such arcane points is the study of English in Japan based.

Some Japanese like to think learning a foreign language is especially hard for them because of their unique grammar and pronunciation, but that's a bit hard to believe when you hear Koreans, for instance, who have an equally abstruse language speaking perfectly acceptable English. Not to mention Tibetans, citizens of Zanzibar and Easter Island, and a friend of mine who managed to hold down the job of Reuter's correspondent in Rekjyavik, in spite of the fact that the only Icelandic/English dictionary then in existence was dated 1890. Others say it's because the Japanese dislike expressing themselves clearly in their own language — they use much body language, sighs and grunts in place of speech — let alone English.

Our friend Manny, who spent a couple of years in Japan teaching his own brand of English for $60 an hour in coffee shops, had yet another theory. 'It's because they never do anything interesting enough to talk about in any language. It's just work, work, work. You ask them what they do on a Sunday, and they answer "Sleep."' My money, for what it's worth, would be with Gregory Clark, an Australian journalist-turned-academic who is a long-term resident and fluent Japanese speaker. He says the Japanese education system has 'created a generation of linguistic cripples' because of plain bad teaching.

Why, you might ask, aren't these deficiencies remedied when Japanese students reach university? A commendable one in three Japanese will go on to tertiary education — although for many young women this will involve a two-year 'liberal arts' college course, supplemented by lessons in the necessary skills to become a 'good wife'. These include cooking, manners, Japanese culture, the three basic bows (fifteen degrees, thirty degrees and forty-five degrees) and when to use them, and the five steps to rise gracefully from a kneeling position on the tatami-mat-covered floor. I am not making this up.

For the boys, the university entrance examination is what they have worked for all their lives. What, if anything, they learn once they get in is completely irrelevant. The three or four years at university are where a Japanese male really spends the happiest days of his life — dating, playing sport and, naturally, drinking. One day, in the interests — of course — of enlightening my readers on this matter, I went exploring the student drinking culture, and came across the phenomenon of *ikki* — yet another way in which Japan's youth are cutting short their lives.

It was spring, and the bars and bistros around Japan's universities were reverberating to the chant of '*Ikki-ikki-ikki* ...' as thousands of freshmen were inducted with a traditional drink-swilling ceremony. It's a chorus that fills an Osaka businessman, Mr Hitoshi Kaku, with dread. Two years earlier, his nineteen-year-old son Satoshi collapsed and died after a 'chugging' contest (*ikki-nomi* means literally 'drink in one gulp') and Mr Kaku has devoted his life to stamping out the practice.

University students everywhere (remember the drinking song from *Student Prince*) lubricate this rite of passage with the consumption of excessive amounts of liquor. The difference here is that many Japanese people lack the enzyme needed to break down the booze, and are at chronic risk of fatal alcohol poisoning. In the eight years after the Tokyo Fire Department (which runs the ambulances) began keeping records, more than 40 000 people were taken to hospital as emergency cases suffering from alcohol poisoning, and thirty-eight died. This is just the Tokyo area — the figure for the rest of the country could be four or five times as high.

Mr Kaku believes a large number of these were students who, like his son, were killed by chugging their drinks. A breakdown of the figures shows that fully a fifth of hospital admissions for acute alcohol poisoning were teenagers — even though twenty is the legal drinking age in Japan. Satoshi, he says, went on a skiing excursion when he was a freshman at Chuo University near Tokyo. While the other students chanted '*Ikki-ikki*', he downed four or five large glasses of sake, and the same amount of whisky, before he passed out and died. 'I'm so angry — that's murder,' says the boy's father, who has devoted his life to trying to make sure it doesn't happen again.

He has built up a dossier of death-by-*ikki* on Japan's university campuses. In 1993, for instance, a second-year student at Japan's Physical Education University died after downing a 1.8-litre bottle of sake in five minutes to celebrate the day he officially became an adult. At Hiroshima University, an undergraduate passed out face-down and drowned in ten centimetres of water when he went outside to vomit during a drinking session — he was found to have a blood alcohol level of 0.50 (ten times the legal driving limit in Australia). Another student missed his train after drinking heavily on a mountaineering excursion, and was run down and killed while staggering along the tracks.

The fad for chugging among students took off ten years ago when a Japanese pop group called Tonneruzu put out a hit called '*Ikki*', whose chorus translates literally as:

> Burn those who cannot drink!
> Never forgive those who just drink socially!
> Beer, *shochu,* whisky!
> Sake cup, glass, saucepan lid,
> Kettle, ashtray, student's hat!
> If it will hold a drink —
> *Ikki! Ikki! Ikki!*

At the shout of '*Ikki!*' ('Drink!'), the student must down his drink in one go — a tankard of beer, a cocktail called *chuhai* (*shochu,* cheap raw spirit, mixed with soda or fruit juice), sake or straight spirits. It's an extension of the 'bastardisation' rituals often carried on in Japanese high schools. Failure to comply may mean ostracism for the rest of the student's time at university; going along with it may mean death.

Dr Susumu Higuchi, a doctor specialising in alcoholism at Kurihama Hospital near Tokyo, told me that about 45 per cent of Japanese and other Asians are particularly at risk of drinking themselves to death because they lack the enzyme (aldehyde dehydrogenase–2) which breaks down alcohol. Even a small amount of booze can lead to redness in the face and a rapid pulse; serious poisoning can result from just a few drinks. The Japanese are well down the international table of alcohol consumers because of this genetic difference, drinking only half as much as the current world champions, France, Luxembourg, Spain and Germany. The problem is, most students don't realise they are alcohol-intolerant until they get to university because they don't drink at home.

Dr Higuchi, who has saved a number of students suffering from alcohol poisoning, says the only effective treatment is immediate hospitalisation and a transfusion of glucose solution enriched with vitamins, particularly B1 — as well as drugs to aid breathing. Mr Kaku's answer is education. His organisation, the Association For the Prevention of Alcohol Chugging, has — with some funding from Japan's beer- and sake-brewers — launched a publicity blitz on the country's 350 university campuses. Using a cartoon figure of a student spreadeagled on a roulette wheel, the association has distributed more than 300 000 booklets warning of the dangers of chugging. 'We are not trying to stop drinking altogether — just to educate them to drink moderately, have something to eat and not to get involved in these *ikki* situations,' he says.

It is hardly surprising that these young men should want to blast their brains loose when they finally arrive on the campus of whatever university they have been lucky enough to get into. Since their mothers first nervously pushed them in their strollers for their *koen debyu* — their debut in the catty, competitive world of young mums who parade their offspring around the neighbourhood parks for approval — it has been drummed into them that this is their goal in life.

From preschool level, the competition is on to get into the right stream which will take a child to the right university and the right job. A case recently came to light in which a restaurant owner paid a $95 000 bribe to try to get his child into the elite Aoyama Gakuin kindergarten, which is affiliated to a prestigious university. Because of this connection, parents are willing to do almost anything to get in; but the kindergarten has more than 2000 applications for the forty places a year it offers, and the entrance examinations for aspiring three- and four-year-olds are notoriously tough. If you are ever going to be anyone in Japan, however, you have to qualify for one of the country's elite universities — and preferably one of the top half dozen like Todai, as ranked by the difficulty of their entrance exams, the *hensachi* or 'deviation score'.

Much has been written about the headlock which Tokyo University — and especially its ultra-elite law department — has on positions of power in the Japanese bureaucracy. Todai (pronounced 'toad eye') and the slightly less distinguished Kyoto University still produce most of the mandarins who rule Kasumigaseki, Japan's public service command centre. Waseda University is the incubator for Japan's future political leaders and writers — Morihiro Hosokawa, one of their best-known postwar graduates, was both. Keio University produces a disproportionate share of the country's business leaders. There are a handful of others, including Meiji, Sophia and Hitotsubashi universities, which also rank. After that, however, you are in the also-rans. For life.

The curious thing is that, academically, none of these universities rates internationally. They have almost no foreign students, and the five leading universities have never produced a writer, a scientist or a thinker of international note — let alone a Nobel prize winner. They produce generalists, the sort of people who once took liberal arts degrees in the West — not specialists in law, business, communications or whatever. Talk to a typical graduate of Todai's law school, a Kasumingaseki princeling, and you are likely to get a similar reply to the one I received from a suave bureaucrat-on-the-make at a Ministry of Finance Christmas Party one year. He laughed as he described lectures by a dotty Marxist history professor, then said, 'But, you know, university is not supposed to give you any more than a general background, and help you meet people who will be important later in life. Your real learning begins when you start work here. You learn from the people who really know how things work, not from those with only a theoretical knowledge.'

Shinichiro Kurimoto, the chancellor of Kurimoto Musashino University, and an ardent critic of the system is much harsher in his judgment. In a lengthy critique in *Tokyo Business Today* magazine in 1993, he was scathing about 'professors who devote no time to study … write no academic papers for ten or twenty years, and rarely read the writings of other scholars in their field. They give lectures, but the students rarely show up.' Professor Kurimoto went on:

> This miserable system is rooted in widespread social indifference to the actual content of today's university education. While these institutions do have the word 'university' in their names, they are effectively regarded as employment preparatory camps. No-one really cares much about the specific details of the work course. Their main role is that of midwife, delivering young people into corporate society, and serving as a holding-tank for teenagers up to the time they find work. The universities have become playgrounds for overgrown children and venues for competitive sports. What has happened to functions such as research and higher education?

One person who seemed not to mind this approach was Mayu's sister Mioko. She had been attending university for three years, aiming at a qualification in biology. However, that did little to interfere with her life. The winter months saw her on the slopes at Myoko Kogen mountain, teaching toddlers to ski. During summer, she worked in a restaurant, had a busy social life, an interest in a new religion and a series of relationships. However, almost no-one ever fails to graduate from university in Japan. It is often said to be a contract: the students pretend to study, the professors pretend to teach and, as long as no-one rocks the boat, everyone is happy. When, eventually, Mioko gained her degree, she was happy to use her tertiary qualification to get a job with a gardening company.

Hardly surprisingly, an increasing number of young Japanese are dropping out of the system rather than endure the rat-race. Absenteeism has become a major problem in high schools, with thousands of kids staying away rather than submit to the pressure of study and the torment of school bullying. Tertiary entrance scores have been falling at all but the best universities, as they compete for a dwindling number of would-be graduates. Overseas study is an increasing option, and many students are choosing to stay abroad once they graduate rather than return to the grind of corporate Japan.

Those who do stay, the young drop-outs, form a kaleidoscope of subcultures. The street-dancers of Harajuku have been well known for years — scores of amateur bands, ranging from greasy leather Elvis look-alikes to Madonna surrogates (circa 1990) in cake-tin bras who strut their stuff most Sunday afternoons not far from the forbidding portals of the Meiji Shrine. There are a hundred other 'tribes' — the *bosozoku*, bikies on their thundering Harley Davidsons; the fan-waving 'dance tribes' of Julianas and other popular venues; greenies fleeing back to nature; the *kogyaru* and the *femio-kun*, vacant-eyed kids attaching themselves to the latest fad in fashion, music or religious cult.

Visit Shibuya, a funky entertainment district whose bars, restaurants and discos are popular with Tokyo's younger generation, and say goodbye to those images of clean, polite, demure Japanese. It's a whole new Tokyo, worlds away from the serried grey ranks of the city's salarymen. Mayu went there one night, toting her camera, and came back with a story that would shock any parent. Three high school boys are lying unconscious on the footpath outside a busy bar. Two teenage girls in party gear are throwing up. A third, who looks about sixteen, is dressed up like a Dallas Cowboys cheerleader, striking erotic poses in the middle of the street while three boys grope her breasts and buttocks. Ten metres away, a uniformed officer stands outside his police-box, studiously ignoring the scenes of drunken teenage debauchery that have become an almost-nightly event in this part of town.

You do not have to be a psychiatrist to work out that they are rebelling against Miyamoto's 'straightjacket society'. At Shibuya, and a dozen other venues around Tokyo, it's all sex and drugs and rock'n'roll. Particularly the sex. A recent national survey of 3600 fourteen- and fifteen-year-olds by the National Congress of Parents' and Teachers' Associations confirmed every parent's worst fears about what little Yoko and Hiroshi are up to when they aren't in the classroom or at cramming school. One-quarter of the girls admitted that they had frequented *terekura* (Japlish for 'telephone clubs') — the 500-odd dating agencies which have sprung up all over Tokyo, where frustrated salarymen pay for introductions to schoolgirls. The girls boast that they can earn $700 or more in cash and gifts for a date. Two-thirds of the students said they regularly drank alcohol (the legal drinking age in Japan is twenty), one in six said they had shoplifted and 7 per cent said they used drugs — an extraordinarily high figure in a country where possession of even one marijuana joint almost invariably brings a stiff jail sentence.

Hiroshi Itakura, professor of criminal law at Tokyo's Nihon University, told me the survey showed today's Japanese youngsters had 'an undeveloped sense of right and wrong and a general attitude of permissiveness [which] will provide a fertile breeding ground for crime'. He asserted, 'Some day this will lead to Japan's ruin.'

The schoolgirl date-club phenomenon sprang into the headlines when three fifteen-year-olds confessed that they had picked up a 43-year-old office worker through a club and gone with him to a love hotel — one of thousands of specialised hotels in Tokyo which rent rooms with video cameras and erotic themes by the hour. There, the girls squirted him in the eyes with a tear-gas canister and fled with his wallet, containing $1500. The embarrassed salaryman told police he thought the girls were treating him to some kinky S&M, and didn't realise he was being robbed until too late. In the uproar that followed, police were ordered to crack down on the clubs. In a series of raids on places with names like Shinjuku Strawberry and

Madonna, a posse of nearly 300 teachers and police rounded up no fewer than 526 schoolgirls — some as young as thirteen — and charged more than 100 of them with outright prostitution. The clubs, however, soon resumed business with new client lists.

Not far from that Shibuya bar, Mayu chatted to two casually dressed sixteen-year-olds named Yuko and Akiko who were primping at a street corner, waiting for someone to pick them up. They were typical members of the *kogyaru* (literally 'child-girls') 'tribe' — attending school by day, partying by night. One is sucking a lollipop and cuddling a large teddy bear. Yuko denies selling her body, but cheerfully admits she sleeps with strangers who sometimes leave her money. She sold her school knickers, along with a photograph of herself wearing them, to one of the specialised *buru sera* sex shops in Tokyo for $95. *Buru sera* means 'sailor's bloomers', the latest craze among Tokyo's dirty old men, who are also willing to pay for schoolgirls' fingernails, vials of saliva and used tampons which are sold in slot machines and in shops which cater for men with *lolicon* — Lolita complex. Akiko had left home two days earlier and was looking for someone to sleep with. 'I don't want to go back home. I just want to go to Canada and become a snowboard pro,' she confided.

Both girls said they used drugs — amphetamines, marijuana, hash (*choco*) at $40 a gram and LSD (*el*), which costs an extortionate $200 a shot. The latest craze on the Tokyo teen scene is capsules of a substance called D&E (cyclohexyl nitrate), a liquid used for cleaning video recorder heads, which is said to give a high when inhaled. The drugs are freely available at dance parties — schoolkids hire disco venues for afternoon hip-hop raves — and are sold more or less openly by Iranian vendors in streets and parks around Shibuya and Shinjuku. Although Japan still has an enviably low rate of drug use — particularly mainline drugs such as heroin — police figures show a dramatic increase among the young. In 1995, police arrested more than 10 000 juveniles for drug use or dealing, most of the arrests involving paint-thinner abuse. Inhalation of thinners has been blamed for a rash of deaths among teenagers.

The *bosozoku* (literally 'reckless run tribe') have been around Tokyo since the movie *Easy Rider* came out in the early 1970s. However, recently the bikies and their rivals in hotted-up cars have been giving police and law-abiding drivers a bigger headache than ever. Wearing black leather and chains, and sporting gangster-style tattoos and rings through their ears, noses, tongues, belly buttons, nipples and genitals, the young reckless riders nightly turn sections of Tokyo's Shuto expressway into a raceway — defying police and ignoring speed cameras. More than a third of the 1000-odd annual motorcycle deaths involve teenagers, and police are now pushing for tougher laws — including raising the age limit for bikers to eighteen — to try and cut down on the mayhem.

And then there are the *femio-kun* ('feminine lads'), who began appearing in the summer of 1994 in the streets of Harajuku, the centre of Tokyo's teen culture. Although they deny they are gay, anywhere else in the world they would be regarded as having a severe case of gender confusion. Wearing berets over their short 'monkey-hair' cuts, and carrying dainty backpacks, these kids mince around the streets, indifferent to sideways looks, wearing necklaces and make-up, and dressed in tight skivvies over lacy blouses, miniskirts or billowing bell-bottomed trousers, and platform-heeled shoes. A whole new industry has sprung up to cater for this latest subculture — magazines, clothing shops with names like Milk Boy, hair stylists. Social commentators are falling over themselves to explain the appeal of the androgynous look. 'They are very popular with the girls,' said one young woman. 'They are not macho or threatening — it's like having a pet to play with.'

No-one has yet come up with a snappy name like Generation X to describe these tribes. Indeed, they seem to have little in common other than rebellion against Japan's suffocating social straightjacket. The term most commonly used by tut-tutting television commentators was *shiji machi sedai*, which translates clumsily as 'a generation awaiting instruction'. The parents, of course, are appalled. 'The results were very shocking,' said Kazuo Hirose, an association official involved in the survey cited earlier. 'It shows that young people's sense of ethics and judgment of good and bad are in a state of confusion nowadays.' For the moment, however, all they can prescribe for their wayward offspring is a stiff dose of law and order. Parents and teachers have called for tougher policing of the date-clubs, and a ban on the ubiquitous sidewalk slot machines where anyone can buy a keg of beer or a bottle of sake, no questions asked.

The author Hideo Kato, who is sixty-five, puts the blame for this reckless behaviour squarely on the Japanese education system, under which by the time a child leaves primary school his or her — particularly her — options of education, and hence career, have already been mapped out. 'When their future is decided for them in this way, there is often a gap between their parents' expectations and what their teachers say is possible. They develop an inferiority complex and a shaky sense of identity. The future is not worth thinking about, so they pursue the pleasures of the moment — that's why they sell their bodies or their underwear. They don't care any more what society thinks,' he told me.

But what would an oldie know about it young Yuko must be thinking as a couple of lads stop to chat her up on her street corner. 'Look at the way Japanese adults behave,' she said. 'It doesn't matter whether they are politicians, company presidents or even my own father. They go around buying girls' bodies. I hold them in contempt. I want to get married to a foreigner and go overseas to live. That's my dream for the future. I just want to get out of here.'

Dropouts. Bullying. Suicide. A sham of an education system. A straitjacket of a life ahead. It's hardly surprising that Japanese students have a gloomy outlook on life. International surveys consistently show that Japanese youngsters are more discontented with their materialistic society than kids in other countries. They also tend to be more apathetic, less ambitious and more inclined to give 'it can't be helped' as a response to any problem. A poll conducted in 1994 by the government's Management and Coordination Agency found that only 44 per cent of Japanese aged under twenty were happy with their lives — a far lower percentage than in the United States, European countries and even Russia. One Japanese youth in five wishes he had been born somewhere else. For reasons I won't even begin to think about, their country of preference was … Switzerland.

In the wake of young Kiyoteru's death, there were demands from all sides for the government to Do Something. Four million dollars was hastily allocated to hire more school counsellors; various hotlines were set up; a book about bullying was distributed to the schools; Mr Fumio Watanabe, principal of the Gal Detective Agency, said that frantic parents were paying him $4000 a week to bug their children with radio transmitters while he took pictures with a high-powered camera to obtain evidence of bullying. However, at the end of the day, no-one expected much to come of it. There had been a similar outcry in 1985 (and, probably, 1975, 1965 and 1955 if I had dug deeply enough back in the files). Bullying is far too deeply entrenched in the psyche of Japanese society for it to yield to such Bandaid fixes.

Sure enough, almost a year later, another horrific mass killing came to light among students at a boarding school on subtropical Oshima Island. It emerged that there had been systematic and quite brutal hazing by senior students of newcomers, who were required to prove their 'fighting spirit'. In one of these rituals, twelve boys aged fifteen and sixteen were lined up on top of a ten-metre high concrete sea wall and ordered to dive into the ocean and retrieve turban shells from the seabed. A storm warning had been issued and the sea was running high, but, terrified of a beating if they refused, the hapless lads jumped into seven-metre waves. Three of them drowned. The headmaster, Isao Shibata, shrugged off the tragedy, commenting, 'It is safe to jump into the water when the sea is calm. I believe the senior students are quite capable of determining whether or not it is safe.' Police wrote it off as 'an accident'.

Quite recently, alarm has begun to be expressed at the very top of what used to be known as Japan Inc. — the political/bureaucratic/business alliance held responsible for Japan's remarkable postwar economic recovery — about the fundamental deficiencies in the education system. Keidanren, the confederation of Japanese business which represents every major manufacturing group in the country, and MITI, the Trade Ministry, are among those going public with their concerns. They are not, it goes without saying, much worried about bullying. They are worried that the education system is no longer meeting the demands of the Japanese economy.

The gist seems to be that a system that turned out well-disciplined intellectual robots was fine when what Japan needed was loyal production-line workers. However, now the country has moved so rapidly up the economic food chain that Japan's blue-collar workers can no longer compete with the world and its manufacturing industry is being shifted offshore at a rate of knots. What Japan now needs, say people like former MITI chief Makoto Kuroda, are those qualities that will be essential if it is to maintain its lead in the post-industrial world of tertiary industries such as finance, entertainment and leisure, new technology and the much-vaunted information superhighway. Perhaps Japan may be slowly coming to realise that it cannot go on allowing the vitality, creativity and originality to be bled out of its young, as it did with poor young Kiyoteru.

Sadly, however, there was little sign as we left Japan that anyone was willing to tackle the fundamental issues underlying the deep-seated sense of frustration, and desperation, that an increasing number of young Japanese feel. The anti-bullying strategy adopted by the government had been a total failure — the number of cases reported in public schools had more than doubled between 1993 and 1995, from 21 548 to 56 601. Another grieving parent was reading another suicide note, this time from a fourteen-year-old girl who hanged herself in her bedroom with her school scarf. 'I am scared of going to school. I am tired of bullying. I want to die,' she wrote. Another education minister was promising another 'review of education practices'. At the end of the day, the undoubted achievements of Japan's education system had been judged too important —

or too difficult — to risk changing, even at the cost of the lives of some of the students it is meant to serve, and the happiness and self-fulfilment of the rest.

O white-faced wonder,
O matchless sight,
O sublimity,
O beauty …
O eternal Fuji!

— YONE NOGUCHI

GLISTENING IN THE SUNLIGHT, IT FLOATS ABOVE the photochemical smog, the ticky-tacky housing estates and the plantations of power pylons, like a four-kilometre high Bombe Alaska in a swamp of grey custard. In the depths of midwinter, with its cape of pristine snow spreading down to the 1000-metre contour, the vast volcanic cone of Mount Fuji lives up to its publicity as Japan's most impressive international icon.

From a hillside across the polluted plain, nothing seems to have changed over the millennia since Shinto pilgrims first came to worship here, since poets composed haiku on its slopes and the great artist Hokusai commemorated the sacred mountain with his famous cycle of thirty-six woodblock portraits.

'From a distance, it's true, it looks just the same as centuries ago,' says Yuzo Nakagawa, a conservationist who has been chronicling the decline of the mountain for twenty years. 'But get up close and, when summer comes and the snow melts, you can see the damage. Pollution is killing Mount Fuji.'

The legendary abode of the goddess Konohana Nasayuki Hime — until last century women were banned, and men who worked on the mountain exposed their genitals to placate her — Mount Fuji was sacred to the Ainu people, long before the modern Japanese came to Japan. Trouble is, with the advent of mass tourism it is being worshipped to death.

Over the five decades since the war, development has remorselessly encroached up the flanks of the mountain — an artificial ski slope scars one side, the military uses the eastern foothills as an artillery range, roads and housing developments expand and the twenty-metre golf ball of a radar dome sits on a site bulldozed out of the very lip of the crater. On the upper levels of the mountain, a plaza of restaurants and gaudy souvenir shops does a roaring business. Soft-drink vending machines line the climbing tracks. More than fifty wooden barracks where climbers sleep and eat disgorge untreated sewage onto the slopes. There are plans for more roads, even a chairlift.

'This is what you find in summer,' says Mr Nakagawa, throwing a file of colour pictures on the table. Piles of refuse, including a toilet bowl and bits of a demolished building, almost block one of the climbing tracks. Dead animals lie squashed on the roads. Food wrappers, disposable nappies and discarded clothing litter the slopes — he guesses that 500 tonnes of drink cans alone are dumped on the mountain every year.

Many people still regard the arduous five-hour pilgrimage to the summit of Japan's tallest mountain as a sacred rite. The nineteenth-century writer Lafcadio Hearn called it 'the supreme altar of the sun'. More recently, the *Wall Street Journal* described it as a 'grotesque fusion of Jerusalem and Woodstock'.

During the two midsummer months of the official climbing season, around 300 000 people trek to the top. 'A wise man climbs Mount Fuji once; only a fool climbs it more than once,' goes the saying — but every year the trampling hordes get thicker. Up to 35 000 people have attempted to climb the mountain in a single day.

Chanting, bell-ringing pilgrims in sandals, straw hats and white robes jostle school excursions, tour groups led by guides with banners and US troops from nearby bases, causing people jams on the narrow tracks that can take hours to untangle. People occasionally die in the crush.

The idea is to reach the 3776-metre summit in time for sunrise, when — if the smog isn't too thick — you may be able to make out the office towers of Tokyo, 100 kilometres away. In practice, rather than a solemn moment of contemplation, it is a celebration of commercialism, with the whirr and clatter of thousands of cameras.

Junko Tabei, the first woman (in 1975) to climb Mount Everest, trained on Mount Fuji in the winter. She recently climbed it in the summer and was disgusted by the rows of public telephones, stalls and vending machines, and the litter, right to the summit. 'When the snow melts, you can see that it is full of garbage,' she said. 'It is a dirty mountain. It stinks. Something should be done.'

What Ms Tabei, Mr Nakagawa and other conservationists want is for Mount Fuji to be placed on UNESCO's World Heritage list — foreign supervision, they believe, is the only way to protect it. They have gathered 2.2 million signatures on a petition to this effect, and succeeded in having a resolution promising to 'study the problem' passed in the Diet (Parliament) a couple of years ago.

Mount Fuji is already part of a 38 000-hectare national park, the first, in fact, to be proclaimed in Japan — fifty-nine years ago. The problem is that in Japan there are national parks and there are national parks — the Mount Fuji kind offers very little real protection.

Hunters are permitted to shoot deer and bears and badgers on Mount Fuji. Foresters are allowed to fell

POSTCARD FROM MOUNT FUJI

timber. There are no full-time rangers in the 'park' and volunteers like Mr Nakagawa have no legal authority to stop the desecration.

More than 1000 private landowners have little restriction on what they can build on their land. Local government authorities are the worst vandals of all — Yamanashi Prefecture, which controls half the mountain, has just sent in bulldozers to clear twenty hectares of virgin forest … on which to build an environmental science research centre, of all things.

'We already have far too many restrictions on what we can do on Mount Fuji,' declares Mr Kikumi Sasuga, who owns five of the huts on the mountain and leads the development lobby on the prefectural government. 'Why should we bring in foreign academics? They wouldn't understand the Japanese way.'

Mr Sasuga sees no problem with felling trees, hunting, building or even discharging raw sewage onto the mountain. 'It is a large area. Parts of it should be protected — a particular tree, for example, or a special rock — but not everything.'

In the meantime, says Mr Nakagawa, the mountain is slowly dying. Wildlife is being pushed to extinction. Erosion is scarring its flanks. The springs that feed the five famous lakes in its foothills, and supply drinking water for the towns, are drying up and being poisoned by bacteria. 'Fuji-san is supposed to be our national symbol,' he says. 'Surely we can do something to save it before it is too late.'

NINE
ECOCIDE

'The Japanese are environmental terrorists.'

— ROGER MCMANUS. DIRECTOR OF THE (US) CENTRE FOR MARINE CONSERVATION

IT'S A WARM, BRIGHT AFTERNOON in early summer and the first tourists of the season have migrated to the pretty resort island of Sado, an hour by sleek hydrofoil out in the Sea of Japan. Here, they head for the latest attraction, clustering around the guardrails, peering through binoculars, using their longest lenses and the zoom on their video cameras to try and capture a small creature cowering in a massive cage of steel and concrete 100 metres away. Somewhere behind the bars, perched on a log and oblivious to all the attention, sit two birds the size of geese, with stilt-like legs, a long black beak and a belly of the palest pink. *Nipponia nippon,* the scientists call them; *toki* to Mr and Mrs Sato; the Japanese crested ibis to Western ornithologists.

This pair of birds, a female called Kin and a male, Midori, are the sad stars of Japan's newest wildlife sanctuary, in a grove of red-pine trees, the last remnant of the forests which once covered Sado. More than $4 million has been spent building their quarters, a staff of four attends their every need, 1000 visitors a week pay $3 to visit the museum devoted to them and queue to try and catch a glimpse of these birds.

Why all the attention? Kin and Midori are the last of their kind. When they die their species will be extinct in Japan. This handsome bird, which has featured in Japanese legend and literature for fourteen centuries, whose image graces medieval screens, whose feathers adorned the sword handles of samurai, whose name is a part of the language (*toki* is a colour, the subtle pinkish hue of the bird's belly feathers) will be no more. Deceased. Dead. Departed. Gone to meet its Maker. Fallen off the twig.

Indeed, a year or so after we visited Sado, Midori was dead. He had just finished mating (unsuccessfully, as it turned out — the eggs were all barren) with an ibis specially flown over from China, when the excitement proved too much and he keeled over. Kin was left alone in her splendid new quarters, the last of her species. Before the century ends — Kin is middle-aged in human terms, and has passed the avian equivalent of menopause — the *toki* will most likely have joined the growing toll of plants and animals which have paid the price of extinction for Japan's postwar progress, yet another dark side of the economic miracle.

There is no more dramatic illustration of the way in which Japan has raped its environment than the plight of species such as the *toki*. You can publish all the statistics you like about pollution of the air and the water, uncontrolled industrialisation, the destruction of virgin forests and the damming of wild rivers, and on most of them Japan will be near the bottom of the international league. The death of a species, however, that is something you usually hear about in far away places like the Amazon rainforest, not in the backyard of the planet's richest nation.

The curious thing is that the Japanese are constantly holding themselves up as the world's greatest nature-lovers. From the magic badgers of legend to the chains of paper cranes that festoon memorials and the boozy parties thrown to admire the spring cherry blossoms, 'nature' is an integral part of Japanese culture. Can you imagine the *Sydney Morning Herald* publishing a front-page colour picture every Saturday of its 'flower of the week'? Well, the *Japan Times* does. Would ABC news devote two or three minutes every night to an item on luminous freshwater prawns, a change in hierarchy in a troupe of red-bottomed monkeys or close-ups of interesting snow-flakes? NHK, Japan's national broadcaster, does. Traditional Japanese households, even in high-rise blocks of apartments, will usually have a symbolic 'garden' — perhaps as minimal as a tiny bonsai pine in a pot. Formal business letters should always begin with a seasonal reference to the rain, the spring blossoms or the autumn colours. Literature swarms with nature-lovers such as the Buddhist monk Ryokan who slept under a mosquito net in summer — not so he would not be bitten, but to avoid inadvertently squashing one of the insects in his sleep.

So it comes as a surprise to discover that the monk's heirs, in many respects, have the worst environmental record in the developed world. At the turn of the century, Japan was still a stunningly beautiful archipelago, two-thirds of it covered by primordial forests of oak and beech which were a treasure trove of biodiversity. Today, two-thirds of the country is still forested, but these are man-made forests of larch and pine and cryptomeria (a sacred cedar), each the bore of a telephone pole, marching across the mountainsides in serried, uniform ranks. They provide the timber for Japan's insatiable wooden housing industry (and, incidentally, afflict the population with the most chronic annual hayfever epidemics). With the destruction of the old-growth forests, hundreds of species of plant and animal have become extinct — and the clear-felling continues.

Only about 2 per cent of those original, magnificent, ancient trees are left, and even these are threatened by acid rain and by loggers. Not even the slopes of Mount Fuji, Japan's most sacred symbol, are safe. The slippery concept of conservation in Japan allows logging and hunting even in national parks such as this. Japan, says the conservationist Nic Nicol, has 'the worst forestry policies of any presumably civilised or environmentally aware nation on earth. Until Japan's forests are saved, there is little hope for the rest of the world where Japanese big money has invaded.'

We got to know Nic well during our time in Japan. A big, boozy, sandy-haired Welshman, he has spent his life in the wild — Arctic expeditions, gamekeeping in Ethiopia, conservation in Canada. He came to Japan twenty years ago to study karate — and stayed to fight for the environment. With the proceeds of a blockbuster novel (he went and lived for a year in the whaling village of Taiji to research his epic *Harpoon*), he bought some land at the foot of Iizuna mountain. We were almost neighbours — Nic's place is not far from the stunningly beautiful Lake Nojiri, about 200 kilometres from Tokyo, where Mayu's parents have their holiday home.

As an author, columnist, activist, adventurer, consultant to government and star of television wildlife programs, Nic is fluent in Japanese and passionate in his concerns. He has become Japan's best-known conservationist, and in recognition of this, the government appointed him deputy head of the country's first wildlife ranger training academy. If they were hoping to buy his silence, however, they were wrong. I spent several evenings helping Nic through the barrel of wine he imported from an estate in Galicia, while he denounced Japan's environmental record in no uncertain terms. 'They have destroyed their own wild places, and now they are raping the forests and the seas all around the Pacific rim,' was one of his milder lines.

One winter's day he took Mayu and me on a snowmobile high up into the mountains above his house, to admire the last stands of 300-year-old beech trees he was fighting to protect from the loggers. The destruction of the environment around Nojiri is a microcosm of the havoc being wreaked from the icy marshes of Hokkaido to the steaming tropical jungles of the Ryukyu islands — a lot of it by the government itself. Nic reserves his fiercest anger for the government — for the Construction and Forestry Ministries which he describes as 'vast juggernauts rampaging through the country, destroying the last shreds of virgin forest, damming the last wild rivers, without any real consideration for the consequences'.

Golf courses and ski slopes have carved great swathes out of the forests, precipitating landslides and pouring poisonous pesticides and nutrients into the rivers and lakes. Lake Nojiri had its first outbreak of toxic algal blooms a few summers back, and it is mainly the mad foreigners — missionaries who have built an estate of summer homes on its banks — who still dare to swim and fish in it. Housing developments have spread haphazardly, and billions of dollars-worth of roads and tracks for a new bullet train were being bulldozed through nearby national parks in preparation for the 1998 Nagano winter Olympics.

Another man who cares is Koki Chikatsuji, a wildlife curator who came to Sado island nearly thirty years ago to try and save the *toki*, and has been the birds' guardian ever since. 'It is tragic,' he told me, peering through a closed-circuit television monitor which constantly watches the unfortunate birds. 'We have tried everything, but I am afraid we were too late. I think the *toki's* last message to us is "Look at me — I am nearly extinct. Please don't let it happen to anyone else."'

The *toki* is a paradigm for the destruction of Japan's unique and once-teeming wildlife. Widespread for millennia through the main island of Honshu, hunting (for sport, food and feathers which were used to stuff doonas), habitat destruction, the poisoning of rivers with industrial effluent and the contamination of rice paddies by agricultural chemicals ravaged the birds. By the 1960s, they were reduced to a tiny flock on the island redoubt of Sado; by the time Japan's fledgling environmental movement blew the whistle, it was already too late.

When Mr Chikatsuji arrived on Sado in 1967, there were only eight left. The death knell appears to have been the introduction of the Japanese marten — a kind of weasel which was brought to Sado to control rabbits, but quickly polished off the eggs and young of the vanishing *toki*. By 1981, the numbers were down to five, and Mr Chikatsuji led a group of scientists who captured the last survivors with rocket-powered nets. For the next twelve years he cared for them, living in a primitive hut beside their cage on a mountainside — freezing in two-metre snowdrifts in winter — while zoologists tried with no success to artificially inseminate the birds and keep the species alive. He has lived with the birds so long his mates say he has begun to look like one, especially when he goes drinking and his neck takes on a rosy hue. Now, he sits waiting and watching. Far too late, the last *toki* now has splendid new quarters in which to die.

The price Japan paid for its place on top of the world's economic league ladder has been a heavy one: clear-felling forests, damming rivers, unchecked industrialisation, the unrestricted spread of urbanisation and uncontrolled use of agricultural chemicals. Stunned by the extent of the destruction, Japan did begin to clean up its image — if not its act — as the 'dirty man of Asia' in the early 1970s. An environment protection agency was formed, laws were passed. Once again, however, this turned out to be the *tatemae* solution; the *honne*, the truth of the situation, is that Japan's environment protection regime is among the least effective in the world. Even Ethiopia, says Nic Nicol, who once worked there as a ranger, takes better care of its national parks. Canada, with one-fifth Japan's population, spends 400 times as much on conservation.

In a very few areas Japan now does better than the other industrialised countries with which it must be compared — the G7 group of the world's seven richest nations. Although, like almost every country, Japan will not make the ambitious greenhouse gas reductions it signed on for at the Rio 'Earth Summit', the levels of sulphur dioxide and nitrous oxide in the air are less than half those of the United States. However, this is due less to anti-pollution measures than to the fact that the Japanese do not drive as much as other people, and the country generates more of its electricity from nuclear plants, which pollute the ocean, but not (except in extreme cases like Chernobyl) the atmosphere. I also feel suspicious about the official figures. Go to the top of any tall Tokyo building, like the forty-storey Yasuda insurance skyscraper in Shinjuku, and all you can see is a grey blanket of gritty smog, with the ghostly outlines of office blocks and smokestacks poking up like concrete stalagmites, all the way to the foreshortened horizon.

The rest of the picture is much grimmer. Japan has the worst record for sewage disposal in the developed world, with less than half the households connected to a main. The rest (like Mayu's parents' old holiday home) rely on septic tanks or holes in the ground. Only Italy has a smaller proportion of land devoted to national parks, and even this is a dubious proposition because Japanese national parks don't mean what they mean elsewhere in the world — an area of strict conservation. You can not only hunt and chop down trees in Japanese national parks, but you can also build houses and even factories. Some parks contain whole towns.

Japan is responsible for two-thirds of all the industrial waste in the world that is dumped into the ocean — 4.4 million tonnes a year. The government is trying to reduce that, by 20 per cent. However, in other cases of potentially disastrous environmental pollution, Japan is unwilling to take even this modest action to protect its citizens at the expense of its industrialists. The rain is so polluted by factory smoke that in Kawasaki City it is said to be as acidic as grapefruit juice. All over Japan you can see poisoned trees turning brown, and ancient bronze statues literally dissolving. Rather than clean up its own smokestacks, the Japanese government points the finger across the sea to China, which it says is responsible.

Similarly with nuclear waste. In 1994, there was a huge hoo-hah when Russia dumped spent reactor fuel in the Sea of Japan. The government denounced it; the media fulminated. Few commentators pointed out that one reason this was done was that Japan had failed to come up with the money it had promised for a recycling program. Only Dr Jinzaburo Takagi, a nuclear chemist who runs the Citizens' Nuclear Information Centre, was game to mention that, in fact, the waste Japan's nuclear power stations are legally licensed to discharge into the sea amounts to considerably more radioactive pollution than the Russians were guilty of dumping. When I asked an expert at the Science and Technology Agency about this, he launched into a scientifically incomprehensible explanation of how Japanese nuclear waste was completely different from, and much safer than, Russian waste.

As for garbage, among the G7, only the United States and Canada generate more per head, and dispose of it in a more irresponsible way. It sometimes seems as though Japan is a country of Christos, with a bag to contain the wrapping around the packaging around the container around every book, bicycle and bar of soap. Because Tokyo Bay is rapidly filling up with all this waste, the government is building incinerators with giant, futuristic smokestacks all over Tokyo in which to burn it. Citizens' groups warn of the dangers of toxic gases and campaign for more recycling. Mayu's mother was active in one such group and one day she even marched down to City Hall to glare at the legislators. All to no avail.

The disaster that focused the eyes of the world on a little town in Kyushu called Minamata is merely the most dramatic of the consequences of Japan's heedless destruction of its environment. Some may think that, because it happened forty years ago, it is unfair of me to bring it up here. But Minamata is a story that is still not over. Nearly half a century after the first victims began to sicken and die, thousands of people were still begging for recognition and compensation. Nearly half a century after scientists proved that effluent from a factory on the bay was responsible, the company responsible continues to deny its guilt. Nearly half a century after it was shown that negligence by local and national governments allowed it to happen, the Japanese government continued to fight the sick and ageing victims through the courts.

It happened at an obscure little fishing village whose name would be catapulted into the international headlines, eventually achieving the dubious distinction of entering the medical encyclopaedias as a crippling man-made affliction — Minamata disease. What occurred here still ranks as one of the greatest environmental tragedies in history. Many more people were killed here than died when the Ukrainian nuclear reactor at Chernobyl exploded. Unlike Bhopal, the Indian chemical plant that erupted one sultry morning poisoning thousands, Minamata's deadly pollution would keep on killing, slowly and silently, for decades. The town became, a quarter of a century before protecting the environment became fashionable, a symbol of the damage that can be done in the name of progress, and a rallying cry for the Green movement around the world. The Japanese call Minamata kogai-gen, the birth of pollution.

Half a century ago, it is true, the world had not yet woken up to the dangers of industrial pollution. Japan had been bombed back to developing nation status. If they thought of it at all, Japanese governments, both local and national, probably considered the environment something they could worry about after everyone had a job, a roof over their heads, and enough to eat. What this simplistic analysis ignores, however, is the wilful wickedness displayed by the company involved long after it knew it was killing people; and the cover-up and conspiracy with the government persists to this day. Japan has not yet learned the lessons of Minamata — that is why I went there.

With a disaster of this magnitude, you expect to find stark and moving mementos — the pulverised pillars of the Catholic cathedral in Nagasaki; the pyramids of skulls preserved on the killing fields of Cambodia. One hundred thousand people were exposed to the deadly effluent that was discharged into Minamata Bay. At least 1500 of them died, and another 12 000 were injured, many of them poisoned in the womb and condemned to a life of frightful physical deformity and intellectual deficit. More than anything, it was the images of these 'Minamata children', seared into the consciousness by the disturbingly beautiful photography of Eugene Smith, that alerted the world to the catastrophe.

Walk around Minamata today, however, and you have to search diligently for the relics. Like so many Japanese seaside towns, it defiles the stunning natural assets of its location. Located halfway down the southwestern coast of Kyushu, Minamata is washed by the shining, silver waters of the Shiranui Sea. Where the sky meets the sea is silhouetted an archipelago called the Amakusa islands. The town itself, though, is grimy and depressing, with the only sign of life the night we arrived the gaudy neons of the inevitable *pachinko* parlour, a few down-at-heel bars and a low-rent business hotel.

Look carefully, however, and you begin to find the clues to the town's decline. A wasteland of reddish soil sparsely sown with scraggly grass shows where a great section of the bay had to be filled with millions of tonnes of earth and rock to contain the pollution. A double line of yellow buoys marks a netted area where the fish are still deemed too dangerous to catch and eat. Then, on the outskirts of the town, you come across the factory.

The Chisso Corporation plant (originally the New Japan Nitrogen and Fertiliser Co. Ltd) is a Dickensian nightmare, something built quite obviously with as little thought for safety as aesthetics. Still, in 1993, smokestacks belched fumes, pipes discharged foul-smelling effluent into drains and pipelines carrying sulphuric acid festooned the buildings. The factory dominates the town and is still (although the workforce has fallen from a peak of 2000 to about 700) its biggest employer.

The locals called Minamata 'Chisso Castle Town' and paid the company the respect that in bygone days would have been accorded the local *daimyo*, the warlord — one reason Chisso got away with what it was doing for so long. As recently as 1973, the mayor could boast, 'What is good for Chisso is good for Minamata.' Chisso, for its part, treated its employees with the same contempt it showed the environment. Its founder, an entrepreneur named Jun Noguchi who originally established the factory here to cash in on the war with Russia, advised his managers to 'treat the workers like cows and horses'. During World War II, Chisso opened new plants in occupied Korea and Manchuria, where it showed no compunction about using slave labour.

It was in the 1930s that the seeds of the disaster were sown when the company began to manufacture acetaldehyde at Minamata, a chemical rootstock used in making plastics. In the process, the 'liquid metal' mercury was used as a catalyst. The poisonous residue was dumped, untreated, into the sea in staggering quantities — the equivalent of ten tonnes a year, when only a few grams can kill. In Minamata Bay, which older inhabitants remember as a favourite swimming and fishing spot with sandy beaches, the mercury was absorbed by marine organisms and inexorably climbed the food chain — until it reached man.

We sailed across the Shiranui Sea to the island of Goshonoura one sunny spring day, passing a fleet of strange wooden boats a little like Arab dhows, tacking into the breeze under triangular sails. Husband-and-wife teams cast nets over the side of these traditional *ukase*, as they are called, for prawns and ribbonfish, in a technique that cannot have changed for thousands of years. Fish is the main protein for all the people who live around the Shiranui, which made its contamination with mercury doubly dangerous. Goshonoura, which was home in the 1950s to 10 000 people, did not have a single butcher's shop.

'Without fish, we would have starved,' said Masamori Murakami, a wrinkled walnut of a man seventy-seven years of age who had lived on the island all his life — apart from a brief excursion to Bougainville and Rabaul as a hospital orderly during World War II. I talked to him and his wife Kozue over a typical Amakusa banquet — grilled sardines, sashimi of black sea bream and something else fishy simmered in sake that doesn't appear in any dictionary. We knelt on the tatami mats in their ancient wooden house with low ceilings, a portrait of Emperor Hirohito on the wall and flowers decorating a small Buddhist altar. Through the window, you could see blue-tiled roofs held down with fishing nets to prevent tiles blowing away in the typhoons that occasionally swoop down on the island during the August Obon festivities.

Like his grandfather and father before him, Murakami was a fisherman, until the disease got the better of him. The first time he noticed something odd was around Showa 25, in the way they count time around here. That is the twenty-fifth year of the reign of the Emperor Hirohito, posthumously (some would say preposterously) renamed the Showa or Shining Peace Emperor; that is, 1950. First it was the fish — whole shoals would be found floating belly up, beds of clams would inexplicably die. Then seagulls began to drop from the sky. Then the village cats started foaming at the mouth, racing around in circles and leaping in a frenzy into the sea to drown. One night, Murakami's beloved German shepherd dog came down with what superstitious villagers thought was demonic possession — he began barking madly and dashing around, crashing into walls. In the morning he was dead.

Then it was the turn of the people, starting with the fishing folk who ate fish three meals a day, to succumb to 'dancing cat disease'. Whole families began to experience the symptoms of heavy metal poisoning — muscular spasms, slurred speech, blurred eyesight and a numbing of the extremities known as 'glove and sock syndrome'. In the worst cases, chronic brain damage ensued and the patients descended into a vegetative state from which the only release was death. The ocean which for millennia had nurtured the people of the Amakusa islands was now beginning to kill them in a mysterious and horrible way.

Even that, however, was not the end of the suffering. In the town of Minamata, and a score of villages up to 100 kilometres away, an epidemic of stillbirths and babies with tragic physical and mental deformities was breaking out. The mercury was penetrating the placenta to poison the foetus in the womb. The Murakamis' second child was one of the first to be affected. 'He could do nothing except cry,' says his mother. 'He couldn't crawl. He couldn't hug me. He couldn't even hold his head up.' The little boy died at the age of five — and so did their next-born, also diagnosed as suffering from cerebral palsy. The Murakamis buried them in the family grave on a hill above the house where they still go to pray for the repose of their souls.

We met some of those who survived in the Meisui-en Municipal Hospital, surrounded by pink cherry blossoms on a hill overlooking the sea. 'Met' is probably not an appropriate word, since most of the sixty patients in the hospital live in a twilight zone of minimal consciousness and are totally dependent on the nursing staff. Some of these 'Minamata children' have lived here for twenty years. All will die here, since there is no cure for the disease once it has attacked the central nervous system. 'All we can do is keep our patients happy and comfortable, and guard them against infection,' said Dr Hiroyuki Moriyama, the medical superintendent of the hospital and a world authority on Minamata disease.

Information about the epidemic spread slowly, because people feared it might be a contagious or — horror — an inherited disease. No-one suspected the fish, and even if they had what could these poor people have done? 'People kept quiet about having it in the family, for fear their children would not be able to find husbands and wives,' Mr Murakami remembers. Employees' children showing the now-familiar symptoms were brought in increasing numbers to the Chisso factory hospital, where doctors misdiagnosed their condition as due to anything but what now appears the obvious. Minamata disease was blamed on encephalitis, alcoholism, syphilis, infantile paralysis and cerebral palsy, as the doctors tried to protect their paymasters.

It is not so much the ravages of the disease that arouse the fury of the survivors like Mr Murakami. It is the callous way in which Chisso, and the government departments which were supposed to be the public watchdogs against such abuses, proceeded to cover up their guilt, not for years but for decades. Principal among these was MITI, the national government's mighty Ministry for International Trade and Industry. These were the years of Japan's frantic postwar economic reconstruction — then prime minister Hayata Ikeda came to power in 1960 with the simple slogan 'double your income' — and nothing could be allowed to stand in the way of 'progress'. Chisso was a showpiece of the 'economic miracle' and was even honoured with a visit by the emperor. A MITI official summed up the ministry's attitude when he admonished a would-be whistle-blower from the fisheries department: 'Don't be so hard. Japan thrives only through trade. If the coast of Japan is dirtied in the process, it can't be helped. Why not fish abroad in the open seas?'

By 1956, one of the few heroes of this sordid saga, a doctor named Hajime Hosokawa, had reported to the authorities that 'an unclarified disease of the central nervous system has broken out'. Working with a team at nearby Kumamoto University Hospital, he found traces of mercury in the brains of people who had died of the disease. In 1959, the medical detective hunt for the cause was over — in a simple experiment, Dr Hosokawa sprinkled 100 grams of the effluent from Chisso's factory on the food of a laboratory cat, and watched as within days it duplicated the symptoms of Minamata disease. He took his results to Chisso, and they responded by confiscating his data and banning further research. Dr Hajime's warnings did not become public until 1970, when he testified to court officials from his hospital deathbed.

For nine years, Chisso continued pumping its pollution into Minamata Bay, poisoning thousands more people. It was only in 1968 — and then for economic rather than environmental reasons — that the company stopped manufacturing acetaldehyde. For nearly a decade Chisso's dark secret had been kept by senior management, and by the local, prefectural and national governments which were all supposed to be regulating the company. As far back as 1959, Takeyuki Wanibuchi, the former president of Kumamoto University — who was head of a special government-appointed taskforce on Minamata disease — presented the Health Ministry in Tokyo with irrefutable evidence that Chisso's pollution was responsible for the epidemic. His voice trembling with anger, he was later to tell a court how the minister responded the very next day — by abolishing the committee and burying its report.

While the government and the company engaged in this massive cover-up, a second outbreak of Minamata disease occurred in 1965, 900 kilometres to the north in the Japan Sea prefecture of Niigata. The symptoms and the cause were identical — a factory owned by a major chemical company, Showa Denko, had been discharging mercury waste into the environment. Again, a cover-up took place — and again, it was years before the government and the company stopped the pollution. More than seventy people were killed and 600 injured in this so-called 'second Minamata disaster', a tragedy that could have been prevented if the Japanese government had heeded the warnings years before of Dr Hosokawa, Dr Wanibuchi and other eminent scientists brave enough to speak out against the system.

With nowhere else to turn, the victims of these two disasters looked to the courts for justice in the early 1970s. This is where, at the end of 1995, the issue was still mired. Remarkably, considering the usual glacial speed of the Japanese judicial system, no fewer than five decisions had been handed down in favour of the plaintiffs. All five excoriated Chisso for its negligence and, in three cases, the government was also criticised for its failures. However, each time the decision was appealed to a higher court, and as the years dragged by, fewer and fewer of the ageing survivors could drag themselves in front of the judges or up to Tokyo to picket the government offices. The lawyers soldiered on, but their clients were dying at the rate of one a week.

At last count, 13 000 people had claimed compensation for mercury poisoning at Minamata and Niigata, registering themselves with the Environment Agency which was put in charge of the mess. However, because of the strict medical criteria enforced to keep the compensation bill down, fewer than a quarter had been accepted as genuine cases. Attempting to explain this, a former Environment Agency chief, Buichi Oishi, outraged the victims when he declared at a medical conference, 'A fake patient is a fake ... he's not a real patient. Such a person is none other than a deceitful citizen of Minamata City.' Hiroaki Hokimoto, one of those 'deceitful citizens', who suffers the classic symptoms of numbness in the hands and feet, unsteady gait and hearing trouble, told me how he came to fail the medical test for Minamata disease. 'When the [government-appointed] doctors test you to see if you can feel anything they jab the needle in so far blood spurts out.'

Even the 3000 or so people who have been accepted as suffering from Minamata disease are hardly generously compensated for their decades of suffering. Those who are totally disabled are eligible for a lump-sum payment of about $200 000, a monthly pension of up to $2200 and free medical care. The final bitter irony is that the bill, far and away the largest ever damages for pollution-related injury, is being footed not by Chisso, but by the Japanese taxpayer. The payout by the end of 1995 (even excluding several big-ticket items such as the cost of rehabilitating Minamata Bay) was in excess of $1.5 billion, and pensions and medical care were mounting at the rate of more than $100 million a year. The money is raised by the issue of government bonds and 'lent' to Chisso to meet its claims. However, since Chisso claims the actions have technically bankrupted it, the loans will never be repaid.

We called on Chisso to hear their side of the story and were met by Mr Kosaku Ito, whose card described him as the 'manager of administration, accounts and human resources'. Like all the other managers in this old-fashioned, hierarchical company, he wore a grey dustcoat to show that he was just one of the boys — and a green armband to show that he was really very important. I will not bore you with his tendentious account of Chisso's lack of responsibility, since every statement the company has ever made on the issue has been demolished in court and shown to be a pack of lies. However, I was curious to know why the taxpayers of Japan should have to pay for the company's sins.

Chisso is a huge, diversified corporation. It lists twenty-eight subsidiaries in its glossy annual report, and its products, arrayed in a display case in the factory foyer, range from perfume to Christmas tree decorations, greenhouse plastic, liquid crystals and tins of Russian tea. In 1993, it made a profit of $80 million. 'Why not break it up and sell it off to provide compensation for the claimants?' I asked. 'It's all mortgaged to the bank,' said Mr Ito. He claimed the company had debts of $1.5 billion and if the government withdrew its lifeline, 'We would go bankrupt — then there would be no money to pay anyone.' Because of the opaqueness of corporate accounting in Japan, there is no way to tell whether or not this is the truth. Certainly, many of the victims' lawyers believe the cover-up is still continuing, with assets being shuffled around into related companies so that Chisso can continue to avoid its responsibilities.

As for personal accountability, it is true that in the 1970s Chisso did offer two sacrificial lambs on the altar of public opinion. Two of the company's executives were convicted of 'voluntary manslaughter', but given only suspended sentences. There was no question of prosecuting a luminary such as Yutaka Egashira, a director of the Industrial Bank of Japan who was seconded to the Chisso board in 1962 — when the company knew its pollution was poisoning the population — and served as the company's president and then chairman during the years of the great cover-up, from 1964 to 1973.

Even though he was never prosecuted, Egashira's responsibility for what went on at Minamata almost ruined Japan's royal romance of the decade. His granddaughter, a career diplomat named Masako Owada, was betrothed to Crown Prince Naruhito, the heir to the Chrysanthemum Throne, in 1993. Egashira was then still alive, aged eighty-five, and listed in *Who's Who* as an 'adviser' to the Chisso Corporation. The Imperial Household Agency, which is responsible for keeping the royal bloodlines pure, considered forbidding the marriage because of the embarrassment it might cause if Egashira's background came out. They need not have worried. Discreet telephone calls to the major media outlets ensured that no-one in Japan would touch the story. Overseas, even *Time* magazine swallowed the line that Egawa 'was not connected to the company at the time' when even the most cursory glance at his curriculum vitae would have shown that this was simply untrue.

Late in 1995, forty years after Minamata disease was first identified by Dr Hosokawa, and twenty-five years after the first case was taken to court, one last initiative began to settle the issue before all involved died of old age. It was not just about the money, but also about seeking a sincere apology from the company and the government for all those years of deceit and denial — and, in particular, for branding the victims 'fakes'. The government proposed a relaxed certification procedure under which most of the 7000 to 8000 remaining claimants could expect to be accepted as Minamata disease patients. The compensation, however, would be a pittance — $35 000 each, after nearly half a century of struggle.

The five main groups representing Minamata claimants all voted to accept the offer as a basis for negotiation. The sweetener was the shrewd inclusion of $66 million to pay each team of lawyers for their decades of work, much of it done on a *pro bono* basis, which is highly unusual in Japan. If the settlement is finally accepted by all 8000 patients, Chisso's payout (underwritten by the government) would be $610 million, of which the lawyers would get more than half — $330 million, compared with $280 million for the victims. It was by no means certain, however, that this would really be the end. 'The government has finally got off its fat arse,' said Makoto Toyoda, a lawyer representing the largest group of 2000 claimants. 'This is a major turning point in the history of Minamata, but we cannot say it is a happy ending. There are still problems, and I doubt that everyone will accept the offer.'

Minimata, of course, is a story of the damage Japan has done to its own people and their environment. Abroad, Japan's record is, if anything, even more appalling. Its trading companies turn vast swathes of Asian rainforest into furniture — forests that are vital for the planet's health because they regulate regional and global climatic conditions, soak up moisture and absorb solar radiation and carbon dioxide. In spite of recent lip service to 'sustainable harvesting', Japan still consumes about a third of the world's tropical hardwood and throws away twenty billion pairs of chopsticks a year, four for every person on earth. Its mining companies ravage the landscape. In North Borneo, for instance, Mitsubishi, Mitsui and Sumitomo, aided by the Japanese government, have developed a copper mine on Mount Kinabalu, Southeast Asia's highest mountain. Heavy metal pollution has contaminated the rivers, killed the fish and made local residents sick.

Until international outrage forced a ban, Japan's fishing boats roamed the oceans of the earth vacuuming up every living creature in 60-kilometre-long driftnets environmentalists called the 'wall of death'. Its proud record as the world's largest donor of foreign aid (in dollar terms, not percentage of gross domestic product) is tainted by the havoc wrought by some of the projects the yen has sponsored. In Kenya, for example, Japanese money built a dam which threatens Lake Nakuru, a Ramsar-listed wildlife habitat near Nairobi which is home to internationally famous flocks of pink flamingoes.

Stung by international criticism, in the early 1990s, Japan decided to devote a slab of its ODA (Official Development Assistance) to environment protection projects. It also, belatedly, signed the CITES treaty outlawing international trade in endangered species — although, from my own observations, I do not believe it is enforced effectively, if at all. Specialist shops around Tokyo still carve and sell ivory artefacts, particularly *hanko* — the seals with which the Japanese still sign contracts. And in Nagasaki, there is a thriving trade in traditional hairpins, carved from the shells of the endangered hawksbill turtle, which would get you arrested if you were caught with one at Sydney airport. 'Old stock' is the official explanation.

'As far as protecting the environment is concerned,' confesses Dr Masaaki Yoneda, a biologist and spokesman for the government-sponsored Japan Wildlife Research Centre, 'Japan is a developing country. I would put it somewhere between Italy and Poland.' We called on Dr Yoneda, in his cramped, under-resourced office in the backstreets of the Tokyo suburb of Hongo to try and find out how many Japanese species were in the same boat as the *toki*. He told us that it was not until 1991 that his agency even completed an inventory of just what animals live in Japan. The results, published in what is known as the *Japanese Red Data Book*, were chilling.

Of the 5300 plants native to Japan, 895 or 17 per cent are either already extinct, endangered or reduced to tiny local populations, often on remote offshore islands. Twenty per cent of the country's 665 birds, 30 per cent of the 188 mammals and 34 per cent of the 146 reptiles and amphibians are officially in danger. There has been no confirmed sighting of the Japanese otter for years. Blakiston's fish-owl, the Okinawa rail (a small bird) and the unique Japanese dormouse are all most likely doomed. The giant Hokuriku salamander may be heading for extinction, only ten years after it was first identified.

Within living memory (Japan has thousands of centenarians), the last Japanese wolf was killed — it sits, stuffed, in a showcase at the British Museum in London — the last Okinawa flying fox, the last Ogasawara bat and the last of a unique type of sea lion. And those are just the ones Dr Yoneda's agency knows about. Environmentalists claim the Red Book is far from comprehensive — eleven species of butterfly which lepidopterists believe are on the brink of extinction are not even mentioned. Many Japanese animals were already doomed before they had even been officially discovered.

The crested ibis is only the most dramatic example — because it is so visible and so rare — of Japan's vanishing wildlife. Once when driving along the wild coastline of the Shiretoko peninsula, we came across a gaggle of 'twitchers', Japanese bird-watchers, intent on a black and white bundle the size of a small turkey crouching in a tree. It was a Steller's sea eagle, a magnificent migratory predator with a two and a half metre wingspan, that swoops like a dive-bomber to snatch fish from the ocean. Once common in Hokkaido in the winter, they are now so rare folk come from far and wide to jostle for a photograph.

In the Amami islands, a rare species of hare sues the government (via its 'best friend', a local wildlife organisation) to stop a golf course being built on its habitat. The judge throws out the case. In Hokkaido, an open season is declared on deer which have been protected since 1923, because they are said to be damaging crops and young trees. On the beaches of Shizuoka, dune buggies destroy the nests of the disappearing loggerhead turtle. Poachers capture and sell those that survive to pet shops for $400 each, and the eggs and blood to gourmet restaurants, where they are devoured as a delicacy.

In the hills above Nojiri, we hear gunshots as hunters armed with 'pest control permits' shoot the supposedly protected black 'crescent moon' bears emerging from hibernation, even inside national parks. Nic Nicol was once given a wounded cub which he nursed back to health and donated to what he thought was a wildlife park. He fumes as he describes discovering that it was butchered for its meat and its gall bladder, which is worth $7500 for its supposed medicinal properties. Naturalists fear that, like the *toki*, the crescent moon bear (so called because of a white marking on its chest) will be extinct in fifty years.

Japan is unable or unwilling even to protect animals which have attracted international attention. The Iriomote wildcat, for instance, caused a worldwide sensation when it was identified for the first time in 1972 because it had previously been thought that all the planet's large mammals were known. The government classified it as a 'living national monument', but does almost nothing practical to protect it. The wildcat lives only in mangrove swamps on the tiny island of Iriomote, part of the Ryukyu chain which is known as Asia's Galapagos islands because of a profusion of unique 'living fossil' species. It is a singularly odd creature, like a large domestic cat, which swims through the mangrove swamps, using its tail for a rudder, catching fish and birds.

To show his concern at threats to their environment — principally from holiday resorts — Prince Phillip, president of the Worldwide Fund for Nature, visited the islands a few years ago. To no avail. There were originally thought to be around 100 wildcats left, but pressure from farming and tourism has probably slashed their numbers below the survival threshold. Ten per cent of all the Iriomote wildcats left in the world have been run over and killed by cars. The government recently sold a large chunk of their dwindling domain for farmland. Few believe it will survive, and even fewer Japanese understand why its extinction would be such a loss. Not because of the cat's individual importance as a species, but because of its symbolism. If a country as rich and technologically sophisticated as Japan cannot find the will to save it, what hope is there for the rest of the planet?

Even more outrageous is the plight of the *todo*, a type of sea lion. Here is a rare creature being killed not by neglect and indifference, but by gunshot — and with a bounty paid by the government. I stumbled across this story one night when Mayu and I wandered into a cosy basement restaurant in Sapporo, the capital of Hokkaido island. She couldn't work out some characters on the menu, and asked the waitress for help. That was when we learned that the Japanese were dining out on an endangered species — a true-life version of that sick movie *The Freshman*, where gourmets pay an escalating price to eat endangered animals, ranging up to $50 000 if it's the last one on earth. We drove through the snow to find out more, to a town called Rausu.

Rausu is on the northerly tip of Hokkaido, a place the Ainu tribes called Shiretoko, the 'end of the world'. In midwinter, that is just what it looks like — desolate, snow-covered mountains jutting out into the frozen waste of the Sea of Okhotsk. We chose February because it is then that, out of sight of the world, blood stains the ice. While conservationists rail against the killing of the minke whale, which most marine scientists believe number nearly one million and can be sustainably culled, they ignore a genuinely endangered species. The victims of the annual slaughter are Steller sea lions, the largest of the seal family, which are protected under the Endangered Species Act in the United States, and just about every other country in the world — including Australia, where its cousins are a tourist attraction at Kangaroo Island in South Australia.

But not in Japan. There they are called *todo*, but nicknamed *umi no gyangu* (the 'gangsters of the sea') because of the volumes of fish that they eat — up to twenty or thirty kilograms of salmon a day — and the damage they do to fishermen's nets. They are marked for extermination. Every winter, fishermen and professional hunters shoot dead around 1000 of them, hacking off the tips of their flippers to claim a $75 bounty from the Hokkaido government, the local council and the fishing cooperative in the village of Rausu. No-one knows for sure how many of these sea lions are left alive — probably fewer than 100 000 in the entire basin of the North Pacific that stretches from Japan to Siberia, Alaska and down the coast to California.

The sea lion massacre also gets other official endorsement. Until a few years ago, the army base at nearby Niikappu used to use them regularly for target practice. Local newspapers reported that on one occasion crowds lined the beach cheering 'Bulls-eye' as the troops emptied Ml9 and M15 automatic gunfire into a colony of sea lions sunning themselves on 'Todo Rock'.

The killing season runs from December through to March. This is when an armada of ice floes drifts down through the Sea of Okhotsk past the Kurile Islands where the Russian government has established sanctuaries for the sea lions to breed. With the icebergs floats a cloud of plankton. Following the plankton come the fish. Feeding off the fish are the unsuspecting sea lions. They travel in harems with one huge bull sea lion — they grow up to four metres long and can weigh a tonne — and a dozen or more females half that size. Their fur is a mottled reddish brown, and they are called sea lions because of the blood-curdling barking roar they make when they are agitated. You can see unfortunate captives perform in the zoo at nearby Abashiri.

As soon as they reach Japanese waters it is open season. 'The place to hit them is under the ear when they stick their heads up to breathe,' says Hajime Takahashi, a local hunter, proudly screening a video of himself blowing sea lions out of the water from a small skiff manoeuvring between the ice floes. He points out the blood spurting in the air and staining the ocean and the ice. Mr Takahashi is one of twenty government-licensed sea lion hunters based in Rausu. There is no bag limit — he gets forty in a 'good' season, and estimates that he has killed more than 3000 over the years.

Some of the kill finishes up on the menu of the restaurant he owns. The Takasago restaurant is a Mecca for Japanese gourmets — and every conservationist's worst nightmare. Just about everything on the menu is an endangered species: bear, deer, seal and, of course, *todo*. Mr Takahashi serves it raw as sashimi, stir-fried with onions, or as a tourist takeaway in tins. The Japanese seem not to mind — photographs around the walls show television stars, authors, musicians and even the family of Japan's last emperor tucking into fricassee of endangered species. Nor does Mr Takahashi. 'It is not just for the food and the money,' he told me over a glass of sake. 'When I kill a *todo*, I feel I am doing my duty. Think of all the salmon they eat.'

Shuzo Hoshino, a director of the Rausu fishermen's cooperative, also defended the price on the sea lion's head, saying they do tremendous damage to the fishery. Rausu, population 8000, has an economy based on the salmon, squid, turbot and pollack its fleet of 350 boats brings in. Lately the catches have been declining. So have the sea lions. Four years ago the cooperative and the council paid a bounty on more than 300 dead sea lions; in 1993 it was fifty. Even Mr Takahashi concedes they may have to be protected one day. 'But why should I worry — I'll be dead then,' he laughed.

I was unable to find anyone in Japan willing to speak out against the slaughter — perhaps because, unlike whales and pandas, the sea lion is a large, loud and very ugly creature. It is a sad fact of life that concerns over wildlife increase according to its cuddliness. Eventually I telephoned across the Pacific to Seattle and found Dr Howard Braham angry about Japan's lack of action to protect the sea lion. Dr Braham was the director of the National Marine Mammal Laboratory (part of the US government's National Marine Fisheries Service) which recently published the most comprehensive international survey of sea lion numbers. That survey concluded that there were probably only 116 000 sea lions left in the world — about half the population of thirty years ago. Although Dr Braham believes that the Japanese sea lion slaughter is only one factor in this dramatic decline, he told me, 'No-one wants to see a local population go extinct, and that is what could happen. I can appreciate that the local fishermen want to protect their fishery, but it does not make good ecological sense to wipe out one species to benefit another.'

Where, it would be legitimate to ask, was Japan's Environment Protection Agency (EPA) while all this was going on — the destruction of habitat, industrial pollution, species such as the sea lion becoming extinct? Good question. Formed in 1971, the Environment Protection Agency is basically a toothless tiger. According to Hideyuki Kawana (author of the definitively hefty, nine-volume *Pollution in Japan*), it is grossly underfunded, and the Basic Environment Law which provides it with a legal framework is completely inadequate. Early drafts calling for environmental impact statements before major construction projects were quietly dropped; Japan remains the only developed country where such assessments are not mandatory.

In the bureaucratic bear pit of Kasumigaseki, where money equals numbers equals power, the Environment Protection Agency is a shrimp among whales. It is not even regarded as a real career option — its senior bureaucrats are seconded for a year or two at a time from other more powerful ministries. It is the least important of Cabinet portfolios.

In 1993, the Environment Protection Agency had fewer than 1000 employees, compared with 59 495 at the Health and Welfare Ministry; its budget was $965 million compared with $201 billion. By contrast, the United States Environmental Protection Agency, even after the cutbacks of the Reagan/Bush years, has 15 000 employees. Even allowing for the fact that the United States is more than twice the size and population of Japan, this is a gross under-resourcing. As well, there are striking qualitative differences. In the United States, for example, 450 substances are recognised as harmful to the environment, whereas in Japan only ten are officially classed as pollutants. The Japanese Environment Protection Agency has neither the power nor the legislative authority to overrule the big ministries which are responsible for much of Japan's pollution. Industrial and household waste is controlled by the Health and Welfare Ministry; the sewerage system by the Construction Ministry; and noise pollution and vehicle emissions are under the control of the Transport Ministry.

As Dr Yoneda, the wildlife expert, and I were discussing the agency's feeble and contested mandate, the phone rang and he began an apologetic discussion with someone. When he hung up, he said, 'That was NHK [the national broadcaster] in Hokkaido wanting to know what we are doing to control the bears which are damaging crops.' He shrugged his shoulders. He knew he couldn't win — not against the hunters, nor the farmers nor especially against the develop-or-bust government construction agencies. 'The reality is that these agencies are extremely powerful, and the Environment Protection Agency is not,' he said. 'Maybe in five or ten years' time we will have more power ...' he paused, 'but then again, maybe it will be too late.'

Time and again during my three years in Japan, I came across examples of the Environment Protection Agency either failing to act, or being overruled, if it sought to intervene to protect the environment. It approved a bitterly disputed reclamation project in the Wajiro tidelands of Hokkaido, an internationally important bird sanctuary on which many of the Australia-bound migrating species depend. It said nothing about the needless damming of rivers — even the epic battle over the building of a colossal and quite useless barrage across the Nagara River near Nagoya, a national cause célèbre in which conservationists, intellectuals, residents, fishermen and canoeists fought for twenty-three years to stop the damming of Japan's 'last wild river'.

Probably the classic example of the Japanese government's willingness to put short-term economic considerations ahead of the long-term interests of the environment occurred in the summer of 1993, near a city in northern Hokkaido called Kushiro. The Kushiro that man built is not much of a town — a grimy fishing port with an ugly sprawl of smokestacks, gas storage tanks and a belching power station. The Kushiro nature made, however, is another story. On the outskirts of the town, you pass an endless expanse of lonesome lakes and marshes, home to more than 100 species of waterfowl, including the throat-catchingly beautiful migratory cranes. That is why, in June that year, Kushiro was chosen as the first Asian city to host a conference of Ramsar, the international wetlands preservation organisation.

Just as the ibis, the wildcat and the sea lion are not as glamorous as the panda — but no less worth preserving — the earth's wetlands do not have the drama of the mountains and the coastlines, nor the romance of the rainforests. Drive past the Kushiro wetlands, and you could be forgiven for thinking they are nothing more than a boring bog. But they are — a whole lot more. The coastal wetlands are as vital to the earth's ecosystem as the tropical forests. Two-thirds of the world's fish breed in them, they are vital to the survival of hundreds of species of waterfowl and they act as filters to protect fragile rivers and lakes from pollution. In a poor part of the world such as Bangladesh, half the country's timber, fish and honey come from the mangrove swamps of the Ganges delta. The Japanese are playing the leading role in destroying this vital habitat — not only in their own archipelago, but all over Southeast Asia, where the mangroves are being cleared so that prawns can be farmed for Japanese dinner tables.

Almost everywhere wetlands are under threat — threat from drainage, from reclamation and from pollution. The Kushiro wetlands are a classic case. Around their edges farms, golf courses, housing estates and industries press in relentlessly on the lakes and marshland. This is Ramsar's concern — named after the town in Iran where it was first convened in 1971, it is an international watchdog, research organisation and guardian of the earth's wetlands. Kushiro was very proud to have the 172 delegates from thirty-seven countries meeting there. So proud, the council voted $60 000 to close and conceal with soil the local garbage tip, where it had been dumping 300 tonnes of rubbish a day into the fragile and precious wetlands. But just for a month. As soon as the international delegates departed, tipping resumed.

However, this was to be only a minor embarrassment. By the time the conference came to an end, Japan had been rewarded for its hospitality with the most scathing international denunciation of its hypocrisy and lies about the environment. The row was over the future of Lake Utonai, a large expanse of water rich in wildlife at the southern end of Hokkaido, which had been listed seven years before by Ramsar as one of Japan's five most important wetlands. When the conference began, each of the member nations was required to submit a progress report on how his country's listed wetlands were faring. Japan's report, prepared by the Environment Protection Agency, showed that all was well — so there was uproar when an enterprising reporter from the *Mainichi* newspaper disclosed that one significant fact had been omitted.

The Hokkaido Development Agency was pressing ahead with

a scheme to build a gigantic canal that was likely to drain Lake Utonai. The wetland would become a dryland because the canal would divert the water from its major tributary, the Bibi River. This was no minor piece of water engineering that could have been overlooked — the canal was to be 200 metres wide and thirty-eight kilometres long, two-thirds the size of the Panama Canal, someone calculated. Nor was it something new — the plan had been approved back in 1986, when the Hokkaido Development Agency was headed by one Fumio Abe, a notorious crook who was later arrested for taking kickbacks from construction companies. The canal was ostensibly for flood control, but no-one was in any doubt that it was really a giant *dango*, a bid-rigging scandal. A substantial portion of its $3 billion cost was intended to be siphoned off as bribes, spread generously around the construction companies, the politicians and the various levels of the bureaucracy involved.

The Japanese delegates spluttered indignantly when this was raised, but there was very little they could say. Even the $150 000 they slipped into Ramsar's Wetlands Protection Fund could not buy the silence of the delegates, who unanimously condemned the deceit. Nor could it conceal the fact that the Japanese government was unable to protect even a piece of the environment of such global significance as Lake Utonai. It is highly unlikely that, much as they love the attention such prestigious gatherings attract, Japan will ever again risk exposing its appalling environmental record to international scrutiny.

So, if the government refuses to abide by international environmental norms, where is the Japanese Green movement? Where are the pressure groups you would expect to fill the vacuum — the lobbyists, demonstrators and politicians? This brings us to another oddity. On the whole, the Japanese are the least aware, and the least active, environmentalists of which I know. They seem vaguely to understand that their environment is a mess. It is hard not to when loudspeaker networks warn people to stay indoors because of air pollution and electronic billboards alert hayfever sufferers to potentially lethal pollen levels. A survey a few years back by the prime minister's department found that 54 per cent of people were worried about noise, dirty air and foul water in their environment.

However, like the weather, it is not seen as something about which ordinary people can do anything. Where Australians blockade noisy airports or defeat koala-unfriendly environment ministers in elections, the Japanese shrug and go '*shoganai*' — it can't be helped. Fewer than 20 000 of a population of 125 million supposedly nature-loving Japanese belong to any conservation organisation, and most of those are bird-watchers, the Japanese male's favourite pastime after sleeping and watching television. As a result of this tiny support base, those clubs and associations which do exist are dependent on government or on industry for their funding. As 'captured' organisations, their voices are muted and their influence non-existent.

I wondered for years, for example, why I could never get a forthright criticism from WWF Japan (the local branch of the Worldwide Fund for Nature, which is the world's largest environment group) of Japan's policies towards its endangered species. I then discovered that nearly all its $3 million annual income is provided by twenty major companies. The Wild Bird Society of Japan is another 'tame' organisation which is largely financed by industry. The Nature Conservation Fund was actually founded under the auspices of Keidanren, the federation of Japanese business organisations, which provided most of its 1993 budget of $4 million. Greenpeace Japan (the world's most confrontational environmental lobby) is the despair of its radical founding fathers. Whenever there is a big issue in Japan, such as opposition to shipping plutonium or protecting whales, Greenpeace International has to send in foreign spokespeople. The local 'activists' refuse to comment, let alone sponsor direct action, if it is likely to offend.

Curiously enough, the environmental issue over which Japan has been pilloried the most loudly by the rest of the world is the one where Japan, for a change, has a measure of right on its side. I do not intend to canvass here all the pros and cons of whaling, nor do I include it in my list of gourmet delights. I was put off whale meat for life when my mother used to fill the house with its nauseating, blubbery stench as she boiled it up for the dog. How quickly we forget that this is not some weird and disgusting Asiatic perversion — the English sold and ate whale meat well into the 1950s. However, I agree with Nic Nicol that all the scientific evidence now shows that one species, the minke whale, has now recovered to sufficient numbers for a small, sustainable harvest. I respect the feelings of those who disagree with killing any creature (and, for consistency, who do not wear wool or leather, use most cosmetics or take any modern medicine). There is a fundamental dishonesty, however, in demanding an end to whaling whilst tolerating shooting certain species of wild duck or catching bluefin tuna.

Yet, for all the money it spent hiring an expensive New York public relations firm and flying a columnist colleague of mine up from Australia, the Japanese Ministry of Agriculture, Forests and Fisheries (MAFF) is losing the propaganda battle. It does not help its cause by telling lies. Whale meat is not now, and never was, a part of the Japanese traditional diet, as MAFF claims. It was consumed, when they could catch one with their fleet of frail canoes, by villagers in a few small towns such as Taiji, which now makes more money from tourists fascinated by its colourful history than it ever did from whaling. The heyday of its consumption was the postwar decade, when whale provided cheap protein in desperate times. In today's Japan, whale meat is a delicacy for rich gourmets, not the food of the common folk — a tiny piece the size of a cigarette packet can cost more than $100. Ninety per cent of young people have never eaten it and have no particular desire to do so.

Not one Japanese in 100 could give a toss about maintaining whaling — although even Japanese conservationists bridle at being seen to submit to *gaiatsu*, foreign bullying. The people who are fighting for it are the bureaucrats of MAFF and their cronies, who fear a loss of power and money. Japan's 'scientific' whaling expeditions fool no-one. The whales that are caught are chopped up under MAFF's auspices and sold through a devious distribution channel, leaving much of the money sticking to the fingers of bureaucrats, politicians and their business accomplices. Even then, paradoxically, there is an oversupply. Most people cannot afford it, and many rich folk who remember the postwar years look down on whale meat. There is no hiding the fact that demand has collapsed. Before long, whale meat will be as alien to the Japanese as goanna stew or cockatoo pie to modern Australians.

Accelerating this trend is the booming new industry of whale tourism. In 1995, for the first time, more money was made from watching whales in Japan than from eating them. Mayu and I travelled north to a former whaling town called Muroran at the southern tip of Hokkaido to look into this phenomenon. Muroran is the story that never gets told when demonstrators gather at the annual International Whaling Commission conferences to protest Japan's latest outrage — most lately, the decision to continue whaling in the Antarctic sanctuary on which most other countries agreed. It is the story of how a country changed its eating habits in just one generation. Whale meat, once a third of Japan's meat intake, is now a gastronomic oddity, eaten mainly by wealthy older folk. Consumption is down to less than 1 per cent of what it was thirty years ago. It is the story of how the whales are being welcomed back to the waters where they were once hunted to the brink of extinction; and of how tourism is rescuing the economies of dying whaling towns. Some of the very men who once fired exploding harpoons into the brains of whales are now making a living showing them off to holidaymakers.

Muroran is a drab industrial port that, until a few years ago, featured on no known tourist itinerary. It is the sister city of Knoxville USA, home of the Tennessee Valley Authority — America's largest power utility — which will give you the flavour of the place. Muroran's only claim to fame (apart from the cement works and the steel mills) is that it stands on Volcano Bay, the northernmost reach of the mighty Black Current. This is the oceanic superhighway that sweeps up from the tropics, bearing with it a rich stew of plankton, shrimp, sardines and squid — and the whales that feed on them.

For nearly half a century, it was one of Japan's great whaling ports. Old photographs show whales the size of semitrailers hauled up on the beach for butchering. In its heyday, two whales a week were winched ashore, the boardwalk ran red with blood and the air was rancid with the stench of rendering blubber. At its peak, in the early 1960s, more than 20 000 whales a year were being hunted down and killed in all the earth's oceans to satisfy Japan's demand for a cheap source of protein — and the companies' greed for profit. There was no thought of conservation, 'sustainable yield' or any of the other buzz words that now abound when you talk to Japan's fisheries bureaucrats. Species such as the magnificent great whale were driven to the brink of extinction.

Then, in Muroran and a score of towns like it around Japan, the whales began to disappear. We tracked down Eikichi Honma, a weathered 73-year-old, whose parents were whale-meat wholesalers and who remembers playing around the great factory by the bay where the big whales were winched ashore to be dismembered and turned into meat, fertiliser and oil. Whale was the only meat the townsfolk got to eat, apart from a bit of pork or chicken for New Year. Mr Honma was working at the cauldrons, rendering the blubber into oil, when word came one day in 1950 that the factory was to close. There are many fanciful theories about why the whales disappeared, but the most obvious seems the most likely — the whalers had all but committed genocide on the larger, and more profitable, species. 'They chased them further and further north, right to the Kurile Islands … and then one day there were no more whales to catch,' said Mr Honma. And no more work for the hundreds of men like him who were dependent on the Toyo Whaling Company for a livelihood. *Isana*, the 'brave fish', was almost extinct.

It was nearly forty years later, the late 1980s, that Dr Tadao Furuya — a local dentist and keen game fisherman — began to notice that the whales were returning to Volcano Bay. By a stroke of luck, the local council was looking for an opportunity to brighten up the town's stagnant smokestack economy with a new image. And so Muroran, Whale City, was born. The new coat of arms — a smiling whale, for some reason balancing a black and white soccer ball on its water spout — emblazons every structure from the Toyota dealer to a gas tank at the oil refinery. A whale bus plies the streets. Whale tiepins, T-shirts, bottle openers, postcards and even whale wine fill the shop windows. A town that once subsisted on whale meat now does not have a single shop that sells it or a restaurant that serves it. In the arcade, colourful banners illustrating the seventeen varieties of whales and dolphins that can be sighted in its waters flap from the roof. 'They are beautiful things,' says Hiroshi Matsubara, chief of the council's tourism bureau. 'Like most younger people today, I prefer to watch them than to eat them. Besides, whale meat is too scarce now, and much too expensive.'

Dr Furuya began taking tourists out on whale-spotting trips in 1992, using two pleasure cruisers. Three years later he hired two skippers, and added a third boat. By 1996 — he was already taking bookings for the season, which around Muroran runs through the three midsummer months — he hoped to have five boats, three of them converted squid-fishing boats whose owners fell on hard times. 'I just can't keep up with demand,' said Dr Furuya. There were 20 000 inquiries one year, but only room for 1200 people on the half-day cruises, which cost sixty-five dollars. Grimy Muroran can hardly believe its eyes — it is now a tourist town, attracting visitors (and their yen) from all over Japan.

Out on the green-grey plankton-rich waters of the North Pacific, they pay to watch the porpoises spring from the waves, and sea lions and otters gambol in the wake. Occasionally, a spume of water marks the surfacing of a great whale — the grey hump of a minke; the dazzling black and white patches of orca, the 'killer whale', like an enormous seagoing Friesian cow. Dr Furuya plays spot-the-generation-difference. 'When we sight a pod of whales,' he says, 'the older people start counting them and working out how much they weigh, how much they would be worth as meat. The younger ones, especially the women, are incredibly moved by the experience ... they want to jump overboard and swim with them.'

Today, the citizens of Muroran stand on the frontier of Japan's newest, fastest growing and most politically correct industry. They have rediscovered the whale ... not as a delicacy for the hotpot, but as a visual treat for tourists. It is only a few years since a Tokyo cartoonist, Kyusoku Iwamoto, led the first group of forty-seven Japanese whale-watchers on an expedition to the Ogasawaras, a chain of semitropical islands 1000 kilometres south of Tokyo. The media treated it all as a bit of a joke, but the idea took off like wildfire with the public.

Each year since, town after town around the Japan coastline has started whale-watching tours — nine of them at last count. In 1994, they catered for more than 30 000 people. That was the year the fisheries agency, which initially regarded it as a one-day wonder, conceded the industry was worth more than $40 million and had overtaken whale meat in importance. The industry was booming in the unlikeliest spots, providing work for the sons and grandsons of whalers in declining fishing villages.

Off the rocky capes of Shikoku, the smallest of Japan's main islands and a whaling centre for more than a century, grizzled former Antarctic whalers are conducting guided tours to the grounds where the giant sperm whales were once hunted. More than forty fishing boats are used for whale-watching, and fishermen say the industry now accounts for about a third of their income. In the Kerama islands around Iwo Jima (of World War II fame), Japanese youngsters are clamouring for the chance to ride out in rubber Zodiacs to encounter the humpback whale — the 'singing whale' whose tapes have become best sellers — and to swim with porpoises. In the Amami islands, between Japan and Taiwan, the humpbacks, which had not been seen since the 1960s when whalers slaughtered twenty or thirty a day, including mothers with calves, are back. A dozen five-tonne diving boats are in operation, providing employment for the young men who had been leaving the islands in droves. The town of Oshika, five hours by train from Tokyo, has built a Whale Land with models, exhibits, films and artefacts. At Kamogawa Seaworld, people pay to frolic in a pool with a 'killer whale'.

The boom shows no sign of abating. Thousands of schoolchildren are being taken on whale appreciation trips. Tokyo bookshops have set up special displays of whale books, tapes and videos. Whale documentaries were the summer's television ratings hits in 1995. The Whale and Dolphin Conservation Society of England — which surveyed the infant Japanese whale-watching industry two years ago — says that Japan is now plugged into a global network involving thirty countries and millions of whale-watchers, which is worth a fast-growing $500 million a year. It believes the simple arithmetic of the industry should eventually persuade Japan to stop whaling altogether. A pod of sixteen Bryde's whales (it calculates) is worth about $5.5 million for the meat, but $7 million over a fifteen-year period in direct whale-watching revenues, and $55 million if all the tourism spin-offs are counted.

In spite of this, Japan — and other countries such as Iceland and Norway — continues to argue at the International Whaling Commission that the whaling industry is an integral part of its culture, and that the minke whale is in no danger of extinction. It is an argument that is increasingly out of touch with public opinion in Japan. The government operates a whaling fleet — technically for 'scientific purposes' — which kills 330 whales a year, and turns them into fifteen-kilogram 'scientific' boxes of whale meat. Another 154 whales are killed on special licence, mainly for local consumption, by four traditional whaling communities. However, total consumption is now down to about 2000 tonnes a year — less than one-hundredth of what it once was — and even dealers concede that it is no longer a part of Japan's culinary mainstream. A poll by the *Asahi* newspaper found that only 11 per cent of the Japanese would fight for the right to eat whale.

What sticks in the throat is the refusal of the government, and the industry, to accept this fundamental change that has come over the Japanese public. People now mostly prefer to watch, rather than to eat, whales. In spite of this, the whaling industry — with national and local government backing — has tried all sorts of ploys to try and turn the tide of public opinion and protect its vested, and highly lucrative, interests. At Oshiki, a declining whaling community northeast of Tokyo, children are forced to eat a whale-meat school lunch once a month and are lectured on its alleged cultural importance. A national advertising campaign was launched extolling its nutritional and medicinal properties (it is supposed to cure skin ailments, asthma and anaemia). Speciality whale-meat restaurants (such as the one in the Tokyo suburb of Shibuya where generations of foreign television journalists have come to do their 'shock, horror' stand-ups) have declared the ninth of every month 'whale day' and offer cut-price specials.

However, none of this has halted its steady decline in popularity. Ms Mutsuko Onishi, a whale-eating enthusiast who owns the Tokuya Restaurant in Osaka — and who travels to IWC meetings offering free whale meals to delegates — says bluntly, 'It has ceased to be something that people eat at home.' To keep its clientele, the restaurant has begun using cheaper cuts of meat, and cutting its prices to what passes for a bargain in Japan — $48 for a bowl of whale stew. The price of whale meat, incidentally, has been another major factor in its fall from gastronomic grace — per kilogram, whale steak goes for around $100, a piece of reddish whale bacon can cost $350 and the choicest cuts of tailmeat go for an astronomical $950. Even Dr Seiji Ohsumi, executive director of the Japanese Whale Research Institute and a member of the IWC scientific committee for twenty-eight years, acknowledges that there has been a 'generational change'. Young people in Japan, he says, have been 'deprived of a feeling of closeness to the whale that comes from eating it'.

And that, says Dr Furuya, is no bad thing for his business. The whales are returning to Volcano Bay in ever-greater numbers now that they are chased for fun, rather than hunted for food, by the people of Muroran. 'It's almost as if they understood,' he mused. 'They are no longer shy. Before, we used to just sight a spray of water on the horizon, but now they come right up to the boat, and rub themselves against it. It is a beautiful sight.'

The decline of whaling in Japan is the one bright spot in an environmental picture of otherwise unremitting gloom. After a minor surge in popularity around the time of the Rio de Janeiro 'Earth Summit' in 1991, the environment has all but vanished off the radar as a popular issue. It is seen as a responsibility of government, not the individual, and — as in so many areas — government alternately ignores and cynically exploits it. At the 1995 Upper House elections, after waiting for a month hoping the issue would go away, the parties vied with each other to condemn the resumption of French nuclear testing at Mururoa Atoll in the Pacific. However, the government confined its objections to a mild diplomatic tut-tut, and pointedly avoided advocating anything practical like a boycott of French products, such as happened in Australia. Finance Minister Masayoshi Takemura joined the protest in Tahiti, but tried to avoid upsetting the French by pretending he was there as a 'private citizen'.

Not that it would have mattered. Your stereotypical Tokyo 'OL' (Office Lady) knows little of conservation, and would sooner die than be caught without her uniform of Hermès scarf, Louis Vuitton handbag and Chanel cosmetics. In a popular hand-held electronic game in Japan a few years ago, the player had to club to death as many cute little baby harp seals as possible — a kill was confirmed by the seal acquiring a halo and going to heaven at the top of the screen.

As a postscript to the sad story of the *toki*, Japanese scientists were offering the hope of a techno-fix for something as fundamental as the extinction of a species. Before Midori's body was cold, a team of experts headed by Professor Susumu Ishii, professor of biology at Tokyo's Waseda University, rushed to Sado island. Professor Ishii had been preparing for this moment for several years — he is an expert in cryogenics, the science of freezing tissue. Using a technique pioneered at California's San Diego Zoo — where the genes of 150 exotic species are preserved for posterity in a 'frozen ark' — he has developed a protocol that he hopes will one day enable the crested ibis to be brought back from the dead; a real-life Jurassic Park.

Midori's body was dissected and samples of each type of tissue placed in 800 test tubes. These were then stored in liquid nitrogen at minus 196 degrees Celsius in a special vault at a facility in Tsukuba Science City near Tokyo. This facility is used by the Japanese Agriculture Department to preserve genetic material from domestic plants and animals. If all goes well — and Professor Ishii says cryogenetics is advancing at such a pace that this might be in only ten years' time — it may be possible one day to thaw it out, inject the genetic material into the embryo of a related species of ibis and bring the *toki* back from extinction. The technique, he says, may also be used on other endangered species — even on ones already extinct such as the Japanese wolf.

However, Professor Ishii's scientific enthusiasm was abruptly doused when I asked him where the *toki* would live if it is ever reincarnated — and whether or not a better solution to preserving this and other endangered species would have been not to destroy its habitat in the first place. 'Perhaps an island will be available …' he said, rather uncertainly. Then he blurted out what seemed to me to be a more honest answer. 'Of course, preserving the environment would be better … but that costs a lot of money, whereas preserving cells, tissue and genes is relatively cheap.'

IT IS THE QUINTESSENTIAL FASHION STATEMENT of traditional Japan — the silken kimono in its luminous colours, with long sleeves almost sweeping the floor, bound around the middle with an intricately knotted sash. However, like the rickshaws, tea ceremony and *noh* dramas of Edo-era woodblock prints, the kimono is in danger of extinction — the victim of its own time-consuming tradition, excruciating discomfort ... and ruinous cost.

At the annual 'Adults' Day' when the two million Japanese who turn twenty during the year celebrate their majority, the Buddhist temples, Shinto shrines and municipal reception halls of Tokyo are alive with a multi-hued flock of kimono-clad young women. Despite this, the numbers of women wearing kimonos are falling year by year — more and more, they are turning up in less colourful, but more practical, Western suits and dresses. Toray Industries, Japan's largest ready-made kimono-maker, says sales have halved over the past decade.

Naomi Nishimura, a company spokesman, says that women of her age (she is a thoroughly modern salarywoman of twenty-seven) are turning away from kimonos because of their cost, difficulty and the lack of opportunity to wear them. Nowadays, apart from professionals like restaurant madams and the vanishing geisha, you are only likely to see kimonos worn at weddings, funerals, Shinto ceremonies and occasions such as university graduation or induction into a new job.

'I like to wear one, because it makes me feel special,' says Ms Nishimura. However, when offered a hypothetical choice between a new kimono and a Western designer gown she says, 'I suppose I shouldn't say this, but I'd rather have the Western outfit because I would have more chance to wear it.'

NOT
A THING

Across the road, in the glittering halls of the Mitsukoshi department store, you can compare the two. If you wince at the thought of a Gianni Versace blouse for $3400, a Lagerfeld dress for $3900 or an Armani suit at $4700, avoid the kimono department. The prices make the top European designer stuff look like St Vincent de Paul. Here, it is easy to spend more outfitting yourself in a kimono than buying a small apartment in Sydney or Melbourne.

A top-of-the-line number in handspun black silk and pure gold thread will set you back a little over $20 000 — and, if you want a signed *obi* (sash) to go with it, the most expensive I saw had a $64 000 price tag. Add on accessories such as carved combs for the pomaded hair, handbag, special silk underwear, white 'toe socks' and *zori* (clogs) and it wouldn't be too extravagant for a woman to be wearing $100 000 on her back.

Why not hire, do I hear you ask? By all means. There are shops in the Ginza which will lend you the complete outfit — but it will cost at least $3000 a day for the costume, plus $100 for removing each stain, should you slop a little sake down the front.

And woe betide the unfortunate woman who selects the wrong one. There is a strict etiquette of styles, colours and designs which depend on your age, the occasion and the season of the year. Pure white is for brides, corpses and theatre ghosts. Wear a pattern of parasols or paper lanterns and you may be mistaken for someone in the bar or brothel business. People will sniff if your kimono is embroidered with willow in winter, when pine, plum and bamboo are the approved texts. An older woman in bright colours or with long sleeves is 'mutton dressed up as lamb'. Even the set of the collar can be a faux pas.

Then there is the problem of putting it on. Mayu's sister Mioko, celebrating Adults' Day with friends at the Zojoji Temple, made her kimono debut. However, as most girls do, she had to visit a special 'dresser' where her mother paid $225 for the hour and a half it took to swaddle her in her new outfit.

'I hope it looks good,' she said, hobbling along with twenty-centimetre steps, slightly stooped under its three-kilogram weight and rubbing her stomach where the four-metre-long *obi* was cutting into her, 'because it sure is uncomfortable.'

In an effort to win women back to traditional costume, the Toray company has undertaken the first major re-engineering of the kimono since it reached its exquisite height in the Heian court nine centuries ago. Using new fibres, and modern technology such as plastic fasteners and Velcro straps, they have produced an outfit called 'Cinderella Time'.

At $9000 for the complete outfit, it is lighter and cheaper than conventional silk kimonos. And instead of an hour or more, it can be slipped on and off in just two minutes, with no assistance. However, since it was launched two years ago, sales have been only a disappointing 2000 a year. The new high-tech kimono has failed to capture the younger market, but is selling well to older women whose stiff joints make it hard for them to tie a traditional *obi*.

Hereby lies yet another tale. For some Japanese feminists, the kimono — like the topknots, shaved eyebrows and blackened teeth that Japanese women used to affect — is a symbol of oppression and exploitation. The historian Murakami Nobuhiko has gone as far as to write, 'The kimono has a criminal record. For hundreds of years, up until the 20th century, [it] insulted the female sex and caused women to suffer ... when women finally removed their kimono they burst the shackles of feudalism.'

Men stopped wearing kimonos — except very rarely, at very formal occasions — not long after Japan opened to the world in the 1860s, and the Emperor Meiji abolished them as court dress, declaring that they were 'un-Japanese and effeminate'. The kimono, which literally means 'thing to wear' was adapted in Japan from Chinese court dress.

Anti-kimono feeling reached a peak after the Great Kanto Earthquake of 1923, when critics charged that many thousands of women were incinerated because, hobbled by their kimonos, they were unable to run away from the fires fast enough. They were too modest to strip them off — traditionally, Japanese women did not wear bras or knickers underneath.

During World War II they were banned as extravagant, and the population reverted to the indigenous smocks and *mompe* pants. It was really only during the affluent 1960s and 1970s that the kimono began to make a comeback. Now, after a few short years of *'boomu'* when kimono magazines sprang up and kimono schools did a roaring trade, the gradual decline has resumed.

'I don't think we will ever see the end of the kimono,' said Ms Nishimura. 'It is such an important part of Japanese tradition. But it will never be as popular as the old days — Western clothing is so much more practical ... and less expensive.'

TEN
TOXIC DOC

Iatrogenic: ... any adverse condition in a patient occurring as the result of treatment by a physician or surgeon ...

— DORLAND'S MEDICAL DICTIONARY

WE SAT AROUND A LOW TABLE IN THE comfy upstairs office of one of Tokyo's leading attorneys — sitting on chairs, instead of kneeling on the floor, Japanese-style, because of the obvious discomfort this would have caused the other visitors. Some of them leaned on canes and crutches, others moved their arms and legs with a stiff, arthritic awkwardness. These people, all of them men, most of them young, were haemophiliacs. They suffer from a rare, congenital condition in which the blood lacks the ingredient needed to clot. If they cut themselves —or, more commonly, bang a knee or elbow, causing an internal haemorrhage — they would rapidly bleed to death without an injection of a clotting agent known as factor VIII, a white crystalline substance extracted from human blood.

We were not here, however, to discuss haemophilia. For an hour or more we had been tip-toeing around the real issue. Finally, when I thought they might have sufficient confidence in me, I asked the question. 'Does anyone here actually have HIV, the AIDS virus?' The eight men looked at each other nervously for ten seconds, twenty seconds. Finally, one raised his hand, a pale gangling young man whose voice was not much more than a monosyllabic whisper. 'I do,' he said.

Even now, I am ethically bound to protect his real identity, and will use a pseudonym, Toshi Mitsui. Only half a dozen of Japan's 3000 AIDS patients have been brave enough to risk social isolation and 'come out' using their real names. Such is the fear, ignorance and prejudice against people with the virus in Japan that identifying him would most likely bring instant ostracism by his friends, the sack from his workplace, and a refusal by doctors and hospitals to treat him. Toshi had confided in his family, but dared not trust his friends or workmates.

Having the virus would be bad enough for anyone who contracted it through what, in the West, are the most common routes — sex and intravenous drug use. In Japan, however, the majority of people with HIV contracted it not through their lifestyles, but from a medical treatment that was supposed to save, not shorten, their lives. Of the 5000 or so haemophiliacs in Japan, at least 2000 have been handed a death sentence, a virus lurking in the injections of Factor VIII on which they depended. And, ten years after it was conclusively shown that this silent epidemic was caused by the grossest medical negligence, patients like young Toshi are dying weekly, almost literally on the steps of the courts, as they seek justice from the doctors and the drug companies responsible.

The 'blood AIDS' controversy is not unique to Japan. Many countries, including Australia, have been caught up in this global scandal. In Melbourne, the law firm of Slater and Gordon had obtained around $100 million in compensation by 1993. In the United States, awards as high as $2.5 million had been made in individual cases. In France, four government officials, including the former head of the blood bank, had actually been jailed for negligence.

What is unparalleled is the scale of the epidemic in Japan — nearly half the haemophiliacs in the country will eventually die — and the fact that after almost a decade the drug companies, and the government which was supposed to regulate them, had not unequivocally admitted their guilt or agreed to compensate the victims adequately. It was beginning to look like a re-run of Minamata.

This was not the first time such a sordid tale of the government failing to protect the public against the greed of the drug companies and the negligence of the medical profession had transfixed Japan. Far from it. This chapter will deal with two of at least a dozen major medical scandals of recent years that have damaged more than 20 000 innocent people and cost many their lives. That is probably an absurdly conservative figure — no comprehensive study has ever been done in Japan on the number of patients killed by their doctors. Nor does it include the tens of thousands of people who have been condemned to a lingering death because of bans or restrictions in Japan on drugs and procedures commonplace elsewhere, such as organ transplants.

Iatrogenic (doctor-caused) sickness and death is nothing new. One hundred and fifty years ago, the Hungarian physician Ignaz Philipp Semmelweis campaigned in the face of scepticism and ridicule to stop doctors coming straight from the morgue to plunge their putrid, bloody hands into the wombs of pregnant women. Forty years, and countless thousands of unnecessary deaths from septicaemia later, his warnings were finally heeded and he is now recognised as the pioneer of safe, hygienic childbirth. Japan today does have a few brave men like Dr Semmelweis campaigning to improve the country's notorious reputation as a 'first world economy with third world medicine'. Tragically, however, no-one is listening to the likes of Yoshio Kato, a Nagoya-based lawyer who founded an information network called *Iryo no Anzen ni Kansuru Kenkyu-kai* (Society for the Study of Medical Safety) after his mother became a victim of a killer drug called (in the West) Enterovioform.

Before we get into the horror story of Japanese medical malpractice, however, there is one apparent contradiction that needs to be dealt with: if Japanese medicine is so bad, how come the people are so healthy? Why do the Japanese live longer than anyone else and have the world's lowest infant death rate?

I puzzled about this for some months in 1995, sitting in hospital and doctors' waiting rooms waiting for treatment for a knee I wrecked in a skiing accident in the Japan Alps. Medical care in Japan gives you plenty of time to think about things. It is something like the British national health scheme. Everyone is covered (through a medical insurance levy) for most of the cost of a basic service by a busy government-paid practitioner and a bed in a crowded public hospital. And I mean busy and crowded. Forty per cent of patients (according to a survey by the Japan Medical Association in 1993) wait two hours or more to see a doctor; the length of an average consultation is four minutes twenty seconds. My own private doctor, a charming old former US Army medic who came to Japan during the Korean War and never left, told me he left public health because he would have had to see 120 patients a day just to break even and he couldn't, in all conscience, continue doing that.

I have no technical complaints about my own treatment, though I did think $700 for a plaster cast was a bit extortionate. Hospitals make their money from 'peripherals' such as casts and drugs, and so tend to excessively prescribe and charge like wounded bulls. The real surprise came when I discussed with Dr Fujii, an orthopaedic specialist, an operation to repair a damaged cartilage. Dr Fujii informed me that I would have to spend three weeks in the public hospital where he practised. Since I couldn't afford the time, and did not like the look of the grungy wards and the crowded corridors where patients wait for hours for the most cursory attention, I questioned this. Dr Fujii's face lit up when he learned that I was not covered by the government medical insurance scheme. 'If you are a paying patient,' he promised, 'a friend of mine has a private hospital where you can have the operation in three or four days.'

Why would the same procedure, by the same surgeon, take six times as long in a public hospital I asked in amazement. 'Public hospitals are very bureaucratic,' said Dr Fujii. However, that was not the real reason, as I later learned. Hundreds of private hospitals were thrown up during the 1980s, creating a bed glut. On a population basis, Japan now has more hospital beds than any country in the world — three times as many as Australia or the United States, for instance. There are 10 000 hospitals in the country, and 80 per cent of them are estimated to be operating in the red. As a result they compete fiercely for patients — and once they get you in, they refuse to let you go.

Fearing this, not to mention the deadly 'golden staph' that infests Japanese hospitals, I telephoned my doctor in Sydney for a second opinion. Just as well. He said that in Australia this particular surgery was usually a walk-in walk-out procedure, and I should be back at work the following day. Dr Fujii looked disappointed when I told him I'd have the operation done in

Sydney. As well as his fee, he would have been looking forward to the traditional *orei*, an envelope which should contain anything from $1300 to $13 000 handed to the doctor before the operation, just to make extra sure nothing goes wrong.

Having seen it in action, it was even more puzzling that this decrepit, overworked, underfunded, kickback-riddled system should have produced the world's healthiest society. By the two most widely used international standards, longevity and infant mortality, Japan leads the world, and has done for a decade. Yet it spends less of its gross national product on health care than almost any other developed nation — 6.8 per cent, compared with 8.6 per cent in Australia and almost double, 13.3 per cent, in the United States. It has far fewer doctors — one for every 610 people, compared with 438 in Australia and 420 in the United States. Yet in 1993 Japanese life expectancy was 78.6 years, compared with 76.7 in Australia and 75.6 in the United States. As for infant mortality, only two babies per 1000 die before their first birthday in Japan, compared with seven in Australia and nine in the United States. These are exactly the opposite of the results you would expect if money and availability of doctors had any bearing on health.

Finally, as I waded through the data, the penny dropped. Bizarre and illogical as it may seem, the statistical picture is clear. Beyond a certain point, the amount of money a country spends on health care has little relationship to the actual health of its population. It is well established that other factors — good housing, adequate nutrition and clean water — have been much more significant in the dramatic improvement in the health of the developed world in the past half century than advances in medicine. Many public health specialists now argue that the most urgent dilemma facing modern medicine is that, beyond the delivery of certain basic services — competent birthing, vaccination and lifestyle education included — all the miracle drugs and high-tech surgical procedures that consume so much of the global health budget deliver ever-diminishing returns. In fact, with the current epidemic of iatrogenic disease, the medical system is shortening, rather than prolonging, many lives.

In the case of Japan, where much of this advanced, Western-invented medicine is not available, and where medical malpractice is rampant, it seems pretty obvious that something else is responsible for the robust good health of the community. Japan already has more than 6000 centenarians; inside a generation it will be the greyest society on earth. The obvious cause is not medical care, but lifestyle, in particular the relatively low level of heart-disease-causing fat in the diet.

Even with hamburger joints, pizza-on-wheels, fried chicken and the rest of the familiar Western junk food diet spreading across the country, the Japanese still eat more vegetables and get more of their protein from fish, and less from red meat, than people in any other developed country. They have the lowest rate of death from heart disease in the developed world — one-sixth the rate of Australia or the United States. Cancer is Japan's biggest killer. In 1995, lung cancer overtook stomach cancer as the most common cause of death — hardly surprising in a place where more than half the men still smoke and a government monopoly over domestic tobacco production ensures that health messages are so muted as to be inaudible.

In short, Japan's famously good health appears to be in spite of its doctors, not because of them. In 1992 — when the country had more doctors practising, more drugs prescribed, and more operations performed than at any time in its history — the life expectancy of men actually dropped for the first time since World War II. More health care equals a higher death rate? In Japan, that may just be so. However, it is much more likely to be due to changes in the Japanese diet, which has become steadily more unhealthy over the past twenty years. Meat has overtaken fish as the main source of protein, fat consumption is up 6 per cent and consumption of carbohydrates has fallen by 15 per cent. The traditional Japanese meal of rice, fish and vegetables is slowly dying, and so are the people — although, it must be said, the trend is not yet one to cause alarm. Men's life expectancy fell from 76.11 to 76.09 years, cutting about one week off their life span.

One other factor may be involved in this hopefully

temporary drop in male life expectancy. Although epidemiologists say the evidence is as yet inconclusive, it coincides with an increase in doctor-caused disease such as that which is wiping out half Japan's haemophiliacs. However, before I can begin to explain this particular tragedy, it is necessary to understand a little of Japan's medical culture.

Japanese doctors demand an almost god-like reverence from their patients. It is not even acceptable to call them *isha* (doctor); they insist on *sensei* (master). Older GPs conduct their surgeries like royal courts with the patients as courtiers, sitting on benches, waiting for the hands to be briefly laid on and the prognosis shared with the rest of the waiting room. They enjoy an incredibly low tax status (introduced after the war and never repealed) and are said to own more Rolls-Royces than any other group in the world. *Setsumei to doi* ('informed consent'), the basis of Western medical ethics, was only grudgingly, and on a non-binding basis, adopted by the Japan Medical Association in 1990. It is still an exotic and little-understood concept.

Surveys show that still, in 1995, 76 per cent of Japanese doctors refused to tell patients if they were suffering from a fatal disease. Among other atrocious consequences are scores of people who are not informed they are carrying the AIDS virus, and who unwittingly infect their partners. Many doctors will not even condescend to discuss their diagnosis, let alone tell patients what medication they are prescribing. Drugs dispensed by doctors and clinics are repackaged in plain plastic with no name and no product information. Patients prescribed experimental drugs which later killed them were told only 'I am going to try a new treatment on you.' In my own case, when I insisted on knowing what was prescribed, I was told the white pills were anti-inflammatory, the greenish ones were painkillers and the pink ones were to protect me from any ill effects from the white ones and the greenish ones. Or was it the other way round?

As well, there is another dark shadow hanging over the profession, of which all Japanese doctors — but few foreigners

— are aware. Today's extraordinarily powerful and self-perpetuating medical Establishment are the heirs and successors of the most evil medical empire the world has ever seen — the infamous Unit 731 described in Chapter three on World War II. When the war ended, the doctors in charge of the unit fled to Japan where they did a deal with the occupation forces — they handed over their experimental data, which the Americans wanted for their own biological warfare research, and were spared prosecution as war criminals.

According to a meticulously documented fifteen-page report headlined 'Black Blood and White Genes' published in 1989 by *Days Japan* magazine, no fewer than 700 of Unit Commander Shiro Ishii's men escaped prosecution in this Faustian bargain. These doctors went on to become the cream of Japan's postwar medical elite, heading most of the major university medical schools, and the key research and policy-making organisations such as the National Cancer Centre, the National Institute of Health and the Japan Medical Association. They took top positions in the Health and Welfare Ministry. They brazenly published the results of their murderous experiments for years after the war, disguising their true nature by referring to the human victims as 'Korean monkeys', 'Chinese monkeys' and so on.

Dr Masaji Kitano, who succeeded Dr Ishii as commander of Unit 731, went on to head Green Cross, Japan's largest pharmaceutical company. Dr Hisato Yoshimura, who froze babies to death to determine their resistance to cold, became an adviser to the Japanese government's polar expeditions. Those who argue that this was all so long ago the system must have long since purged itself of this evil know nothing of Japanese education. The *sensei* is never wrong. Generation after generation passes on his teachings, his beliefs and his attitudes, never changing a single comma even when all the evidence is against it. As we have seen, some Japanese leprosy experts still insist that Hansen's disease is hereditary, fifty years after the bacillus was first identified.

So Dr Shiro Ishii lives on in the hearts of his followers,

today's Japanese medical Establishment. They control the Health and Welfare Ministry which is supposed to be the public's watchdog against medical malpractice, and they have for decades dictated national health policy. Even now you hear of medical experiments so senselessly sadistic and scientifically worthless they remind you of Dr Ishii's doctors amputating prisoners' arms and legs, then trying to sew them back on in the wrong place.

The Japan Anti-Vivisection Society has been campaigning for years to stop Japan Tobacco, the government-controlled monopoly, funding experiments designed to 'prove' smoking cures Alzheimer's disease. It seems not to have occurred to anyone that Alzheimer's, although an awful affliction, is not fatal, and lung cancer is. Mice have their brains doctored to simulate symptoms of the disease and are then forced to inhale tobacco smoke. At a time when the rest of the world is turning in revulsion from live experimentation, Japan (according to JAVA) kills twenty million dogs, cats, monkeys and mice a year in the name of this sort of pseudo-science. Not to mention the human beings who, without their knowledge or consent, are used as guinea pigs by unscrupulous doctors testing new drugs and procedures.

If there is no effective government regulation, surely aggrieved patients can turn to the courts for redress for medical malpractice. Well, actually, no. As Japan's legal system is so slow, so expensive and so biased against plaintiffs, almost no-one bothers to sue doctors who saw off the wrong leg or prescribe pills that kill. Only 400 malpractice suits are filed annually in the entire country, of which fewer than one in five will end in a decision of any sort. Only one in five of those rulings will be in favour of the patient — odds of 25/1 against. With appeals taking years, even decades, to resolve, you can almost guarantee that with diseases like AIDS the undertaker will arrive before the judgment.

The ministry does, I was surprised to learn, have a medical ethics council which can in theory cancel the licence of a doctor guilty of malpractice. However, this power is never used.

'Disciplinary action,' says a spokesman, 'is limited to doctors filing improper billing claims, or those convicted in a criminal case. We do not take action on malpractice.' The message appears to be that killing a patient is OK, as long as you don't overcharge him or her.

Also, do not expect it to be a painless death. Japanese doctors have little training or interest in pain management, and prescribe for the terminally ill only a fraction of such widely used painkillers as morphine as do doctors in other countries. Nor is there much understanding of euthanasia. In 1991, Masahito Tokunaga, a 38-year-old former physician at Tokai University Hospital in Kanagawa, became the hero of the fledgling Japanese 'right to die' movement. Dr Tokunaga was charged with killing a 58-year-old man who was dying of cancer with an injection of potassium chloride. However, he appears to have overlooked one essential ingredient of the euthanasia moral contract. The patient's family had repeatedly demanded that the doctor end the man's life, but the patient himself had never been consulted. Never mind, said the judges of the Yokohama District Court. They let Dr Tokunaga off with a two-year suspended prison sentence.

With such total freedom from any legal or regulatory safeguards, it is hardly surprising that almost every month the papers — the only place aggrieved patients can turn — are full of some new medical outrage. The haemophiliac scandal cited at the opening of this chapter was a double tragedy because, whereas patients damaged by drugs or disabled by medical negligence might expect some sympathy from the community, those with AIDS can look forward to nothing but fear and loathing. They are treated like plague-carriers in the Middle Ages.

A low-key and underfunded government education program has made little impact on public understanding of AIDS. A 1993 poll by NHK, the national broadcaster, found that half the Japanese population believed you could contract the virus from a mosquito bite, and one in four believed you could catch it by sharing a cup. Even reputable international companies such as Matsushita 'offer' their employees AIDS tests which are, to all intents and purposes, compulsory. Employees fear a positive test would mean the sack. Little wonder that there is at least one support network which helps HIV-positive people leave Japan to live in the United States, where they believe they will not only receive better medical care, but more tolerance and compassion from the community.

The prejudice is reinforced by the fact that, for reasons that are not fully understood, Japan has fewer people known to be infected with the AIDS virus than almost any country in the world. It is regarded as a *'gaijin* disease' and media coverage focuses on mass round-ups of Thai prostitutes, rather than the majority of patients, who are Japanese. In early 1996, only about 4000 people living in Japan were known to be HIV-positive, and the numbers were growing at a snail's pace compared with the epidemic engulfing the rest of Asia. In stark contrast, the United States, with double the population, had 50 000 cases. Australia, with 16 000, had forty times as many cases as Japan, on a population basis.

Some explanations are obvious. Condoms, which offer protection against disease transmission, are Japan's favourite contraceptive as the Pill is illegal. The Japanese do not travel abroad much, and wives are said to put a packet of condoms in their husbands' suitcases if they suspect them of planning a sex holiday somewhere like Thailand. Intravenous drug use is extraordinarily rare. The overtly homosexual community is considerably smaller, less flamboyant and less assertive about its rights than in other countries. People with HIV are still very reluctant to speak out, and many, even those like Toshi who have decided to sue, are so ashamed they are identified in court papers by numbers, not names.

This sense of guilt is heightened by the shameful way in which the Japanese medical Establishment has dealt with AIDS in the decade since the first case (a haemophiliac) was detected. Ignoring government guidelines, three-quarters of hospitals still turn away patients with HIV. Those that do treat people carrying the virus do so secretly, for fear they will be boycotted by all their other patients and by the medical staff.

The overwhelming majority of dentists, doctors and nurses in Japan will have nothing to do with anyone carrying the virus. One patient describes a doctor 'examining' people with AIDS by fastidiously lifting their pyjama legs with the tip of his umbrella to inspect their sores. At other hospitals, AIDS patients have hanged themselves after staff left their food on the floor, refused to clean their rooms and banned visitors. No publicly funded counselling is offered and little treatment; in 1993, only 200 of 3000 HIV-positive people were receiving the only drugs then known to be effective, AZT and DDI. Murao Kusabuse, another haemophiliac AIDS patient I spoke with, described it like this, 'Once you are found to be HIV-positive, you are treated, even in hospital, like a virus yourself — and your relatives attending at the bedside are treated in a similar way.'

When they first began to sicken with the virus, it came as a shock, but no surprise, to most Japanese haemophiliacs. They had known since 1982, when they read a *Washington Post* report republished in a local newspaper, that US scientists had discovered that the AIDS virus could be transmitted by factor VIII, the blood product they depend on to stop uncontrolled bleeding. The following year it was official: screening for the virus and heat-treatment of the blood-clotting factor were made mandatory in the United States, virtually eliminating the risk. Old, infected product was withdrawn and destroyed. That should have been the end of the story.

However, in Japan, the authorities (that is, the Health Ministry) refused to act, even though they were officially informed in April of 1983 of the terrible risk. For another twenty-eight months they continued to allow Japanese haemophiliacs to be treated with the potentially contaminated product, eventually handing 2000 people a death sentence. 'We begged the doctors to change to domestic blood products, but they refused,' Yukio Yasuda, a haemophiliac who is president of Tokyo Friends of Haemophiliacs and a lawyer involved in the litigation, told me. Japanese blood was then uncontaminated;

the virus had not yet entered the country.

As is usual in cases of such wicked negligence, money was the major factor. Imported blood products were more profitable. Toshihiro Suzuki, the attorney who represents Toshi and 120 other haemophiliacs who contracted HIV, has conclusive evidence Green Cross and four other Japanese and American pharmaceutical companies involved were aware of the danger. However, factor VIII was an extremely lucrative product — the Japanese market was worth around $100 million a year. Japanese companies did not have the necessary heat-treatment technology, and they refused to hand this market on a platter to foreign companies which did. They asked for, and were given, two years to bring themselves up to speed. During those two years, the majority of the 2000 haemophiliacs were needlessly, and negligently, given infected products.

In fact, Japan became a dumping ground for infected blood and by-products from around the world as country after country acknowledged the risk and banned non-treated products. An investigative journalist named Ryuichi Hirokawa whom I came to know has dug up evidence showing that this led to a price war, with the cost of imported blood products being cut by up to 50 per cent. This, argues Hirokawa, suited some unscrupulous hospitals and doctors fine, because they are reimbursed by the health funds on a fixed, rather than actual, cost basis. Suddenly, haemophiliacs represented big profits, as much as $20 000 a year per patient, if they were given cut-price infected blood.

Attorney Yasuda told me, 'They rounded us up like milking cows.' Doctors urged haemophiliacs to use more factor VIII, and to inject themselves at home as a 'preventative' measure, an unwise practice at the best of times. Couriers used to dump dozens of bottles of it in insulated boxes on people's doorsteps. In those two years there were windfall profits of around $100 million made by doctors and hospitals, as the five companies unloaded their 'dumped' imported factor VIII on thousands of unsuspecting haemophiliacs. One Tokyo private hospital which 'recruited' 300 haemophiliacs, paid off debts of $7 million and began a major expansion program with the profits. It was a feeding frenzy which only ended when the government could no longer ignore the fact that it was committing genocide on its haemophiliac population.

If any one man has to take the blame for this deadly profiteering it is Professor Takeshi Abe, the guru of Japanese blood doctors and head of the key government advisory committee. Documents prized a decade later from ministry files show that Professor Abe, a man now in his eighties who was vice-president of Tokyo's prestigious Teikyo University, warned the Health Ministry back in April 1983 that untreated blood products could infect Japan's haemophiliacs with HIV. However, that warning was later retracted in circumstances so morally sordid they defy belief — Professor Abe was bribed with more than $500 000 from the drug companies to set up a research facility. Green Cross, the company with most to lose, gave him $100 000 and found seats on company boards for Abe and six Health and Welfare Ministry bureaucrats involved in the monstrous cover-up.

For twenty-eight months, 'Dr Death' as he became known, refused to acknowledge reports flooding in from all over the world of haemophiliacs contracting the AIDS virus, and insisted publicly that there was no conclusive connection with infected blood products. For twenty-eight months, he protected the Japanese pharmaceutical giants and their profits from foreign competition. It was not until July 1985 that the Japanese government finally approved the use of safe, heat-treated factor VIII in Japan — although, incomprehensibly, there was still no recall of the infected batches. Of course, by then it was too late. The first AIDS case in Japan was detected that very month — not a homosexual or a drug user, but a haemophiliac. More cases followed — although even now doctors, fearful of the consequences of their reckless profiteering at the cost of their patients' lives, continue to conceal the true extent of the epidemic.

One mother who had been injecting her haemophiliac son with factor VIII was told by his doctor that the boy was OK, but she should sterilise the household eating utensils anyway.

Another mother said she thought it 'very strange' that her doctor told her her son did not have HIV, but advised her to take out a life insurance policy on him. In a third case among Suzuki's clients, a fifteen-year-old haemophiliac boy who had been reassured that he did not have the virus was invited by his doctor to a discussion group with other patients. There, the doctor proposed that the students form a 'society for male virgins'. Another haemophiliac was thinking of getting married and prudently went to have an AIDS test. His doctor reassured him that everything was fine. Three years after their wedding day, his wife was admitted to hospital with what they initially thought was pneumonia ... and was dead a month later of AIDS. The doctor had lied, and the lie killed his bride.

'There is no doubt in my mind,' says attorney Suzuki, 'that the doctors knew they had the virus and deliberately concealed this.' He believes that several hundred haemophiliacs are still going about their lives accepting their doctors' false assurances that they are free from HIV. 'They are afraid to admit their mistake ... they are allowing their patients to infect their loved ones, and they are preventing them from getting proper treatment that could prolong their lives. It is scandalous that their gross negligence has caused the unnecessary deaths of so many people.'

Late in 1995, only four years after the litigation was launched, lightning fast by the standards of Japanese justice, courts in Osaka and Tokyo proposed a settlement. By now, the epidemic was in full swing, with half the victims already dead and one more haemophiliac added to the toll every five days. The courts suggested an admission of guilt by the government and the drug companies, and a payment of $600 000 to each patient — or to the relatives of those who had died of AIDS in the meantime. A few months later, a new health minister called Naoto Kan invited the media to film him belatedly apologising to relatives and patients, many of whom had been staging sit-in demonstrations outside his ministry for the best part of a decade.

If this had been accompanied by a pledge by the

government to purge the ministry's medical Establishment and introduce tough, independent safeguards against the repetition of such an outrage, that might have been some reassurance. However, the bureaucracy was arrogantly refusing to acknowledge its culpability, allowing the minister to carry the can. Also, the drug companies were bickering over compensation, claiming the eventual payout could exceed $1 billion and send many of them bankrupt. As for putting Professor Abe on trial for murder, as had occurred with those responsible for the French blood/AIDS disaster, that was unthinkable. Still protesting his innocence, he was allowed to resign his university job in full and final atonement for his awful crimes. It looked as if 'The System' — surprise, surprise — was going to win once again.

This was not the first, probably not even the forty-first, time the Japanese medical Establishment had connived in the release of a profitable, but dangerous, product on the market. The most authoritative critic of the system is Dr Hirokuni Beppu, the deputy medical director of Tokyo Metropolitan Hospital and the Ralph Nader of Japan's drug industry. Or perhaps I should say the Ignaz Philipp Semmelweis. He edits the monthly *Informed Prescriber* magazine, which blows the whistle on bad drugs. In the past forty years, Dr Beppu told me, he had analysed eleven major drug disasters in Japan, which had affected a minimum of 20 000 people, killing several hundred of them. This does not include those killed by infected blood products, since they are not technically drugs. However, it does include a new 'wonder drug' called Sorivudine which was launched on an unsuspecting public in 1993.

If anything, the scandal that erupted over Sorivudine caused even more public outrage than the slaughter of the innocent haemophiliacs. Although the number of people who would eventually die was far smaller — 'only' fifteen — the almost-daily disclosures of faked research, sloppy government controls, lies, bribery and blatant profiteering that surrounded the release of the drug are a medical horror story. First, however, I should explain why the Japanese are more vulnerable than people in almost any other country to a rogue drug like this slipping through what passes for the regulatory safety net and onto the market.

Japan has a major drug problem, a multibillion-dollar drug problem that kills thousands of people every year. Unlike other countries, however, Japan's drug crisis is not on the backstreets and in the shooting galleries — it is in the country's hospitals and surgeries. The Japanese are the world champion pill-poppers. They spend around $85 billion a year on pills, potions and injections — more than the country's entire defence budget and almost double what they pay for their staple food, rice. They swallow twice as much medicine as Americans and three times as much as the British. There is a phrase for this — *kusuri zuke shakai* which means literally 'drug-pickled society'. It is almost impossible to walk out of a doctor's surgery without your pockets clattering like a baby's rattle. It is common for older patients like Mayu's ailing grandmother to be taking six or eight different medications. At one stage Grammy (as she calls herself) had to be hospitalised to 'dry out' from the drugs her doctor was pumping into her. Death from overdose, and from reaction between the different drugs, is common.

You only have to look in Tokyo's bookshops to see how concerned the public is about this. When I last counted, no fewer than 1237 books were available to try and help Japanese consumers understand what all these mysterious chemicals are doing to their bodies. The No. 1 best seller for the past ten years is the annually updated *How to Understand the Drugs which Doctors Prescribe*, which has sold an amazing 1.8 million copies.

There are a variety of reasons for this infatuation with drugs. One is cultural. Since the Nara period, beginning in the eighth century, *kanpo*, or herbal medicine, has been the traditional remedy for any ailment — imported Chinese concoctions of tiger penis and dried seahorse for the wealthy; infusions of wild bark and berries for the common folk. Belief that a 'magic bullet' exists for whatever ails you is deeply embedded in the Japanese psyche.

However, nowadays money is the main cause of the 'drug-pickled society'. Under the Japanese national health scheme, the government pays doctors, clinics and hospitals for the drugs which they hand out to their patients. The more you prescribe, the more you earn. As Japanese national health doctors are paid a pittance they also rely on kickbacks from the drug companies, secret discounts on the approved prices. As much as one-quarter of that $85 billion-a-year is pocketed by the profession. The doctors also willingly connive in the lucrative exploitation of their patients as unwitting guinea pigs for experimental drugs. Drug companies pay hospitals up to $2500 a head for such 'research', which would be regarded as unethical, if not illegal, in most other countries.

For the past fifteen years or so, since overprescribing became a public issue, the government has been trying to put a lid on the soaring cost by progressively cutting the reimbursement price on established drugs. This has been singularly ineffective — a survey by an Osaka medical group in 1993 found that forty-nine common prescription drugs on sale in Japan were still three times as expensive as the overseas average. The policy has had the perverse effect, however, of causing an explosion of 'new' (and so not price-capped) drugs, unparalleled anywhere in the world. At latest count, Japan had an astonishing 14 000 approved drugs, compared with only 600 in Australia. This enabled the drug companies and the doctors to maintain their profits in spite of the price squeeze. Although established drug prices were cut by half between 1980 and 1990, the drug companies' total sales actually increased 5 per cent. It also ensured that, in their rush to the marketplace with new products, the drug companies would cut corners.

According to Dr Beppu, many of these new drugs are either ineffective or dangerous, or both. Some of them were imported, like Enterovioform (an anti-diarrhoea drug which killed scores of people and may have blinded as many as 11 000 in the 1960s and 1970s) and Thalidomide, which was supposed to prevent morning sickness, but which penetrated the placenta and caused thousands of shocking birth deformities around the world. Many of these drugs continued to be used in Japan long after they had been banned in every other country. Steroids are still referred to by Japanese doctors as 'magic medicine' and prescribed holus bolus for conditions such as skin ailments; Interferon is still a best seller for hepatitis treatment in Japan, is in spite of having been linked to chronic depression resulting in thirty-two suicide attempts — twelve of them successful — and two murders.

Other drugs, such as Sorivudine, are Japanese-produced, if not invented. Deaths have resulted from bizarre fads like the injection of vitamin K and other useless 'tonics' claimed to help Alzheimer's disease patients. The massive overprescription of antibiotics has led to an epidemic of the lethal MSRA (methicillin-resistant *Staphylococcus aureus* or 'golden staph' bacteria) in Japanese hospital wards. Some Japanese regard hospitalisation as a potential death sentence — and with good reason. In one hospital near Tokyo alone 190 people were infected with MSRA in a matter of months in 1990–91, of whom eighty died. A simple endoscope examination, a procedure regarded as routine in other countries, can also kill you in Japan. According to the Japan Gastroenterological Society, between 1988 and 1992, 225 patients were killed during botched examinations.

There are hundreds of home-grown cancer drugs on the Japanese market which are unheard-of anywhere else in the world. This is an enormously profitable market — Japan has more than a million cancer patients, desperate for anything that may offer hope. If you are lucky, these drugs will turn out to be merely useless, like Krestin and Picibanil, two only-in-Japan drugs which made their makers more than $13 billion. If you are unlucky, the treatment will kill you quicker than the cancer.

Irinotecan hydrochloride, claimed to be a cure for stomach cancer, killed fifty-five people — one in twenty of those who took it — during clinical trials. Yet the Health and Welfare Ministry approved it for general release, where it is known to have killed at least nine more people. The ministry's official response will convey some idea of the contempt with which patients' rights are regarded in Japan. A spokesman was quoted as saying, 'Doctors at the National Cancer Centre said that since it is a cancer medicine such deaths resulting from side effects cannot be helped.' According to Dr Beppu only two of the hundreds of Japanese 'anti-cancer' drugs have ever been able to pass the rigorous safeguards to be approved for use in the United States.

Many Westerners in Japan take their children to Hong Kong or the United States for their inoculations because Japanese vaccine has a deadly reputation. In 1988, a new MMR vaccine (to protect children against measles, mumps and rubella) was rushed onto the $45 million-a-year market after being tested on only 313 people. It killed and maimed thousands with meningitis before the government withdrew it. As with the haemophiliacs, distraught parents are still fighting for acknowledgment and compensation years later. Those Japanese who have the money and the *nous* go overseas for their medical treatment. Ichiro Ozawa, for instance, the Japanese coalition strongman, used to disappear at regular intervals for heart surgery at the US Naval Hospital in Bethesda, Maryland (where former President George Bush was treated), and at the exclusive Royal Brompton Hospital in London.

Partly as a result of their terrible record, Japanese drug companies are global minnows, almost unknown outside their own captive market. While Toyota, Sony and Fuji have become internationally admired brand-names, who has ever heard of even Japan's largest drug companies, Takeda, Sankyo and Shionogi — let alone Nippon Shoji Kaisha, the company responsible for the Sorivudine nightmare?

Nippon Shoji was actually not a drug company at all. It was a trading firm based in Osaka, which wanted to diversify into pharmaceuticals to boost its flagging profits. In the mid-1980s, it began planning for a 'smash hit' drug to boost its share-price when it went public in 1991. Having no research expertise, Nippon Shoji did what many Japanese drug companies do — it began scouring the world for a drug which other companies, for whatever reason, had discarded.

The drug the company eventually plumped for was called Sorivudine, a potent anti-viral agent, which had been trialed and rejected as too dangerous in Europe for the fairly obvious reason that, if used in combination with certain anti-cancer drugs, it could be fatal. During their own trials, Nippon Shoji's doctors discovered the same thing; three patients died within days of being given Sorivudine. Two of these deaths were kept secret, and a former executive of the company has explained why, with chilling candour:

> It is normal [in the pharmaceutical industry] to close your eyes to bad data … it would be a big problem if a drug which cost billions of yen to develop was not approved.

However, one of the deaths — as well as an animal trial, in which every rat died — *was* reported to the Health and Welfare Ministry's Medical Deliberation Committee, the Japanese equivalent of America's Food and Drug Administration (FDA) which is responsible for ensuring that new drugs are both safe and effective. So why didn't the government act to ban the drug or at least order further trials?

In a post-mortem on the disaster, *Nature,* the prestigious British science magazine, pointed out one reason: Japan's drug-approval bureaucracy is woefully understaffed — it has just two inspectors to verify the integrity of clinical trials, compared with 100 in the United States. 'We are notorious for this,' says Dr Beppu. 'We are way behind the United States in the evaluation and monitoring of drugs.' He also points out that Japanese doctors are generally abysmally ignorant about drugs, have no hope of knowing about more than a tiny fraction of the 16 000 on the market and rely on salespeople for their information. Only half a dozen of the eighty medical universities in Japan even have pharmacology on the syllabus.

However, as with the 'blood AIDS' scandal, money was the most important cause — the barely concealed bribery and collusion between the industry and the people who are supposed to be its watchdogs. A former manager at Nippon Shoji described how the company wined and dined Health and Welfare bureaucrats to get Sorivudine approved — the monthly budget for entertainment was $13 000 a head. As well, if they do the 'right thing,' bureaucrats can expect to be rewarded with highly paid seats on drug company boards when they take early retirement in their fifties — the practice known as *amakudari* or 'descent from heaven'. Said Shoichi Sugiyama, another lawyer involved in negligence actions against drug companies, 'Unlike the US FDA, the ministry has no independence and no specialists. The system is one of rotation and transfer, then retirement to the drug companies. The bureaucrats know that is who will provide their rice in the future.'

On September 3, 1993, Sorivudine was released in a blaze of hype. It was claimed, on completely phoney data, to be 6000 times as effective in treating herpes as Zovirax, an American drug which was the world leader for treating this painful and contagious viral condition. Nippon Shoji's president, Mr Takakazu Hattori, crowed that it was 'the most expensive drug in the world'. Each pill cost $30, and the prescription was three a day. Within ten days, the company racked up sales of $13 million, and its shares went through the roof.

Typical of the patients who were prescribed the new drug was Koei Nishino, a 74-year-old retired farmer from a little village called Chosei, some eighty kilometres from Tokyo. Five years earlier he had had an operation for cancer of the spleen and stomach. He was prescribed anti-cancer drugs which kept the malignancy at bay, but weakened his immune system so that he suffered an outbreak of herpes. Impressed by the publicity (and the profit), his doctor prescribed Sorivudine. The pain of the herpes soon faded, but within days Mr Nishino noticed weird changes in his body. He then collapsed and had to be rushed to an emergency hospital ward where he lay in a coma for three weeks, with his family at the bedside preparing for his death.

When we spoke to him nearly a year later, Mr Nishino still suffered the aftereffects of his close encounter — keloids (painful scarring of his face and body), swollen legs that make it difficult for him to walk and trouble urinating. 'It is the drug company that has done this to me,' he said. 'It is hard to believe I am still alive. How can anyone ever feel safe again?' Although he didn't realise it at the time, Mr Nishino, in fact, was one of the lucky ones. Within a month of its release, the new 'wonder drug' had killed fifteen people and injured scores more. Many survivors, like Mr Nishino, will have long-lasting aftereffects.

Yes, there was a tiny warning on the box — merely that it was 'inadvisable' to take Sorivudine in conjunction with anti-cancer medication. Most doctors paid no attention to it. Certainly, no patient was ever warned there might be lethal side effects. On September 19, just a fortnight after the launch, the first death was reported to the company and the ministry. By September 27, the toll was eight. Still there was no public warning. Minutes of a meeting at company headquarters in Osaka show that the deaths were to be a 'secret within the company'.

Nippon Shoji and the Health Ministry knew by now that the drug was deadly. However, before the public was warned, there was one much more important task: to make sure that, even if more patients had to lose their lives, no-one at the company lost any money. Between September 27, when the whistle should have been blown loud and long, and October 12, when the Health Ministry issued a belated warning, 200 employees of Nippon Shoji and two associated companies dumped their shares on the Osaka stock exchange. They saved millions — after the announcement Nippon Shoji shares plummeted from forty-seven dollars to twenty-two dollars.

During that fifteen-day period while the drug company's employees kept silent and scrambled to save their money, eight more people died. Masanori Fukushima of the Aichi Cancer Centre describes it as 'the most shameful episode in Japanese medical history'. As we have seen, there is keen competition for this title.

When the *Asahi* newspaper broke the story, public outrage was such that the government felt it had to take some action. However, extraordinarily, they did not dare challenge the fraudulent experimental data, the incompetent evaluation by the Health and Social Welfare Department nor the lies and bribery engaged in by Nippon Shoji. The company itself was ordered to cease production for a few weeks, a typical thrashing with a feather. Some of the victims sued, but, as we have seen, they are unlikely to see any result this side of the twenty-first century. Twenty-five people were eventually charged over the scandal — although not for homicide as they should have been. They were booked for insider trading and fined amounts ranging from $2500 to $7000 for their part in the wicked conspiracy.

So far, we have looked at 'active' medical negligence, cases where doctors, drug companies and the government have colluded to kill people with defective products. However, 'passive' deficiencies in Japan's medical system in all likelihood result in much greater unnecessary suffering and death. These are cases where, for whatever reason — usually to protect the Japanese market for Japanese companies — drugs and procedures which are universally found to be safe and effective overseas are banned or severely restricted. Organ transplants are a classic example.

Transplants are a particularly touchy issue in Japan for cultural, as well as medical, reasons. Many people are opposed to the donation of body parts because of a quasi-religious feeling that it is wrong to 'mutilate' the body. As well, Japan has no legal definition of brain death. The only time a heart transplant was attempted, in 1968, just a year after Dr Christiaan Barnard performed the first such operation in South Africa, the surgeon wound up being charged with manslaughter. Late in 1995, the latest of many hundreds of heart patients on transplant waiting lists died. Yasushi Nagai, aged forty-four, who had been on an artificial heart machine for more than a year, had been waiting three years and four months for the Diet to approve legislation permitting the operation that might have saved his life.

As a result of this mixture of popular superstition and

government failure to provide a proper legal framework, many tens of thousands of Japanese are denied the operations to restore their sight and other functions which are routine in other developed countries. In 1993, for example, there were only 468 kidney transplants in Japan, compared with 11 000 in the United States. About 14 000 people were being treated on dialysis machines, with little hope that they would ever live to see the day a kidney was available for transplant.

Those Japanese who can afford it travel overseas for transplants. Television is always showing footage of cute kids recovering from transplants in foreign hospitals. It has become quite a lucrative industry for American and Australian hospitals — 100 Japanese have had liver transplants in Queensland alone. The other way, for those who can pay, is to use an imported organ. This is where we enter another murky area where profit for the doctor can override the interests of the patient.

Transplants are highly profitable operations in Japan. A simple kidney transplant costs about $15 000. However, there is a chronic shortage of donors in Japan, and most countries are extremely reluctant to allow the export of transplantable organs. No kidneys means no operation means no money.

Dr Kazuo Ota, Japan's leading transplant surgeon and the head of the Japanese doctors' transplant society, thought he had the answer. Using a friend and colleague based at the University of Southern California, he managed to obtain dozens of American kidneys, which had been rejected as unsafe for transplantation by the US organ transplant network, UNOS. The kidneys had been taken from the bodies of people with cancer, with hepatitis and, in one case, from a man aged seventy.

Dr Ota, who was head of transplant surgery at the prestigious Tokyo Women's Medical College, imported the kidneys by falsely claiming they were for 'research purposes'. They were not declared to the Japanese transplant network which is supposed to supervise all kidney transplants in Japan. To round up patients, Dr Ota used Parramatta Road car-dealer tactics; he put up fliers near dialysis centres advertising 'kidneys available' and giving his hospital's telephone number. Hundreds of desperate people suffering chronic kidney disease inundated the hospital and Dr Ota's team began to transplant the rejected kidneys into them. On top of everything else, it was now more than seventy-two hours after some of the kidneys had been removed from their host bodies — they were well past their use-by date.

No-one knows just how many operations this greedy, wicked man conducted before he was caught and exposed by the NHK television network. Hospital sources said it was at least thirty. Of these, several patients contracted hepatitis C, one of the deadliest strains of the virus. In at least six cases, the 'reject' kidney failed immediately — so Dr Ota presumably collected a second fat fee for operating to remove them. Secure in the knowledge that he would neither be successfully sued nor delicensed, nor even disciplined, Dr Ota did not appear to even understand that what he had done was wrong. 'We're trying to see the possibility of broadening the use of kidneys,' he was quoted as saying. As for the government, as usual there was no response.

If the non-availability of transplants causes distress — and death — to tens of thousands of Japanese, just think about a world without the Pill. Since the first oral contraceptive was approved in the United States in 1960, it has become the most popular form of birth control in the world, used by more than sixty million women. It is said that the Pill, more than anything else, has been responsible for female emancipation. Only two countries of the nearly 200 which now make up the United Nations ban it — North Korea and Japan. Both, feminists point out, are notoriously chauvinist societies.

Just why it remains banned in Japan, after three generations of women have shown it to be their preferred form of contraception, is a matter for speculation. The Japanese government's official reason has changed dramatically over the years, as each position was shown to be absurd. First, they said the Pill was unsafe — which many of the early, high-dosage brands surely were. When the low-dosage 'mini-Pill' was shown to be both safe and effective, the government said it was worried about the effect on the country's morals. When the West failed to degenerate into Sodom and Gomorrah, the Japanese government came up with its trump card — the Pill would promote the spread of AIDS.

The real reason for this 35-year display of intransigence, speculate critics of the Japanese Establishment, was to protect two of the country's most profitable medical monopolies: abortion and condoms. About a quarter of all pregnancies in Japan end in abortion — 386 807 in 1993 — which is an extremely lucrative operation for Japanese doctors and private hospitals. This is a higher figure than in most other countries. The real (as opposed to the artificial official) abortion rate is probably around eighty-four per 1000 women, compared with twenty-seven per 1000 in the United States. Abortion carries a small, though significant risk to the woman. Although death rates in Japan are not available, it is believed that more than 100 women a year die of complications, and many hundreds more suffer serious injury, including infertility.

Apart from the absence of the Pill, there are cultural factors at play here. Japanese women plainly do not like abortion and regard it as a 'necessary evil'. Seven out of ten abortions are performed on married women who already have children, as opposed to ignorant unmarried teenagers. The millions of Jizos in cemeteries around Japan — stone statues of children wearing little red bibs and holding plastic whirligigs in their hands — erected to commemorate unborn babies, testify to the grief involved. Yet, particularly among the older generation of women, taking contraceptive precautions before having sex is regarded as somehow unseemly.

Perhaps because of this, Japanese men are the most enthusiastic users of condoms in the world. Japan's condom manufacturers — protected, as is every domestic industry, against competition from abroad — are highly profitable. More than half a billion condoms (one-fifth of the entire world output) are used every year, and it is the preferred contraception option of eight out of ten couples. By contrast, in

Australia the Pill is still far and away the most popular method. Although condoms, IUDs and other methods of contraception are becoming increasingly popular, 28 per cent of women aged eighteen to fifty take the Pill.

One glaring anomaly of the outlawing of the Pill is that Japanese doctors are still allowed to prescribe the outdated 'maxi Pill' — although it is only supposed to be for medical reasons, such as regulating menstruation, rather than contraception. Thus, several hundred thousand women are exposed to the risks of high blood pressure, thrombosis and so on associated with the high-dosage Pill which caused it to be taken off the market in every overseas country twenty years ago.

Japanese women have been fighting to have the Pill legalised for decades, and in some quite imaginative and original ways. During the 1970s, an organisation of women called the Chupiren (an abbreviation of the Japanese for women's liberation) terrorised Tokyo's suits. Wearing pink crash helmets painted with the female symbol, they demonstrated, disrupted government meetings and invaded workplaces to denounce married men who were having affairs. This attracted the predictable media attention and resulted in a predictable lack of action by the medical Establishment. Most women, conditioned to a passive role and deprived of information about contraception, regarded it as rather scandalous behaviour and failed to support the cause.

However, late in 1995, to the surprise of people like Yuriko Ashino, deputy director-general of the Family Planning Federation of Japan, who had almost given up hope, the Establishment appeared to be about to change its long-standing policy. The about-face appears to have come about not, it goes without saying, as a result of public pressure, but because of intensive lobbying by nine Japanese pharmaceutical companies itching to break into a major new market, which had applied to import or manufacture the Pill. Approval by the Central Pharmaceutical Affairs Council — the government/industry screening committee — was expected soon. 'It's about time,' Ms Ashino told me, 'that Japanese women had the same right to choose what they want to do with their bodies, as women in every other country.'

It would be absurd to draw too many conclusions from this overview of medical malpractice in Japan. There are clearly some doctors, a minority, who like Dr Beppu are ethical, talented and dedicated professionals. However, there is a disproportionate number who are not — doctors who see no conflict of interest in taking money from drug companies to push their products, drug companies which bribe bureaucrats to turn a blind eye to their criminal profiteering, a legal system which does nothing to redress the imbalance of power between the patient and the medical Establishment. These are themes that are persistent throughout Japanese society — the powerlessness of the individual in the face of an arrogant and unaccountable bureaucracy. Japanese medicine is not going to improve in any more rapid or dramatic way than any other aspect of life in this authoritarian country. It would be a brave, or foolhardy, pundit who would predict that that is about to happen any time soon.

THE SUPERLOO

IT'S NOW OFFICIAL. THE JAPANESE REALLY ARE different. Their poo doesn't stink.

From the country that brought you Super Nintendo, tofu ice cream and the cellular car-fax, stand by for the latest revolution in household habits — the Neorest, an odour-devouring superloo that does everything but wipe your bottom. In fact, looking through the thick specification book, I've just discovered it does that, too. And dries it.

This miracle of modern engineering is the proudest achievement of Mr Hiroshi Kobayashi, a brilliant design engineer from the sunny island of Kyushu. For four years he and a team of seventeen engineers, designers and electronic specialists have been beavering away in the top-secret Fukuoka R & D laboratories of the Toto company, Japan's largest loo-maker.

If there was ever any creature comfort you desired in the smallest room, Mr Kobayashi has thought of it. And patented it — no fewer than 155 patents in Japan and seven worldwide have been applied for before the 'new age toilet', as it's billed, is unveiled to the public.

So revolutionary is the design, it doesn't even look like a loo — more like a discreet piece of pastel hued ceramic sculpture. There is no chain, no lever, in fact no cistern. Instead, at the touch of a button, a mere eight litres of water hisses almost silently through a series of microprocessor-controlled valves to flush the bowl.

The hush-flush created an unexpected problem when it was found during extensive consumer testing that women rather like the rush of a good flush to drown out any other incidental sound effects, explained Mr Kobayashi.

Never, however, underestimate the Japanese genius for improvisation. To go with your Neorest you can now buy a wall-mounted unit, named an 'Otohime' after a mythological Japanese Mother Neptune, which automatically broadcasts the tape-recorded sound of a good old-fashioned flush when anyone approaches the throne.

It goes almost without saying that it has an electrically warmed seat — that's hardly anything new in Japan. However, the Neorest also comes with an optional heating element that can keep the whole room warm — a feature deemed desirable because elderly Japanese are terrified of dying of a stroke while visiting their unheated dunnies during the icy winter nights. A fully integrated bidet — with the nozzle adjustable from a remote-control keypad — is also regarded as essential to the modern ablution, as is a stream of warm air to dry the bottom gently afterwards.

Then there is the matter of the smell. Japanese consumers, it seems, are no longer satisfied with the sickly scent of those little bars of crystals dangling under the dunny seat. A number of companies have been working towards the ultimate solution.

Inax (a sister company of Toto, part of the Morimura group that also owns Noritake) uses 'sepia light' deodorisation, a secret process involving a special ceramic finish that is said to absorb ammonia. Matsushita, an upstart rival which built its reputation on an electronic sensor which automatically springs the lid open when you approach, has unveiled a 'honeycomb catalytic converter', named 'The Bashful'.

However, Toto is confident that its new system, a cunning combination of extractor fans and electrically generated ozone gas, will leave the bathroom smelling as sweet as cherry blossom after even the most seismic event.

THE SUPERLOO

The company — which has fifteen subsidiaries from France to the United States and Indonesia — is still considering whether to launch the Neorest on the international market. Initially, it is waiting to see how sales go in Japan, where it was recently launched with a modest target of 1000 superloos a month.

There is still one major problem, says Mr Kobayashi, that his team needs to work on with this Rolls-Royce of lavatories — the price. At $6000 (for the top-of-the-range model with built-in bathroom heater), 'I couldn't afford one myself,' he laments.

And, for those who have difficulties programming their VCRs, don't even think about installing one. The whole thing is computer-controlled from a complicated-looking keypad. Failing to record the late-night movie is one thing. Not being able to go to the loo because you've forgotten your PIN number is quite another.

Even if your poo won't stink.

EPILOGUE

As 1996 DREW TO A CLOSE, the media pundits began once again to talk excitedly about the next election. But this time, my reading of the news reports and conversations with friends indicated that there was little of the excitement of 1993. The mood seemed more one of surly apathy, as though finally it had dawned on the Japanese electorate that no matter who they voted for, the system would never change.

The conservative rhythms of the previous half century had been re-established, hardly missing a beat. The Liberal Democratic Party, still as politically bankrupt and systemically corrupt as ever, despite the promises of reform, was enjoying a renaissance under the leadership of Ryutaro Hashimoto, the disciple and latest inheritor of the soiled toga of Messrs Tanaka, Takeshita and Kanemaru. Public opinion polls showed the LDP enjoying a three-to-one lead over Ichiro Ozawa's New Frontier Party, which was wracked with dissent and wallowing in a policy vacuum. The socialists, unable to re-invent themselves, had disappeared into the dustbin of history. The electorate, said one prominent conservative commentator, had swung back to the LDP as 'the least worst party'. Morihiro Hosokawa, the standard-bearer of reform just four short years ago, lounged smirking on the back benches while a new generation of 'young Turks' tried vainly to stir public interest.

Most saw this as the end — for at least another generation — of dreams of a brave new world in which the bureaucrats surrendered authority to the politicians; of Ozawa's 'more normal' Japan, in which parliament becomes the supreme authority, and two clean and credible alternative governments competed for power.

Not even Japan's long-delayed bail-out of its giant financial institutions — many of them bankrupted by reckless and corrupt investments during the 1980s — could shake the government. It caved in to the demands of the Finance Ministry and reached into the pockets of the taxpayers for the first instalment of what could be a $1 trillion rescue package. The greed and incompetence of the bankers — and the cover-up by the ministry of its own ineffectual supervision and collusion in crooked practices — went unpunished. The taxpayers will be socked with an increase from 3 to 5 per cent in the hated consumption tax. And yet, even though polls showed 90 per cent of Japanese rejected the bail-out, there was a shrug of resignation. *Shoganai* — what can we do? The opposition, equally ineffective, resorted to a kindergarten-style protest, attempting to prevent the measure passing by sitting and obstructing the corridors of parliament.

Economically, it is true, things had improved a little. After five years of recession — boosted by a yen that had fallen by as much as 50 per cent against competing currencies such as the Australian dollar — the factories were humming once again, corporate profits were up, and the stock exchange had staged a nervous recovery, although it was still at little over half its level at the hysterical heights of the boom. But this was a recovery very unlike anything postwar Japan had seen before. The dole queues continued to grow as manufacturing was exported to low-wage economic colonies in mainland Asia, and the 'kudoka' or hollowing-out of Japanese industry continued. Without further major structural reform — impossible, of course, unless Japan changes political direction — few saw any prospect of a return to the heady 6.5 per cent growth of the past three decades. Doomsayers such as Johnsen Takahashi, an economist at the Mitsui Research Institute, even discussed Japan degenerating into a 'senile state' such as Britain.

Diplomatically it was back to the ice-age. The fifty-first anniversary of the end of World War II came and went with the new government showing even less enthusiasm than its predecessor for finally exorcising the demons of the past. Hashimoto travelled to Cheju Island to meet the South Korean President Kim Young-sam, an excruciatingly embarrassing performance at which nothing of any significance could be discussed because of Hashimoto's refusal to apologise, in a forthright way, for Japan's wartime conquest of the peninsula. Journalists derided it as the 'soccer summit' because all the two leaders could agree on was to share venues for the 2002 World Cup, an issue over which national pride had been whipped up to such an extent that it threatened relations between the two countries. As if on cue, an odious LDP parliamentarian named Tadashi Itakagi chose this moment to announce that the 200 000 principally Korean 'comfort women' kidnapped by the Imperial Army and forced to work in front-line brothels, were volunteers who did it for the money.

On some of the issues raised in this book, kicking and screaming to the end, the bureaucracy was dragged reluctantly to the bar of public opinion. Fifty years after the cure for leprosy was discovered, Japan finally abolished the law confining Hansen's disease patients to their devil's islands — though, as their doctors had predicted, they were all by now so old, so infirm and so institutionalised that few could take advantage of their newly granted freedom. A new Health Minister (the sixth, or seventh, in four years ... I have lost count) made a hero of himself by apologising to the dead and dying haemophiliacs, infected with AIDS because of a wicked conspiracy to cover up the dangers. By now, thousands more victims had come to light, and the death toll had exceeded 2000. However, the Health Department and the drug companies were still arguing over compensation for the living — and there was no likelihood of murder charges being laid to atone for the dead. More than forty years after the victims of Minamata began their crusade for justice, the majority — though by no means all — of the victims had finally been offered some modest compensation.

On other fronts, the progress seemed to be mainly backwards. The trial of Shoko Asahara meandered aimlessly on at the rate of a day or two a month, while police searched in vain for six of his mass-murdering henchmen believed still to be at large. Nearly two years after it masterminded the most horrific terrorist attack in Japanese history, the Aum Shinri-kyo cult was still flourishing, and Asahara's two infant sons had been installed as its new leaders. An advisory board to the National

Police Agency finally conceded what had been obvious to everyone else for years — 'Japan is proceeding down the path to becoming a Western-style crime society' — but had made no sensible recommendations to reform the antiquated law-enforcement system, beyond suggesting hiring a few thousand more Mr Walkabouts. Down in Kobe, tens of thousands of people were still living in 'temporary' accommodation, while the city fathers squabbled over the spoils of redevelopment.

And for those who were hoping the twin disasters — the subway gas attack and the earthquake — may have jolted the government into establishing more effective emergency planning systems, 1996 threw up yet another example of a man-made disaster. Thousands of people were stricken — and at least a dozen killed — by a strain of *e.coli* bacterium. The national government refused to intervene for fear of causing a panic, leaving the disaster to local government officials to handle. These officials blundered around for weeks unable — or unwilling — to identify the source of contamination as children's school lunch-boxes, probably for fear of exposing their own lack of supervision, but almost certainly also because of a reluctance to upset some hidden vested financial interest. While the children died, ludicrous 'precautions' were taken to prevent the outbreak, such as closing swimming pools and spraying school desks with disinfectant. Australian correspondents contrasted the schemozzle with the speed with which health threats in their own country, such as the contaminated peanut-butter scare, were identified and contained.

It is common for a foreign correspondent to imagine that he lives through unprecedentedly interesting times. It is also part of that conceit to suppose that one is in a unique position to observe and prescribe for the social ills which afflict that society. I make no apology, but I would like to say that I have tried, even if not always successfully, to avoid glib and generalised judgments about the people whose guests Mayu and I were for those three years. Where I have levelled criticism, it is meant in a constructive way, and is a criticism not of the Japanese but of what many Japanese themselves see as the failures of their peculiar system of social organisation to respond to their legitimate needs and aspirations.

I am reluctant to exit on this rather down note, so I was overjoyed to read the other day that, no matter the state of the economy and the distrust in politicians, some Japanese institutions keep plugging away. The Toto company has just come up with its latest contribution to global bathroom comfort. The 'Zoe' model, which supercedes the obsolete Neorest, is so advanced it looks more like the pilot's seat from the starship *Enterprise* than a humble lavatory. I won't begin to describe its lengthy list of patented innovations, save to say that those who have trouble programming their VCRs should not apply. The functions are so varied you need a hand-held remote control pad to operate it.

GLOSSARY

The glossary is a guide to the Japanese and 'Japlish' (transmogrified English) words and phrases used in this book. This is not intended as a literal translation, as many Japanese words have several meanings and some have no English equivalent. It is an attempt at interpretation to help readers understand the words in the context in which they are used.

AINORI 'riding together', used to describe the Left/Right coalition which ruled Japan after 1994.

AINU Japan's aboriginal inhabitants.

AISHI a rank given to Aum Shinri-kyo priests.

AKAGAI — edible shellfish.

AKAONI 'red-faced devils', a phrase used to describe the invading Americans in World War II.

AMAKUDARI 'descent from heaven', the practice of retired public servants taking lucrative jobs in the private sector.

ANAGO edible sea eel.

ARIGATO thank you.

AUM SHINRI-KYO the Aum Supreme Truth cult.

AWAMORI Okinawa rice spirits.

BAKA stupid or fool.

BANZAI exclamation of victory, as in *tenno heika banzai*, 'May the emperor live 10 000 years'.

BENTO takeaway boxed lunch.

BOCHO a rank of Aum priest.

BOOMU boom or fad.

BORYOKUDAN 'violence group' or organised crime gang.

BOSOZOKU 'reckless run tribe' or bikie gang.

BURAKU 'village', euphemism for neighbourhood regarded as low-caste.

BURAKUMIN people who live or lived in a *buraku*.

BURU SERA 'sailor's bloomers' worn by schoolgirls.

CHAWAN MUSHI savoury custard.

CHUHAI cocktail of *shochu* and soda or fruit juice.

DAIDAI type of citrus fruit.

DAI JISHIN the 'big one', a giant earthquake.

DAIKON large white radish.

DAI KU 'Number Nine' or Beethoven's Ninth Symphony.

DAIMYO a local ruler in feudal times.

DANGO a bid-fixing ring of contractors.

DANNA husband or master, also used for a geisha's patron.

DASHI stock made of seaweed and dried bonito.

DEBU plump or fat.

DIET Japan's bicameral parliament.

DOBIN MUSHI broth, served in a small teapot.

EDAMAME green soy beans.

EDO old name for Tokyo; the Edo period is post-1868, when Tokyo became Japan's capital.

EKI-BEN *bento* sold on trains and at railway stations.

ENKA popular ballads.

ENOKITAKE a type of edible fungus.

ETA 'filth galore', an insulting way of referring to *burakumin*.

FEMIO-KUN 'girl buddies', young men who dress effeminately.

FUGU puffer fish.

FUTON bed covering like an eiderdown.

GAIATSU 'outside pressure', as in foreigners trying to change Japan.

GAIJIN 'outside person' or foreigner.

GANBATTE! go for it!

GEISHA female entertainer.

GINGKO a nut-bearing tree, Tokyo's city symbol.

GOSHI rank of Aum priest.

GOYU GAKUSHA 'official scholars', such as government-approved historians.

GUZU sluggish.

HAIKU a seventeen-syllable verse.

HAKOFUGU a type of *fugu* fish.

HANAMI cherry-blossom viewing, often an alfresco party.

HANKO the personal seal Japanese use for official documents.

HANSEI self-reflection.

HARA KIRI more correctly *seppuku* or suicide by ritual disembowelling.

HEA pubic hair; abbreviation for pictures in which pubic hair is visible.

HEIAN the period from 794–1868 when Kyoto was Japan's capital.

HENSACHI the method of grading examination papers for university entrance.

HIBAKUSHA victim of bombing; particularly the atomic bombs.

HIMEYURI 'princess lily', the name given to the schoolgirls who served as nurses during the battle for Okinawa.

HINANJO HAIEN 'shelter pneumonia', suffered by survivors of the Kobe earthquake.

HINOMARU Japan's 'risen sun' national flag.

HONNE a person's true beliefs or feelings.

IJIME extreme bullying, particularly in schools.

IKAMESHI squid stuffed with rice.

IKKI-NOMI 'chugging' drinks.

IREZUMI Japanese traditional tattooing.

ISANA 'great fish', the old word for whale.

ISHA 'doctor'.

JAKUSHIN a type of earthquake.

JCP Japan Communist Party.

JIKATA geisha who plays musical instruments.

JIMINTO abbreviation of Jiyu Minshuto, the Liberal Democratic Party (LDP).

JIMUJIKAN government departmental head.

JINSAI man-made disaster.

JIZO small statue of a Buddhist deity often sponsored by women who lose children.

JOMON Japan's neolithic period, from 10 000–300 BC.

JUKU cramming school.

KABUKI pantomime-like Japanese theatre.

KAISEKI RYORI traditional Japanese banquet.

KAITEN miniature 'suicide submarine'.

KAKI-MESHI a dish of rice and oysters.

KAMIKAZE 'divine wind' pilots of World War II suicide missions.

KAMPAI! cheers!

KANJI written characters of Chinese origin.

KAN-KAN SETTAI lavish entertainment of government officials by other officials.

KANPO traditional herbal medicine.

KANRYO SENGEN 'completion declaration' when a *buraku* has its facilities raised to satisfactory standards.

KANTEI the prime minister's official residence in Tokyo.

KARAOKE 'empty orchestra', a sing-it-yourself entertainment system.

KAROSHI death from overwork.

KARYUKAI the 'world of flowers and willows' of the geisha.

KATA correct form or method.

KATAKANA one of the two Japanese syllabaries.

KEIDANREN the peak organisation of Japanese industry.

KEIRETSU the business 'families' into which Japanese industry is organised.

KEISHIN type of earthquake.

KEMPEITAI wartime security police.

KENDO traditional swordsmanship.

KIDOTAI riot police.

KIMIGAYO 'His Majesty's Reign', the national anthem.

KIMONO Japanese formal dress, now worn mainly by women.

KINOME tiny sprigs of fragrant, edible prickly ash.

KISHA KURABU *'kisha* clubs' of reporters who monopolise most news centres.

KISHIMEN flat wheat noodles like fettucine.

KITANAI dirty.

KOAN KEISATSU the Public Security Agency.

KOBAN street-corner police box.

KOEN DEBYU the 'park debut' of a new baby in its stroller.

KOENKAI politicians' electoral support groups.

KOGAI-GEN the 'origin of pollution' at Minamata.

KOGYARU young girls who dress up provocatively.

KOKUGO the study of Japanese.

KOMBU a type of seaweed.

KOSEKI register of household occupants.

KOTATSU a heated 'well' beneath a low table.

KOTSUZUKI a hand drum used in *noh*.

KUDOI garrulous (a term used in sake-tasting).

KUROGO the 'man in black' or puppeteer.

KYOGEN a comic interlude in *noh* drama.

LDP the conservative Liberal Democratic Party which ruled Japan for thirty-eight years up to 1993.

LOLICON 'Lolita complex'.

MAFF the Ministry for Agriculture, Fisheries and Forests.

MAGURO the best part of prime tuna, used for sushi and sashimi.

MAHO magic.

MANGA comic book.

MARUGARI close-cropped hair favoured by schools and the military.

MATSURI a festival.

MATSUTAKE edible 'red pine' mushrooms.

MEIJI the emperor who ruled from 1868–1912 as Japan entered the modern world.

MFA the Ministry for Foreign Affairs.

MIKOSHI a portable shrine used during *matsuri*.

MINSHUKU inexpensive dinner/bed and breakfast places.

MIRIN sweet rice wine used in cooking.

MISO bean paste.

MITI the Ministry for International Trade and Industry.

MOF the Ministry of Finance.

MOMPE baggy pants worn by peasants.

NABE a simmered pot-meal.

NAMAZU a catfish; in legend, one sleeps beneath Japan, causing earthquakes when it stirs.

NAMEKO a type of mushroom.

NARA PERIOD AD 710–794 when Nara was Japan's imperial capital.

NATTO fermented soy beans.

NHK Nippon Hoso Kyokai, the government-owned national radio and television broadcaster.

NIHONJINRON the study or science of Japaneseness.

NIKKEI *Nihon Keizai Shimbun,* Japan's leading business newspaper.

NINNIKU-BARA 'garlic bellies', a pejorative phrase for Koreans.

NOH traditional dramatic theatre.

NOKYO network of agricultural cooperatives.

NOMIYA a humble bar.

NOREN the cloth which hangs over restaurant entrances to indicate that they are open.

OB an 'old boy' or alumnus; often used for former government ministry officials.

OBI the sash that goes around the waist of a woman wearing a kimono.

OBON the midsummer holiday festival.

OISHII delicious.

OKA-SAN mother; used by some men to refer to their wives.

OKIYA geisha house.

OKONOMI-YAKI savoury pancake popular in Osaka.

OKYO-YOMI sutra-chanting; politicians making meaningless speeches.

OL 'office lady'.

OMAWARI-SAN 'Mr Walkabout', a beat policeman.

OREI a gratuity, often given to doctors or teachers.

OTSUYA a Buddhist wake or period of mourning.

PACHINKO pinball.

POA-SURU an Aum phrase meaning to send someone to heaven or murder them.

PONZU   a dipping sauce made of soy, citrus and other ingredients.

RAMEN   noodles, most commonly of the instant variety.

RENRITSU-YOTO   the ruling coalition of (political) parties.

ROBATAYAKI   a restaurant where the chef sits behind the counter barbecuing at a fire.

RYOKAN   a hostelry, often high class, for food and accommodation.

RYOTEI   an expensive traditional establishment where meals are served in screened rooms, often by geisha.

SAKANA   light snacks served with drinks.

SAKE   rice 'wine' (*see* chapter 2 on food for proper description, along with different varieties).

SALARYMAN   sometimes 'salariman'; salaried office worker.

SAMURAI   the warrior class of feudal times.

SANSHO   prickly ash, used as seasoning.

SARU GAKU   'monkey music', the travelling entertainments that preceded *noh* and *kabuki*.

SASHIMI   raw food, usually fish.

SATYAM   'place of worship', the Aum name for its buildings.

SDPJ   Social Democratic Party of Japan, the English name for the main opposition party 1955–95.

SEIFU   government.

SENSEI   respectful form of address for leading authorities, such as in medicine and education.

SEPPUKU   ritual suicide by disembowelling.

SHAKAITO   see SDPJ.

SHAKEN   motor vehicle roadworthiness inspection system.

SHAMISEN   a three-stringed musical instrument like a banjo.

SHIITAKE   a type of mushroom.

SHINGI-KAI   study group, usually connected with government policy formation.

SHINKANSEN   high-speed 'bullet train'.

SHINSHINTO   Japan's main opposition group since 1994. Official translation: New Frontier Party.

SHINTO Japan's native animistic 'religion'.

SHISO broad-leafed aromatic herb used as a garnish, especially for sashimi.

SHOCHU vodka-style spirit.

SHOGANAI it can't be helped.

SHOGUN feudal ruler.

SOBA buckwheat noodles.

SOKA GAKKAI Buddhist 'lay religious' organisation.

SOMEN thin wheat noodles.

SOSHI founder; for instance, of a religion.

SUDACHI a type of citrus fruit.

SUKIYAKI beef hotpot.

SUMO Japanese wrestling.

SUNOMONO vinegared dish, typically of fish or vegetables.

SUPARUTA KYOIKU the concept of 'spartan education'.

SUSHI cold cooked rice, often topped with fish.

TAKOYAKI octopus fritters.

TARENTO 'talent' as in singer or television performer.

TATAMI straw floor matting.

TATEMAE outward pretence, the opposite of *honne*.

TEMPURA fish or vegetables deep-fried in batter.

TENSAI natural disaster.

TEREKURA telephone dating club, often a front for prostitution.

TESSA 'gun sashimi', Osaka dialect for raw puffer fish.

TODAI the ultra-elite Tokyo University.

TODO the Steller sea lion.

TOFU bean curd.

TOKAI a region of Japan, also a type of earthquake.

TOKI the Japanese crested ibis.

TOKUGAWA the shogunate that ruled Japan from 1603–1868.

TORII the vermillion archway that marks the entrance to a Shinto shrine.

TOSA a breed of fighting dog.

TSU connoisseur.

TSUBUGAI edible shellfish.

TSUNAMI earthquake-caused tidal wave.

UDO a type of vegetable. No English word.

UDON thick noodles.

UKASE traditional Kyushu sailing boat used for fishing.

WAGYU fatty, premium-quality Japanese beef.

WAJIN Ainu word for majority Japanese, who are of Yamato ethnic origin.

WASABI a type of horseradish.

YAKI-NIKU barbecue-style cooking at the table.

YAKITORI small pieces of chicken, skewered and grilled.

YAKUZA Japanese gangster.

YOKOZUNA highest rank of sumo wrestler.

YUKAR Ainu epic recitation.

YUKATA light cotton robe.

ZENECON 'general contractors', Japan's construction companies.

ZOKU 'tribe', often a grouping of special-interest politicians.

ZOSUI rice gruel.

BIBLIOGRAPHY

The following is my (usually reliable) regular reading list, which I have used for ideas and background.

NEWSPAPERS

Asahi Evening News, Asahi Shimbun, Daily Yomiuri, Japan Press Service, Japan Times, Japan Times Weekly, Mainichi Daily News, Nikkei Daily Fax, Nikkei Weekly.

MAGAZINES

Aera, Asia Week, the *Economist, Far Eastern Economic Review, Gekkan Sentaku, Intersect, Shukan Bunshun, Shukan Kinyobi, Spa, Tokyo Business Today, Tokyo Journal.*

BOOKS

Abegglen, James C. & George Stalk Jnr. *Kaisha: The Japanese Corporation.* Charles E. Tuttle. An impressive business school style account of how the modern Japanese corporation works.

Agency for Cultural Affairs. *Japanese Religion.* Kodansha, Tokyo. Solid, scholarly reference.

Alletzhauser, Al. *The House of Nomura.* Bloomsbury. A terrific account of the rise of the world's most powerful security company. Needs another chapter to bring readers up to date on the scandals of the 1990s.

Benedict, Ruth. *The Chrysanthemum and the Sword: Patterns of Japanese Culture.* Charles E. Tuttle. An attempt, fifty years ago, by an American 'cultural anthropologist' to explain a country she had never visited. Still on the Australian Embassy recommended reading list, which may explain a lot.

Bornoff, Nicholas. *Pink Samurai: Love, Marriage and Sex in Contemporary Japan.* Pocket Books. Everything you wanted to know from Shinto fertility rites to the love hotel to a ceremony involving a young woman, a silver tray and men with chopsticks.

Buruma, Ian. *The Wages of Guilt: Memories of War in Germany and Japan.* Farrar, Straus, Giroux, New York. Masterfully written account contrasting Germany's agonising acknowledgment and Japan's official rejection of their respective roles as the aggressors in World War II.

Dalby, Liza. *Kimono.* Yale University Press. The definitive English-language cultural history of Japan's garment icon. Tragedy it's not in colour.

Davis, F. Hadland. *Myths and Legends of Japan.* Graham Brash, Singapore. Compendium of curiosities, folk literature and legend.

Discover Japan: Words, Customs and Concepts (vols 1 & 2). Kodansha. Bite-sized vignettes on everything from climbing Mount Fuji to *tachishoben*, the pleasure of urinating while standing up in a public place.

Emmott, Bill. *Japan's Global Reach*. Century, London. Emmott is less opinionated and a better writer than most of his colleagues on the *Economist* magazine on (not again!) 'the influences, strategies and weaknesses of Japan's multinational companies'.

Feiffer, George. *Tennozan: The Battle of Okinawa and the Atomic Bomb*. Ticknor and Fields, New York. One of the best histories, and most gripping reads, of World War II.

Fingleton, Eamonn. *Blindside: Why Japan Is Still on Track to Overtake the US by the Year 2000*. Houghton Mifflin, Boston. An interesting and original book that challenges conventional wisdom, but ultimately fails to live up to its title.

Flannigan, Thomas & Ellen. *Tokyo Museums: A Complete Guide*. Charles E. Tuttle. One hundred and ninety-five of them, no less, showcasing everything from internal parasites to oxygen.

Glynn, Paul. *The Smile of a Ragpicker* and *A Song for Nagasaki*. Marist Fathers Books, Sydney. Two books by a Marist missionary who, with his brother Tony, did much to reconcile Australia and Japan after the war. Both deal with unsung Japanese heroes — one a doctor who cared for the survivors of the second atom bomb, the other a noblewoman who worked among the destitute in postwar Tokyo.

Goodman, David G. & Masanori Miyazawa. *Jews in the Japanese Mind*. Free Press, New York. Fascinating account of Japan's weird racist stereotyping, including the little-known facts that the first sanitary napkin designed in Japan was named after Ann Frank and that Shakespeare's most popular play is *The Mysterious Breast-Meat Trial* (known to the rest of the world as the *Merchant of Venice*).

Goto, Takanori. *Japan's Dark Side to Progress*. Manbousha, Chiba. A lawyer's account of the 'struggle for justice' by thousands of victims of defective drugs.

Greenfeld, Karl Taro. *Speed Tribes: Children of the Japanese Bubble*. Boxtree, London. A ripping read in the genre known as 'infotainment' taking you inside Tokyo subcultures including pornography, bikie gangs, drugs and thieves.

Hadfield, Peter. *Sixty Seconds That Will Change the World*. Pan. First-rate whistle-blowing on Tokyo's failure to prepare for the inevitable Big One — and what that means for the rest of the world.

Harris, Sheldon H. *Factories of Death: Japanese Biological Warfare 1932–1945 and the American Cover-up*. Routledge, London. Chilling and meticulously researched history of the 'Asian Auschwitz'.

Hearn, Lafcadio. *Glimpses of Unfamiliar Japan*. Charles E. Tuttle, Tokyo. Celebrated in Japan and unknown elsewhere, this Irish/Greek/American brought the 'Hey, Martha!' school of journalism to Japan a century ago.

Hicks, George. *The Comfort Women: Sex Slaves of Japan's Imperial Forces*. Yenbooks, Tokyo. A moving and well-researched history of one of World War II's most sordid episodes.

Inoguchi, Rikihei, Tadashi Nakajima & Roger Pineau. *The Divine Wind*. Greenwood Press. An excellent account of the kamikaze pilots, researched from both sides of the Pacific War.

Johnson, Chalmers. *Japan: Who Governs?* (W. W. Norton, New York. The latest weighty tome on Japan's economy/government from the man who likes to be called the 'Godfather of Revisionism'.

Kayano, Shigeru. *The Romance of the Bear God.* Taishukan, Tokyo. One of many books written by Japan's last surviving Ainu elder, in an attempt to preserve his people's language and culture.

Kennedy, Rick. *Good Tokyo Restaurants.* Kodansha. That rarity among Japanese guides — an honest, accurate, readable account of some of the city's best Japanese and foreign eating places. Badly needs an update.

Kennedy, Rick. *Little Adventures in Tokyo.* Stone Bridge Press, Berkeley, California. Charming stroll through thirty-nine off-the-beaten-track locations, from jazz clubs to jacuzzi parlours.

Kinoshita, June & Nicholas Palevsky. *Gateway to Japan.* Kodansha. Forget about the rest — since 1990 (with regular updates), this has been the most comprehensive, accurate and enlightening guide to Japan available in English.

Kojima, Setsuko & Gene A. Crane. *A Dictionary of Japanese Culture.* Chopmen Publishers, Singapore. Handy, accurate reference.

Lazarus, David. *Japan Seriously.* Japan Times, Tokyo. Quirky encounters by a former columnist on the country's best-selling English-language newspaper.

Maitland, Brian. *Japanese Baseball: A Fan's Guide.* Charles E. Tuttle. Entertaining primer on Japan's national sport, complete with translations of such traditional calls as *pinchi hitta* (pinch hitter).

Masuji, Ibuse. *Black Rain.* Kodansha. Meandering, sententious, fictionalised account of the Hiroshima bombing by one of Japan's most awarded authors.

Martineau, Lisa. *Caught in a Mirror: Reflections of Japan.* Macmillan, London. An entertaining, neatly written, hit-and-run job by someone who was the Guardian's correspondent in Tokyo for three years.

Mishima, Akio. *Bitter Sea: The Human Cost of Minamata Disease.* Kosei, Tokyo. A committed account by a former senior *Asahi* journalist of this environmental disaster.

Miyamoto, Masao. *Straightjacket Society: An Insider's Irreverent View of Bureaucratic Japan.* Kodansha. One of the most entertaining reads of 1995 — a bureaucrat breaks the code of *omerta* and blows the whistle on his former employers. They had the last laugh, however. Miyamoto was fired.

Nicol, C. W. *Harpoon.* Cignet, New York. 'A vivid epic … James Clavell move over!' says the cover note, quoting from something called *Rave Reviews*. What more can I say? Don't read it if you are squeamish about whaling.

Oppenheim, Phillip. *Trade Wars: Japan versus the West.* Weidenfeld & Nicolson, London. A competent account of Japanese industrial policy — but, again, shows how much five years of recession can render the insights of 1992 obsolete.

Ota, Masahide. *Genocide.* Okinawa Times. Blood-curdling illustrated history of atrocities through the ages, from Japan's Rape of Nanking to the holocaust on Okinawa in which Ota, who became governor of the island, was wounded as a schoolboy.

Ozawa, Ichiro. *Blueprint for a New Japan*. Kodansha. 1993's politician-of-the-moment writes about everything he failed to do in government.

Peng, Fred C. C. & Peter Geiser. *The Ainu: The Past in the Present*. Bunka Hyoron, Hiroshima. Turgid sociological tract.

Ritchie, Donald. *Geisha, Gangster, Neighbour, Nun*. Kodansha, Tokyo. Forty-eight sharp, beautifully observed portraits by Japan's premier resident *gaijin* writer.

Sakaiya, Taichi. *What Is Japan? Contradictions and Transformations*. Kodansha. Why did the Japanese never have slavery (except for a few million Koreans, Chinese, Filipinos etc)? Simple. Because the country had no tradition of animal husbandry! A journey into the wacky world of ethnicity as icon by a former senior bureaucrat.

Seward, Jack. *The Japanese*. Passport Books, Illinois. Describes himself as 'America's foremost authority' on Japan. He isn't.

Sharnoff, Lora. *Grand Sumo*. Weatherill, New York. The most comprehensive book in English about this mysterious sport — even answering the most often asked question: 'Do they do it?'

Shelley, Rex. *Culture Shock: A Guide to Customs and Etiquette*. Times Books, Singapore. A compendium of the bleedin' obvious that would be useful to anyone who couldn't find Japan on the map.

Tsuji, Shizuo. *Japanese Cooking, a Simple Art*. Kodansha. The most comprehensive account in English that I have come across of the principles and practice of one of the world's great cuisines.

Vogel, Ezra F. *Japan as No. 1: Lessons for America*. Charles E. Tuttle, Tokyo. Influential 1970s analysis of the reasons for Japan's economic success.

Warner, Dennis, Peggy Warner & Sadao Seno. *Kamikaze: The Sacred Warriors*. Oxford University Press. Another excellent account of the kamikaze pilots, researched from opposite sides of the Pacific War.

Wolferen, Karel van. *The Enigma of Japanese Power*. Papermac. Still the definitive account of how government really works in Japan. Overdue for an English-language update.

Wood, Christopher. *The Bubble Economy: The Japanese Economic Collapse*. Sidgwick & Jackson, London. *Economist* journalists, no matter how gifted as writers, should know better than to leave the theatre in the middle of act two to try and write the review.

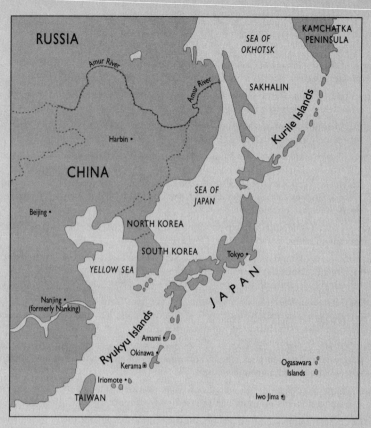

RUSSIA

KAMCHATKA
PENINSULA

SEA OF
OKHOTSK

Amur River

Amur River

SAKHALIN

Kurile Islands

Harbin •

CHINA

SEA OF
JAPAN

Beijing •

NORTH KOREA

SOUTH KOREA

Tokyo •

JAPAN

YELLOW SEA

Nanjing •
(formerly Nanking)

Ryukyu Islands

Amami •

Okinawa •

Kerama ⊚

Ogasawara
Islands

Iriomote • •

TAIWAN

Iwo Jima ◔

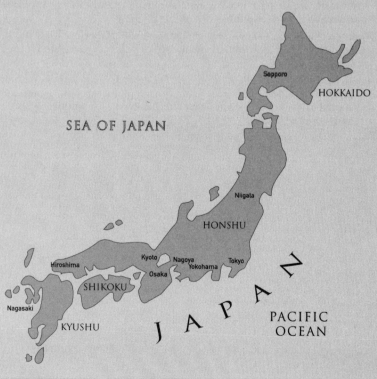

SEA OF JAPAN

Sapporo

HOKKAIDO

Niigata

HONSHU

Hiroshima

Kyoto

Nagoya

Tokyo

Osaka

Yokohama

SHIKOKU

Nagasaki

JAPAN

PACIFIC
OCEAN

KYUSHU

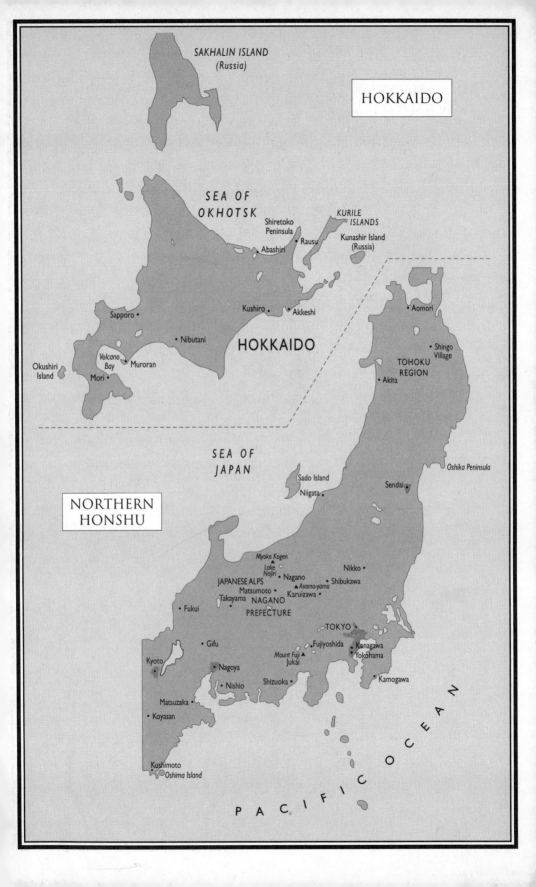

SAKHALIN ISLAND
(Russia)

HOKKAIDO

SEA OF
OKHOTSK

Shiretoko
Peninsula
• Rausu

KURILE
ISLANDS

Kunashir Island
(Russia)

Abashiri

• Aomori

Kushiro   • Akkeshi

• Sapporo

• Nibutani

HOKKAIDO

• Shingo
  Village

TOHOKU
REGION

Okushiri
Island

Volcano
Bay
Mori   Muroran

• Akita

Oshika Peninsula

SEA OF
JAPAN

Sado Island

Sendai •

Niigata •

NORTHERN
HONSHU

Myoko Kogen
Lake
Nojiri

Nikko •

JAPANESE ALPS

Nagano •

Shibukawa

Matsumoto •

▲ Asama-yama

Takayama •

Karuizawa •

NAGANO
PREFECTURE

• Fukui

• Gifu

TOKYO •

Fujiyoshida •

Kanagawa

Mount Fuji ▲

Yokohama

Kyoto •

• Nagoya

Jukai

• Nishio

Shizuoka •

• Kamogawa

Matsuzaka •

• Koyasan

Kushimoto •
• Oshima Island

P A C I F I C   O C E A N

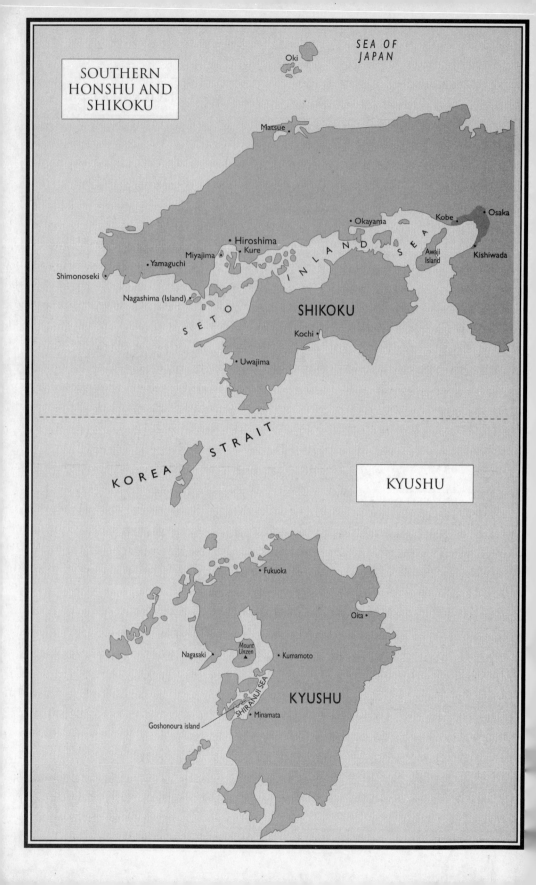

SEA OF
JAPAN

SOUTHERN
HONSHU AND
SHIKOKU

Oki

Matsue

Kobe • • Osaka
• Okayama
INLAND SEA
Hiroshima • Kishiwada
Miyajima • • Kure Awaji
• Yamaguchi Island
Shimonoseki •
S E T O
Nagashima (Island) • SHIKOKU
Kochi •
• Uwajima

K O R E A   S T R A I T

KYUSHU

• Fukuoka

Oita •

Mount
Unzen
Nagasaki • ▲ • Kumamoto
SHIRANUI SEA
KYUSHU
Goshonoura island • Minamata